Engaging Nature

Engaging Nature

Environmentalism and the Political Theory Canon

Peter F. Cannavò and Joseph H. Lane Jr., editors

The MIT Press
Cambridge, Massachusetts
London, England

© 2014 Massachusetts Institute of Technology

All rights reserved. No part of this book may be reproduced in any form by any electronic or mechanical means (including photocopying, recording, or information storage and retrieval) without permission in writing from the publisher.

MIT Press books may be purchased at special quantity discounts for business or sales promotional use. For information, please email special_sales@mitpress.mit.edu.

Set in Sabon by the MIT Press. Printed and bound in the United States of America.

Library of Congress Cataloging-in-Publication Data

Engaging nature : environmentalism and the political theory canon / Peter Cannavò and Joseph H. Lane, Jr., editors ; foreword by John Barry.
    pages cm
Includes bibliographical references and index.
ISBN 978-0-262-02805-9 (hardcover : alk. paper) — ISBN 978-0-262-52656-2 (pbk. : alk. paper)
1. Political ecology. 2. Political science—Philosophy. 3. Environmentalism—Philosophy. 4. Philosophers—Biography. I. Cannavò, Peter F., editor of compilation. II. Lane, Joseph H., Jr., 1968–
JA75.8.E56 2014
363.7001—dc23
2014012488

10 9 8 7 6 5 4 3 2 1

Contents

Foreword by John Barry   vii
Acknowledgments   ix

    Introduction: How We Got Here   1
    Peter F. Cannavò and Joseph H. Lane Jr.

1 Plato: Private Property and Agriculture for the Commoners—Humans and the Natural World in *The Republic*   29
   Sheryl D. Breen

2 Aristotle: Phusis, Praxis, and the Good   45
   Özgüç Orhan

3 Niccolò Machiavelli: Rethinking Decentralization's Role in Green Theory   65
   Francisco Seijo

4 Thomas Hobbes: Relating Nature and Politics   83
   John M. Meyer

5 John Locke: "This Habitable Earth of Ours"   99
   Zev Trachtenberg

6 David Hume: Justice and the Environment   117
   Andrew Valls

7 Jean-Jacques Rousseau: The Disentangling of Green Paradoxes   133
   Joseph H. Lane Jr.

8 Edmund Burke: The Nature of Politics   153
   Harlan Wilson

9 Mary Wollstonecraft: "Systemiz[ing] Oppression"—Feminism, Nature, and Animals   173
   Barbara K. Seeber

10 John Stuart Mill: The Greening of the Liberal Heritage   189
   Piers H. G. Stephens

11 Karl Marx: Critique of Political Economy as Environmental Political Theory   205
   Timothy W. Luke

12 W. E. B. Du Bois: Racial Inequality and Alienation from Nature   223
   Kimberly K. Smith

13 Martin Heidegger: Individual and Collective Responsibility   239
   W. S. K. Cameron

14 Hannah Arendt: Place, World, and Earthly Nature   253
   Peter F. Cannavò

15 Confucius: How Non-Western Political Theory Contributes to Understanding the Environmental Crisis   271
   Joel Jay Kassiola

   Conclusion: The Western Political Theory Canon, Nature, and a Broader Dialogue   287
   Peter F. Cannavò and Joseph H. Lane Jr.

About the Authors   293
Index   295

Foreword

When the past no longer illuminates the future, the spirit walks in darkness.
—Alexis de Tocqueville

Engaging Nature is a landmark contribution to the overlapping fields of political theory/history of political thought and green/ecological political theory. It is the first publication of its kind. Effectively marking out a new area for both green scholarship and those working within the history of political thought, it clears a scholarly path that others will follow. Outlining distinctively novel readings and interpretations of classical texts and thinkers in the political theory canon, it marks a maturing of the field of green political theory scholarship. It also displays the talent and breadth of scholarship within the community of green political theory.

The question animating this book is, simply, "What can we learn from re-reading classic political and ethical thinkers from the past?" Or, more specifically, "What can they tell us about our current ecological predicament?" Doubtless we live in difficult and turbulent times, but, while the scale and urgency of the challenges and opportunities we face are of course different from those of previous eras, there is much to be gained from critically analyzing the ideas of those who lived through unstable and unsettling periods in the past.

But the thinkers discussed in this volume speak to us also because they reflected upon some of the enduring and foundational political and ethical questions for human society. Questions such as "What is the good life?" and "What is the good society?" are as important and relevant today as they were for these thinkers, and there is much we can learn from how our predecessors answered these questions. At the same time, how we think about and answer these questions will have profound consequences for how we think about nature and for how we interact with, use, or choose not to use the nonhuman world.

All political thinking, self-consciously "green" or not, has ecological assumptions and consequences. Whether explicit or implicit, all forms of political theory have particular understandings of concepts such as "nature," "the nonhuman," "the environment," "human-animal relations," and "human nature." This volume questions conventional readings of canonical theorists—readings which maintain that these thinkers saw nature, land, agriculture, animals, the nonhuman, and human-nonhuman interaction as somehow uninteresting from a political or an ethical point of view, as somehow "pre-political."

Of course we cannot simply or simplistically "read off" (or "read into") these canonical thinkers specific recommendations on contemporary ecological issues such as climate change, peak oil, ecosystem degradation, or animal welfare. This volume does not claim that these canonical thinkers and the bodies of knowledge that they produced would describe themselves as "greens" or "environmentalists," or that they could be so described from the point of view of current green/environmental political theory. There is, of course, always a temptation to read canonical thinkers as supporting particular positions. But this volume does not do that. Instead it allows each contributor to speak for himself or herself while offering an ecologically sensitive reading of that thinker and, in the process, offering a fresh and illuminating interpretation to either sit alongside or directly challenge more established views. Part of what this volume does is restore ecologically interesting and significant (and for that reason perhaps hidden or neglected) aspects of the canon. Equally important, the discussions in this volume deploy imagination and creativity in thinking about how canonical political thinkers would address the complex of issues that make up "actually existing unsustainability." And in so doing, the analyses in this book contribute to informing how our current ecological reality should be conceptualized in terms of causes, consequences, coping mechanisms, solutions, and so on.

In part, the scholarship displayed in this volume can be viewed in terms of revealing how older thinkers can enable us to better understand modern environmental terms, concepts, and concerns. For example, Locke's account of private property in land and the political regulation of it and his famous "spoilage proviso" can provide an insightful account of what we would now term "weak sustainability," Aristotle's important distinction between *chrematistics* (short-term money-making) and *oikonomia* (prudent long-term management) as the over-arching objective of the human economy can enrich green/ecological reconstructive critiques of capitalist economic theory and practice, and Marx's "metabolic" understanding of the material and interdependent relationship between humanity and the nonhuman world can shed light on the social organizations required to yield the energy and resources that power the human economy. Though we may have more sophisticated scientific knowledge and different conceptual tools than older thinkers had, many of the issues they discussed are still relevant.

Green political theory, like mainstream contemporary political theory, is more appropriately seen as one contribution to the ongoing conversation about "the human condition" (as Arendt put it)—a conversation enacted within the canon of political theory. But green political theory and its engagement with canonical thought offer distinctive contributions to the material, moral, and political dimensions of the complex and ever-changing relations between *zoon politikon* (Aristotle's telling phrase for the human individual as a political/social animal) and the ecological context. This volume is testifies eloquently to the vibrancy of that conversation and to how each new generation brings its own particular concerns to this intergenerational dialogue.

A very welcome feature of this volume is the inclusion of some nontraditional thinkers within what we usually understand as the political theory canon. Marking a positive departure from the standard description of the canon as European or Western and essentially the work of white men, we find thinkers such as Wollstonecraft, Du Bois, and Confucius. This volume also broadens the list of thinkers who have been discussed or interpreted from a green point of view (prominent here are Rousseau, Marx, Mill, and Locke) by including such relatively underanalyzed thinkers as Hume, Burke, Machiavelli, and Arendt.

The green reading of the thinkers in this volume also reminds us of the importance of having a historical sensibility when contemplating our present situation and possible future trajectories. By reading these great thinkers from the point of view of today's globalized, unequal, carbon-addicted, and unsustainable societies, we can gain salutary lessons from previous human societies and civilizations that have faced (and usually lost) major challenges, some of them ecological and some having to do with resources.

The readings in this volume raise the question of why anyone would confidently think that current ways of life and currently dominant views of the good life and associated forms of economic development, which are at most decades old, will continue into the foreseeable future. Here re-reading the canon is rather like looking back in the rear-view mirror as a sensible part of looking ahead, helping us plan, make decisions, and inform our judgment on specific courses of action. Looking back and reflecting on the evolution of political thought is to my mind a salutary and sobering experience, an opportunity to pause and reflect rather than rush headlong on the basis of ungrounded confidence. In this way a volume such as this can help guard against a certain "presentism" and "exceptionalism" in which the present generation thinks it is unique and so different from all previous human generations or thinks that it has solved perennial human-nature problems. A thorough knowledge of the political theory canon—especially a knowledge that places each thinker within his or her social, historical, and ecological context, as this volume does—can help prevent or at least militate against a dangerous ahistorical arrogance based on ignorance and amnesia.

I would like to congratulate all the contributing authors, but especially the editors, Peter Cannavò and Joe Lane, for collectively producing an exceptional publication. In looking backward and offering green readings of the canon, this volume also charts a new and exciting future research agenda. Hopefully it will be read as an invitation for further conversations and responses from "mainstream" political theory and scholars of the history of political thought alike, as well as charting new areas for scholarship in green political theory. And who knows, perhaps from this exchange we may get some insight into what Plato would think about peak oil.

John Barry
Reader in Green Political Economy
Queen's University Belfast
October 2013

Acknowledgments

A collection such as this is clearly the product of a number of contributors. We heartily thank our authors for their hard work and for their patient willingness to accept numerous editorial suggestions and subject their essays to several rounds of revision.

We would also like to thank John Barry for lending his considerable reputation to this project by contributing a foreword. We also have enormous gratitude for those behind the scenes of this project. First of all, we would like to thank our colleagues in the Environmental Political Theory community (many of whom contributed essays to this book), who regularly gather for a workshop at the annual meeting of the Western Political Association. Our small but growing community has, over the past twenty years, created the academic field that made this book both possible and necessary. Moreover, our colleagues' inspiration, academic insights, and encouragement, each year at the annual EPT gathering, have been tremendously valuable. We owe especial thanks to Joel Kassiola, whose enthusiastic support and practical guidance were truly essential in getting this project off the ground.

Thanks also go to the three anonymous, diligent reviewers whose comments and criticisms made for a vastly better book.

We would also like to thank Colin Christensen, Anne Marie McLean, Rachael Sharp, and Tara Mueller, undergraduates at Emory & Henry College, who did the painstaking work of formatting and proofreading the manuscript. Colin deserves particular thanks for reading and re-reading the manuscript to check and correct notes and references. At times, he has carried the work of a third co-editor, and we hope this apprenticeship in the world of scholarly publishing will serve him well as he starts graduate school in political theory in 2014.

Perhaps most of all, we would like to thank Clay Morgan, our editor at the MIT Press. Over the years, Clay has arguably done more than anyone else in putting EPT scholarship into published form and building the reputation of our field. He has been incredibly patient with our countless delays and missed deadlines, and we owe him enormous gratitude.

Our families certainly deserve our sincere gratitude for making it possible for us to invest so many hours in this project. Without their support and encouragement, this volume would certainly never have been completed.

Finally, we would like to dedicate this book to our students. Their enthusiasm for political theory and environmental politics continually re-energizes us, and their willingness to ask tough, insightful questions makes this whole project worthwhile.

Introduction: How We Got Here

Peter F. Cannavò and Joseph H. Lane Jr.

Environmental, or green, political theory is a relative newcomer to the field of political thought. Not until the late 1980s did a significant number of political theorists begin considering the fundamental political implications of what is often termed "the environmental crisis"—modern society's increasingly dangerous impact on the biophysical world, including such problems as climate change, pollution and toxicity, habitat and biodiversity loss, resource exhaustion, ozone depletion, and acid rain—and of humanity's moral and material relations with the rest of nature. However, theorizing about the political and moral aspects of humanity's impact on the natural world goes back at least as far as the nineteenth century, to the writings of Henry David Thoreau, George Perkins Marsh, and John Muir. All three of those writers criticized American society for its environmentally destructive practices (from distinct perspectives and philosophical commitments), but none of them elaborated a systematic theoretical account of human society and its relations with the rest of the natural world.

In the twentieth century, a wide range of thinkers, epitomized by Aldo Leopold and Rachel Carson, took such critiques further and began articulating a more coherent ethical and political perspective in explicit opposition to the dominant paradigm of crude, unrestrained anthropocentrism. Leopold offered a new ecological conception of citizenship: "[A] land ethic changes the role of *Homo sapiens* from conqueror of the land-community to plain member and citizen of it. It implies respect for his fellow-members, and also respect for the community as such."[1] Carson, with her dire analysis of the environmental impacts of DDT and other artificial chemicals, provided a powerful critique of America's veneration of technological progress and urged an ethic of ecological interdependence.[2]

By the early 1970s, a number of authors, many of them scientists, were refining or developing important conceptual frameworks to analyze humanity's relationship with the environment. These frameworks included

Garrett Hardin's "tragedy of the commons" and Barry Commoner's "four laws of ecology."[3] William Ophuls, building on Hardin's work, explained the environmental crisis in terms borrowed from Thomas Hobbes and other early modern philosophers. Ophuls framed contemporary environmental problems as classic examples of the need for constraints on individual liberty. In essence, Ophuls argued that human material relations and their physical impacts on the Earth and its resources were pushing at the limits of our planet's "carrying capacity." The resulting ecological crisis, in Ophuls's view, forced a critical reappraisal of the individualist political philosophy inherited from classical liberal thinkers of the seventeenth and eighteenth centuries.[4]

Also in the 1970s, Murray Bookchin was diagnosing human domination and degradation of the natural world as an outgrowth of hierarchical relationships within society.[5] He developed a decentralist, anarchist political perspective that would become highly influential. Soon a wide range of environmentalist thinkers were analyzing the ecological crisis in terms of a critique of hierarchies and centralization of authority. Françoise d'Eaubonne saw the domination of nature as connected with the domination of women by men, and Carolyn Merchant traced the intellectual history of that connection.[6] André Gorz saw ecological problems as related to labor alienation.[7] Wendell Berry, a major figure in modern agrarian thought, connected the environmental crisis to our disconnection from place and the related industrialization and consolidation of agriculture.[8] Kirkpatrick Sale, Peter Berg, and other American activists developed the concept of ecologically defined place into the perspective of bioregionalism.[9] Meanwhile, the emergence of Green parties around the world during the 1970s and the 1980s signaled the rise of the ecologically oriented organized political movement; those parties also articulated a critique of industrial society that tied ecological issues and values to other political principles, including nonviolence, social justice, and participatory democracy.[10] Starting in the 1980s, the environmental dimensions of social justice and inequality were further highlighted by the environmental justice movement. Robert Bullard, Dorceta Taylor, Laura Pulido, and others analyzed connections among race, class, and environmental degradation as they developed a theoretical articulation of the movement.[11] Writings on environmental injustice also emerged from the global South—for example, the Indian scientist and activist Vandana Shiva criticized globalization from a social justice and ecological perspective.[12]

In the 1970s and the 1980s, Christopher Stone, John Passmore, Peter Singer, Robin Attfield, Tom Regan, Paul Taylor, Holmes Rolston III,

Richard Routley (Sylvan), Val Routley (Plumwood), Bryan Norton, and other philosophers began to offer rigorous philosophical analyses of the extent of human moral responsibilities toward individual organisms or natural systems, thus developing the field of environmental ethics.[13] Arne Naess pioneered the influential ecocentric and spiritual concept of deep ecology,[14] and so offered a radical re-imagining of the place and self-realization of human beings within the natural world.

However, it was not until the late 1980s that social and political theorists began to significantly and systematically consider the implications of the environmental crisis for such fundamental political concepts as rights, community, citizenship, justice, property, democracy, civic virtue, the state, and membership, and to consider how nature and politics materially and conceptually constitute one another. Such analysis goes beyond environmental ethics' focus on moral responsibility regarding nature and involves more intellectual rigor and conceptual depth than activists' social critiques and political programs. During the 1980s and the early 1990s, pioneering works in environmental political theory were authored by John Dryzek, Mark Sagoff, Robert Paehlke, Joel Kassiola, Andrew Dobson, Robyn Eckersley, and Robert Goodin.[15] These works may be distinguished from the first stirrings of environmental political thought a generation earlier by a more systematic political analysis that considered material relations, social institutions, power structures, conceptions of community and membership, and humanity's ecological context. These writers successfully fused accomplished theoretical analysis and critiques of both mainstream political thought and contemporary environmentalist writings with a recognition that they were participating not only in a debate among academics but also in a growing public discourse about our increasingly serious ecological challenges. Their works were more rigorously engaged with the terms of social-scientific analysis of politics and power while being accessible to a broad audience.

Since the 1990s, environmental political theory has become an established subfield within academic political theory. Timothy Luke, John Barry, Val Plumwood, Kate Soper, Ted Benton, Andrew Dobson, Jane Bennett, Bill Chaloupka, John Meyer, Andrew Biro, and other theorists, joined by environmental historians such as William Cronon and Donald Worster and historically minded philosophers such as Max Oelschlaeger, have gone beyond the original bounds of environmental political theory to interrogate the intellectual discourse and foundational assumptions of the environmental movement, including leading "green" ideologies such as deep ecology and concepts such as "sustainability," "place," "wilderness," "animal rights," and "nature" itself.[16] Often such authors draw upon postmodern or poststructuralist thought or upon the intellectual resources provided by critical theory or analytic philosophy.

Other current thinkers, such as David Schlosberg, have drawn on a wide range of influences from political activists, particularly those in the environmental justice movement, to articulate new possibilities for realizing justice and for democratizing our politics and polities.[17] A number of theorists have also drawn preexisting traditions of social and political thought into a dialogue with environmental politics: liberalism (Marcel Wissenburg, Robyn Eckersley), theories of the state and law (Robyn Eckersley) and of globalization (Robert Paehlke), pragmatism (Andrew Light), democratic theory (Terence Ball), Marxism (Ted Benton and John Bellamy Foster), feminism (Val Plumwood, Karen Warren, and Ariel Salleh), African-American thought (Kim Smith), capabilities theory (David Schlosberg and Breena Holland), communitarianism (Avner de-Shalit and Robyn Eckersley), French political thought (Kerry Whiteside), agrarian thought (Kim Smith), civic republicanism (John Barry, Peter Cannavò, and Thad Williamson), virtue ethics (Ronald Sandler and Philip Cafaro), and materialism (Jane Bennett).[18]

Environmental, or green, political theory is an increasingly rich and diverse field. The growing community of green political theorists disagree on many issues of both method and conclusions, but they share certain philosophical aspirations: Environmental political theory aims at a deeper understanding of human relations with the rest of nature, challenges mainstream political theory to recognize environmental concerns, challenges environmental ethics to consider political and social context, and interrogates the often unexamined assumptions and conclusions of environmental activists. While generally sympathetic to the aims of the environmental movement, environmental political theorists are not bound by these goals and try to prioritize intellectual rigor above ideological commitment. Though still committed to ultimately reshaping public discourse, environmental political theorists are now writing on a more academic level for an audience steeped in contemporary and historical social and political thought and its conceptual categories.

As green political thought has become less a theoretical elaboration on environmentalism and more a rigorous philosophical enterprise, a growing number of environmental political theorists have set out to situate this "new" field within the broader compass of the tradition of political philosophy, reaching back into the history of political thought to uncover both recurring narratives and neglected insights. After all, the uncomfortable embedding of the human animal in a broader nature has always been a source of philosophical inquiry and political importance and has raised truly perennial questions.

Scholars engaged in exploring the connections between environmental theory and earlier philosophical traditions have engaged a wide range of thinkers, including Aristotle, John Locke, Jean-Jacques Rousseau, Karl Marx, John Stuart Mill, Martin Heidegger, Hannah Arendt, and more recent but equally fundamental thinkers such as Iris Marion Young, Michel Foucault, Martha Nussbaum, and John Rawls. Some scholars have focused on individual thinkers and elements of their thought that address or shed insight on our relations with the rest of the natural world—Melissa Lane (Plato), John O'Neill (Aristotle), Kerry Whiteside (Arendt), Joe Lane and Rebecca Clark (Rousseau), Jane Bennett (G. W. F. Hegel), John Bellamy Foster and Ted Benton (Marx), Kim Smith (Frederick Douglass and W. E. B. Du Bois), Breena Holland and David Schlosberg (Nussbaum), John Meyer (Aristotle and Hobbes), Andrew Biro (Rousseau, Marx, Theodor Adorno, and Herbert Marcuse), and Charles Miller (Thomas Jefferson), to cite a few examples.[19]

Nevertheless, there is a need for a comprehensive volume presenting the environmental implications and insights of leading thinkers in the political theory canon, particularly those thinkers who are not animated by or explicitly focused on environmental matters. It is vitally important that we apply the perspectives of mature green political theory to reinterpreting the political theory canon and that we explore the forgotten or unexpected insights of canonical theorists to enrich the theoretical dialogue about ecological issues.

Consequently, after discussions with various colleagues in environmental political theory, we came up with the idea for this volume. Although some other works have tried to connect environmental political thought and politics with the broader tradition of political philosophy, none have taken the approach that we have followed here. However, several excellent volumes deserve special mention. We highlight the limits of their coverage not for the purpose of criticism but to demonstrate the need for our own collection.

Andrew Dobson and Robyn Eckersley's *Political Theory and the Ecological Challenge*[20] surveys the implications of environmental politics for several ideological traditions (conservatism, liberalism, socialism, feminism, nationalism, communitarianism, cosmopolitanism) and several political concepts (democracy, justice, the state, representation, freedom and rights, citizenship, security). However, Dobson and Eckersley's focus on traditions and concepts doesn't provide a sustained treatment of the environmental perspectives and insights of specific thinkers and texts. In many ways, then, their project is complementary to ours.

Explorations in Environmental Political Theory, edited by Joel Jay Kassiola, covers connections between a few of the thinkers covered herein and environmentalist thought, but the focus is squarely on latter-day green theorists bringing their own insights to bear on today's ecological challenges.[21] In fact, Kassiola's introductory essay essentially calls for a book such as ours, as he notes that the connections between environmental issues and the history of political philosophy haven't received the attention they deserve from political theorists.

In *Environmentalism and Political Theory*, Robyn Eckersley analyzes several major thinkers, including Locke and Marx. However, she confronts these theorists primarily for the purpose of evaluating their fit with ecocentrism.

John Meyer's *Political Nature* provides insightful interpretations of Aristotle and Thomas Hobbes, but with a more particular focus on illuminating how conceptions of nature interact with conceptions of politics.

In *Denaturalizing Ecological Politics*, Andrew Biro undertakes close, detailed readings of Rousseau, Marx, Adorno, and Marcuse. However, he looks at those thinkers through the lens of one specific concern: our purported alienation from nature.

David Macauley's edited volume *Minding Nature*—a valuable collection of essays on significant thinkers and their environmental insights[22]—anticipated our project in some ways. However, a number of the thinkers explored most deeply in *Minding Nature* are explicitly environmental theorists or writers—Bookchin, Carson, Commoner, Paul Ehrlich—who are already extensively covered in the literature on green theory and, with the exception of Bookchin, don't theorize about fundamental political concepts. As regards the social and political theorists featured in the other essays, the historical coverage is fairly circumscribed, as only two of them—Thomas Hobbes and Charles Fourier—date from before the twentieth century.

The Purpose of This Volume

But why a collection on the political theory *canon*, and why is it organized in such canonical fashion—each essay focused on a single thinker and presented in a distinctly chronological order (with the exception of the final essay, on Confucius)? We are convinced that those theorists whose work focuses on modern understandings of environmental issues must recognize that the most insightful and influential political theorists of the past still have much to say to us, even though their questions, concerns, and conclusions are historically and geographically situated in eras in which many of our most pressing issues didn't exist in their current forms. Important thinkers of the past, *including those not directly concerned with environmental issues*, can offer profound insights into how our ecological situation affects our politics, and vice versa. Political theorists, in addressing their own historical and geographic situation and in touching on more transhistorical issues (justice, equality, liberty, rights, difference, membership, the good life, gender, family, property, economy, war and peace), provide a number of ecologically relevant insights: how we get our living from nature, adapt to ecological conditions, distribute natural resources and amenities, and assign property rights; how the harvesting and distribution of resources organizes political and social institutions, from state to family, and creates power relations and conflict within and between communities; how conceptions of place and landscape help define political community; how conceptions of citizenship, rights, and moral obligation are situated in deeper conceptions of human nature and identity that relate back back to our placement within, and our ideas about, the biophysical world and to our conceptions of nonhuman animals. Individual theorists' thought processes, insights, internal tensions, inconsistencies, and conclusions all reflect the challenge of trying to understand a political society that is inescapably situated in the resources, rhythms, and limitations of the natural world and yet also partly governed by its own operative principles. Moreover, there are important insights to be gained from how a particular theorist grappled with the specific problems, limitations, and opportunities (including those related to ecological context) provided by his or her particular time and place. Understanding those insights often involves contesting standard readings of theorists' conceptions of humanity's relationship with nature. Many of these essays do just that.

The essays in this volume place canonical thinkers in dialogue with questions raised and theories advanced by recent environmental political thought. Such a dialogue advances a deeper understanding of the many dynamics that complicate the relationships among human beings, their political societies, and the rest of nature. Far too often, "traditional" political theory is oblivious to important consequences of applying such principles as right and justice to human societies without considering the much broader web of ecological relationships within which these societies are situated. Bringing environmental thought into a dialogue with canonical works may thus enable us to correct contemporary political theory's shortsightedness regarding the natural world. Scholars of canonical thinkers would do well to consider their subjects' critical engagement with humanity's ecological context more fully.

By the same token, however, environmentalist thought too often avoids or minimizes broader political issues that should be recognized and considered. Green political theory, like any school of thought, risks falling into overfamiliar and too comfortably utilized conceptual categories that may stultify our reasoning or exclude necessary challenges. When we get thoroughly caught up in discussions of nature, sustainability, environmental justice, and other familiar "green" concepts, we tend to forget the centuries-old intellectual, political, and historical traditions from which these concepts have emerged. In this regard, we should heed Peter Euben's reminder that all political theorists are too prone to falling into "presentism," an intellectual myopia that he defines as "a proclivity to analyze contemporary culture and politics using only contemporary texts, theories, and methods."[23] Euben warns that this tendency leads us to reflect back our antecedent concerns in our diagnoses of our own problems and to dismiss as irrelevant those thinkers who had different problems or who reached conclusions different from our own. "Presentism" occludes our perspective on our own position within the larger context of human efforts to understand the world, convinces us that our problems are unique, and thus reinforces conceptual categories that may not be helpful. Thus, Euben argues that we "need distant mirrors that are premodern texts, unpopular theories, peculiar locutions, and political or cultural non-sequiturs to better map the outlines of the contemporary." If we don't avail ourselves of the vantages that such texts provide, we are likely to make the false conclusion that "we here and now are the culmination of history" and that "what came before was aiming to be what we are."[24] "Depressingly," Euben writes, "this view is often held by those who regard themselves as repudiating narratives of progress."[25]

No group of thinkers has been more determined to "repudiate narratives of progress" than environmentalists. But at the same time, environmentalists, especially the most radical ones, often tend to speak as theoretical progressives of a peculiarly definitive sort; we might even infer from some environmentalist writings that really great *thought* emerged only in the last 150 years or so—beginning, perhaps, when Thoreau went to Walden Pond in 1845—and that only the faintest glimmers of valuable insights are discernible in the works of earlier writers.[26] Although environmentalists aver a genuine respect, which in many cases may involve nostalgic, patronizing, and racially insensitive caricature, toward pre-modern or aboriginal peoples who didn't have our problems, they are most interested in reading writers who are focused exclusively on the self-conscious articulation of our times and our issues. In doing so, they are particularly vulnerable to the trap of "presentism" that Euben identifies. In writing on canonical thinkers, the authors in this volume have tried to uncover the useful interactions that may be generated by a conversation between these historical thinkers and contemporary green thought without slighting either. In part through the chronological treatment of the essays, we have tried to view contemporary questions more clearly through "distant mirrors" that may help us to better understand where we are *and* how we got here.

Our approach has been greatly influenced by our experience as teachers. In teaching courses on the history of political thought, we have repeatedly seen that when students recognize the broad implications of a thinker's understanding of the nexus between the political and the natural worlds they begin to appreciate why earlier works have real implications for today's political issues and policy debates. They are consequently much more motivated to delve further into the texts. We have encouraged all our contributors to write as if addressing students and scholars who will be engaging the primary texts alongside their commentaries, thus guiding students into the implications of those texts and toward a reconsideration of their enduring importance, relevance, and value.

Furthermore, these essays are written for scholarly colleagues on both sides of the "divide" between green political thought and historical or canonical political philosophy, so as to introduce them to one another. The authors draw theoretical connections between these two branches of political thought and raise questions for future scholarly explorations at the interface between green and canonical theory. As was noted earlier, these essays offer new readings of canonical theorists and texts and thus should have an effect on scholarly debates. Some of these readings—notably Zev Trachtenberg's surprisingly "green" take on Locke and the limits of Locke's understanding of property and Piers Stephens's revisionist reading of John Stuart Mill's seminal essay "Nature"—are particularly provocative. In short, we have encouraged our contributors to show how a new reading of each theorist might expand and complicate the debates that we have about both political theory and political theorists. Indeed, we hope that this volume will stimulate more scholarship and expand the circle of political theorists exploring human embeddedness in the natural world.

Ultimately every collection of essays rests on decisions about which topics to cover and which to exclude. Questions of inclusion and exclusion were particularly acute in the case of this volume. We relied on two main criteria in selecting topics and essays, and we also made some meaningful exceptions. Both the rules and the concessions warrant brief explanation.

We began with the resolution to focus as much as possible on the traditional figures in the standard canon of political theory. The political theory canon, like all canons, is defined by contested borders and problematic prejudices about those issues that matter and those that can be safely ignored. Nevertheless, we can safely say that almost any scholar of political theory would include Plato, Aristotle, Machiavelli, Hobbes, Locke, Rousseau, Mill, and Marx among the most important thinkers in the 2,500-year history of Western theorizing about politics. Moving beyond those obvious choices to other central figures, we have included Edmund Burke and David Hume, yet we are aware that some scholars might find the absence of essays on Thomas Aquinas, Baruch Spinoza, Francis Bacon, Montesquieu, Immanuel Kant, Adam Smith, or G. W. F. Hegel troubling. To some degree, these decisions were dictated by the most mundane of constraints: the availability of appropriate scholars willing to contribute essays. Yet economy of space also set limits. For example, including Smith would have provided an opportunity to explore both free-market capitalism and the Scottish Enlightenment, yet the inclusion of Locke and Marx on the one hand and Hume on the other meant that these two topics were already at least partly covered.

Despite these potential sources of controversy or criticism, we have done our best to include those theorists who are most widely accepted as major figures in the Western political thought canon. We have done so on the assumption, not unjustified, that these thinkers offer works of a depth and a complexity that present us with "an uncommon opportunity" to rethink what we believe about the causes and contours of our environmental crisis. As John Meyer claimed in his earlier study of Hobbes and Aristotle, "Both [of these canonical authors] ... offer exceptionally thorough treatments of their understandings of nature and politics. Their texts thus provide an uncommon opportunity to explore this relationship in a way that moves beyond the tendentious and ultimately less interesting question of intention."[27] In the same spirit, we think that approaching ecological concerns through the thinkers we have included in this volume offer new perspectives on our recent efforts to understand our place in this world.

We also resolved to avoid discussions of thinkers whose work was already primarily and explicitly focused on environmental problems. Such thinkers—Thoreau, Leopold, and Bookchin among them—may demonstrate prescience and insight into the dynamics of human political life that argue for their inclusion in a larger canon, but their environmental insights are foregrounded in their thought and are widely discussed in many works by green political theorists. To include them here would add little to the extensive scholarship on these authors in the fields of green political thought and environmental studies more generally.[28] Moreover, their inclusion might detract from one of the main objectives of this volume: to approach the environmental problematic from the standpoint of those motivated first by a desire to understand the political problematic.

We have made at least two exceptions to the rigorous application of the primary criteria described above. First, we have included two thinkers—Mary Wollstonecraft and W. E. B. Du Bois—who are less commonly recognized as canonical but whose works offer invaluable, pioneering insights into a crucial constellation of issues arising out of modernity's conflicted relationship with conceptions of race and gender. These insights are highly germane to the concerns of this volume. From Aristotle's notion that Greeks cannot be natural slaves to classical liberalism's conception of the autonomous self as masculine, constructions of race and gender have been central to political theory. Moreover, conceptions of nature and the organization of political society with respect to the natural world are themselves closely bound up with social relations regarding race and gender, as the aforementioned literature on ecofeminism and environmental justice also makes clear.

We have included essays on Wollstonecraft and Du Bois in order to provide a broad theoretical groundwork for interrogating the relationship between these literatures and political theory more broadly. We think that each theorist offers valuable foundational insights into the interplay of race, gender, and conceptualizations of politics and nature. In addition, we have included essays on two theorists, Heidegger and Arendt, who are increasingly recognized as canonical even though are not as central to the canon of political theory as, say, Kant. However, Heidegger and Arendt are enormously relevant for this volume both because of their more fundamental philosophical insights and because they directly addressed the pathologies of modern technological society.

We have also departed from the traditional definition of a *Western* canon by inviting Joel Jay Kassiola's essay on Confucius. Clearly geography alone might explain why Confucius is so often excluded from survey discussions of political theory; the political theory canon, as taught in the West, has confined itself to thinkers who lived and worked in Europe, North America, and, in some cases, the broader Mediterranean world and the Middle East. Environmental political theory has been greatly advanced by some Australian scholars but has nevertheless largely focused on European and American work. At the same time, many environmental activists, particularly deep ecologists, are convinced that a mutually exclusive division between so-called Eastern and Western worldviews is of paramount importance in understanding the dynamics—particularly of Western capitalist states and economies—that have generated our environmental crisis. They have urged greater attention to non-Western philosophical, cultural, and religious perspectives, especially Buddhism, Taoism, and Native American religions.[29] However, we fear that non-Western traditions have perhaps been too easily caricatured, idealized, and excerpted in some environmentalist thought, again without the careful attention and depth of analysis that they deserve. It is thus worth considering non-Western traditions from a more rigorous standpoint, both to glean their environmental perspectives and insights and to treat them as the complex philosophical systems that they are.

Confucian thought is certainly a good place to begin, as it constitutes a profoundly influential tradition within the world's most populous nation, a rising military and economic superpower with an "ecological footprint" rivaling that of the United States. China and its political and philosophical traditions are simply too important to ignore as we confront global climate change.[30] Furthermore, as Kassiola discusses, Confucianism has a good deal to say about our relationship with nature and offers a sharp contrast to the anthropocentric conceptions of humanity and nature that have been highly influential in the West.

Of course, including only one essay on one East Asian thinker is an inadequate basis for reconsidering all the insights that the huge diversity of non-Western (Middle Eastern, South Asian, East Asian, African, Latin American, indigenous) political and philosophical writings and discourse might bring to environmental thought. Space constraints and the shortcomings in our own expertise prevented us from including a broader consideration of these far-too-often-marginalized voices, though Farah Godrej and Fred Dallmayr are also already doing valuable work in this area.[31] We hope that their work and Kassiola's essay may inspire others to explore non-Western environmental and political thought. We would even dare hope that someone might edit a companion book to this one focusing on political theory outside Western confines.

Despite the fundamental unity of this collection, we allowed our contributors to follow their own intellectual interests and dispositions and take a variety of different approaches to how their subject may be best read for enlightening angles on current environmental debates, political or academic. Some provided very general overviews of their assigned thinker and tried to provide a comprehensive summary of the various insights that might inform green political thought. The essays on Aristotle, Hobbes, Hume, Rousseau, Burke, and Heidegger might be considered to take such broad views of their subjects that they can serve as introductions to a more general study of the author's approach to humanity's relations with nature. Other authors chose to focus on a particular aspect of their thinker, highlighting one concept or text that seems particularly insightful from an environmental standpoint. The essays on Plato, Machiavelli, Wollstonecraft, Du Bois, Arendt, and Confucius all fit this mold. Finally, as was noted above, we have a few essays that challenge, as incomplete or wrong, commonly accepted readings of much-discussed thinkers. The essays on Locke, Mill, and Marx take issue with anti-ecological interpretations of them. Moreover, rather than ask the contributors to adhere to a rigid, textbook-style formula, we allowed them to use their distinctive voices and writing styles.

Such divergences in approach should be viewed as a virtue of this volume insofar as it offers a number of models for applying old thinkers to new questions. In fact, we might venture that these essays, read against one another, offer many insights into the various intellectual and stylistic approaches that present-day political theorists take when reading the canon for a deeper understanding of our most pressing political and environmental problems.

Summary of the Essays

Sheri Breen's essay on Plato (chapter 1) is largely critical of his utopian scheme in *The Republic*, and of all the essays it is probably the least sympathetic to its subject.[32] Rather than focus on Platonic idealism or on Plato's account of the feverish city in book II of *The Republic*, Breen looks at the class structure of Plato's ideal city, Kallipolis. Kallipolis, which is initially populated by children with no cultural or historical memory and has a communist ruling elite divorced from manual labor and property ownership is, Breen argues, characterized by placelessness and detachment from nature. Plato, whether he is in fact deliberately suggesting the impossibility of utopia or, as Breen suggests, is more genuinely invested in his ideal city, nevertheless alerts us that attempts to create a selfless governing elite detached from material cares and interests can lead to disconnection from and disregard for nature. Though Breen cites Thomas More's *Utopia* as an example of a propertyless ideal society more closely connected with nature, one cannot help but wonder if a sense of ownership over nature through both work and possession is a more plausible route to environmental responsibility. Breen also challenges us to directly confront the question whether politics or polities can be considered in isolation from their place in the natural world and their relationships to specific nonhuman systems, particular locales, and ecologies. By posing this question directly, Breen opens the volume with an immediate emphasis on the inescapability of the environment in our political thinking.

In chapter 2, Özgüç Orhan challenges anthropocentric interpretations of Aristotle. Such interpretations often focus on Aristotle's statement in the *Politics* that plants and animals were "made" for human use. Orhan puts this statement in its proper context of Aristotle's discussion of household economics rather than in the context of a more general account of the ends and purposes of nonhuman nature and notes that the anthropocentric sentiment seemingly articulated here isn't repeated in Aristotle's other works. He notes how Aristotle's "scientific" writing emphasizes the kinship between human beings and other animals. He also suggests that Aristotle's teleology and his notions of human virtue and flourishing, which put limits on material acquisition, continue to offer a philosophical basis for ecological responsibility. In fact, Orhan partly blames our environmental crisis on modernity's rejection of the Aristotelian conception of nature and directly calls into question the assumption—common among environmentalists—that Aristotelian thought represented a turn *away* from nature.[33] Aristotle thus continues to offer a useful counterpoint to modern conceptions of nature, the human good, and property.

In chapter 3, Francisco Seijo puts heavy emphasis on Niccolò Machiavelli's institutional insights. Seijo takes issue with contemporary greens who argue that maximalist approaches to political decentralization—eco-anarchism or bioregionalism—are most conducive to ecological sustainability. Seijo notes that Machiavelli sees changing *Fortuna* (roughly, fortune) as destabilizing the conditions for peaceful coexistence among small polities and providing an impetus for expansion. Drawing on Machiavelli's account of Rome, Seijo argues that issues of security and (today) large-scale ecological problems make a somewhat loose partnership between a large central government and its constituent smaller polities—perhaps a kind of eco-federalism—superior to maximalist approaches to decentralization. Seijo's work suggests that Machiavelli's emphasis on the innately precarious character of political union in a world full of threats and the imminent possibility of collapse into chaos may be understood in a broader way than Machiavelli himself might recognize. Machiavelli's insistence on the political imposition of order may be understood as a valid response to both political and ecological instabilities, perhaps anticipating works such as Robin Eckersley's *The Green State*.

John Meyer's discussion of Thomas Hobbes (chapter 4) focuses on how Hobbes, who offers thoroughly realized accounts of both the natural world and the political community, illuminates the relationship between conceptions of nature and conceptions of politics. Meyer rejects two leading interpretations of Hobbes: the dualist interpretation that sees Hobbes as sharply contrasting a violent, brutal nature with a peaceful, orderly political commonwealth and the derivative interpretation that sees Hobbes as simply deriving his political theory from his mechanistic view of nature. Meyer in fact sees in Hobbes's political theory a mutually constitutive relationship between human beings' participation in and interaction with nature on the one hand and their political life on the other. Based on his discussion of Hobbes, Meyer goes on to criticize environmentalists who try to derive political principles or prescriptions from ecological science. Though Meyer in no way claims that Hobbes had an ecological sensibility, he argues that recognition of a mutually constitutive relationship between nature and politics would provide a more politically promising approach for environmentalism than reductionist attempts to insist that a purified and sustainable politics may be directly derived from a "corrected" or "ecological" view of the natural world. Indeed, Meyer's insights are focused on meta-theoretical lessons from Hobbes rather than on Hobbes's substantive views about nature. The attentive reader may also notice that Meyer's arguments are in some tension with the essays by Orhan and Kassiola, which both emphasize how foundational worldviews of nature shape political theory and practice.

In chapter 5, Zev Trachtenberg challenges standard readings of John Locke as sanctioning the more or less unlimited exploitation of nature and a very strong conception of property rights. Trachtenberg agrees that Locke, who doesn't recognize either the contribution of ecosystem services to the value of land or the ecological interconnections between separate parcels of property, is not a proto-environmentalist. However, he develops a nuanced and novel view of Locke as offering a theory of sustainable habitation, not exploitation, of the natural world.[34] (Peter Cannavò, in his essay on Arendt, draws on Trachtenberg's concept of habitation.)

Trachtenberg draws not only on Locke's familiar moral limitations on the appropriation of property—the "Lockean Provisos" that no man should appropriate so much that it spoils and that one should leave enough and as good for others—but also on Locke's arguments against Robert Filmer's notion of the divine right of kings, and on James Tully's reading of Locke as advocating only usufructory, not full ownership, rights to nature. Trachtenberg presents Lockean theory as justifying a significant role for government in the management and conservation of natural resources. In so doing, he underscores the limits of individual property ownership even under a classic liberal theory such as Locke's. (Interestingly, Trachtenberg's reading of Locke is strongly at odds with that of Piers H. G. Stephens, who touches on Locke in his chapter on Mill. Moreover, Cannavò, in discussing Arendt's theory of habitation and drawing some contrasts with Locke, presents perhaps a more anti-environmental reading of Locke than does Trachtenberg.)

Andrew Valls, in his essay on David Hume (chapter 6), takes up the common claim that liberalism and environmental values are fundamentally incompatible. Valls's reading of Hume, much like Trachtenberg's reading of Locke and Stephens's reading of Mill, suggests that green critiques of liberal thought may mischaracterize liberalism and unduly foreclose the prospects for a greener liberalism. Because Hume, Valls argues, isn't limited by the political constraints associated with Locke's conception of natural property rights, a Humean perspective doesn't face the same strictures on the regulation of property to achieve environmental justice and other green policy goals. Moreover, Hume emphasizes human beings' embodied, physically situated natures. Consequently, Hume underscores our commonality with other animals. Although he sees justice as limited to relations among human beings, he also sees human beings as having duties of benevolence toward other animals—an idea that emerges again in Barbara Seeber's chapter on Mary Wollstonecraft. In fact, Valls notes, Hume sees benevolence as a higher virtue than justice. Finally, Valls argues that Hume's emphasis on our embeddedness in the physical world can show the way to a conception of biotic community not unlike Aldo Leopold's and yet still open to the humanistic political claims of liberalism.

In chapter 7, Joseph Lane builds on his earlier published work to argue that Jean-Jacques Rousseau anticipated many key environmentalist narratives and themes. Although Lane argues that Rousseau's *Discourse on the Arts and Sciences*, *Discourse on the Origins of Inequality*, *Social Contract*, *Julie*, and *Reveries of the Solitary Walker* all contributed influential narratives that recur in subsequent environmentalist theorizing, he insists that it is through recognizing the *interdependence* of these disparate works in Rousseau's *corpus* that his most important contributions to green theory can be recognized. Rousseau's works appear to offer self-contradictory understandings of the relationship between nature and the political world, but Lane insists that Rousseau was explicating the complexity of that relationship as it was being transformed by the Enlightenment and the emergence of modernity. Rousseau's writings articulate a complex and interdependent system of thought that explores the paradoxes inherent in modern life, and as such, they may help us understand both the promise and the limits of enshrining "Nature" as the value to be preserved in our efforts to temper and control the destructive powers of modern technologies. Lane argues that Rousseau's writings are essential to understanding the complex interrelationships among various strands of modern environmentalism and our prospects for controlling humanity's impacts on the natural world.

Though environmentalism and green thought have largely been associated with the political left, there are strongly conservative elements in the green impulse toward sustainability and preservation. And, as even Corey Robin, a trenchant critic of conservatism, has noted, "it remains an unfortunate reality of American higher education that social scientists and historians can get through their training with only the most passing acquaintance with conservatism."[35] Consequently, the inclusion in this collection of Edmund Burke, a foundational conservative theorist, is doubly important.

Harlan Wilson's essay on Burke (chapter 8) brings out the affinities and tensions between green and conservative thought. Wilson first cites Burke's aesthetics, especially his writings about gardens, as favoring a cooperative relationship between nature and art. More significant, though, is Burke's emphasis on complexity in both nature and society, which feeds into a focus on intergenerational obligation and caution about risks and innovation. Thus, Wilson argues, Burke anticipates many green values, such as an intergenerational time horizon, sustainability, stewardship, and the precautionary principle. On the other hand, Wilson notes, Burke's emphasis on prejudice and tradition might serve to uphold long-standing crude anthropocentric values that sanction the exploitation and unrestrained development of nature, and Burke's defense of private property and his later writings extolling the free market as a source of inequality and lower-class deference also present obvious tensions with environmentalism. These tensions are not unlike those separating greens and conservatives today.

Though Mary Wollstonecraft is often identified as a pioneering feminist theorist, Barbara Seeber shows in chapter 9 that she offers considerable insights into the relationship between human beings and nature. Like Aristotle and Hume, Wollstonecraft sees commonalities between human beings and other animals. She attributes sentience and emotion to animals and accords them ethical consideration. Seeber, revealing an ecofeminist perspective in her subject, argues that cruelty toward animals is, in Wollstonecraft's view, part of a broader matrix of gender, class, and species oppression. Tyrannical behavior toward animals and toward other human beings is mutually reinforcing. However, Seeber notes, Wollstonecraft's perspective on nature goes beyond moral consideration for animals. Wollstonecraft's written observations of the Scandinavian landscape assess the environmental degradation wrought by human beings and also break down the distinction between subject and object, as she immerses herself in an interactive, reciprocal relationship with the natural environment and also sees agency in the landscape's nonhuman inhabitants. In contesting the subject/object distinction, Wollstonecraft also criticizes, as patriarchal and oppressive, the ideal of the detached observer of nature. In developing these ideas, Seeber anticipates Kim Smith's discussion, in her chapter on Du Bois, of the relationship between racial oppression and abuse of nature.

In chapter 10, Piers H. G. Stephens discusses John Stuart Mill. Like other authors in this volume, Stephens considers the compatibility of liberalism and environmental values. From his discussion of Mill, he concludes that individualism, the hallmark of liberalism, isn't necessarily opposed to environmentalism. The key is to distinguish Mill's brand of individualism from possessive individualism. Stephens dispenses with a common criticism of Mill, based on his 1874 essay "Nature," as sanctioning the human conquest of nature. Though he agrees that Mill is anthropocentric, Stephens shows that the standard reading of "Nature" misses the actual point of the essay, which was a critique of the use of nature to support conservative, religiously based ethics. Stephens also highlights Mill's embrace of a stationary-state economy, his willingness to accept regulation of the market, and his support for small-scale agriculture and land preservation. However, Stephens's revisionist reading of Mill goes even deeper. Citing Mill's affinities with Romanticism, Stephens shows that Mill rejects the self-interested, economistic individualism espoused by Jeremy Bentham and others and instead posits an individualism, or individuality, that is relational, complex, and oriented toward natural spiritedness. Mill, Stephens argues, also connects appreciation of nonhuman nature to the development of character. For Stephens, such a Millian individualism suggests a strong affinity between freedom and diversity on the one hand and ecological consciousness on the other.

As was noted earlier, environmentalism is generally associated with the left. However, environmentalism has had a highly conflicted relationship with at least one major leftist tradition: Marxism. In addition to the ecological devastation wrought by communist regimes, perceptions of Marx as an advocate of unbridled resource exploitation, technological progress, and industrial development account for his many environmentalist critics.[36] In chapter 11, Tim Luke, drawing both on Marx himself and on a growing eco-Marxist literature, offers a very different reading of Marx. Marx, Luke argues, sees humanity and the natural world as fully implicated and interdependent with one another and as mutually constitutive, all of which entails that we treat nature with care. Through commodification, however, capitalism exploits and dominates both labor and nature. Capitalism transforms human society and the physical metabolism of the planet into hybrid assemblages for the production of commodities. Luke argues that Marx enables us to truly understand the global ecological crisis, as Marx offers us a holistic view of the material metabolisms encompassing the globalized market system, its class relations, and the reengineered, regimented, degraded natural world forced to yield up raw materials for commodity exchange. This holistic view also forces us to take a more critical stance toward supposed solutions to the environmental crisis, such as the emerging "green economy," which Luke sees as yet another stage in the capitalist rationalization and reorganization of nature.

Kimberly Smith's essay on W. E. B. Du Bois (chapter 12) reveals another side of a thinker who helped pioneer scientific sociology and, even more significant, developed a rich empirical and theoretical analysis of race relations, identity, and politics. As Smith notes, Du Bois's insights into our relations with nature are largely unrecognized. In fact, as Smith shows, Du Bois wrote on agriculture, the urban environment, the importance of place, and perceptions of wilderness. Du Bois, she argues, articulates how racism distorts our relationship with the natural world. For African-Americans, according to Du Bois, racial segregation and prejudice resulted in a persistent sense of placelessness and alienation from a landscape to which they were denied ownership rights (note the connections here to Breen's discussion of Plato and to Seeber's discussion of Wollstonecraft) and thus contributed to poor agricultural stewardship and urban decay. Moreover, segregation prevented African-Americans from traveling to national parks and wilderness areas and thus limited their access to the scenic landscapes and proto-environmentalist narratives that transformed how white Americans spoke about nature. In fact, Du Bois shows how racism also distorted white Americans' relationship with nature by legitimating and fostering a willful blindness toward suffering and oppression. Such blindness meant that many whites could not comprehend complex landscapes and their often troubled human histories, but could only appreciate phony, picture-perfect idealizations of nature. For Du Bois, healing Americans' relationship with nature involves more than having equal access to wilderness or appreciating the landscape in its historical complexity. For African-Americans in particular, the experience of slavery and long-standing disenfranchisement from land ownership mean that overcoming alienation from nature requires property ownership—either private or collective—and physical transformation of the land through agriculture and gardening. Here we have, of course, a powerful contrast with contemporaries of Du Bois, among them John Muir, who saw nature largely in terms of a purportedly untouched wilderness, a landscape preserved but yet abstracted from the historical legacies of slavery, genocide, inequality, and exploitative possession. There is also a connection to Trachtenberg's discussion of the relationship, in Locke, between private property and habitation of the Earth.

Of all the theorists discussed in this volume, Martin Heidegger has perhaps been most explicitly and repeatedly cited as a major influence by environmentalists. However, in chapter 13, W. S. K. Cameron, in keeping with the unconventional readings pursued in this book, doesn't focus much on Heidegger's most ecologically oriented works, such as "The Question Concerning Technology" (1954). Those writings, Cameron argues, diagnose modernity's problematic will to power to "enframe" nature—i.e., control it as a stock of resources—but don't offer any solution, insofar as exercising the will to try and stop the domination of nature only feeds into the pursuit of control. Cameron seeks his main insights into Heidegger in *Being and Time*.

He argues that Heidegger sees our mode of being, Dasein, as fundamentally shaped by prevailing convention but also open to surprises and new insights when it reaches the limits of commonly accepted perspectives. Cameron argues that this view of Dasein can validate a micropolitics of individual action on issues such as climate change. For example, an individual who rejects reliance on the automobile and instead chooses to bicycle to work can create surprises and challenges for others' existing mode of being and can help to set political change in motion.

In chapter 14, Peter Cannavò considers Hannah Arendt, another thinker whose ecological insights have scarcely been noticed. Scholars have focused on Arendt's concepts of the public sphere and the realm of the social, her agonistic politics, her connections with civic republicanism, and her analysis of totalitarianism. Yet Cannavò notes that Arendt, in developing her concept of the human artifice—a world or second nature created through work and action—also articulates the value of *place*, though she doesn't actually employ that word. Arendt sees a stable, coherent geography and an enduring relationship with one's physical surroundings (both built and natural) as critical in making the world a reliable human home. Yet Arendt, unlike many environmentalists who emphasize the value of place, also highlights the complexity and ambivalence of humanity's relationship with nature and habitation of nature. Not only do we exist as part of the natural world and depend on its stability; we must live *in* the natural world and must struggle with and transform nature. Arendt, Cannavò argues, shows how our relationship with the natural world involves both care and violence, and also shows how this complex relationship is fundamentally endangered by modern consumer society. Cannavò's presentation of a theory of human habitation has much in common with Trachtenberg's discussion of Locke. However, Cannavò contrasts Arendt's approach to habitation with Locke's.

As was noted earlier, Joel Jay Kassiola's essay on Confucius and the Confucian tradition (chapter 15) takes the discussion beyond Western thought. This one chapter violates the book's chronological treatment. It is meant as an opening to a broader, more global perspective on environmental political theory. Kassiola argues that looking beyond the Western tradition makes obvious sense in an era of globalization and planetary environmental crisis; moreover, such a move enables us to escape the narrow perspectives that have contributed to our ecological predicament.

Confucius may provide a particularly valuable understanding of our times for several reasons. First, he wrote in response to a society confused and bewildered by a transformative moment in history and widespread sense of perceived crisis. Kassiola sees parallels between the violence and moral decadence of Confucius's sixth-century-BCE China and the challenges now facing globalized consumer society. Moreover, perhaps not unlike Burke, Confucius values past teachings and thus offers an intergenerational perspective. Even more immediately germane to environmental values, the later Confucian tradition advanced a cosmology attuned to an ecological perspective. Neo-Confucian thought sees nature as always existing in an endless, ongoing process of creation. This is in contrast to the Western notion of a discrete moment of creation by a divine creator, a cosmology that fosters a dualism of humanity and nature. Furthermore, the Confucian tradition is non-anthropocentric, as it sees a fundamental continuity and unity among humanity, Heaven, and Earth (a view that, in turn, entails respect and care for nonhuman nature—ideas somewhat marginalized though not wholly absent in Western thought, as the chapters on Aristotle, Hume, Wollstonecraft, and Marx suggest).

Looking Back and Looking Ahead

We hope that this volume will serve as a source of new insights and challenging connections for the diverse scholars and students who have entered the study of political theory and its various subfields. We hope it will help establish the continuity of environmental political thought with the *many* traditions of political thought that preceded it or run concurrently with it. Green political theory didn't result from a radical, decisive, and final departure from earlier political theory any more than the emergence of Christian political thought involved a clean break from earlier Aristotelian schools or modern liberalism a complete rupture with the Classical and Christian thought that preceded it.

It is appropriate to the environmentalist sensibility that we recognize the history of political thought to be *organic*. Environmental political thought has brought new concerns, insights, and challenges into existing traditions of theorizing about humanity's political choices. Rather than an entirely new, distinct, and original species of thought, it represents an adaptation and an evolution of earlier modes of thought to generate new perspectives on emerging environmental and social realities. We hope that it will help all of those interested in theorizing our environmental problems understand the complex interrelationships among environmental politics, the various streams of environmental thought, and the historical works that shaped our discourse about both politics and nature. We look forward to the debates these essays will sow and to the new conversations that may bloom.

Notes

1. Aldo Leopold, *A Sand County Almanac* (Oxford University Press, 1949), p. 204.
2. Rachel Carson, *Silent Spring* (Houghton Mifflin, 1962).
3. See Barry Commoner, *The Closing Circle: Nature, Man and Technology* (Knopf, 1971); Garrett Hardin, "The Tragedy of the Commons," *Science* 162, no. 3859 (1968): 1243–1248.

4. Ophuls first articulated his understanding of the implications of Hardin's work in "Leviathan or Oblivion?" in *Toward a Steady State Economy*, ed. Herman E. Daly (Freeman, 1973). He has since explored his political theory of environmental crisis in three books, each heavily dependent on the preceding one: *Ecology and the Politics of Scarcity* (Freeman, 1977), *Requiem for a Modern Politics* (Westview, 1977), and *Plato's Revenge: Politics in the Age of Ecology* (MIT Press, 2011).

5. Murray Bookchin, *Post-Scarcity Anarchism* (Ramparts, 1971), *Toward an Ecological Society* (Black Rose, 1980), and *The Ecology of Freedom* (Cheshire, 1982).

6. Françoise d'Eaubonne, *La Feminisme ou la Morte* (Horay, 1974); Carolyn Merchant, *The Death of Nature: Women, Ecology, and the Scientific Revolution* (HarperCollins, 1980) and *Ecological Revolutions: Nature, Gender, and Science in New England* (University of North Carolina Press, 1989).

7. Andre Gorz, *Ecology as Politics* (Black Rose Books, 1980) and *Farewell to the Working Class* (Pluto, 1982).

8. Wendell Berry, *The Unsettling of America: Culture and Agriculture* (Sierra Club Books, 1977).

9. Kirkpatrick Sale, *Dwellers in the Land: The Bioregional Vision* (Sierra Club Books, 1985); Peter Berg, *Envisioning Sustainability* (Subculture Books, 2009).

10. See Charlene Spretnak and Fritjof Capra, *Green Politics: The Global Promise* (Bear, 1986); Rudolf Bahro, *Building the Green Movement* (GMP, 1986); Jonathon Porritt and David Winner, *The Coming of the Greens* (Fontana, 1988); Brian Tokar, *The Green Alternative: Creating an Ecological Future* (Miles, 1992).

11. Robert D. Bullard, ed., *Confronting Environmental Racism: Voices from the Grassroots* (South End, 1983); Dorceta E. Taylor, "Can the Environmental Movement Attract and Maintain the Support of Minorities?" in *Race and the Incidence of Environmental Hazards*, ed. Bunyan Bryant and Paul Mohai (Westview, 1992); Laura Pulido, *Environmentalism and Economic Justice: Two Chicano Struggles in the Southwest* (University of Arizona Press, 1996).

12. See Vandana Shiva, *Biopiracy: The Plunder of Nature and Knowledge* (South End, 1999) and *Making Peace with the Earth* (Fernwood, 2013).

13. Christopher D. Stone, "Should Trees Have Standing?—Toward Legal Rights for Natural Objects," *Southern California Law Review* 45 (1972): 450–501; John Passmore, *Man's Responsibility for Nature: Ecological Problems and Western Traditions* (Scribner, 1974); Peter Singer, *Animal Liberation: A New Ethics for our Treatment of Animals* (Random House, 1975); Robin Attfield, *The Ethics of Environmental Concern* (Columbia University Press, 1983); Tom Regan, *The Case for Animal Rights* (University of California Press, 1983); Paul W. Taylor, *Respect for Nature: A Theory of Environmental Ethics* (Princeton University Press, 1986); Holmes Rolston III, *Environmental Ethics: Duties to and Values in The Natural World* (Temple University Press, 1988); Richard Routley and Val Routley, "Against the Inevitability of Human Chauvinism," in *Ethics and Problems of the 21st Century*, ed. Kenneth E. Goodpaster and Kenneth M. Sayre (University of

Notre Dame Press, 1979); Richard Sylvan and David Bennett, *The Greening of Ethics: From Human Chauvinism to Deep-Green Theory* (University of Arizona Press, 1994); Bryan Norton, *Toward Unity Among Environmentalists* (Oxford University Press, 1991).

14. Arne Naess, "The Shallow and the Deep, Long-Range Ecology Movement: A Summary," *Inquiry* 16 (1973): 95–100. See also Bill Devall and George Sessions, *Deep Ecology: Living as if Nature Really Mattered* (Peregrine Smith, 1985).

15. John S. Dryzek, *Rational Ecology: Environment and Political Economy* (Blackwell, 1987); Mark Sagoff, *The Economy of the Earth* (Cambridge University Press, 1988); Robert C. Paehlke, *Environmentalism and the Future of Progressive Politics* (Yale University Press, 1989); Joel Jay Kassiola, *The Death of Industrial Civilization: The Limits to Economic Growth and the Repoliticization of Advanced Industrial Society* (SUNY Press, 1990); Andrew Dobson, *Green Political Thought* (HarperCollins, 1990); Robyn Eckersley, *Environmentalism and Political Theory: Toward an Ecocentric Approach* (SUNY Press, 1992); Robert E. Goodin, *Green Political Theory* (Polity, 1992).

16. See Timothy W. Luke, *Ecocritique: Contesting the Politics of Nature, Economy, and Culture* (University of Minnesota Press, 1997); John Barry, *Rethinking Green Politics: Nature, Virtue, and Progress* (Sage, 1999); Val Plumwood, *Feminism and the Mastery of Nature* (Routledge, 1993); Kate Soper, *What is Nature? Culture, Politics, and the Non-Human* (Blackwell, 1995); Ted Benton, *Natural Relations: Ecology, Animal Rights, and Social Justice* (Verso, 1996); Andrew Dobson, *Justice and the Environment: Conceptions of Environmental Sustainability and Dimensions of Social Justice* (Oxford University Press, 1999); Jane Bennett, *Unthinking Faith and Enlightenment: Nature and the State in the Post-Hegelian Era* (New York University Press, 1987); Jane Bennett and William Chaloupka, eds., *In the Nature of Things: Language, Politics, and the Environment* (University of Minnesota Press, 1993); John M. Meyer, *Political Nature: Environmentalism and the Interpretation of Western Thought* (MIT Press, 2001); Andrew Biro, *Denaturalizing Ecological Politics: Alienation from Nature from Rousseau to the Frankfurt School and Beyond* (University of Toronto Press, 2005); William Cronon, "The Trouble with Wilderness, or Getting Back to the Wrong Nature," in *Uncommon Ground: Toward Reinventing Nature*, ed. Cronon (Norton, 1995); Donald Worster, *Nature's Economy: A History of Ecological Ideas* (Cambridge University Press, 1977); Max Oelschlaeger, *The Idea of Wilderness: From Prehistory to the Age of Ecology* (Yale University Press, 1991).

17. See David Schlosberg, *Environmental Justice and the New Pluralism: The Challenge of Difference* (Oxford University Press, 1999) and *Defining Environmental Justice* (Oxford University Press, 2007).

18. See Marcel Wissenburg, *Green Liberalism: The Free and the Green Society* (UCL, 1998); Robyn Eckersley, "Liberal Democracy and the Rights of Nature: The Struggle for Inclusion," *Environmental Politics* 4, no. 4 (1995): 169–198; Robyn Eckersley, *The Green State: Rethinking Democracy and Sovereignty* (MIT Press, 2004); Robert Paehlke, *Democracy's Dilemma: Environment, Social Equity, and the Global Economy* (MIT Press, 2004); Andrew Light and Eric Katz, eds., *Envi-*

ronmental Pragmatism (Routledge, 1996); Terence Ball, "Democracy," in *Political Theory and the Ecological Challenge*, ed. Andrew Dobson and Robyn Eckersley (Cambridge University Press, 2006); Ted Benton, "Marxism and Natural Limits: An Ecological Critique and Reconstruction," *New Left Review* 178 (November-December 1989): 51–86; Ted Benton, ed., *The Greening of Marxism* (Guilford, 1996); John Bellamy Foster, *Marx's Ecology: Materialism and Nature* (Monthly Review Press, 2000); Val Plumwood, *Environmental Culture: The Ecological Crisis of Reason* (Routledge, 2001); Plumwood, *Feminism and the Mastery of Nature*; Karen Warren, *Ecofeminist Philosophy* (Rowman & Littlefield, 2000); Ariel Salleh, *Ecofeminism as Politics: Nature, Marx and the Postmodern* (Zed Books, 2000); Kimberly K. Smith, *African-American Environmental Thought* (University of Kansas Press, 2007); Schlosberg, *Defining Environmental Justice*; Breena Holland, "Justice and the Environment in Nussbaum's 'Capabilities Approach': Why Sustainable Ecological Capacity Is a Meta-Capability," *Political Research Quarterly* 61, no. 2 (2008): 319–332; Avner de-Shalit, *Why Posterity Matters: Environmental Policies and Future Generations* (Routledge, 1995); Robyn Eckersley, "Communitarianism," in *Political Theory and the Ecological Challenge*, ed. Dobson and Eckersley; Kerry Whiteside, *Divided Natures: French Contributions to Political Ecology* (MIT Press, 2002); Kimberly K. Smith, *Wendell Berry and the Agrarian Tradition: A Common Grace* (University of Kansas Press, 2003); John Barry, *The Politics of Actually Existing Unsustainability: Human Flourishing in a Climate-Changed, Carbon Constrained World* (Oxford University Press, 2012); Peter F. Cannavò, "To the Thousandth Generation: Timelessness, Jeffersonian Republicanism, and Environmentalism," *Environmental Politics* 19, no. 3 (2010): 356–373; Thad Williamson, *Sprawl, Justice, and Citizenship: The Civic Costs of the American Way of Life* (Oxford University Press, 2010); Ronald Sandler and Philip Cafaro, *Environmental Virtue Ethics* (Rowman and Littlefield, 2005); Jane Bennett, *Vibrant Matter: A Political Ecology of Things* (Duke University Press, 2010).

19. Melissa Lane, *Eco-Republic: What the Ancients Can Teach Us about Ethics, Virtue, and Sustainable Living* (Princeton University Press, 2012); John O'Neill, *Ecology, Policy and Politics: Human Well-Being and the Natural World* (Routledge, 1993); Kerry H. Whiteside, "Hannah Arendt and Ecological Politics," *Environmental Ethics* 16, no. 4 (1994): 339–358; Kerry H. Whiteside, "Worldliness and Respect for Nature: An Ecological Application of Hannah Arendt's Conception of Culture," *Environmental Values* 7, no. 1 (1998): 25–40; Joseph H. Lane Jr., "Reverie as Political Argument: Rousseau and the Experience of Convergence in Environmental Political Thought," *Review of Politics* 68, no. 3 (2006): 474–499; Joseph H. Lane Jr. and Rebecca Clark, "The Solitary Walker in the Political World: The Paradoxes of Rousseau and Deep Ecology," *Political Theory* 34, no. 1 (2006): 62–94; Bennett, *Unthinking Faith and Enlightenment*; Foster, *Marx's Ecology*; Benton, "Marxism and Natural Limits"; Benton, ed., *Greening of Marxism*; Smith, *African-American Environmental Thought*; Breena Holland, "Ecology and the Limits of Justice: Establishing Capability Ceilings in Nussbaum's Capabilities Approach," *Journal of Human Development and Capabilities* 9, no. 3 (2008): 401–425; Holland, "Justice and the Environment"; Schlosberg, *Defining Environmental Justice*; Meyer, *Political Nature*; Biro, *Denaturalizing Ecological*

Politics; Charles A. Miller, *Jefferson and Nature: An Interpretation* (Johns Hopkins University Press, 1988).

20. Dobson and Eckersley, eds., *Political Theory and the Ecological Challenge*.

21. Joel Jay Kassiola, ed., *Explorations in Environmental Political Theory: Thinking About What We Value* (Sharpe, 2003).

22. David Macauley, ed., *Minding Nature: The Philosophers of Ecology* (Guilford, 1992).

23. J. Peter Euben, *Platonic Noise* (Princeton University Press, 2003), p. 7.

24. Ibid., p. 7.

25. Ibid., p. 8.

26. For example, George Sessions, in "Spinoza and Jeffers on Man and Nature," *Inquiry* 20 (1977): 481–528, sees the value of the "perennial philosophy" mostly in terms of its ability to demonstrate the connection between the vital environmentalist philosophies of the present and foresighted prophets who saw hints of what was coming. Robinson Jeffers, much more than Spinoza, is the hero of the piece. Earlier thinkers among the pre-Socratics are "celebrated" only in the equivocal sense that they dimly sensed truths that Thoreau could explain much more clearly and they "failed" insofar as their articulation of this healthy worldview was advanced so ineffectively that it was entirely supplanted by the unhealthy humanistic tradition that followed from Plato and Aristotle.

27. Meyer, *Political Nature*, p. 122.

28. For examples from within environmental political theory and related fields, see Macauley, ed., *Minding Nature*; Jane Bennett, *Thoreau's Nature: Ethics, Politics, and the Wild* (Sage, 1994); Philip Cafaro, "Thoreau, Leopold, and Carson: Toward an Environmental Virtue Ethics," in *Environmental Virtue Ethics*, ed. Sandler and Cafaro; Philip Cafaro, *Thoreau's Living Ethics: Walden and the Pursuit of Virtue* (University of Georgia Press, 2006); William Chaloupka, "Thoreau's Apolitical Legacy for American Environmentalism"; Melissa S. Lane, "Thoreau and Rousseau: Nature as Utopia," in *A Political Companion to Henry David Thoreau*, ed. Jack Turner (University Press of Kentucky, 2009); Bob Pepperman Taylor, *America's Bachelor Uncle: Thoreau and the American Polity* (University of Kansas Press, 1996); Peter F. Cannavò, "The Half-Cultivated Citizen: Thoreau at the Nexus of Republicanism and Environmentalism," *Environmental Values* 21, no. 2 (2012): 101–124; Bill Shaw, "A Virtue Ethics Approach to Aldo Leopold's Land Ethic," in *Environmental Virtue Ethics*, ed. Sandler and Cafaro; Stephen R. Kellert, "Aldo Leopold and the Value of Nature," in *Aldo Leopold and the Ecological Conscience*, ed. Richard L. Knight and Suzanne Riedel (Oxford University Press, 2002); J. Baird Callicott, *In Defense of the Land Ethic: Essays in Environmental Philosophy* (SUNY Press, 1989); Peter F. Cannavò, "Ecological Citizenship, Time, and Corruption: Aldo Leopold's Green Republicanism," *Environmental Politics* 21, no. 6 (2012): 864–881; Andrew Light, ed., *Social Ecology after Bookchin* (Guilford, 1998); John Clark, ed., *Renewing the Earth: The Promise of Social Ecology* (Green Print, 1990).

29. See, for example, Devall and Sessions, *Deep Ecology*.

30. See Joel Jay Kassiola and Sujian Guo, eds., *China's Environmental Crisis: Domestic and Global Political Impacts and Responses* (Palgrave Macmillan, 2010).

31. See Farah Godrej, "Ascetics, Warriors, and a Gandhian Ecological Citizenship," *Political Theory* 40, no. 4 (2012): 437–465; Fred Dallmayr, *Return to Nature? An Ecological Counterhistory* (University Press of Kentucky, 2011).

32. For a more sympathetic reading of Plato, and particularly *The Republic*, as a potential source and inspiration for environmentalist theory, see Lane, *Eco-Republic*.

33. Contrast George Sessions, "Spinoza and Jeffers on Man and Nature."

34. Though Trachtenberg's view is not without support in the literature. See, for example, Kristin Shrader-Frechette, "Locke and Limits on Land Ownership," in *Policy for Land: Law and Ethics*, ed. Lynton K. Caldwell and Kristin Shrader-Frechette (Rowman & Littlefield, 1993).

35. Corey Robin, *The Reactionary Mind: Conservatism from Edmund Burke to Sarah Palin* (Oxford University Press, 2011), pp. 109–110.

36. See, for example, John P. Clark, "Marx's Inorganic Body," *Environmental Ethics* 11 (fall 1989): 243–258.

1

Plato: Private Property and Agriculture for the Commoners—Humans and the Natural World in *The Republic*

Sheryl D. Breen

Whether we are compelled or repelled by Plato's arguments for the ideal city-state and just rulership, his dialogues have driven a significant portion of political debate since classical Athens. Alfred North Whitehead thus famously claimed that the Western philosophical tradition is simply a "series of footnotes to Plato."[1] Perhaps more surprisingly, some 2,300 years after his death, Plato's arguments continue to inform not only scholarship but also daily political debate. As one example, both sides of a 1993 Colorado court case on a state constitutional amendment that excluded gays and lesbians from anti-discrimination protection turned to Plato for legal support.[2] In this and other circumstances, Plato's broad influence has been lauded and, especially during the twentieth century, also loudly lamented. Yet both supporters and critics agree that Plato sits squarely at the center of the political theory canon.

As a student of Socrates, the founder of the Academy, a teacher of Aristotle, a traveler, and an unsuccessful political consultant to the tyrannical Dionysius II of Syracuse, Plato inhabited a world that witnessed the collapse of Athenian imperial ambitions but the continued dominance of Greek learning. In his early political dialogues, Plato presented his teacher's trial by jury (*Apology*) and refusal to escape from jail (*Crito*) under a recently restored Athenian democracy. Socrates later served as a mouthpiece for Plato's mature political philosophy in the latter's most famous dialogue, *The Republic*, which outlines an ideal *polis* and probably was written just after the founding of the Academy. The *Statesman*, written by Plato in his later years, uses the voice of the Eleatic Stranger to examine the role of the ruler as shepherd. In the *Laws*, unfinished at the time of Plato's death, the Athenian Stranger describes an achievable state ruled by a virtuous council.

Despite its prominence in political theory, Plato's philosophy generally has been rejected as a model for environmental thought. In fact, Greek political philosophy as a whole—with some accommodation for Aristotle but almost none for Plato—has been charged with spreading flawed understandings of the natural world. J. Baird Callicott, for example, blames Plato's belief that the immortal soul is "essentially foreign to the hostile physical world" for inspiring the early modern view of nature as a place of misery, temptation, and fear.[3] Likewise, Max Oelschlaeger argues that Plato's dualism "has infected virtually all Western philosophy, science, and religion," convincing us that the invisible world of knowledge is sacred while the experiential world around us is corrupt and profane.[4] Carolyn Merchant traces modern science's mechanistic view of nature to a tradition arising from Plato's mathematical understanding of the universe.[5]

Criticism of Plato's influence on environmental thinking has not been universal, however. Laura Westra and Thomas Robinson, in a volume that seeks to re-evaluate Greek environmental ethics, present several favorable analyses of Plato's vision of nature. These range from arguments for Plato's connections to deep ecology to contentions that his dialogues *Timaeus* and *Critias* provide firm foundations for ecological thought.[6] More recently, Melissa Lane has argued that Plato's *Republic* offers methodologies for questioning the givens of our particular regimes and reigning philosophies; such questioning may foster a more ecological understanding of virtue, thus leading us to view our place in the world in more sustainable terms.[7]

This chapter continues the examination of Plato as an environmental thinker with a different goal in mind. Whereas earlier considerations emerged primarily from the field of environmental ethics, I focus on Plato's political theory, particularly on his presentation of the ideal *polis* and its structures of property ownership in *The Republic*. Drawing from this dialogue, I use Plato's theory of property and the role of agriculture as a way to examine the boundaries of the relationship between humans and the natural or external world. First, I summarize Plato's ideal political model and examine his rejection of private property for the warrior and ruling classes. Second, I examine the necessary role of property ownership in the *Republic* among the majority of the population with special attention to those engaged in agriculture. Third, I argue that Plato's distinction between communalism among the elite and ownership among the commoners takes place within a citizenry divorced from their nonhuman environment and within a political model built upon an assumption of placelessness. Fourth, I present and reject several defenses of Plato's presentation of external nature and then examine the ways in which his presentations of property and agriculture reinforce a split between external nature and political life while maintaining a hierarchy of power and just rule. In the final section, I identify and summarize five concluding points of this analysis.

The Ideal Republic and the End of Property

As Joel Kassiola notes in his examination of Confucius in this volume, innovative political theory often arises from significant political unrest, and Plato's political theory is no exception.[8] His teacher Socrates, born in 469 BCE, witnessed the rise of Athenian power after the defeat of the Persians and the consolidation of Athens's empire under the aegis of the Confederacy of Delos. This was the height of Athenian democracy under the leadership of Pericles. Plato, born more than 40 years later, witnessed the gradual collapse of Athenian political and moral power during the long Peloponnesian War, which ended with the defeat of Athens in 405 BCE and the establishment of oligarchy under the Thirty Tyrants. Plato refused to work with the oligarchs, who included Critias (an interlocutor of Socrates and, according to some sources, Plato's great uncle), but also scorned the democracy, restored two years later, that soon silenced Socrates through trial and execution.

In *The Republic*, Plato lays out a model of life for the hypothetical city-state of Kallipolis that differs radically from the Athens he knew. The good of the whole overrides all other interests in this *polis*, and the division of labor ensures that each person fills a particular role within a harmonious and just society. Some are worthy of serving as rulers; some are meant to be warriors who protect the *polis* from external and internal threats; others are suited to be artisans, merchants, and farmers, who provide society's economic base. Metics (non-Athenian residents) and slaves fill other economic and social roles. Such a world represents *dike*, constituting behavior in accordance with nature, a Greek concept that is generally (but unsatisfactorily) translated as "justice."[9]

Socrates' probing questions to his companions about the meaning of *dike* constitute the dialogue's framework. Plato frequently draws comparisons between *dike* at the individual level and within the city-state, pointing out the hierarchical relationship among intellect, spirit, and appetite that must be manipulated at both the individual and the collective level through carefully controlled education and manipulative myths. Only when wisdom rules by means of unchallengeable philosopher-kings, when spirit is harnessed in the realm of incorruptible soldiers, and when appetite is exercised within the economic base of the *polis* can a good and just political life emerge.

senting this model, Plato rejected a political culture in which Athenian-born adult males ruled jointly through democratic deliberation. Athens's system of direct democracy during the classical age relied on and demanded extensive participation: Rotation by *demos* (or *deme*, the local administrative district) and selection by lottery determined who would temporarily assume administrative duties. In large part, Athenians achieved the status and leisure to engage in Assembly debates and assume these rotating positions of political service through ownership of property, including slaves. Thus, in classical Athens, private ownership of both land and humans was the economic lever that provided the foundation for democratic citizenship.

Athenian law in Plato's time made the connection between private property and citizenship even more determinative. Each son had an unquestioned right to an equal share of the family household after his father's death. Agricultural land was the primary form of household property, passed along through generations. In addition, prospective inheritance of family property directly affected a son's future role as a citizen. The paternal *demos* examined each son's lineage as a rite of passage into citizenship. Once deemed worthy, the son was formally registered on the *demos* list within the property class dictated by the economic status of his father's *oikos* (household).[10] Metics, in contrast, could not become citizens or own land without rare dispensation, even though some of them were wealthy merchants who had helped fund the Athenian war effort against Sparta. As a result, private land ownership was a filter for an Athenian's role as citizen as well as a condition for the maintenance of that role within the democratic *polis*. For citizens of classical Athens, the three concepts of democracy, property, and the public good were inextricably linked.

Plato was far from convinced of the interdependence of democracy, property, and the public good, however. Instead, he believed that Athenian democracy and political decision making by private property owners resulted in division and strife. *The Republic* offers his alternative vision of a unified, harmonious, hierarchical *polis* ruled not through direct participation but rather through laws determined by the truly deserving elite—identified as the guardians, or philosopher-kings, who understand universal truths—and enforced by the auxiliaries, or the warrior class. The majority of those who qualify as citizens of Kallipolis play no active political role but instead support the elite classes through skilled work within their appropriate craft or trade. This ranked classification is enforced through propagation of the myth of the metals, a "noble lie" designed to convince the ordinary citizens of Kallipolis that the gods have mixed their bodies with iron or bronze, the auxiliaries' bodies with silver, and the philosopher-kings' bodies with gold (415a–c).[11] In this way, citizens accept the hierarchical organization as natural rather than imposed.

In conjunction with his rejection of democracy, Plato disavows the Athenian norms and institutions of private property for the elite classes. His alternative, a communalistic theory of property, is enacted to secure unity in the *polis* and common devotion to the public good. The guardians and auxiliaries must "possess nothing" (465e–466a; see also 543a,b). Instead, they eat, study, train, and live together in communal camps (458c) with no more than essential supplies, which are stored in common rooms (416d,e) and provided by the rest of society. Because private possessions engender greed and because association with valuable goods unavoidably leads to covetousness, members of the ruling and auxiliary classes may neither handle nor be in the vicinity of gold or silver, an edict they accept because they have been taught that such contact would violate the gods' gift of gold and silver to their natures (416e–417a). This prohibition of private property and luxury for the elite classes is, according to Plato, necessary so that the guardians and the auxiliaries will remain devoted to the public good. Access to private property would turn them into cruel masters (416b). Plato thus anticipates the socially corrosive influences of wealth accumulation and/or material consumption discussed later in this volume in the chapters on Aristotle, Karl Marx, and Hannah Arendt.

Plato also connects private property to political decay through his discussion of corrupt cities. First, Plato describes the ways that fear of poverty leads to a love of money that dominates both individuals and the city in the corrupt form of timocracy (553b,c). He then identifies the property-driven triggers of revolution within democracy: debt and loss of property among the poor paired with the soft, lazy lives of the rich (555d–556c). Desire for property also promotes the rise of the "dictatorial man," who spends all of his resources, borrows as much as possible, then takes property from others (573d–574e). Again and again, Plato puts the loss or gain of private property at the center of political corruption.

Plato's distrust of possession among the guardians and auxiliaries extends to abolition of familial bonds and prohibitions on ongoing relationships with sexual partners. For these two elite classes, family is nonexistent. Reproduction is controlled through eugenically designed festivals. Children are selected or discarded on the basis of breeding heritage, and those worth raising are communally reared by nurses in separate encampments (457d–460d). No guardian or auxiliary knows his or her own ancestors or descendants, and therefore each regards all children born in the appropriate months as sons or daughters. Likewise, auxiliaries of reproductive age treat all within certain age cohorts as their own siblings and therefore off limits for sexual relations (461c–e). As a result, in every aspect of their lives, guardians and auxiliaries experience only common ownership (464b) and understand their welfare only in common terms (463e-464a). Because the guardians and the auxiliaries have nothing of their own, their good is identical to the good of the whole. Neither those who lead nor those who guard have incentives or experiences that allow them to differentiate among "mine," "yours," and "ours."

Agricultural Property for the Commoners

Analyses of *The Republic* routinely note the radical extent of its communalist theory of property. Often obscured, however, is the fact that Plato's prohibition of private property doesn't apply to the rest of the citizens. Aristotle muddied this distinction with his misleading criticism of his teacher in book 2 of *Politics*, where he reminds us that Plato, through Socrates, contends that women and children and property should be in common (1261a5–7). Aristotle goes on to reject Plato's formula without mentioning class. Aristotle's presentation of "a flawed version of Plato's ideas on property" misled later Platonists[12] and influenced modern scholars concentrating on Plato's model of elite rule, who often ignore the class aspects of communal property.[13]

Plato's own inattention to the topic might be responsible for this lack of notice. He devotes relatively little of *The Republic* to the life of the commoners, but it is important to observe he also doesn't wholly ignore them or their property status. In describing what guardians and auxiliaries cannot possess, Plato implies that private ownership continues by default among the lower class of society. The guardians and auxiliaries, "alone among the city's population," are forbidden to be near gold and silver, for example; no such restriction is provided for the rest of the citizenry (417a,b). One of Socrates' partners in conversation, Adeimantus, confirms the property-owning potential of other citizens when he challenges the relative hardships imposed upon the guardian and auxiliary classes: "Others own land, build grand and beautiful houses, acquire furnishings appropriate to them, ... have gold and silver and all the possessions which are thought to belong to people who will be happy." (419a) Not only does Socrates fail to object to Adeimantus's characterization; he adds the observation that if members of the auxiliary guardian and auxiliary classes were to acquire "private land and houses and currency" they would be "household managers and farmers instead of guardians" (417a). In this way, Plato defines these occupations in terms of ownership and further establishes the class-restricted nature of his property prohibition.

This class distinction makes sense within Plato's overall scheme. The social and political positions of the majority of citizens raise no barriers to the retention of private property and family blood ties. Furthermore, the role of non-elite citizens requires the maintenance of private property for the sake of economic and political stability. In this ideal model, workers, farmers, artisans, and merchants provide the essential economic means of support for the rulers and guardians. This necessary role doesn't overturn the fact that they occupy a lower rung within the hierarchical relationship or the fact that their behavior must be controlled; their lives represent the appetitive part of the city, comparable to the bodily appetites of individuals (442a,b), and they too are subject to corruption by both wealth and poverty (421c,d). Nonetheless, the relationship between the classes is one of mutual reliance, a foundational aspect of Plato's theory of *dike* and political harmony. In the early stages of the conversation, Socrates' interlocutor Adeimantus speculates that "justice" itself is "somewhere in some need that these men have of one another" (372a).

At the same time that the guardians benevolently rule the *polis* and the auxiliaries protect the commoners and maintain order among them, the workers, artisans, and farmers control the necessities of sustenance and produce the minimal comforts that the guardians and auxiliaries must be allowed. Without the products generated by the commoners, the elites either must support themselves, which would reintroduce "hating and being hated, plotting and being plotted against" (417b), or must die out. True to the Platonic sense of harmony through unity, everyone must fit neatly and willingly (although without full knowledge of the circumstances) into his or her proper place.

Separation and Placelessness

The dualistic approach to property ownership—forbidden to the elites, necessary for the commoners—highlights the role of productive land as the essential economic resource held in private hands. After all, as Socrates says in the dialogue, food is a city's "first and greatest need" (369d). Furthermore, for agricultural land to be successful, some members of the population must have knowledge of livestock breeding and grazing, seed storage and production, and weather patterns. Just as a doctor has knowledge of the human body and a ship's captain understands the many factors necessary for navigation (428b,c), farm owners must have a specific kind of necessary and valuable agricultural knowledge that allows them to achieve sufficient production. Like the knowledge of captains, which is restricted to those with navigational training and experience, this expertise is exclusive to those who have an aptitude for agriculture, have practiced it for life, and have assiduously avoided all other crafts (374b,c). Laborers who work under them, like sailors who work under captains, simply follow directions.

In environmental terms, however, it is not clear to what extent farm owners' knowledge of their craft goes beyond technical management of production. Historically, close relationships with land parcels arise through storytelling, experience, and inheritance. Though Plato makes no mention of changing the inheritance aspect of Athenian law, his vision for the founding of this new city-state narrowly restricts its residents' exposure to environmental, social, and cultural history. In fact, the founding of the new *polis*, Socrates tells his companions, demands a radically clean slate. In contrast to time-tested connections to land based on narratives passed through generations, Socrates calls for excising the community's historical knowledge of people and their environment through enforced exile of anyone older than ten years (540e–541a).

What does this separation from the environment's history and traditions mean for ownership of agricultural land? In Kallipolis, a farm owner's level of knowledge is tied to management of that owner's *oikos*, including slave laborers, and to the output of foodstuffs for the collective; it is not inherently tied to the land's ecosystemic peculiarities. The farm owner's management craft must be finely honed, according to Plato's model of the ideal *polis*, yet it appears to be a technical set of skills tied to specific geographic settings only to the extent necessary to yield the desired production.

The role of agricultural laborers, who are primarily slaves and therefore non-citizens, also raises doubts about the degree of connection between land owners and the natural world. Unlike the rebellious and ignorant sailors in *The Republic*'s cautionary parable, who fail to recognize their captain's extensive knowledge of navigation, agricultural laborers of long standing may possess more specialized understanding of husbandry than the owners of both laborers and land. Experienced goatherds, for example, are far more likely to know the shifting locations of good grazing spots than are the actual owners of the grazing lands. While farm owners and privileged slaves who rise to the position of overseers would presumably handle administrative issues,[14] daily contact with the agricultural landscape and the physical labor of farm practices remain the devalued work of slaves within Plato's model, as in his contemporaneous Athens. No inherent value is attached to contact with the soil itself or to the labor that connects humans to nonhumans and to their non-urban surroundings.[15]

What of the environmental relationships of those in other trades in the ideal city-state of Kallipolis? Under Plato's plan, citizens have a spiritual connection of a sort with the Earth. As a part of the myth that their class-bound natures contain gold, silver, iron, or bronze, residents are told that the Earth, their mother, has fully prepared and equipped them for life and then has brought them into the world. They now must defend that Earth and regard each other as "Earth-born brothers" (414e). This Earth-as-mother metaphor continues past the creation story: Socrates tells his companions that, although parties to a civil war will kill one another, they will never ravage their city's land, which is their "nurse and mother" (470d).

Nonetheless, separation from the natural world may be even greater for commoners who make their living from shoemaking, carpentry, and other non-agricultural work. The origin myth of the Earth-mother is a tool for manufacturing social bonds rather than for creating links to the land of a particular place, and a prohibition on harming land during a civil war need not reflect attachment to nature of more than an instrumental kind—and Plato offers no sign that citizens' relationship with the Earth is likely to go any further. The workers' role in Kallipolis is to maintain the economic, social, and political bounds of society, and the workers' environment is no more than a means for them to achieve that end. With agricultural duties assigned to certain members of the community, other residents of Kallipolis have no encouragement to think about their environment in other than perfunctory ways. Farming is a specialized occupation; the citizenry as a whole requires no further knowledge of the land as a particular place. As a result, Plato's presentation of the natural world is strikingly devoid of a sense of place.[16] Kallipolis has no apparent attachment to any particular geographic setting. Subjects are tightly bound to their city-state; however, the attachment is to the *polis*, not to a specific landscape or ecosystem. As an ideal model, Kallipolis can be picked up and dropped down anywhere at any time without changing its internal structure. This is a political society that is independent of, rather than constructed from, its environment.

Politics, Nature, and the Hierarchy of Power

It might be argued that the separation between citizens of Kallipolis and their environment is a function of the utopian model: an ideal society, by definition, must be applicable anywhere and anytime. However, Plato undermines this argument through Socrates' refusal to label Kallipolis as mere conjecture. In *The Republic*, Socrates tells his companions that the constitution he describes would be a difficult to make happen, though not impossible (499d). This argument also fails to meet the evidence of the history of utopian thought. Sir Thomas More, the author of *Utopia*, was a careful student of Platonic philosophy, yet his imaginary state demands an intimate connection between its citizens and the environmental specificities of their land. Whereas Plato's division of labor restricts agricultural work to specialized farm owners and their slaves, More's narrator Hythloday tells of a country that prohibits property ownership to all citizens regardless of class. Furthermore, Hythloday reports, the nation of Utopia requires all subjects (with a few exceptions, including scholars) to live and work full-time on farms during regular two-year rotations, in addition to offering periodic help with harvest chores in other years.[17]

In *Utopia*, More, often characterized as a neo-Platonist, emphasizes the moral virtue of hands-on farm labor for all members of society. Plato sees no such universal link; for him, virtue is tied to the division of labor and political leadership on the basis of intellectual knowledge, not on the basis of knowledge of one's environment. For Plato, political stability is achieved through individual and collective balance among the intellect, the spirit, and the appetites, and achieving such balance requires an understanding of one's place in society and the cosmos rather than an understanding of one's place in the natural, material world.

We also might soften the environmental critique of Plato by regarding *The Republic*'s structure of separation as an anomaly within his dialogues, but this potential defense of Plato's understanding of the natural world also fails when we examine separation and placelessness in his other dialogues. For example, in *Crito*, as Socrates prepares to drink the hemlock, his eloquent explanation of why he must stay in Athens rather than escape is founded on his duty to the Laws of Athens and includes no allegiance to or longing for the place itself. In Socrates' prison cell, as in Kallipolis, the *polis* doesn't assume any particular concrete physical presence.

Phaedrus, another of Plato's dialogues, provides an especially striking example of his lack of interest in place. At first, love for nature seems to be present in *Phaedrus* (which is unusual among Plato's dialogues because its conversation takes place outside of the city walls). Socrates' companion leads him to a spot beneath a tree that Socrates calls a "charming resting place." Socrates seems enchanted with the locale, praising the breezes and the "delightful" grass. His companion, puzzled by these comments, remarks that Socrates seems to be someone who never goes outside the city's walls. Socrates replies that he is "fond of learning," and that he believes "the country places and the trees won't teach me anything, and the people in the city do" (230b–d).[18] Here again, Plato—perhaps anticipating a contemporary rootless urban intellectual—finds the nonhuman world to be irrelevant to the higher search for knowledge in the immaterial world.

In another dialogue, *Phaedo*, Plato also explicitly separates the natural, visible world of opinion and representation from the goodness and beauty of the immaterial world. Socrates, describing "the form of the Earth" and its regions, is comparing the perspective of the Greeks who live by the sea "like ants or frogs about a pond" to those who might live below in the depths of the sea but believe that they are on its surface (108e).[19] Both sea dwellers and land dwellers are too feeble and sluggish, he says, to realize that true beauty lies in another world above them:

> For this earth of ours, and the stones and the whole region where we live, are injured and corroded, as in the sea things are injured by the brine, and nothing of account grows in the sea, and there is, one might say, nothing perfect there, but caverns and sand and endless mud and mire, where there is earth also, and there is nothing at all worthy to be compared with the beautiful things of our world. But the things in that world above would be seen to be even more superior to those in this world of ours. (109e–110b)

The comparatively few scholars who have found an ecological sensitivity in Plato's philosophy[20] point to two other dialogues, *Timaeus* and *Critias*, to support their argument. *Timaeus* is Plato's cosmological work, presenting the origin of the universe by the Demiurge, who imposes order on two levels: the world soul and the world body. According to Madonna Adams, this cosmology "affirms a positive view of the cosmos that engenders respect, awe, and joy, all of which seem to be essential for a complete human response to the natural world and to our human reality."[21] A more careful and cautious reading of *Timaeus*, however, finds Plato providing a summary of physics and biology as known in his time and suggests that Adams may be giving more environmental kudos to this summary than it deserves. *Critias* tells the story of ancient Athens and its rival, the city-state of Atlantis, and includes a description of soil loss to the sea due to earthquakes and deforestation of the mountains around Athens. However, as Eugene Hargrove points out, Plato's matter-of-fact report lacks any sense of ecological judgment.[22]

Plato's other dialogues, then, don't refute the conclusion that *The Republic* presents an understanding of nature and the environment founded on separation and lack of place. Plato's perspective is an exclusively human one, grounded firmly within the walls of the city-state and nestled within a *polis* that is supported by but not bonded to the pre-political peculiarities of place. Although connections to landscape emerge from direct and continuing intimacy with one's environment and its interconnected human and nonhuman dwellers, Plato's presentation of the ideal *polis* devalues the skills and knowledge that arise with pastoral and agricultural experience and a resulting sense of place. Reflecting this vision of land and the non-urban world as pre-political, *The Republic*'s prohibition of ownership among the auxiliaries and guardians and consequent mandate of ownership among the class of commoners are tied to the belief (Plato would say knowledge) that the division of labor and balance among the rational, spirited, and appetitive parts of both city and soul are the only means by which human beings may be justly ruled.

Although *The Republic* finds little of importance in the natural world in an ecological sense (as Socrates says in *Phaedrus*, "country places and trees" have nothing to do with knowledge), there is a concept of nature that lies more broadly at the center of *The Republic*'s vision of harmonious hierarchy. Plato's theory of the forms finds the Good in the eternal, intelligible, non-visible world of reason rather than in the ephemeral, material world of sense and opinion; however, his demotion of the physical world is not a rejection of nature but a claim for what Plato takes to be our "true" nature. Plato is calling for a political world that is governed by the essential nature of things (*physis*) and not by custom or convention (*nomos*). When we recognize that knowledge is the prerequisite for rulership, according to Plato, and have seen that only those who would least like to govern may be entrusted with governance, we will have moved an important step toward what political life ought to be. Plato's understanding of "nature," we might conclude, is itself a type of anthropological re-creation of the world in which the primacy of a specifically human "reason" becomes the "natural," and thus the measure by which all things must be judged. This is the reverse of the—itself admittedly flawed—notion often held by environmentalists that earthly nature and its ecological relationships provide a standard for how things, human and otherwise, should best be ordered.[23]

Conclusion

What conclusions can we claim to make after this examination of property and agriculture within Plato's *Republic*? I believe that five useful points can be drawn from our analysis.

First, we must recognize that Plato's theory of property is only half-told when we focus only on his rejection of private property for the auxiliaries and the philosopher-kings, who constitute a small fraction of the population. The vast majority of citizens necessarily remain property owners in the ideal city-state of Kallipolis and, through that ownership, provide the economic and social foundation for the political elite.

Second, by using agriculture as a framework for our analysis of property, we see that private possession is exercised within the limits of the agricultural support structure. Ownership of farm and pastoral property is a means to Plato's politico-economic end. Although possession of property among the general citizenry might bring with it greed and conflict, which Plato abhors and works to prevent among the ruling elite, he offers as a solution a class of guardians who know only common property and serve only the public good and are therefore both determined and able to control such problems. Thus, for Plato, property ownership by commoners and prohibition of private property among the auxiliaries and guardians serve mutually advantageous goals.

Third, although Plato emphasizes physical training for war, he devalues labor connected to land. A just society requires just citizens who fulfill their appropriate functions as producers and distributors of goods, including those who maintain the food system, but neither social nor individual justice depends upon virtue gained through physical labor in that production. Yet Plato doesn't overlook the physical body; on the contrary, he devotes considerable attention to the rigorous standards of athletic training that the auxiliaries and guardians of the *polis* must meet. On both the individual and collective levels, the spirit must be strong and able if it is to control appetites and serve the intellect. The physical prowess of the guardians and the auxiliaries is important in attaining the virtue of courage (429a–430e), one of the four necessary virtues of the city-state. The physicality of farm labor, on the other hand, falls outside of the necessary virtues of citizenship.

Fourth, although Plato tightly conjoins internal (i.e., human) nature and politics, his model portrays a theoretical chasm between politics and the external nature of humans' physical and ecological surroundings. For individual humans and the politics they collectively create, internal nature and the political body are mutually constitutive; the city of Kallipolis is built upon the foundations of what Plato sees as our essential needs and possibilities. We are, he believes, inherently constructed of reasoning, spirited, and appetitive parts, and our path to *dike* and a just society must be based on our ability to recognize, control, and develop those aspects of human nature. External nature, in contrast, is a pre-political resource rather than a constitutive element of our lives. For Plato, the political structures of class hierarchy, elite rule, and "noble lies" have no intimate connection with the particularities of the ecological landscape of the *polis* beyond the extent to which those differences will affect military strategy and agricultural management from city to city. The political structure stands independently, regardless of place.

Fifth, Plato's bifurcated theory of property and the split between external nature and politics work to maintain the hierarchies of power. As was noted earlier, Plato argues that property ownership unavoidably leads to destructive activities such as "hating" and "plotting" (417b), and he emphasizes the central importance of harmony achieved through unity. This decision to lodge ownership and management of the land with the commoners further strengthens the need for an elite police force in Kallipolis and for political rule by guardians detached from the land. If private property were to be prohibited universally within the *polis*, denying ownership to both elite and commoners, at least one element of the argumentative logic for elite rule would weaken. Under this alternate scenario, and in conjunction with the unifying "myths" of creation and class, citizens of the lower class would have less reason to require domestic control; lack of property would mean reduced levels of covetousness and greed. Moreover, in a Kallipolis wholly devoid of private property (a model that would be paralleled in More's *Utopia*) the guardians and auxiliaries would have little reason to refrain from taking their own turns at agricultural work. In Plato's ideal republic, by contrast, such participation in agriculture would presumably distract from or undermine the development of elite characters suited to war and governance; meanwhile, the preservation of property ownership for the general populace maintains the exertion of force by a landless warrior and guardian elite as an important aspect of just rule.

The separation of external nature from politics and the close link between internal nature and politics uphold Plato's class-based distribution of power. Kallipolis is constructed upon a foundation of human possibility: With the right breeding heritage, education, athletic and military training, and study of philosophy's truths, the best of all possible republics can be attained under the just and absolute rulership of philosophers. The nature of what it means—and could mean—to be human is directly and inextricably linked to *The Republic*'s construction of an ideal city and its model of authoritarian elite rule. Furthermore, this certainty about the possibilities of just leadership discounts (and perhaps even ignores) the uncertainties caused by the variability and particularities of external nature. Ecosystems, terrains, climatological factors, coastlines, and mountains are relevant in a secondary, not a primary, way. For Plato, internal nature is fully integrated with political life and elite governance; external nature remains in a separate and subsidiary pre-political sphere, the realm of commoners shut out from rule.

In conclusion, Plato's theory of property ownership, as it applies to the elite and the commoners of *The Republic*, directly affects the boundaries of the relationship between humans and the natural or external world. The subjects of Kallipolis are bound intimately (and, for Plato, harmoniously) to their city-state; the bond fits the internal nature of what it means to be human. Yet external nature, including the ecosystemic identities of specific agricultural lands, remains apart. Kallipolis is a placeless political model that arises not from its environment but from Plato's vision of unchanging and universal forms that constitute the true nature of political life.

Notes

1. Alfred North Whitehead, *Process and Reality* (Free Press, 1978), 39.

2. Melissa Lane, *Eco-Republic: What the Ancients Can Teach Us about Ethics, Virtue, and Sustainable Living* (Princeton University Press, 2012), chapter 1.

3. J. Baird Callicott, "Traditional American Indian and Western European Attitudes toward Nature: An Overview," *Environmental Ethics* 4 (1982): 293–318, at 298.

4. Max Oelschlaeger, *The Idea of Wilderness: From Prehistory to the Age of Ecology* (Yale University Press, 1991), 57.

5. Carolyn Merchant, *Radical Ecology: The Search for a Livable World* (Routledge, 1992), 57.

6. Timothy Mahoney, "Platonic Ecology, Deep Ecology," Madonna Adams, "Environmental Ethics in Plato's *Timaeus*," and Owen Goldin, "The Ecology of *Critias* and Platonic Metaphysics," in Laura Westra and Thomas M. Robinson, eds., *The Greeks and the Environment* (Rowman and Littlefield, 1997).

7. Lane, *Eco-Republic*.

8. See also Joel Jay Kassiola, *Explorations in Environmental Political Theory: Thinking About What We Value* (Sharpe, 2003), chapter 15.

9. Thanks to an anonymous reviewer for this point.

10. W. K. Lacy, *The Family in Classical Greece* (Cornell University Press, 1968), 125, 128–130.

11. Plato, *Republic*, translated by G. M. A. Grube (Hackett, 1974). All subsequent citations of Plato's *Republic* follow this translation.

12. Peter Garnsey, *Thinking about Property: From Antiquity to the Age of Revolution* (Cambridge University Press, 2007), 27.

13. Ibid., chapter 1; Robert Mayhew, *Aristotle's Criticism of Plato's Republic* (Rowman and Littlefield, 1997).

14. See Xenophon, *Oeconomicus*, translated by Sarah B. Pomeroy (Clarendon, 1994).

15. American slavery parallels this Platonic divide. See Kimberly Smith's book *African-American Environmental Thought* (University of Kansas Press, 2007) and her chapter on W. E. B. Du Bois in this volume.

16. See, by way of contrast, the discussion of Arendt's concept of the human artifice in chapter 14 of this volume.

17. Sir Thomas More, *Utopia*, translated by Robert M. Adams, second edition (Norton, 1992), 32–33.

18. Plato, *Phaedrus*, translated by Harold North Fowler (Harvard University Press, 1977).

19. Ibid.

20. Westra and Robinson, eds., *The Greeks and the Environment*.

21. Adams, "Environmental Ethics in Plato's *Timaeus*," 72.

22. Eugene C. Hargrove, *Foundations of Environmental Ethics* (Prentice-Hall, 1989), 30.

23. For a critique of this environmentalist view, see John Meyer's chapter on Thomas Hobbes in this volume.

2

Aristotle: Phusis, Praxis, and the Good

Özgüç Orhan

Aristotle's environmental relevance has been challenged on the basis of the charge of anthropocentricism. As Sheryl Breen points out in this volume, Greek philosophy in general and Plato or Aristotle in particular have been held responsible for the modern ecological crisis. Whereas the environmentally problematic aspect of Plato's philosophy is ontological dualism, in the case of Aristotle it is "anthropocentric teleology."[1] It has been claimed that the ancient Greek definition of man as a rational animal privileges human beings at the expense of other living beings, and this view, in turn, underlies the anthropocentric bias in the Western tradition.[2] More recently, though, the holistic view of nature in Aristotle's natural philosophy has been found compatible with the ecological ideas of interconnectedness and interdependence.[3]

It is also possible to assess Aristotle's environmental relevance from the angle of his practical philosophy. The concept of nature in general and the question of the right relationship between humanity and nature in particular are central to contemporary environmentalism. But the concept of ecology or nature as used in the environmental movement and literature isn't merely about the state of the physical environment. It signifies a much deeper existential concern about industrialized society and technology, a yearning for an alternative vision of the good life, and the appropriate means and practices to realize the good society.[4] This chapter argues that this vision of the good implicit in the ecological critique of modern society finds support in Aristotle's ideas on the workings of nature and human agency.

Aristotle's Philosophical Legacy and the Rise of Modernity

Though he was not a citizen of Athens, Aristotle (384–322 BCE) resided there for most of his life, first as a student and lecturer at Plato's Academy and then as the founder of his own school, the Lyceum. He wrote on a wide variety of subjects concerning nature and human beings, inventing not only scientific disciplines, which had not previously existed, but also the very idea of a "discipline" itself. He marked out the boundaries of several academic disciplines as well and formulated the fundamental questions and principles that have come to be associated with each.

Aristotle's critique of his mentor, Plato, is of particular philosophical importance. At the core of his critique lies the Platonic doctrine of Ideas or Forms (*eidē*; singular *eidos*), which postulates an intelligible realm of true and real beings behind or beyond the sensible world of appearance. Against this dualist ontological view, Aristotle put forth his own theory of being that has come to be known as hylomorphism. Actual beings, for Aristotle, are composite entities made of matter (*hule*) and form (*morphe*). Unlike Plato, Aristotle saw no reason to look for another reality beyond this world. Aristotle's biological interest is indicative of his rejection of a Platonic division between a transient world of becoming and an eternal world of Being. The environmental significance of this critique is that, as Friedrich Nietzsche would later recognize in relation to Platonism and Christianity, the postulate of another, more valuable world of "being" could devalue this world of "becoming," and even justify a promethean or hubristic stance toward it.[5]

The implications of this philosophical difference between Plato and Aristotle are especially visible in their approaches to ethics and politics. The priority of the universal and unchangeable realm of Being over the particular and changeable realm of becoming can result in the exclusive valuation of the former as the only worthy object of human understanding. A distant consequence of this epistemological stance in the modern era was the coupling of the "theoretical" with the "productive" and the disappearance of human agency or action (*praxis*).[6]

Unlike Plato, Aristotle was not suspicious of the realm of becoming, as he believed that human understanding of transient phenomena was possible. Aristotle distinguished the domains of the theoretical, practical, and productive knowledge (*episteme*), and while granting the value and superiority of contemplation (*theoria*), he nonetheless gave more credit to the different aspects of practical knowledge such as experience, sense perception, desire, action, and practical judgment than did Plato. With these epistemological and psychological elements of (human) nature, Aristotle effectively demarcates an autonomous place for the practical dimension of human existence, separate not only from contemplation but also production (*poiesis*) and its corollary mode of knowledge, art or craftsmanship (*techne*). Hence, Aristotle vindicates human agency against possible encroachment by hubristic science and technology.[7]

Aristotle's philosophical authority, highly respected during antiquity and the Middle Ages, eventually came under attack in the early modern period with new scientific discoveries and theories. The leading figures of the Scientific Revolution were all critical of the medieval scholastic tradition, which they associated with Aristotle. Thomas Hobbes mockingly called scholastic philosophy "Aristotelity." Hobbes's negative assessment of Aristotle signaled an enormous shift in Western thought: "Scarce anything can be more absurdly said in natural philosophy than that which now is called Aristotle's Metaphysics; nor more repugnant to government than much of that he hath said in his Politics, nor more ignorantly, than a great part of his Ethics."[8]

The worldview behind this paradigmatic shift has come to be known as "modernity." Its driving force was the mechanistic conception of nature underlying the new science. In particular, Aristotle's natural philosophy was targeted, as its central concept of the final cause (*telos*) was deemed to be a superfluous factor in explaining natural causation. An outcome of this modern scientific view has been the growing Cartesian chasm between human and nature. Nature as a whole or living beings individually were conceived as machines, driven by chance or necessity. As nature was no longer capable of agency, Francis Bacon could reinterpret humanity's relationship to nature in terms of the increase of technological power for "the relief of man's estate." The new worldview shaped by modern science has turned man into a subject (i.e., creator) and nature into an object, or rather a stock of resources waiting to be exploited in the service of human goals.[9]

Today, the material effects of this intellectual transformation are increasingly visible in the exponential growth of ecological problems. The problem of modern civilization isn't confined to the ecological fallout of the human "conquest of nature." The modern view of nature has actually infiltrated all spheres of human life, and, in particular, the study and practice of economy. As various contemporary philosophers from Hannah Arendt to Jürgen Habermas have recognized, the new worldview has allowed the invasion of the human world by technology and instrumental thinking.[10] The environmental relevance of Aristotle's philosophy can best be appreciated within this historical and philosophical framework. Hence, the so-called ecological crisis can be understood not so much as an unintended consequence of misguided technology or economy but as the failure of human action at a more fundamental level, which in turn rests on an inadequate view of nature and the role of nature in human life.[11]

Aristotle's Conception of Nature

Among Aristotle's foremost philosophical interests was biology, or rather zoology.[12] At the center of Aristotle's natural and practical philosophy is the concept of *phusis*, whose meaning in the Greek language was "growth"; the concept was originally applied, especially, to plants. The English word *nature* and its variants in other European languages were derived from the Latin *natura*, which was used to render the Greek *phusis* in the Latin literature. This lingua-historical connection alone cannot, however, ensure commensurability between the concepts of *phusis* and *nature*. Indeed, *nature*, just like any other concept, has varied in meaning across time and space. While it is important to attend to the semantic differences between Aristotle's *phusis* and modern usages of *nature*, suggestive comparisons can still be made with due caution.

Accordingly, it should be noted that Aristotle uses *phusis* primarily in relation to the particular natural processes or elements rather than in a general sense for the natural world as a whole or the natural world set apart from the realm of human civilization (as in "wilderness"). Still, some of his usages resemble our conception of nature, as, for instance, in his oft-repeated maxim "Nature does nothing in vain." Furthermore, his usage of the Greek word *kosmos*, which means an orderly reality or totality of beings with moral and aesthetic connotations of fitness and beauty, echoes the idea of interconnectedness in the modern concept of ecology. Aristotle depicts a teleological *kosmos* as an interlocking natural order: "All things are ordered together somehow, but not all alike—both fishes and fowls and plants; and the world [*kosmos*] is not such that one thing has nothing to do with another, but they are connected." (*Metaphysics*[13] 1075a17–19)

The semantic plurality and ambiguity of *phusis* is actually noted by Aristotle himself as he mentions a number of its different usages by his philosophical predecessors. Aristotle accepts the relevance of these different senses to the nature of a being but argues that *phusis* in the strict sense is an immanent source of motion and rest for the beings that move on their own. Unlike artificial beings, the source of motion of natural beings lies within them. Plants or animals move on their own, while a mass of rock is transformed into a statue by the sculptor.

For Aristotle, both natural and artificial beings are composites of form and matter; neither can exist apart from each other. Matter remains inchoate, potential, and passive until an active principle of form works on it and actualizes its potential. The form and matter are inseparable but the *phusis* of a being is primarily its form or the end (*telos*), which it shall attain when fully developed and if not hindered. Aristotle identifies the form of living beings as their *psuche* (soul), which fulfills varied functions such as nutrition, reproduction, sensation, desiring, and thinking.

The completed being, for Aristotle, is the best or most excellent; the intermediary stages of a being during the process of becoming exist for the sake of its final state. Hence, Aristotle explains natural processes or beings (and their parts) in relation to their natural ends, goals, and functions. Aristotle's typical example is an acorn destined to become an oak tree; an acorn is potentially an oak tree but fulfills its nature only when it fully becomes an oak tree. In Aristotle's words, "whenever there is plainly some final end, to which a motion tends should nothing stand in the way, we always say that the one is for the sake of the other; and from this it is evident that there must be something of the kind, corresponding to what we call nature" (*Parts of Animals*[14] 641b23–26). This view of nature has come to be known as *teleological* or goal-directed.

The concept of motion lies at the center of Aristotle's conception of nature, but this concept is much richer than how we typically understand it today. First, Aristotle explains "motion" (*kinesis*) through two affiliated concepts: *entelecheia* ("having an end within itself") and *energeia* ("being-at-work"). These two uniquely Aristotelian terms are typically rendered as "actuality" and "activity," respectively.[15] For Aristotle, both of these concepts signify the process of becoming during which a being actualizes its potential features or powers. To use Aristotle's example, the oak tree is the *entelecheia* of the acorn and growing is its *energeia*. Second, Aristotle mentions four kinds of motion at work in nature: change of place, quantitative changes (e.g., something becoming smaller or larger), qualitative changes (e.g., something getting hotter or colder), and substantive changes (e.g., the generation or death of a being).[16]

Moreover, in the process of becoming and change, beings are moved or affected by four kinds of factors or causes: the material, formal, efficient, and final. With his typical example of a bronze statue, Aristotle illustrates the material cause as the matter of bronze, the formal cause as the form of a statue, the efficient cause as the sculptor, and the final cause as the intent or plan of the sculptor (*Physics* 194b23–35). When applied to a living being, the material cause can be thought of as its flesh and bones, the formal cause as soul (*psuche*), the efficient cause as its parents, and the final cause as its peculiar function (*ergon*).

Since the natural principle of motion and rest is common to all living beings, Aristotle presumes a fundamental unity and interconnectedness across the species of plants, animals, and human beings. Nature isn't marked by uniformity, however, as Aristotle doesn't reduce everything to a single constituent principle or material. A second important feature of Aristotle's conception of *phusis* is that "necessity" doesn't apply to nature, as natural processes take place not in a deterministic way but "for the most part." Aristotle acknowledges that *phusis* may, at times, err and produce aberrations or monstrosities.

Furthermore, *phusis*, for Aristotle, is a source of order as it aims to reach a limit (*peras*) or end (*telos*). In this sense, it can be contrasted with "chance" (and likewise "fortune" for the human world), which affects beings contrary to the tendency of nature. Chance events are not aimed at ends, but natural events and beings are.

The end or purpose, for Aristotle, is critical to the understanding and explanation of natural and human phenomena. The natural element in living beings seeks completion or perfection by actualizing its inherent potential. The natural process isn't a ceaseless or infinite activity; rather, it seeks (not always successfully) to come to an end, which is expectedly the best and complete condition for that being.

Aristotle's conception of *phusis* also treats the "natural" as a normative standard. This understanding can be gathered from certain conceptual categories that run through his works. Aristotle classifies human activity into three broad categories, which carry both ontological and epistemological implications: *theoria* (contemplation), *praxis* (action), and *poiesis* (making). Each activity exists in relation to a certain domain of human life and requires a certain type of knowledge. *Theoria* refers to the philosopher's leisurely quest for theoretical knowledge of the universal causes in nature; *praxis* takes place in the realm of human affairs constituted by human agency; *poiesis* creates the realm of useful artifacts, which corresponds to activities such as art, technology, production, and construction. The cognitive faculties needed for the competent execution of these activities are *episteme* (scientific knowledge), *phronēsis* (practical reason), and *techne* (art), respectively.[17]

What is noteworthy about these ontological and epistemological categories is that Aristotle holds a more affirmative view of *theoria* and *praxis* than of *poiesis* and *techne*. The reason is that *theoria* and *praxis* resemble *phusis*, which is considered as a norm. He says, for instance, that "virtue is something more precise and better than any art, just as nature is," suggesting that *praxis* is superior to *techne* because it possesses its end in itself rather than outside of itself.[18] Whereas *praxis* of virtue contains its goal (i.e., the noble) within itself, arts and crafts aim at producing an external product. In this sense, *praxis* is a more complete or nearly perfect type of activity than *techne*. Still, *theoria* is the best and highest possible human activity for being the most nearly complete, since one would need other humans or things to engage in *praxis* (i.e., to be just or generous). Hence, for Aristotle, what is complete (*teleios*) and self-sufficient is better than what is incomplete and dependent, just as nature is better than art in these senses.

Besides normative implications, *phusis* carries an aesthetic dimension. *Kalon* ("beautiful" or "noble"), an important term in Aristotle's ethics, combines both aesthetic and moral overtones. The following passage, for instance, affirms the value of studying nature by appealing to nature's aesthetic dimension: "Every realm of nature is full of wonder. ... We should venture on the study of every kind of animal without distaste, for each and all will reveal to us something natural and something beautiful. For what is not haphazard but rather for the sake of something is in fact present most of all in the works of nature; the end for the sake of which each animal has been constituted or comes to be is a form of the beautiful." (*Parts of Animals* 645a16–25) This quotation highlights the essential connections among order, purpose, and beauty in Aristotle's thought. What is natural is beautiful because it is purposeful and orderly.

Yet according to some contemporary critics Aristotle's conception of nature, organized around ends (*teloi*), betrays an anthropocentric worldview, as was noted earlier. This criticism implies that Aristotle's "anthropocentric teleology" is not only mistaken but also pernicious because it justifies an exploitative attitude toward nature. In particular, the claim of Aristotle's critics is that his drawing a sharp distinction between human beings and animals underlies the unjustifiable claims that human beings enjoy a moral superiority over animals and that human ends are higher or more choiceworthy than those of other beings.

The *locus classicus* of this view is found in Book I.8 of *Politics* (1256b15–22): "It is clear in a similar way, therefore, that for grown things as well one must suppose both that plants exist for the sake of animals and that the other animals exist for the sake of human beings—the tame animals, both for use and sustenance, and most if not all of the wild animals, for sustenance and other assistance, in order that clothing and other instruments may be got from them. If, then, nature makes nothing that is incomplete or purposeless, nature must necessarily have made all of these for the sake of human beings."[19] This passage, according to Aristotle's contemporary critics, illustrates an "external teleology" and an offensively anthropocentric outlook. The purpose of a lower species is reduced to subservience to human ends.

This passage and similar ones in Aristotle's corpus are not as straightforward in their meanings as they may at first appear to be. There is no doubt that Aristotle understands the realm of art in terms of external teleology, but whether he extends this understanding to the realm of nature is debatable. The surface reading of this passage as an instance of Aristotle's defense of "external teleology" has been challenged by scholars who found this passage consistent with Aristotle's innocuous "internal teleology" (i.e., the immanent ends of natural beings).[20] These scholars point out that there is no trace of a similar passage anywhere else in Aristotle's corpus. The natural treatises lack any assertion to this effect. This fact suggests that the passage isn't central to Aristotle's philosophy, as we seldom find an essential idea that isn't repeated across Aristotle's works.[21]

Furthermore, this passage appears in a chapter in which Aristotle discusses household management (*oikonomia*), and specifically a precise category of economic activity: the business expertise (*chrēmatistikē*) that seeks after the acquisition of possessions and sustenance. What is at issue here is the relationship between *oikonomia* and *chrēmatistikē*. Aristotle's purpose is to determine whether the latter is part of the former or something separate. His answer to this question is "both." Since obviously it isn't possible to live without sustenance, nature must provide the means of sustenance to all living beings both not only at their birth but also while they grow. For human beings, one kind of *chrēmatistikē* serves this purpose by gathering the necessary goods from nature for the household use (*oikonomia*), so this kind must be considered as part of and subservient to *oikonomia*.

Therefore, Aristotle may very well be speaking, in this passage, of the fact that nature provides for the needs of human beings without implying that their sole purpose of existence is service to human beings. The tentative tone of Aristotle's voice in this passage—notice the verb *suppose* in the first sentence—casts doubt on the unequivocal interpretation of this passage as an endorsement of a wholly anthropocentric, let alone exploitative, attitude toward nature. Such an attitude would require a justification for unlimited acquisition, and this is exactly what Aristotle denies at the close of this section. Goods acquired by *chrēmatistikē* are "necessary for life and useful for partnership in a city or a household ... [but] self-sufficiency in possessions of this sort with a view to good life is not limitless" (*Pol.* 1256b27–30). Later in this chapter I shall return to this topic and discuss the second kind of *chrēmatistikē*, which is limitless and unnatural and therefore not part of *oikonomia*.[22]

Aristotle certainly places plants, animals, and human beings in a hierarchical relationship. However, it is better to picture this relationship in terms of concentric circles than as a pyramid with mutually exclusive compartments. The living world is no "caste system." The plant world in the outermost circle is primarily characterized by the capacities of nutrition and reproduction. Within the next circle are the animals, which possess perception in addition to their vegetative capacities. Human beings in the innermost circle have all these capacities but are distinguished primarily by their faculty of thinking, which is made possible by their capacity for language.

It should be noted that Aristotle grants the kinship of human beings with animals in his biological works (*Parts of Animals* 645a3) and allows for certain common emotional and intellectual traits shared by animals and humans alike: "As regards man and animals, certain psychical qualities are identical with one another, whilst others resemble, and others are analogous to, each other." (*History of Animals*[23] 588b2, 3) This is due to the principles of gradation and continuity in nature: "Nature proceeds little by little from things lifeless to animal life in such a way that it is impossible to determine the exact line of demarcation, nor on which side thereof an intermediate form should lie." (*HA* 588b3–5) This view of nature, called *scala naturae* or the Great Chain of Being, was quite influential in late medieval and early modern times.[24]

We should also remember that the moral superiority of human beings doesn't rest purely on nature but on the condition of "perfection" and guidance by law and justice: "Man, when perfected, is the best of animals; but if he be isolated from law and justice he is the worst of all." (*Pol.* 1253a31–33) Human superiority over other living beings thus presupposes ethical perfection.[25]

Moreover, Aristotle denies that humanity occupies the highest position in the cosmos. In the context of his argument for the superiority of wisdom (*sophia*) to politics or practical reason (*phronēsis*), he remarks: "A human being is not the highest thing in the cosmos. ... For there are also other things that are much more divine in their nature than a human being, such as, most visibly the things out of which the cosmos is composed." (*NE* 1141a20–1141b2) This passage suggests a cosmocentric view, as Aristotle gives priority to the whole of existence. According to Aristotle's axiological view, beings derive their value from their approximation to the activity of mind—and consequently to God—which is conceived as being-at-work (*energeia*) of mind (*Metaphysics* 1072b13–30, 1074 b15–35; *NE* 1177b25–32). The concept of *energeia* that we encounter in Aristotle's physics and metaphysics is also central to his conception of *praxis*, to which I now turn.

Aristotle's Conception of Human Agency and Flourishing

The most important feature of Aristotle's conception of *praxis* is its normative or virtue-oriented framework, in which issues of ethics and politics are coupled without being conflated. Ethics and politics, for Aristotle, constitute the two fundamental aspects of human life: the individual and the collective. Ethics is concerned with the right conduct of the individual, whereas politics is related to the affairs of the political community. although these two domanins of human life are inescapably interrelated, they don't fully overlap. Both the "ethical" and the "political" are situated within the natural context of human desire for living well.

The opening sentences of Aristotle's most important works of practical philosophy, *Nicomachean Ethics* and *Politics*, are quite similar in this regard. In both of those works, Aristotle refers to an ultimate "good" aimed at by every human action or association. At the end of *Nicomachean Ethics*, he also explains the rationale of politics by pointing out the inadequacy of ethical discourse: "discourses appear to have the power to encourage and stimulate open-natured [free-spirited or liberal] young people, and would make a well-born character that loves what is truly beautiful be inspired with virtue, but they are unable to encourage most people toward what is beautiful and good" (*NE* 1179b6–11). Aristotle is well aware of the logic of political realism: "Most people are more obedient to compulsion than to argument, and are persuaded by penalties than by what is beautiful." (*NE* 1180a3,4)

But compulsion isn't the only purpose of politics. More important, politics is responsible for providing proper education to the citizens of a political community: "someone who is going to be good needs to have been raised and habituated in a beautiful way," "he needs to live in that way amid decent practices and not do things that are base either unwillingly or willingly," and his life must be "conducted with some intelligence and right ordering" (*NE* 1180a14–18). The role of intelligence in politics is played out by the "law," which "has a compulsory power, while being speech [*logos*] that comes from a certain thoughtfulness [*phronēsis*] and intelligence [*nous*]" (*NE* 1180a21, 22).

Aristotle is no legal positivist, however. The law has to order what is decent or fair (*epieikēs*) and fulfill an educative purpose for the public: "Public concerns are brought about by means of laws, and that decent ones are brought about by laws of serious merit." (*NE* 1180a24, 34, 35) And one needs to learn how to make good laws: "For someone who wants to make people better by giving care ... what one ought to do is to try to become knowledgeable about lawmaking." (*NE* 1180a23–25) Aristotle sees the role of statesman and the art of politics in the legislation of good laws, and that of political philosophy in teaching this art (*NE* 1181a23–b2).

The ethical horizon of Aristotle's political philosophy is reflected in expressions such as "the *polis* exists by nature" and "man is by nature a political animal" (*Pol.* 1253a2, 3). What these statements mean is that the end of political association is happiness, and this can come about only through political cooperation. It is noteworthy that Aristotle counts human beings as political animals along with bees, wasps, ants, and cranes, all of which engage in a single common activity peculiar to their species (*HA* 488a7–10). But the human species is more political than others because of its capacity for reason and language, which allows judgment of what is good and bad as well as of what is just and unjust (*Pol.* 1253a7–15).

Aristotle's account of the origin of political association is twofold. The political community stems from a natural impulse for living or survival but continues to exist due to human striving for the good life and self-sufficiency (*Pol.* 1252b27–1253a1). The first step toward the *polis* (city) is the formation of the household (*oikos*), which results from the natural desires of reproduction and preservation. But self-preservation alone isn't fully satisfying for human beings. What is really sought after by human species is the good life. Those who possess every good necessary for survival but no friends, for instance, would not be deemed as living a good life. But as the good life necessitates some division of labor, human beings naturally form not just families but political groups. This natural impulse of sociability and the striving after the good life, according to Aristotle, lie at the origins of political community.

The origins of political community in natural strivings confer on politics certain standards and limits derived from (human) nature. The ultimate human good, *eudaimonia*, is the standard by which human action and association can be measured and evaluated. *Eudaimonia* is often translated into English as "happiness," "flourishing," or "well-being," but literally it means "being in good spirits." It can also be understood as "living well and doing well." Aristotle considers *eudaimonia* as a universal aspiration and motive of human action unique to the human species. This is evident in constant human striving for a better quality of life. Thus, all human actions and associations, knowingly or not, are oriented toward this end. Happiness is the supreme and the intrinsic good for all human beings, as everything is desired for its sake and nothing else is attained beyond happiness.

Aristotle treats happiness as fundamentally an activity (*energeia*) of the human soul emerging from a stable condition of character and intellect rather than as a passive and momentary experience befalling us. According to Aristotle, barring an unbearable misfortune it isn't possible to be happy one day and miserable the next. To be more precise, Aristotle defines happiness as the activity of the soul in accordance with virtue, and, if there is more than one virtue, in accordance with the best and most complete virtue (*NE* 1098a17, 18). In doing so, Aristotle draws attention to the common mistake of confounding true happiness with a life devoted to the pursuit of crude pleasure, political power, and material comfort. His contrast of true happiness with the semblance of happiness highlights their differences in terms of completeness and self-sufficiency. For Aristotle, happiness is an activity of the soul that is complete and self-sufficient, whereas all other human pursuits would be lacking in these crucial aspects (*NE* 1097a15–b21). However, Aristotle allows for the psychological pleasures that necessarily accompany the functioning of natural faculties or happiness in general (*NE* 1153b7–14). Thus, pleasure is not flatly rejected, but a clearer understanding of pleasure to attain true happiness is needed (*NE* 1172a19–1176a29).

To understand Aristotle's practical philosophy properly, we should remember that *aretē* means "virtue" in Greek but also carries a number of amoral connotations, such as skill, prowess, excellence, and valor. It typically refers to the best or excellent qualities of a living or a non-living being. In Aristotle's usage, however, *aretē* must be understood primarily as those qualities of character and mind that contribute to human perfection and happiness. Aristotle calls these *ēthikai aretai* (virtues of character or ethical virtues) and *dianoetikai aretai* (virtues of mind or intellectual virtues). Both ethical and intellectual virtues emerge from proper education, that is, the training of potential capacities of human beings.

For Aristotle, human beings fulfill their natural function or work (*ergon*) when they exercise their distinct capacity or potential. Ethical virtues regulate character, whereas intellectual virtues govern thinking. Both kinds of virtue are necessary for the excellence of a human being, but the latter is superior and more conducive to human happiness and perfection. The intellectual virtues can be taught by instruction, whereas ethical virtues are acquired by habituation. After a period of habituation in childhood, the practice of ethical virtues depends on the exercise of practical reason (*phronēsis*), the intellectual virtue of deliberation about practical matters (e.g., economic, political, or ethical). *Phronēsis* enables the making of right choices in practical affairs.[26]

Since one cannot live permanently in a state of contemplation, striving for intellectual excellence consummates (but doesn't nullify the need for) ethical virtue. One of the characteristics of *eudaimonia* is its self-sufficiency, and it is the contemplative activity that best fulfills this criterion (*NE* 1177a28–b1). Aristotle acknowledges that contemplation needs a minimum amount of material goods, yet "we must not think that the man who is to be happy will need many things or great things, merely because he cannot be supremely happy without external goods; for self-sufficiency and action do not involve excess, and we can do noble acts without ruling earth and sea" (*NE* 1179a1–5).

Aristotle's view of contemplation as most conducive to perfect or complete happiness ties in with his questioning of the temptations of material wealth, pleasure, status, and comfort (*NE* 1177a1–1179a33). Restlessly pursuing these objectives and turning them into ultimate ends impairs the sound judgment of what is good and just and leads eventually to moral decay, both individually and socially. The most common signs of moral decay are obsession with sex and obsession with money, which often go together and which are both caused by insatiable desire. Aristotle refers to the pleasure-based desire as *epithumia* (appetite) and the excessive desire to possess more and more things as *pleonexia* (literally "having more"). Aristotle characterizes the latter as a combination of greed and ambition. It is something unnatural and a fundamental motive of injustice in human relations. The problem with *pleonexia* is that it doesn't recognize limits, whereas the *telos* functions normatively as a limit for natural beings or activities (*Metaphysics* 994b8–16; *Pol.* 1257b28).

Here an important and ecologically relevant aspect of Aristotle's philosophy of *praxis* emerges: his moral conception of economy. As was mentioned earlier, Aristotle draws a distinction between two types of economic activity, *oikonomia* (household management) and *chrēmatistikē* (business expertise). He further divides the latter into two types. One type of *chrēmatistikē* is limited and natural, as it recognizes the limit of "good life" and serves *oikonomia* to fulfill its task toward the attainment of this end. The other type, on the other hand, is unnatural, as it doesn't recognize natural limits to its activity.

The more fundamental difference between *oikonomia* and the second (unnatural) type of *chrēmatistikē* is that, whereas the former takes the use value of goods as a reference point and is concerned with essential human needs, the latter is solely organized around the exchange value of goods and accordingly ignores limits in the acquisition and accumulation of property (*Pol.* 1257a1–1258a14). The effective goal of this distinction is to keep *chrēmatistikē* within limits, which cannot be achieved without virtue in general and justice in particular (*Pol.* 1259b17–20). Whereas unnatural *chrēmatistikē* is driven by unlimited striving for wealth and status, *oikonomia* is bounded by an ethical perspective that is grounded in nature.[27]

A parallel can be drawn between Aristotle's discussion and the discourse of ecological limits and sustainability in contemporary environmental literature. Modern economic theory rests on the assumption of an infinite nature composed of unlimited resources, but the concept of ecological sustainability traces the origins of most environmental problems to overexploitation of natural resources for the sake of perpetual economic growth. The field of ecological economics aims to remedy this flawed economic model. Accordingly, the distinction between *chrēmatistikē* and *oikonomia* has been revived by environmental scholars.[28]

A related issue that also suggests limits to accumulation is Aristotle's discussion of property ownership in *Politics* Books II and VII. Aristotle defends the private ownership of property for the most part but permits the common use of property for certain situations. Anticipating Garrett Hardin's "tragedy of the commons" argument, Aristotle asserts that common ownership leads to neglect of the thing owned (*Pol.* 1261b32–40, 1262b14–24).[29] While he mainly argues that private property is essential for the practice of citizenship and virtue (such as moderation and generosity), he also allows for common use of property in certain contexts to reinforce civic partnership and friendship (*Pol.* 1263a20–40).[30] However, this notion of common use opens the way to a more communitarian understanding of property that is open both to notions of ecologically responsible private ownership and to notions of public environmental regulation.

Aristotle's name has also come up in the literature of environmental virtue ethics and ecological citizenship in relation to his practical philosophy, particularly in connection with his emphasis on the virtue-oriented understanding of human agency.[31] The interest in environmental virtue ethics is motivated by a practical concern to turn environmental scholars' attention from the arcane questions of "the intrinsic value or moral considerability of non-human nature" to more practical "questions concerning human happiness and flourishing."[32] Ecological problems may have certain intellectual roots, but remedies for them cannot be found by theory alone. One environmental scholar put it this way: "How a person interacts with the environment is influenced by her attitudes toward it, and ... a central cause of reckless environmental exploitation is the attitude that nature is merely a resource for satisfying human wants and needs."[33]

An attitudinal change in this regard requires an environmental ethic, which must be embodied in everyday practices and support the necessary social, economic, and political changes. The purpose of ethical discourse, as Aristotle would remind us, is not simply knowing what is good, but putting it into practice (*NE* 1095a5, 6, 1179a35–b4). The concept of human agency or *praxis*, which runs through Aristotle's practical works on politics, ethics, economics, and rhetoric, can be quite helpful for this task.[34]

Conclusion

Aristotle's ecological relevance can be seen in his integral approach to *phusis* and *praxis*. Aristotle's perspective, with its emphases on a purposeful nature and on a conception of human agency and flourishing that involves virtue and limits to material accumulation, may offer an ecologically compelling alternative to modernity's mechanistic, instrumentalized conception of nature and relentless pursuit of material wealth and consumption. Indeed, the "reckless environmental exploitation" of nature has its roots in the rejection of Aristotle's *phusis* and *praxis* in the modern age.

Notes

1. See, for instance, John Passmore, *Man's Responsibility for Nature* (Scribner, 1974), 13–14; George Sessions, "Spinoza and Jeffers on Man in Nature," *Inquiry* 20.4 (1977): 483–484; and Eugene C. Hargrove, *Foundations of Environmental Ethics* (Prentice-Hall, 1989), 21.

2. See Robert Renehan, "The Greek Anthropocentric View of Man," *Harvard Studies in Classical Philology* 85 (1981): 239–259; David Sedley, "Is Aristotle's Teleology Anthropocentric?" *Phronesis* 36.2 (1991): 179–196; Michael Soupios, "Greek Philosophy and the Anthropocentric Vision," in *Ethics and the Environment*, ed. Richard E. Hart (University Press of America, 1992); Richard Sorabji, *Animal Minds and Human Morals: The Origins of the Western Debate* (Cornell University Press, 1993), 12–20.

3. See Laura Westra and Thomas M. Robinson, eds., *The Greeks and the Environment*, (Rowman & Littlefield, 1997); Konstantine Boudouris and Kostas Kalimtzis, eds., *Philosophy and Ecology: Greek Philosophy and the Environment*,

2 vols. (Ionia, 1999); David Cooper, "Aristotle," in *Fifty Key Thinkers on the Environment*, ed. Joy Palmer (Routledge, 2001).

4. This is especially true for the European ecology movement and the deep ecology movement in the United States, which has some European elements in it. The ecology movement "was not merely about protecting species and habitats, but encompassed a broader, more expansive meaning: the critique of industrial modernity itself. It entailed ... a choice about what kind of society one wants to live in." See Michael Bess, *The Light-Green Society: Ecology and Technological Modernity in France, 1960–2000* (University of Chicago Press, 2003), 12; Axel Goodbody, ed., *The Culture of German Environmentalism: Anxieties, Visions, Realities* (Berghahn, 2002).

5. See, for instance, Friedrich Nietzsche, *The Anti-Christ, Ecce Homo, Twilight of the Idols, and Other Writings*, ed. Aaron Ridley and Judith Norman (Cambridge University Press, 2005), 166–171. Nietzsche's critique of the metaphysical conception of "two worlds" in the Western tradition had found its way into contemporary environmental discourse. For Heidegger's interpretation of Nietzsche on this issue, see Martin Heidegger, *Nietzsche*, ed. David Farrell Krell (HarperCollins, 1991), particularly volume 1, pp. 200–210 and volume 3, 57–63. On Heidegger's differences with Nietzsche, see chapter 13 in this volume.

6. Stanley Rosen, "*Technē* and the Origins of Modernity," in *Metaphysics in Ordinary Language* (Yale University Press, 1999).

7. Hannah Arendt's political theory builds on these Aristotelian distinctions: "It is through a revival of the Aristotelian distinction between *praxis* (the doing of fine and noble deeds) and *poiesis* (making) that Arendt arrives at her own concept of action." See Seyla Benhabib, *The Reluctant Modernism of Hannah Arendt* (Rowman & Littlefield, 2003), xv. Arendt in particular draws attention to the substitution of making for action in the modern era. See especially Arendt, *The Human Condition* (University of Chicago Press, 1958), 220–230, 289–304. In chapter 14 in this volume, Peter Cannavò takes a somewhat different approach and looks at Arendt's conception of place.

8. See Thomas Hobbes, *Leviathan*, ed. Edwin Curley (Hackett, 1994), chapter 46.

9. See Martin Heidegger, *The Question Concerning Technology and Other Essays*, tr. William Lovitt (Harper & Row, 1977). Also see the chapter on Heidegger in this volume.

10. See the chapter on Arendt in this volume.

11. For detailed discussions of Aristotle's environmental relevance along these lines, see Mulford Q. Sibley, "The Relevance of Classical Political Theory for Economy, Technology, and Ecology," *Alternatives* 2, no. 2 (1973): 14–35; Keekok Lee, *The Natural and Artifactual: The Implications of Deep Science and Deep Technology for Environmental Philosophy* (Lexington Books, 1999); Trish Glazebrook, "Global Technology and the Promise of Control," in *Globalization, Technology, and Philosophy*, ed. David Tabachnick and Toivo Koivukoski (SUNY Press, 2004).

12. Aristotle's biological interest was taken over by his colleague and friend Theophrastus, whose study of plants earned him the recognition as "the father of ecology."

13. Aristotle, *Metaphysics*, tr. W. D. Ross in Jonathan Barnes, ed., *The Complete Works of Aristotle: The Revised Oxford Translation*, volume 2 (Princeton University Press, 1984).

14. Aristotle, *Parts of Animals*, tr. William Ogle, in Jonathan Barnes, ed., *The Complete Works of Aristotle: The Revised Oxford Translation*, volume 1 (Princeton University Press, 1984).

15. Both words were probably of Aristotle's coinage. See George A. Blair, "The Meaning of 'Energeia' and 'Entelecheia' in Aristotle," *International Philosophical Quarterly* 7.1 (1967): 101–117. Heidegger meticulously explicated Aristotle's conception of nature and its central concepts, *energeia* and *entelecheia*, in various writings. *Entelecheia*, according to Heidegger, is the fundamental word of Aristotle's thinking and represents "that knowledge of being that brings Greek philosophy to its fulfillment." See Heidegger, "On the Essence and Concept of *Phusis* in Aristotle's *Physics* B, I," in *Pathmarks*, ed.. William McNeill (Cambridge University Press, 1998), 216.

16. Murray Bookchin's evolutionary view of nature and society drew upon Aristotle's concepts of "potentiality" (*dunamis*) and "development" (*entelecheia*), which he called "dialectical naturalism." See Bookchin, *The Philosophy of Social Ecology: Essays on Dialectical Naturalism*, second edition (Black Rose Books, 1995).

17. Aristotle also mentions two other intellectual virtues essential to human perfection: *nous* (intellect), which provides intuitive insight into the circumstances of right conduct or the first principles of theoretical knowledge, and *sophia* (wisdom), which involves knowledge of eternal and necessary beings (e.g., God).

18. Aristotle, *Nicomachean Ethics*, tr. Joe Sachs (Focus, 2002) (hereafter cited as *NE*), 1106b14, 15.

19. Aristotle, *Politics*, tr. Carnes Lord (University of Chicago Press, 1984) (hereafter cited as *Pol.*).

20. See, for instance, D. M. Balme, "Teleology and Necessity," in *Philosophical Issues in Aristotle's Biology*, ed. Allan Gotthelf and James G. Lennox (Cambridge University Press, 1987), 279; Monte Johnson, *Aristotle on Teleology* (Clarendon, 2005), 222–237; Mariska Leunissen, *Explanation and Teleology in Aristotle's Science of Nature* (Cambridge University Press, 2010), 40–47; Rich Cameron, "Aristotle's Teleology," *Philosophy Compass* 5, no. 12 (2010): 1096–1106, at 1104.

21. Aristotle adjusts the level of precision according to the subject matter under discussion (*NE* 1094b11–13). For an interpretation of the passage from *Politics* in light of Aristotle's scientific treatises, see Gary Steiner, *Anthropocentrism and Its Discontents: The Moral Status of Animals in the History of Western Philosophy* (University of Pittsburgh Press, 2005), 57–76.

22. For a detailed discussion of this passage along these lines, see Johnson, *Aristotle on Teleology*, 229–237.

23. Aristotle, *History of Animals*, tr. D'Arcy W. Thompson, in *The Complete Works of Aristotle*, volume 1 (hereafter cited as *HA*).

24. See Arthur O. Lovejoy, *The Great Chain of Being: A Study of the History of an Idea* (Harper & Row, 1960), 55–61. For a defense of Aristotle's conception of animal cognition, see Andrew Coles, "Animal and Childhood Cognition in Aristotle's Biology and the Scala Naturae," in *Aristotelische Biologie*, ed. Wolfgang Kullmann and Sabine Föllinger (Steiner, 1997). As the chapters in this volume on David Hume, Jean-Jacques Rousseau, and Mary Wollstonecraft show, diverse conceptions of the continuity (or lack thereof) between humans and animals have been advanced and debated throughout the history of Western thought. To think as though the complexities of this distinction have been discovered only recently is to miss the long history of this perennial debate.

25. Aristotle's notorious defense of slavery in Book I of *Politics* must also be understood in this context; natural slaves are those who, by nature, lack the full rational capacity to make moral choices and are necessarily dependent on another person's guidance and protection.

26. Aristotle's recognition of an autonomous place for the practical dimension of human existence has been the main impetus behind the recent revival of interest in his practical philosophy. For a summary of the neo-Aristotelian literature, see Franco Volpi, "The Rehabilitation of Practical Philosophy and Neo-Aristotelianism," in *Action and Contemplation*, ed. Robert C. Bartlett and Susan D. Collins (SUNY Press, 1999).

27. Aristotle's contrast between *oikonomia* and *chrēmatistikē*, and the corollary contrast between "use-value" and "exchange-value," would be recovered by modern economists, most notably by Karl Marx and Karl Polanyi. See Marx, *Capital: A Critique of Political Economy*, volume 1, tr. Ben Fowkes (Penguin, 1990), 151–152, 179, 253–254, 267; Karl Polanyi, *The Great Transformation: The Political and Economic Origins of Our Time* (Beacon, 1957), 53–54. On Marx's connection to Aristotle, see George McCarthy, *Marx and the Ancients: Classical Ethics, Social Justice and Nineteenth-Century Political Economy* (Rowman & Littlefield, 1990); George McCarthy, ed., *Marx and Aristotle: Nineteenth-Century German Social Theory and Classical Antiquity* (Rowman & Littlefield, 1992). As with Aristotle, there are ecological implications in Marx's analysis. The Marxian concept of "metabolic rift," discussed by Tim Luke in this volume, reflects how, under capitalism, the pursuit of exchange value and commodification without limits fails to respect natural use values and overwhelms nature's metabolic processes.

28. See, for instance, Herman E. Daly and John B. Cobb Jr., *For the Common Good*, second edition (Beacon, 1994), 138–158; John O'Neill, *Ecology, Policy and Politics: Human Well-Being and the Natural World* (Routledge, 1993), 161–175.

29. See Garret Hardin, "The Tragedy of the Commons," *Science* 162 (1968): 1243–1248.

30. See Darrell Dobbs, "Aristotle's Anticommunism," *American Journal of Political Science* 29, no. 1 (1985): 29–46; Fred D. Miller, *Nature, Justice, and Rights in Aristotle's Politics* (Clarendon, 1995), 309–331.

31. See, for instance, Susanne E. Foster, "Aristotle and the Environment," *Environmental Ethics* 24, no. 4 (2002): 409–428; Robert Hull, "All about EVE: A Report on Environmental Virtue Ethics Today," *Ethics & the Environment* 10, no. 1 (2005): 89–110; Ronald L. Sandler, *Character and Environment: A Virtue-Oriented Approach to Environmental Ethics* (Columbia University Press, 2007).

32. Philip Cafaro, "Environmental Virtue Ethics," *Philosophy in the Contemporary World* 8, no. 2 (2001): 1.

33. Sandler, *Character and Environment*, 1–2.

34. The critique of abstract "environmental ethics" by advocates of "environmental pragmatism" agrees with Aristotle in this regard. See Avner de-Shalit, *The Environment: Between Theory and Practice* (Oxford University Press, 2000); and Andrew Light and Avner De-Shalit, eds., *Moral and Political Reasoning in Environmental Practice* (MIT Press, 2003).

3
Niccolò Machiavelli: Rethinking Decentralization's Role in Green Theory

Francisco Seijo

Centralization of wealth and power contributes to social and economic injustice, environmental destruction, and militarization. ... Decision-making should, as much as possible, remain at the individual and local level ... .
Green Party of the United States, Ten Key Values, ratified at Green Party Convention, Denver, June 2000

[Italy] has not been able to come under one head but has been under many princes and lords, from whom so much disunion and so much weakness have arisen, that it has now be the prey not only of barbarian powers but of whoever assaults it.
Niccolò Machiavelli, *Discourses on Livy*[1] I: 12, 138

Niccolò Machiavelli—an Italian civil servant, political thinker, and playwright—lived in Florence from 1469 to 1527. Though Machiavelli was one of the leading political thinkers of the Italian Renaissance, his thought has not been frequently engaged with or alluded to in recent debates about environmental political theory. Perhaps this is because, like many of the leading intellectual personalities of his time, the former Second Chancellor of the Florentine Republic considered himself a humanist. Humanism, owing to its seemingly unrestrained anthropocentrism, may at first sight appear not to be relevant to present-day thinking on the relationship between politics and nature. Furthermore, political theorists still disagree about the philosophical significance of Machiavelli's work, some contending that his reflections and insights don't amount to a full-fledged and coherent theoretical framework.[2] Environmental political theory's lack of engagement with Machiavelli's thought is troubling because the political issues and themes raised in his writings, however unsystematically proposed, have consistently compelled political philosophers of the first rank to engage with his ideas, if only to dismiss them.[3]

The Prince and *Discourses on Livy*, Machiavelli's main political works, are among the most widely discussed and influential texts in the Western canon. As Leo Strauss notes, "the moral-political teaching of the *Discourses* is fundamentally the same as that of the Prince but with one important difference: the *Discourses* state powerfully the case for Republics."[4] In *The Prince*, Machiavelli analyses political power, how to accumulate it, how to preserve it, and how to use it. He does so by using real political and historical events to illustrate his theoretical points, while appearing to withhold ethical judgment. He sets aside the ancient tradition of philosophizing, rejecting what "ought to be" in favor of, as he puts it, considering the theoretical significance of what "is." For this reason, he is often characterized as the first modern political scientist.[5]

In his other fundamental political treatise, *Discourses on Livy*, which he considered his masterpiece, Machiavelli reveals more normative aspects of his political thinking.[6] By the time he wrote the *Discourses*, Machiavelli had abandoned all hope of regaining an important political position in Florence and had comfortably settled into the role of sage, historian, and political theorist with which we identify him today. In the *Discourses* he shows a well-reasoned and empirically rooted preference for the republican form of government over all other imaginable alternatives and meditates, comparing the Italy of his time with the historical experience of the early Imperial Roman Republic and considering the advantages and disadvantages of republican government for what we today would call effective "governance."[7] While doing this, he weighs the relative value for his thought of the fundamental political goals of security and liberty, concluding—in a manner that some scholars believe contradicts *The Prince*—that republics are better at balancing the inherent tension between the simultaneous pursuit of those two goals.[8]

In the *Discourses*, Machiavelli develops an argument that is of paramount importance for environmental political thinking. He makes the claim that republics are the most durable and resilient governmental institutions devised by human beings. Republics, he argues, offer the best possibility for withstanding aleatory catastrophes—environmental and otherwise—provoked by a mysterious factor that Machiavelli calls *Fortuna*. In this sense, Machiavelli's work foreshadows the work of many latter-day environmental political theorists who find in civic republicanism and a strong "green" state an antidote for various environmental and political perils that advanced industrial and post-industrial societies are currently facing.[9]

Machiavelli's main works deal, then, with matters that appear to be among the essential questions posed by environmental political theory. Yet present-day Green theorists have dedicated little effort to a discussion of his ideas, with the possible exception of the aforementioned references among political theorists to his republican preferences as a basis for a civic republican vision of an environmentally sustainable society.[10] As this chapter will argue, Machiavelli's views on the decentralization of power and its implications for the resilience of political systems do indeed merit closer attention and may have significant implications for environmental political theory. This chapter will, therefore, examine both Machiavelli's ideas about the relationship between nature and politics and his ideas about what he argues is the most preferable form of political regime—the republic.

The Struggle Between *Virtù* and *Fortuna*: Bridging Machiavelli's Ideas with Present-Day Concerns about the Relationship between Nature and Politics

Virtù is one of the most essential concepts in Machiavelli's thought.[11] Though there is no scholarly consensus as to its correct translation into English, this chapter will argue that it holds many affinities with what we would call "power." A virtuous prince, or ruler, is for Machiavelli a person who is "able not to be good, or use goodness and abstain from using it, according to the circumstances," with the ultimate goal of "maintaining himself" or achieving "his preservation" as well as preserving "his state."[12] Thus, for Machiavelli there are certain specific political skills that are associated with *Virtù*, such as an ability to transcend human social and moral conventions when that is politically necessary and a capacity to adapt to changing political circumstances without preconceived doctrines or strategies. As Machiavelli states in *The Prince*, *Virtù*'s greatest rewards are worldly success and political survival, two things that weren't easy to achieve in turbulent Renaissance Italy. In this sense Machiavelli prefigures Thomas Hobbes's political philosophy, which places security maximization as the essential function of all political systems.[13]

As a humanist thinker, Machiavelli, then, seems to focus mainly on what conditions lead to the effective functioning of a political system and on the study of political power and how to accrue it, maintain it, and use it so as to further security maximization.[14] When it comes to nature and the natural systems within which human political power is ultimately embedded, however, Machiavelli's views remain largely implicit. This is, no doubt, one of the reasons why Green Theory has had difficulty engaging with his thought. Whereas the writings of Hobbes, Rousseau, and Mills are peppered with reflections on the natural world, references to nature are scarce in Machiavelli. His best-known allusion may be one found in chapter XXV of *The Prince*, where he likens another of his theoretical concepts, *Fortuna*—which for Machiavelli is the eternal nemesis of human *Virtù*—to a river that, in a moment, can sweep away centuries of human toil and prowess:

> I judge that it might be true that fortune [*Fortuna*] is the arbiter of one-half of our actions, but that she still leaves the other half, or close to it, for us to govern. And I liken her to one of those violent rivers, which when they become enraged, flood the plains, ruin the trees and the buildings, lift earth from this part, drop it in another; each person flees before them, everyone yields to their impetus without being able to hinder them in any regard. And although they are like this it is not as if men when times are quiet, could not provide for them with dikes and dams so that when they rise later, either they go by a canal or their impetus is neither so wanton nor so damaging. (*The Prince*,[15] XXV: 98)

Indeed, the tension between human *Virtù* and *Fortuna* that Machiavelli emphasizes in his writings proves essential to understanding his contribution to the elucidation of his position on the relationship between political and natural systems. This relationship is perhaps best understood through a passage in a letter from Machiavelli to a friend, Francesco Vettori: "We are imitating nature which itself is changeable, and whoever imitates nature cannot be blamed."[16]

Machiavelli's conceptualization of *Fortuna* depicts forces that, like the river he uses metaphorically to illustrate his point, function independently of human agency. All human beings can ever do with their *Virtù* is reduce the likelihood that the disturbances (to use the theoretical term employed by present-day ecology to describe what in common language is usually referred to as "natural disasters") unleashed randomly (or probabilistically, as some ecologists wishing to model them would argue) by *Fortuna* will ruin them by designing strategies that emphasize adaptability to ever-changing circumstances. In holding this view on the relationship between *Virtù* and *Fortuna*, Machiavelli proves to be far ahead of his time in embracing a non-static, non-equilibrium view of nature that is only now beginning to emerge as the dominant paradigm in the science of ecology.[17] Present-day ecological concepts such as "transition probability" and "resilience" place stochasticity and randomness at the heart of the scientific explanation of such crucial natural processes as ecological succession and the evolution of species populations in resource limited ecosystems. Indeed, the concept of ecological succession has shifted from a predictable Clementsian linear order (a perspective that, according to some scholars, Frederic Clements borrowed from Aristotle) to a "non-equilibrium" disturbance-centered paradigm more akin to Edward Lorenz's chaos theory.[18] Perhaps Machiavelli's probabilistic guess that there is a 50–50 chance of *Fortuna* or *Virtù* prevailing in any given circumstance may be a quantitatively naive assessment by the standards of present-day ecological science, but the essential insight into how natural processes operate—that is, randomly—is impeccable and indeed shows Machiavelli's insights into nature to have more present-day relevance than those discussed in Mill's essay "On Nature," which emphasizes the regularity and predictability of the laws of nature.[19]

This interpretation of how Machiavelli's ideas on *Fortuna* and *Virtù* bear on present-day preoccupations with the relationship between politics and nature leads to the central question of this chapter: How can environmental political theory's concept of decentralization be reconsidered in light of Machiavelli's thought? A good way to frame this engagement or dialogue between the two theories would be in terms of Machiavelli's reflections on the relationship between human political power—as embedded in the institutional design of humanity's political systems—and nature, as defined by its stochastically determined disturbance regimes. Decentralization, as we shall see, is Green Theory's normative and practical "means" (or strategy) of achieving desirable "ends": environmental sustainability, social and economic justice, demilitarization.[20] For Greens, human *Virtù* (power) should be employed to strike a new balance with *Fortuna* (natural processes) through the strategy of decentralization. Just as the dikes and dams that constrain a river do so by imitating the natural processes by which the river operates, a certain type of decentralization would allow us to live more harmoniously with nature by placing our political entities within the natural whole in a way that would imitate the organic communities of which that whole is itself composed. The remainder of this chapter will examine this Green theoretical and ideological claim in light of Machiavelli's reflections on the matter as derived from *Discourses on Livy*.

The Concept of Decentralization in Environmental Political Theory

Decentralization is one of the preferred Green ideological recipes for political re-organization of present-day nation-states and the creation of more sustainable societies. The concept, however, has meant different things to

Green thinkers and activists. Some environmentalist movements, for instance, have appealed to decentralization to support the abandonment of large cities in favor of smaller, theoretically more ecologically sustainable eco-communes.[21] Still others have employed it to advocate the dissolution of nation-states into smaller, more ecologically harmonious independent political units or bioregions.[22] Green parties around the world[23] have employed it to call for the devolution of environmental policy-making powers from the nation-state to regions, local communities, and citizens and have used this political platform (particularly in Europe) to justify electoral alliances with regional nationalist parties demanding more or less the same things though for different ideological reasons.

Beyond the diverse ideological and tactical uses that Greens have made of it in the recent past, it is clear that the concept is also firmly rooted in environmental political theory. A close examination of these theoretical approaches to decentralization, however, reveals that the concept's exact normative meaning remains elusive. In other words, the questions of exactly what decentralization means and why it is desirable haven't been entirely settled in Green political thought. Thus, decentralization has been alternatively postulated as a remedy for the ailments of ecologically unsustainable centralized political systems and as a method for transcending such purportedly outmoded social, economic, and political structures as the family, business corporations, political parties, and the nation-state.[24] The accumulation of power in these varied political, economic, and social institutions would somehow be, then, linked to the present ecological crisis. Through decentralization, it would appear, this pernicious influence would be deactivated. In this iteration of the decentralization debate, the concept would serve both as a means and an end for the reshuffling of archaic and ecologically and economically unsustainable social and political structures. Once those structures had been transcended, new, decentralized sustainable societies would participate more actively in the governance of their more locally attuned democratic political systems, and decentralized economic habits of local production and consumption would leave less of an ecological footprint.[25] A less transformative and more pragmatic Green variant of this argument holds that some measure of decentralization would, at least, improve the efficiency of present environmental policy making. Additionally, decentralization could simultaneously serve to empower citizens and local communities by enhancing their participation in the day-to-day political process of creating more ecologically sustainable societies.[26]

In sum, decentralization, as the term is used both by environmental political theorists and Green activists, seems to be endowed with both a normative and a pragmatic dimension. It serves simultaneously as a means and as an end for the attainment of sustainable societies. As Andrew Dobson has noted,

> Green radicals are in the same position as Rousseau: the raw material (mankind) is inadequate for the task at hand (building a sustainable society). Greens, however, have to answer political and institutional questions. If human nature (and the societies that have engendered it) is considered, a decentralized politics seems inefficient and naive. However, if mankind and human nature are analyzed with reference to what they could become (their modes of production and patterns of consumption), decentralized politics becomes the preferred option for the Green radicals. In fact, decentralized politics would be the ecological equivalent of Rousseau's legislation: the source of the transformation of mankind.[27]

The remainder of this chapter will compare and contrast Green ideas about decentralization with Machiavelli's political philosophy. By juxtaposing Green ideas about both the theory and the praxis of decentralization with Machiavelli's implicit and explicit views on the matter, this chapter will argue that Machiavelli's analysis of decentralization reveals that the Greens' decentralizing vision remains a largely unexamined assumption that, in its present articulation, fails to answer a key question facing all human political systems, environmentally sustainable or not: How can security and liberty be maximized in political systems that operate within the rules imposed by ever-changing natural systems or processes?

Machiavelli's Reflections on Politically Decentralized Renaissance Italy

The Italy in which Machiavelli lived was by far Europe's wealthiest region. During the Renaissance, Italian city-states controlled Europe's commerce, its budding banking industry, and its most profitable manufacturing sectors.[28] In spite of its economic and cultural achievements, however, Machiavelli's Italy was simultaneously one of Europe's most politically unstable regions, as it was divided into a multitude of city-states. Duchies, principalities, and republics vying for regional hegemony were continually at war. Many of the wars were fought, not by Italians, but by foreign mercenary troops. The wars usually ended in stalemate and the temporary bankruptcy of the contending city-states.

As a result of this deadly combination of economic prosperity and political disunity, Italy was repeatedly preyed upon by more powerful, centralized and expansionist neighbors such as Spain and France.[29] Much of Machiavelli's thought stems from his attempt to analyze this apparent contradiction. One of his main arguments in *The Prince* is that Italy's political division was leading to its political disappearance and/or to subservience to foreign powers. Machiavelli's recipe for averting this outcome was Italian political unification. Normatively he would have preferred republican government for a unified Italy. Because of the pragmatism that governed his thinking, however, he was willing to contemplate a monarchic form of government as a lesser evil, provided that it would unify Italy and rid it of foreign invaders. In chapter XXVI of *The Prince* he writes:

[H]aving considered everything discussed above, and thinking to myself whether in Italy at present the times have been tending to the honor of a new prince, and whether there is matter to give opportunity to someone prudent and virtuous to introduce a form that would bring honor to him and good to the community of men there, it appears to me that so many things are tending to the benefit of a new prince that I do not know what time has ever been more apt for it. And if, as I said, it was necessary for anyone wanting to see the virtue of Moses that the people of Israel be enslaved in Egypt, and to learn the greatness of spirit of Cyrus, that the Persians be oppressed by the Medes, and to learn the excellence of Theseus, that the Athenians be dispersed, so at present to know the virtue of an Italian spirit it was necessary that Italy be reduced to the condition in which she is at present, which is more enslaved than the Hebrews, more servile than the Persians, more dispersed than the Athenians, without a head, without order, beaten, despoiled, torn, pillaged, and having endured ruin of every sort. (102)

Machiavelli, therefore, can be read as a potent critic of the effects of political decentralization in his own time. For the sake of unity, as is apparent in this passage, Machiavelli was willing to sacrifice one of his most cherished normative values—republicanism—in favor of a centralized monarchy. Having witnessed the practical consequences of political decentralization for Italy, he believed that it had planted the seeds of Italy's destruction. Hence the importance for the Green theoretical debate on decentralization of Machiavelli's thought. If decentralization is the means as well as the end for the creation of future ecologically sustainable societies, Green thinkers should come to terms with Machiavelli's criticism of decentralization and what he claims were its empirical political consequences in Renaissance Italy.

Machiavelli's Critique of Decentralization

Most of Machiavelli's normative views on decentralization can be found in *Discourses on Livy*, a work that reveals why republics (of a certain type) endure hardships of all types more effectively than principalities. These are precisely the "ends" that Greens seek through decentralization. For Machiavelli the ultimate test of a political system's success is, as we have seen, its endurance, its resilience, its ability to survive and adapt to a world beset by contingency and random events that can barely be controlled or predicted—that is, by *Fortuna*.[30] In light of this criterion, Machiavelli, in the first few chapters of *Discourses on Livy*, evaluates the various types of republics, principalities, and kingdoms that had existed in the West before his time. At the end of these chapters, he reaches the conclusion that there are two main successful political models for reaching the ultimate goal of political security. Both are republics. The first is the Imperial Roman republic. The second is the model offered by the republics of ancient Sparta and Renaissance Venice.

Chapter VI of book I of *Discourses on Livy* includes a passage that is fraught with implications for the decentralization debate:

> If someone wished, therefore, to order a republic anew, he would have to examine whether he wished it to expand like Rome in dominion and in power or truly to remain within narrow limits. In the first case it is necessary to order it like Rome. … In the second case, you can order it like Sparta and like Venice, but because expansion is poison for such republics, he who orders them should, in all the modes he can, prohibit them from acquiring, because such acquisitions, founded on a weak republic, are its ruin altogether. … Without doubt I believe that if the thing could be held balanced in this mode, it would be the true political way of life and the true quiet of a city. But since all things of men are in motion and cannot stay steady, they must either rise or fall; and to many things that reason does not bring you, necessity brings you. So when a republic that has been ordered so as to be capable of maintaining itself does not expand, and necessity leads it to expand, this would come to take away its foundations and make it come to ruin sooner. … I believe that it is necessary to follow the Roman order and not that of the other republics. (22–23).

Machiavelli sees the model represented by Sparta and Venice as too idealistic for his purposes because it doesn't take into account the inherent instability of all human constructs, political or otherwise, and the political effects of the constant and relentless operation of *Fortuna*. In an ideal, static world in which "the things of men are (not) in motion," free and independent republics—or, for the sake of argument, self-enclosed, environmentally sustainable, decentralized polities—would be able to live tranquilly alongside one another. This would be, as Machiavelli puts it, "the true political way of life and the true quiet of the city." However, for Machiavelli this can never be the case—in a world in which *Fortuna* plays a leading role, a stable, decentralized political system of non-expansive, self-enclosed city-states can be achieved only momentarily. Human fate is, as we have seen, partly determined by *Fortuna*—by random processes, either anthropogenic or non-anthropogenic. It is difficult to imagine a political entity that is immune from the impacts of distant political or economic upheavals (such as wars, depressions, or trade embargoes placed by or upon other nations) or effectively insulated from environmental disasters (such as earthquakes, hurricanes, plagues, and climate change). Even if non-expansive, self-enclosed city-state republics managed to find a way to curb their own expansionary human tendencies and those of other republics, they would always face the danger of a change in *Fortuna* that would surely create the right conditions, in its eternal toss of the probabilistic dice, in which an expansionary centralizing political system would emerge, either locally or elsewhere, not because it may be politically desirable but because it is possible. These expansionary states would not necessarily originate because of any inherent human disposition to expansiveness, which would be the way Hobbes would see it. The likelihood of their emergence would depend entirely on the always dependable, though largely unpredictable, inherent randomness of *Fortuna*. Because human affairs are always in a perpetual state of flux, "necessity" (as determined by *Fortuna*), not "reason," would ultimately force decentralized political systems to expand so as to better defend their independence and even their continued survival against the ever-existing possibility that an expansionary state may arise somewhere. Isolationist self-enclosed non-expansionism, hence, is not an option for any political system, according to Machiavelli, because the possibility that a rival expansionary state will come into being elsewhere is ever present and therefore those leaders who design their systems without taking that possibility into account are courting disaster.

For Machiavelli, therefore, the conclusion is inescapable: In the long run, entralizing republics that are designed to expand face better options of surviving *Fortuna* than decentralized republics that are not designed to expand. It is for this reason that Machiavelli postulates the Imperial Roman republic as his model political regime—the "end" to his "means"—and discards other forms of government. Imperial republics can afford some of the freedom, the good life, and the prosperity for their citizens that decentralized republican forms of government can provide without endangering the political system's survival in an inherently unstable and unpredictable world. They have the resources and the powers necessary to sustain themselves against both ambitious rivals and natural disasters.

Implicitly, Machiavelli depicts the decentralized world of independent city-states that the Italian Renaissance embodied as a sort of political "dead end" experiment. That system can continue to exist only if its political model prevails universally and all other polities in the world also become independent, self-enclosed, republican city-states without any ulterior political or territorial expansionary ambitions. That, according to the inescapable logic of Machiavelli's argument, can never be the case, for two reasons: because the regional orientation of such city-states leads them not to expand and universalize their model and because the random powers of *Fortuna* are likely to engender, at some point, a centralizing political system or internal tendency that is hostile to this ideal elsewhere. Let us note that in Green political thought this idea of a steady, self-enclosed, non-expansionary state is widely posited and is most popularly represented in the works of Herman Daly.[31]

Machiavelli's Defense of Decentralization

Does Machiavelli have any use at all for political decentralization? Surprisingly, he does. Having settled in book I of *Discourses on Livy* on the superiority of the Imperial Roman republic as a political model, Machiavelli turns in book II to explain how Rome reconciled its two driving values, liberty and security, into a regime that eventually prevailed quasi-universally in the West. As Machiavelli puts it, "a city that lives free has two ends—one to acquire, the other to maintain itself free" (*Discourses* I: 29, 66). Machiavelli cites three historical examples of expanding republics that attempted to reconcile these two ideals: a league of republics (the Etruscans), an imperial republic with partners (the Roman Republic), and an imperial republic with subjects (Athens).

Not surprisingly, Machiavelli believed that the second model proved in the long run to be superior and more enduring. Both the first model and the third were proved wrong by historical experience. The third model, exemplified by Athens, failed because it based the control of new territories purely on military force, a force that a small city could never muster sufficiently owing to its own limited size. This makes sense because self-contained, self-centered republics that don't allow membership to conquered outsiders will always be inherently limited in resources, such as population. The Etruscans were successful, according to Machiavelli, only for a limited amount of time, since they were ultimately conquered by the even more successful republican regime represented by the Romans.

The key to the success of the Roman model of expansionary republic was, then, its reliance on partners rather than subjects. It is in this sense that Machiavelli finds a use for the concept of decentralization. The partners of the imperial republic were allowed to share the same laws and the same rights as Rome, but they ceded the final political word on crucial decisions affecting the well-being of all the constituent parts of the imperial republic, all decision-making prerogatives, and their political "brand" or name to the central Roman government. As Machiavelli puts it, "get partners but not so much that the rank of command, the seat of empire, and the title of the enterprises do not remain with you, which mode was observed by the Romans" (*Discourses* II: 4, 136). Thus when Rome conquered new territories, it allowed the inhabitants, in most cases, to live according to their own customs, religions, and laws (as long as the laws didn't contradict the more fundamental imperial Roman laws). This was the extent to which Rome allowed for decentralization. The ability to make new laws and the power to enforce all laws, however, always remained in the hands of the Roman republic's imperial government. This was the liberty for its partners that Rome considered to be compatible with its security.

Green Views on Decentralization Reconsidered in Light of Machiavelli's *Discourses*

Machiavelli's discussion of decentralization in *Discourses on Livy* raises an important issue for present-day Green Theory. For Machiavelli, maximization of security is the primary determinant in the design of a functional political system. However, political systems ought to be designed with other values also in mind. Machiavelli is not Hobbes. He postulates liberty as the most important other value that a political system must simultaneously maximize.[32] In Machiavelli's ideal political regime—the Imperial Roman republic—both of these values were realized in compatible incarnations and even reinforced one another. The liberty of Rome's citizens reinforced the regime's ability to expand, and the regime's capacity to expand reinforced the liberty of its citizens. Decentralization improperly understood, on the other hand, may lead, according to Machiavelli, to the undermining of security in the name of liberty, which in turn may lead to the collapse and extinction of the political system that fails to balance the two values adequately.

Some environmental political thinkers have noted this "security gap" in the Green approach to decentralization. For example, Robyn Eckersley argues in *The Green State* that environmental threats are too large in scope for small communities or political entities to control and that, therefore, a large modern "Green" state is needed to undo the damages that large modern states inflict on the environment.[33] William Ophuls also addresses the issues raised by Machiavelli regarding republics that can foster both security and liberty while adhering to the realities of what Ophuls calls "natural law," which closely resembles Machiavelli's concept of *Fortuna*.[34] Don Alexander's critique of bioregionalism also highlights its theoretical shortcomings and its inability to decide between maximizing security and maximizing liberty. "Groups," he writes, "are not rooted in specific regions; they are constantly migrating and displacing one another. The Welsh and Bretons may seem like the authentic bioregional occupants of their respective bioregions, but they got where they are by displacing even more primordial inhabitants. This process of migration and conquest is a constant throughout human history. How does this fit with bioregional theory?"[35] Garrett Hardin, in his classic essay "The Tragedy of the Commons," makes a similar point when he reflects on of population growth, security, and liberty in the context of the intrinsic finitude of natural systems. As Hardin puts it, human individuals or communities that unilaterally choose to respect these limits will always be threatened by the possible emergence of others who choose not to maximize sustainability: "In a welfare state, how shall we deal with the family, the religion, the race, or the class (or indeed any distinguishable and cohesive group) that adopts over breeding as a policy to secure its own aggrandizement? To couple the concept of freedom to breed with the belief that everyone born has an equal right to the commons is to lock the world into a tragic course of action."[36]

Similar questions could be posed to Green thinkers calling for the decentralization of existing political systems and the establishment of sustainable eco-communes, or even to Green parties that have a minimalist vision of devolving administrative political power to smaller local communities. How can security for local decentralized political entities, however attuned and in harmony they may be with their ecosystem, be guaranteed in a world where constant instability and change both in human and natural systems is the norm and not the exception? Certainly, Greens argue reasonably, some forms of decentralization may be desirable and can enhance the resilience of a natural system, as shown by studies of how communities and organizations respond to external shocks.[37] Conceivably, the future of energy production may also lie in distributed and decentralized systems that are less vulnerable to terrorist attacks or natural disasters. Perhaps centralized political systems also show vulnerability to change in the sense that their centralized "command and control" centers lack resilience and can easily be destroyed by competing political systems. One need only recall that the inefficiency and rigidity of the centrally planned economies of Eastern Europe ultimately resulted in the collapse of their political systems.[38]

Machiavelli's thinking, however, suggests that only political systems that are somewhat centralized and are designed to expand manage to preserve a degree of security in the long run in a world governed largely by random and unpredictable forces that can be viewed as manifestations of what Machiavelli calls *Fortuna*. These Machiavellian theories, of course, contradict the basic point made by many environmental political thinkers and ideologists that, in a closed and finite natural system, political entities and economic entities cannot grow indefinitely but must sustain themselves through efficiency in production and sufficiency in consumption. They must, in the words of the title of the 1972 Club of Rome report, accept "limits to growth." It is not clear that Machiavelli conceived of, let alone accepted, a view of the world that necessitated limits in any ecological sense.

Perhaps a useful middle ground between the Green view of decentralization and the Machiavellian view can be found in the work of Elinor Ostrom, who sought to reconcile the strengths of decentralized sustainable governance of long-enduring common-pool resources by local communities with the harsh political realities of the present-day world as represented by the driving expansionary (or "globalizing," to use the more vernacular term) forces of "markets" and interventionist "states." Ostrom's work shows empirically that common pool resources (CPRs) have been best managed—and under certain strict conditions—by self-regulating, decentralized local communities. However, Ostrom thinks that in a world dominated by the expansionary forces of markets and states this decentralized mode of government is increasingly endangered. In our time, then, there is a growing need to build diverse—one could almost say "customized"—institutions for the administration of local CPRs that are capable of recognizing and reinforcing multiple levels of governance.[39] In this respect, Ostrom's approach differs from Hardin's quasi-Hobbesian model of "command and control" centralized government to prevent "the tragedy of the commons." Ostrom insists that a state needs "partners" (as Machiavelli would have put it) in its governance of CPRs, and that those "partners" (which Ostrom called "local communities") also need a state that can guarantee their security against outside expansionist "market" or "state" intruders such as a multinational corporation seeking to maximize its profits at the expense of a local CPR's sustainability or a foreign state with ambitions to appropriate unsustainably the wealth embedded in local CPRs. Thomas Homer-Dixon's work illustrates how these tensions are becoming an increasing source of conflict.[40]

In light of Machiavelli's reflections and Ostrom's call for multi-level governance of CPRs, it would seem that only two options are left for Green theorists and practitioners of decentralization: either they must strive to design ecologically sustainable centralized "Green" states that have the capacity to establish partnerships or merge with smaller political systems (sustainable or not) or they must adopt the position of partners to a stronger centralized political system that will guarantee them some, if not all, of their freedoms (including, of course, a sustainable relationship with their environment). Either of these alternatives would satisfy Machiavelli's design principles for building political systems flexible enough to "imitate nature which itself is changeable."[41]

Notes

1. All references to Machiavelli's *Discourses on Livy* are to the translation by Harvey C. Mansfield Jr. and Nathan Tarcov (University of Chicago Press, 1996).

2. Cary Nederman, "Niccolò Machiavelli," in *The Stanford Encyclopedia of Philosophy*, ed. Edward N. Zalta (fall 2009 edition).

3. Ibid.

4. Leo Strauss, "Machiavelli," in *History of Political Philosophy* (University of Chicago Press, 1963), 289.

5. Miles Unger, *Machiavelli: A Biography* (Simon and Schuster, 2011).

6. Ibid.

7. Harvey C. Mansfield, introduction to *Machiavelli's Discourses on Livy* (University of Chicago Press, 1966).

8. Ross King, *Machiavelli: Philosopher of Power* (HarperCollins, 2004).

9. John Barry and Kimberly Smith "Civic Republicanism and Green Politics," in *Building a Citizen Society*, ed. Stuart White and Daniel Leighton (LW Books, 2008); John Barry, *Environment and Social Theory* (Routledge, 2006); Peter Cannavò, "To the Thousandth Generation: Timelessness, Jeffersonian Republicanism, and Environmentalism," *Environmental Politics* 19, no. 3 (2010): 356–373; Robyn Eckersley, *The Green State: Rethinking Democracy and Sovereignty* (MIT Press, 2004); Thad Williamson and Martin O'Neill, "Property-Owning Democracy and the Demands of Justice," *Living Reviews in Democracy* 1 (2009): 1–10.

10. Barry, *Environment and Social Theory*.

11. Nederman, "Niccolò Machiavelli."

12. King, *Machiavelli: Philosopher of Power.*
13. Strauss, "Machiavelli."
14. Cary Nederman, "Machiavelli and Moral Character: Principality, Republic and the Psychology of Virtu," *History of Political Thought* 20 (autumn 2000): 349–364.
15. All references to *The Prince* are to the Mansfield translation (University of Chicago Press, 1985).
16. Unger, *Machiavelli: A Biography*, 280.
17. Steward T. A. Pickett and Peter S. White, eds., *The Ecology of Natural Disturbance and Patch Dynamics* (Academic Press, 1985).
18. George L. W. Perry, "Landscapes, Space AND Equilibrium: Shifting Viewpoints," *Progress in Physical Geography* 26, no. 3 (2002): 339–359.
19. John Stuart Mill, *On Nature* (Rationalist Press, 1904).
20. Murray Bookchin, *The Ecology of Freedom* (AK Press, 1982); Fritjof Capra, *The Turning Point: Science, Society and the Rising Culture* (Simon and Shuster 1983).
21. Edward Goldsmith, *A Blueprint for Survival* (Tom Stacey, 1972); Rudolph Bahro, *Avoiding Social and Ecological Disaster: The Politics of World Transformation* (Gateway Books, 1994).
22. Kirkpatrick Sale, *Dwellers in the Land: The Bioregional Vision* (Sierra Club, 2000); Don Alexander, "Bioregionalism: The Need For a Firmer Theoretical Foundation," *Trumpeter* 13, no. 3 (1996); Stewart Davidson, "The Troubled Marriage of Deep Ecology and Bioregionalism," *Environmental Values* 16 (August 2007): 313–332.
23. Examples: Greens/European Free Alliance (2007); Green Party of California (2010).
24. Andrew Dobson, *Green Political Thought* (HarperCollins, 1990).
25. John Barry, *Rethinking Green Politics: Nature, Virtue, and Progress* (Sage, 1999); Herman Daly, "A Steady-State Economy," paper presented to Sustainable Development Commission (UK), April 24, 2008.
26. Greens/European Free Alliance 2007.
27. Dobson, *Green Political Thought*.
28. Unger, *Machiavelli: A Biography*.
29. Ibid.
30. Nederman, "Niccolò Machiavelli."
31. Herman Daly, *Steady-State Economics* (Freeman, 1977); *Beyond Growth: The Economics of Sustainable Development* (Beacon Press Books, 1997); *Ecological Economics and Sustainable Development: Selected Essays* (Elgar., 2007). For another example of the importance of this concept for current Green ideology, see Degrowth Declaration Barcelona 2010 and Working Groups Results at http://barcelona.degrowth.org/.

32. Strauss, "Machiavelli."

33. Eckersley, *The Green State*.

34. William Ophuls, "Leviathan or Oblivion," in *Toward a Steady-State Economy*, ed. Herman E. Daly (Freeman, 1973); William Ophuls, *Plato's Revenge: Politics in the Age of Ecology* (MIT Press, 2011).

35. Alexander, "Bioregionalism: The Need For a Firmer Theoretical Foundation."

36. Garrett Hardin, "The Tragedy of the Commons," *Science* 162 (1968): 1243–1248.

37. Elinor Ostrom, *Governing the Commons* (Cambridge University Press, 1990).

38. John Barry, "Towards a Model of Green Political Economy: From Ecological modernisation to Economic Security," *International Journal of Green Economics* 1 (2007): 446–464.

39. Elinor Ostrom, *Understanding Institutional Diversity* (Princeton University Press, 2005).

40. Thomas Homer-Dixon, *Environment, Scarcity, and Violence* (Princeton University Press, 1999).

41. Unger, *Machiavelli: A Biography*, 280.

4

Thomas Hobbes: Relating Nature and Politics

John M. Meyer

Thomas Hobbes (1588–1679) is among the most prominent and pivotal political theorists in the Western tradition. The first to develop the notion of the social contract systematically, Hobbes argues for the necessity of a unified sovereign in order to escape the violence that he describes as our "natural condition." By his own assertion and the concurrence of many interpreters, Hobbes is among the first *modern* political theorists, distinguished from the ancients and scholastics by (among other things) his emphasis upon agreement as the basis for political legitimacy, freedom as nothing more than the absence of "external impediments to motion," and peace as the only appropriate goal of the sovereign.

Yet it is a mistake to regard Hobbes as strictly a "political theorist," if by this we assume that questions of political order were his sole—or even primary—preoccupation. Although his best-known work, *Leviathan*, is most often read as a work of political theory or philosophy (what Hobbes called "civil philosophy"), even *Leviathan* reflects his deep and abiding interest in "natural philosophy" (i.e., natural science) and his rejection of his era's received Aristotelian wisdom on this subject. Hobbes, a major participant in the Scientific Revolution of seventeenth-century Europe, presented his reflections on the nature of nature as integral to his analysis of political order.[1] His most extensive work to address natural philosophy, *De Corpore* ("On the Body"), published within a few years of *Leviathan*, was offered as the first part of a comprehensive trilogy that included *De Homine* and *De Cive* (Body, Man, and Citizen).

What appears striking when one views Hobbes's work as a whole is its encompassing breadth and its ostensive integration of a revolutionary new understanding of nature itself with a radical new vision of political order. This bringing together of "nature" and "politics"—however each is understood—is also inescapably central in present-day environmental politics and ideas. Yet it is fraught with ambiguity, confusion, and debate.

Turning to Hobbes offers the promise of insight into the relationship between nature and politics, but not necessarily because he got it "right." Indeed, figuring out just what sort of relationship exists in Hobbes's work is difficult. Prominent interpreters offer surprisingly contradictory accounts of the conventional wisdom about Hobbes, accounts that I have termed *dualist* and *derivative*.[2] By recognizing both the insights of each account and the contradictions between them, we will be better positioned to rethink the relationship between nature and politics in his theory. The tensions and contradictions addressed here are also echoed in present-day contests over the idea of nature.[3] But although the current environmental debate is often fraught because assumptions about nature and politics are insufficiently explicated or implications incompletely developed, the clash among interpreters of Hobbes is largely a result of the fact that his understandings of nature and politics *are* thoroughly developed. The aim of this chapter is to better understand the challenges and pitfalls of relating conceptions of nature to politics today by exploring how this relationship played out in the work of Hobbes.

The Dualist Account

One of the most recognizable sketches of Hobbes's political theory has him setting "nature"—conflict-ridden and violent—in opposition to a social contract that creates political order, characterized as a peaceful human construct. This dualist account is at the heart of diverse readings by political theorists—so much so that one scholar recently dubbed it the "iconic" Hobbes.[4] This account treats Hobbes's view of the "state of nature" as adequately descriptive of his understanding of nature and the natural itself.

Early portions of *Leviathan* offer an account of matter and motion—nature in an inclusive sense—and *De Corpore* develops this. Yet many political theorists have treated Hobbes's extended discussion of these matters as a curiosity to be ignored. These theorists are, perhaps, reassured in doing so by the fact that Hobbes is rarely recognized in the pantheon of natural philosophers that included his contemporaries Galileo, Descartes, Gassendi, and Mersenne.[5] Others acknowledge the extent of Hobbes's work on natural philosophy, but regard it as a feint that distracts us from the true character of his political theory. Either way, in this account nature and politics sit on opposite sides of a deep divide.

Two of the most prominent twentieth-century political theorists who read Hobbes as a dualist were Leo Strauss and Michael Oakeshott. The Hobbes that emerges from their interpretations is one whose political ideas developed from consideration of a denatured humanity and whose stance is distinctively anti-natural.

For Strauss, Hobbes's political thought is founded entirely upon his humanistic convictions—convictions that he contends are wholly at odds with Hobbes's professed natural philosophy and that require us to reject any connection with it. Presenting a stark dichotomy, he asserts that "the student of Hobbes must make up his mind whether he is going to understand Hobbes's political science by itself or whether he is going to understand it in the light of Hobbes's natural science."[6] Siding with the first of these understandings, he argues forcefully that

> the conception of nature which Hobbes's political philosophy *presupposes* is dualistic: the idea of civilization presupposes that man, by virtue of his intelligence, can place himself outside nature, can rebel against nature. ... The antithesis of nature and human will is hidden by the monist (materialist-deterministic) metaphysic, which Hobbes *teaches* ... [but] which is not only not needed for his political philosophy, but actually imperils the very root of that philosophy.[7]

The tension, as Strauss describes it, is between a materialist view of human embeddedness in nature—which, he accurately notes, Hobbes teaches—and Strauss's conviction that human civilization requires us to place ourselves "outside nature." To understand Hobbes's political theory "in the light of [his] natural science" would be to accept this materialist view of human embeddedness. Since there is little doubt that Hobbes professed this materialist view, the only question is whether we should take this seriously when reading his political theory. Strauss answers No.

In a similar manner, Oakeshott—in his highly influential introduction to *Leviathan*—characterizes it as the "supreme expression" of an emergent tradition of thought centered on "Will and Artifice," which he contrasts with the previously dominant tradition of ancient and medieval political philosophy founded on "Reason and Nature."[8] He, too, thereby rejects any connection between Hobbes's politics and his natural philosophy. Both Strauss and Oakeshott present this separation of politics from nature as integral to the development of a distinctly *modern* political philosophy. Yet whereas Strauss laments this apparent demise of nature as a touchstone for politics, Oakeshott celebrates it.

The characteristics of Hobbes's political theory highlighted by the dualist view—individual will and voluntarism, agreement, and rhetoric—certainly are important and cannot be jettisoned in any coherent account of Hobbes's theory. However, it is striking and ironic that by dividing human will and artifice from nature, the dualist view places Hobbes in the same camp as his nemesis, René Descartes.

A human-nature dualism has come under frequent criticism from present-day environmental critics. Understood as an unbridgeable chasm, this duality is read as obstructing any meaningful role for nature in relation to human society. Some have argued that dualism is endemic to Western thought. For instance, Val Plumwood has argued that "the Platonic, Aristotelian, Christian rationalist and Cartesian rationalist traditions [all] exhibit radical exclusion as well as other dualistic features" and "there is a total break or discontinuity between humans and nature, such that humans are completely different from everything else in nature."[9] In a similar vein, Peter Marshall asserts that the "traditional Western worldview" has been supported by "the rationalist tradition from Plato onwards [that] also separated the mind from the body ... and humanity from nature."[10] Others narrow their censure to Descartes or the social contract tradition that Hobbes initiated. In a chapter titled "Beyond the Social Contract," Andrew Brennan rejects contractarianism in favor of "the recognition that all human life is lived within some natural context,"[11] and in a book titled *The Natural Contract* Michel Serres asserts that "the world ... is totally absent from the social contract."[12] Yet while Hobbes as dualist and anti-naturalist can make a convenient foil, this account simply cannot be squared with a reading that takes seriously his philosophical preoccupation with the natural world.

Bringing Nature and Politics Together

Here's the problem: Hobbes vehemently rejected Cartesian dualism between mind and body, or artifice and nature, in favor of an argument that *everything* was matter in motion, including our thoughts, senses, and will. Moreover, Hobbes did this in direct conversation with Descartes.[13] His natural philosophy was explicitly materialist and monist. Nature—matter in motion—is the singular organizing principle of the universe and everything in it; thus Hobbes rejects the Cartesian conception of an immaterial mind or soul. As he unequivocally expresses it in *Leviathan*, "every part of the universe is body, and that which is not body is no part of the universe. And because the universe is all, that which is no part of it is nothing (and consequently, nowhere)."[14] Hobbes's expansive conception of "body" is made plain here; he is connecting nature to human nature; human embodiment with our embeddedness in the larger nonhuman world. He is also characterizing human cognitive and sensory processes as "motions of the mind,"[15] despite the lack of visible movement.[16] This conception of body, it should be noted, can be fruitfully compared to Hume's understanding, as described by Andrew Valls in this volume.

This emphasis upon humans' materiality and embeddedness in nature has been a central theme of many recent environmental arguments as well. For this reason, Samantha Frost concludes in her important book on Hobbes's materialism that he "prompts us to adopt an ecological mindset."[17] Thus the question addressed in the remainder of this chapter—what happens to Hobbes's political theory when we refuse to jettison this monistic conception of nature and read Hobbes's philosophy comprehensively?—can inform these debates. To be clear, my focus will be less on the particulars of Hobbes's idea of nature and more on the role this idea might play in his political thinking.

Below, I summarize one answer to that question, in which it appears that Hobbes seeks to derive his political theory from nature itself. Diametrically opposed to the dualist account, this view also has many adherents. Yet, as I subsequently make clear, this is not the only—or the best—possible answer.

Deriving Politics from Nature

In contrast to the influential dualist accounts advanced by political theorists, including Strauss and Oakeshott, others have read Hobbes—and it seems he presented himself—as advancing a derivative account of the relationship between nature and politics. Here, the correct form of politics follows necessarily from an appropriate conception of nature.

Current thinkers often trace our current environmental challenges to the disenchanted conception of nature as "dead" matter developed during the Scientific Revolution. Carolyn Merchant and Freya Mathews offer especially pointed criticisms of Hobbes as the source of these challenges.[18] The core of their concern with Hobbes is their conviction that he successfully derived a new understanding of political power and social order from his problematic view of nature.[19] He is also distinguished, they argue, by his "unsugarcoated" appraisal of the social and political consequences derived from this view of nature.[20] Another author, William Ophuls, presents this especially bluntly:

[the new science] swept away the old worldview and the social order based upon it ... [and] led directly and immediately to the new political thought. ... Hobbes, whose explicit aim was to reconstruct politics in the light of the new Scientific understanding ... made building the commonwealth into a matter of engineering—that is, of applying mechanistic principles to social life. He therefore began

Leviathan with an explanation of the basic principles of *mechanistic* philosophy precisely in order to establish the basis for an *individualistic* theory of politics.[21]

Ophuls, like Merchant and Mathews, rejects the new conception of nature, and consequently rejects Hobbesian politics as well.[22]

Because this sort of criticism leaves the derivative relation of nature to politics untouched, the environmentalist "solution" here entails appealing to a new ecological conception of nature and natural law as the basis for deriving a new, improved political and social order.[23] Even where the explicit subject matter is political order, this approach is notable for its deference to scientists or others whose expertise rests in their understanding of nature. The derivative account grants such experts authority not only over their explicit subject matter (scientific understanding of nature), but over political judgment itself.

This temptation—appealing to nature as a form of authority to transcend the realm of political contest—has long echoed in environmental arguments. For example, we can find it in Al Gore's book and film *An Inconvenient Truth*, which regards public ignorance of climate science as the primary obstacle and so focuses on describing climate change, rather than on confronting the contested meanings and values embedded in particular strategies of understanding, representing, and addressing the problem.[24]

Importantly, it is not just environmental critics that read Hobbes in this way. Indeed, for scholars who read Hobbes's philosophy comprehensively (that is, who take his natural and civil philosophy as parts of a whole) this has been characterized as the "standard account."[25] This account is supported by Hobbes's own statements—for instance:

[H]e that teaches or demonstrates any thing, [should] proceed in the same method by which he found it out; namely, that in the first place those things be demonstrated, which immediately succeed to universal definitions. ... Next, those things which may be demonstrated by simple motion. ... And after these, the motion or mutation of the invisible parts of things, and the doctrine of sense and imaginations, and of the internal passions, especially those of men, in which are comprehended the grounds of civil duties, or civil philosophy; which takes up the last place.

Here Hobbes outlines a hierarchical and derivative sequence in which all subsequent philosophy ultimately depends upon our understanding of nature. Following Galileo,[26] Hobbes regarded geometry as the language of nature itself. In *Leviathan*, Hobbes argues that "senseless and insignificant language ... cannot be avoided by those that will teach philosophy without having first attained great knowledge in geometry. For nature worketh by motion, the ways and degrees whereof cannot be known without the knowledge of the proportions and properties of lines and figures."[27]

The application of the same method to the study of humans and the creation of political order reflected the conviction that the underlying "nature" of these subjects is—despite all other differences—congruent. In the absence of such a conviction, one might just as easily suggest that another, radically different, method was appropriate to understand the realms of human reasoning, passions, and creation—a suggestion that cannot be found in Hobbes's treatises.

Hobbes thus offers a materialist description of human psychology, a basis for an unchanging view of human nature. Once humans are understood as they are "by nature," then (and only then) can reason recommend to us a series of "natural laws" that delineate how sovereignty and society should be organized.[28] The derivation of these "laws of nature," which he also terms "dictates of reason," is for Hobbes as "the true and only moral philosophy."[29] In sum, the derivative account builds upon the overall structure of Hobbes's work, moving from "Body" to "Man" to "Citizen" and thus deriving the theory of the body politic from a proper understanding of the human body, itself derived from a properly scientific view of nature (i.e., "Body").

We saw earlier that dualist interpreters like Strauss and Oakeshott, because they presume that *any* act of will stands apart from nature, require us to remove Hobbes's ideas about nature and natural philosophy from a consideration of his political philosophy. This strategy fails because Hobbes doesn't offer us a way to separate his political thought from the understanding of nature that shapes these concepts in important ways. For Hobbes, the will is always situated within the laws of nature.[30]

Yet a certain impossibility remains in the derivative view: Hobbes cannot move directly from nature to politics. Matter's motion describes every phenomenon in the universe. The consequence of this universalism is that all political systems (or the absence of them) will necessarily be consistent with the laws of matter in motion. In this sense, all political systems are natural. Nonetheless, Hobbes famously promulgates laws of nature specific to humans: "A law of nature ... is a precept, or general rule, found out by reason, by which a man is forbidden to do that which is destructive of his life, or taketh away the means of preserving the same ... ."[31] Law, as Hobbes understands it, is an obligation, not a choice. Where would such an obligation come from? Perhaps all people might unanimously agree that preserving one's own life is a good idea, and Hobbes might succeed in convincing us that the only way to preserve life is to accept unified sovereignty. But such a law of nature would then be violable in a way that the law of gravity is not. Suicide, which Hobbes argues contradicts the laws of nature, is not impossible in the way that resisting gravity is impossible. At the moment Hobbes moves to politics, he must rely on humans' agreement about what *ought* to be, not just what *is*. Not coincidentally, it is precisely lack of agreement on this score that Hobbes hopes to eliminate.

Reconceptualizing the Relationship between Nature and Politics

Hobbes seems to be trying unsuccessfully to have it both ways. His conception of nature as matter in motion is monistic and inescapable. This prevents human creation and artifice from being situated across a conceptual boundary from it. And yet Hobbes's rich contribution to political theory rests heavily upon a vocabulary of will, artifice, and voluntary agreement. If we are not to deem Hobbes incoherent on this score, we must re-imagine the nature-politics relationship. That is the focus of the remainder of this chapter.

We can glimpse in Hobbes's theory a mutually constitutive relationship between nature and politics that entails recognition of both his materialist nature, and the ineliminability of political contest. For reasons that will soon become clear, however, such a relationship threatens to undermine other sources of authority that Hobbes seeks to rely upon.

Hobbes's conception of the "natural condition" or "state of nature" is one that mediates between—and partakes of some qualities from both—his conception of material nature itself and his judgments about the character and scope of politics. I will summarize some of these judgments first.

The social contract, as described by Hobbes, is the singular and definitive means of escaping from the natural condition that he describes as a "war ... of every man against every man."[32] It is, says Hobbes, "as if every man should say to every man *I authorise and give up my right of governing myself to this man, or to this assembly of men, on this condition, that thou give up thy right to him, and authorize all his actions in like manner.* This done, the multitude so united in one person is called a COMMONWEALTH ... ." The "man, or ... assembly of men" is the unified authority whose acts everyone has made themselves the author of, "*to the end he may use the strength and means of them all, as he shall think expedient, for their peace and common defence.* And he that carrieth this person is called SOVEREIGN ... ."[33] Hobbes doesn't merely draw a distinction between a condition in which the structures created by humans predominate (artifice), and one in which they are absent (state of nature). He predicates human artifice in general upon unified sovereignty in particular. In contrast to thinkers for whom civil society or private life exist apart from the sovereign, for Hobbes they can only be understood within it. Commonwealth results only from the creation of sovereign power. There is no other possible location for political activity within his scheme.

Historically, Hobbes directed his argument for unified sovereignty against those that sought to justify independent realms of authority, whether the church, parliament (before its ascension to sovereign power), common law, universities, or experimental science.[34] The goal of politics is said to be the pursuit of peace,[35] and therefore decisions about the form and process of politics and political decision making are dismissed from theoretical consideration and designated as a mere "difference of convenience."[36]

Hobbes cannot rule out disagreement or debate within the (either collective or individual) body of a sovereign. Differences of opinion between individuals, and even within the same individual over time, are *natural*, according to Hobbes.[37] While he seeks to eliminate these differences as a challenge *to* sovereign power, he offers no reason to believe that they can be eliminated *within* the sovereign itself. Nonetheless, by describing politics strictly as unified sovereignty, he can say little or nothing about processes by which disagreement might be channeled into effective decision making.

A major element of Hobbes's attempt to ground unified sovereignty is his nominalism. Nominalism is the philosophical position that abstract concepts have no referent in the external world but exist merely as the names attributed to things by humans. As a nominalist, Hobbes repeatedly emphasizes the absolute importance and temporal priority of defining terms. This is necessary because *quality* is eliminated from the new conception of nature espoused by Hobbes and the other natural philosophers of his time.[38] As Hobbes explains it, "whatsoever accidents or *qualities* our senses make us think there be in the world, they are not there, but are seemings and apparitions only. The things that really are in the world without us, are those motions by which these seemings are caused."[39]

Hobbes is insistent upon distinguishing "accident" from "nature." Because these "accidents" are mental concepts, they are necessarily subject to the distinctly human practice of naming. As one scholar explained, for Hobbes, "conceptions in the mind bridge the signs of language and objects in the external world."[40]

The emphasis is consistent with his reliance upon geometry, which itself utilizes a nominalist method: theorems are deduced from a set of first principles, but these principles themselves are not subject to proof. Sovereign authority thus appears necessary, in order to provide a singular set of definitions. Yet this disrupts the derivative account of his theory, by requiring the artifice of political judgment at a very early stage. Hobbes's insistence, however, doesn't rest simply on the need for singularity. Instead it relies upon his argument that discrepancies in the definition and valuation of terms are themselves a primary cause for war in the state of nature. As he expresses it in *Leviathan*, "divers men differ [in] what is conformable or disagreeable to reason in the actions of common life. Nay, the same man in divers times differs from himself, and one time praiseth (that is, calleth good) what another time he dispraiseth (and calleth evil); *from whence arise disputes, controversies, and at last war*.[41] According to this argument, terminological disagreement itself is the cause of physical conflict. As Hobbes puts it, humans are "so long in the state of war, as … they mete good and evil by diverse measures."[42]

Certainly, Hobbes also blames conflicting passions as a cause of war in the state of nature. However, the argument outlined above is not specifically linked with one about passions. It is an independent claim that the "fact" of nominalism, which leads to varied notions of the good, is itself inherently conflictual in the absence of a sovereign to overcome it.[43]

This claim cannot be reconciled with Hobbes's observation that differing nominal interpretations are commonplace even within a single individual over time. Clearly, we appear able to overcome some differences within ourselves and with others without the imposition of power from above. Therefore, although nominalism—a fact of nature as presented by Hobbes—sets the stage for human artifice, it cannot establish the necessity of unified sovereignty. Only Hobbes's political judgment that conflict will ensue from these differences can lead him to the latter conclusion.

For Hobbes, nominalism draws our attention to a kind of particularism—in the natural condition, we each assign names to concepts on the basis of our particular experiences in the world. Yet, contra Hobbes, the question of whether this particularism will lead us into violent conflict is an open one. Unified sovereignty transcends this particularism by assigning names (and laws), and fear is presented as the motivator to adhere to these definitions. Yet unified authority cannot be derived from a fact of nature; only we humans can determine how we grapple with difference. Though Hobbes asserts that conflict emerges from our attachment to principles originating in our particular experience of the world, peace lies in the denial of those attachments and adherence to the sovereign's proclamations. This political judgment is not derivable from his conception of nature itself; we might challenge this conclusion without challenging our participation in this nature.

Note that Hobbes's sovereign doesn't claim authority over objective fact and on those grounds claim legitimacy. His notion of rationality is of a strictly means-ends, instrumental sort:

> No man can know by discourse that this or that is, has been, or will be, which is to know absolutely, but only that if this be, that is, if this has been, that has been, if this shall be, that shall be, which is to know conditionally; and that not the consequence of one thing to another, but of one name of a thing to another name of the same thing.[44]

The sovereign's definitional authority derives not from some claim to objective, rational knowledge about the status of abstract concepts, but instead from its task of directing us away from attachment to our own particular, phenomenological experiences, providing definitions that can ground subsequent conditional knowledge and thus prevent conflict. Hobbes's conception of nature tells us that humans have no natural ends, because the natural world of matter in motion has no *telos*. Yet, from this, he wishes to characterize sovereignty as having no end other than peace. At best, the relationship between these two claims is an analogy.

It is as a result of what Hobbes defines as the "desire of such things as are necessary to commodious living, and a hope by their industry to obtain them"[45] that human manipulation of the nonhuman natural world takes place. At the same time, Hobbes's depiction of private desire for "commodious living" is presented as a restriction upon the power of the sovereign. Once we see that the restricted end of sovereign power is not derived from Hobbes's conception of nature, however, then we can also see that the particular ways in which the sovereign encourages, discourages, or directs human interaction with the material world are not inevitable or unalterable. Commodious living, for Hobbes, is a construction that defines our relation to the material world, seemingly outside the realm of sovereign power. Yet the absence of teleology in Hobbes's nature doesn't, or shouldn't, inhibit us from considering and questioning the manner of pursuit of commodious living—or even, more particularly, from doing so via sovereign political institutions.

If we understand politics as a contest over visions of the good emerging from our particular interactions with and experiences of the world, then attempts to derive politics from nature aim to eradicate space for this contest. Yet if the political structure of unified sovereignty cannot be derived from a proper understanding of nature itself, then the sovereign generated by Hobbes will not be uniquely positioned to overcome the consequences of nominalism—manifest as a contest over meaning and values. The sovereign cannot transcend political contest in this sense. Our diverse experiences of the world—both the human and nonhuman worlds—will shape political deliberation and will in turn be shaped by it.

Recognizing the mutual constitution of nature and politics in Hobbes's theory can point us toward a more pluralistic and open model of political contest. Such a model may not initially appear attractive to present-day environmentalists, who often rely upon the authority of nature and science to advance their cause. Yet this explicitly political model ultimately provides a more viable basis for this advance.

A Constitutive Approach to the Relationship between Nature and Politics

Re-examining our received understandings of Hobbes's philosophy might lead environmental thinkers and activists to a seemingly anti-Hobbesian conclusion: that any meaningful environmental politics must reconcile scientific knowledge about humans' effects on the rest of the world with the plurality of experience and political values. Viewing the nature-politics relationship in a constitutive manner can model a more *political* science, or a more scientifically informed politics, where two seemingly opposed realms of environmentalism—values and science—can meet. The failure of both the dualist reading and the derivative reading of Hobbes points to such a constitutive approach in which conceptions of nature and conceptions of politics inform each other but don't determine each other.

The occlusion of politics in present-day environmental argument has often been justified on the grounds that it would open a Pandora's Box of skepticism that would undermine belief in climate change and consequently undermine public support for action to mitigate or adapt to it. Yet the current state of environmental politics makes it evident that contests over ends, values and visions of the good cannot be escaped. Indeed, the tendencies of the environmental justice movement, and of other movements focused on attention to place or locality, push in the opposite direction. Explicitly grounded in normative claims for the meaning and value of local community, livelihood, or a particular way of life, they gesture toward an alternative way of *doing* environmental politics. To date, the most prominent movements and initiatives have focused on particularistic concerns, and hence their broader potential hasn't always been recognized. Yet writ large, such movements contest what counts as "nature" in relation to their concerns. They can also contest the familiar political strategies and rhetoric (or the sense of unity surrounding such strategies or rhetoric) of environmentalism—even those of the most global of environmental concerns, climate change.[46]

Thus we ought to reject a rhetoric of political engagement that represents itself as apolitical and objective in spirit. Whereas many fear that such a move might open a Pandora's Box, the avoidance of politics has in fact proved to be the movement's Achilles' Heel. This rhetoric hampers the ability to engage a diverse public and to advance efforts to mitigate climate change and other environmental challenges. Re-reading Hobbes as a materialist yet truly political theorist allows us to achieve greater insight into his philosophy as a whole; it also provides some assistance in navigating this re-thinking of current environmental politics.

Acknowledgments

This chapter draws extensively from my book *Political Nature: Environmentalism and the Interpretation of Western Thought* (MIT Press, 2001). Recent collaboration with Justin Williams was essential to the analysis here. Justin served as co-author of this chapter for a time, but withdrew because of other commitments. Early versions were presented at the 2011 Western Political Science Association annual meeting and by Justin at the University of Michigan Political Theory Workshop. Valuable feedback at Michigan, especially from Lisa Disch, Arlene Saxonhouse, Bonnie Washick, and Elizabeth Wingrove, prompted a restructuring. Comments and suggestions by Lisa Ellis and by Peter Cannavò and Joe Lane were also extremely helpful.

Notes

1. Thomas Hobbes, *Leviathan*, ed. Edwin Curley (Hackett, 1994), chapter 9. See, especially, page 48 for Hobbes's table that surveys all of science ("that is, knowledge of consequences; which is called also PHILOSOPHY"), of which natural and civil philosophy are two branches. As we shall see, however, many interpreters of Hobbes deny this connection between nature and politics.

2. For a more complete description of these accounts, see John M. Meyer, *Political Nature: Environmentalism and the Interpretation of Western Thought* (MIT Press, 2001), especially pp. 35–53.

3. For a useful guide, see Kate Soper, *What Is Nature? Culture, Politics and the Non-Human* (Blackwell, 1995).

4. Samantha Frost, *Lessons From a Materialist Thinker: Hobbesian Reflections on Ethics and Politics* (Stanford University Press, 2008), 2.

5. Hobbes's contribution to modern science has often been granted little more than a footnote by scholars, despite the fact that Hobbes's own seriousness in applying himself to this subject is undeniable. For one exception, see Robert H. Kargon, *Atomism in England from Hariot to Newton* (Clarendon, 1966), 54. For a discussion of the scholarly neglect of Hobbes's contribution's to science, see Steven Shapin and Simon Schaffer, *Leviathan and the Air-Pump: Hobbes, Boyle, and the Experimental Life* (Princeton University Press, 1985), 7–9 and passim. Also see Noel Malcolm, "Hobbes and the Royal Society," in *Perspectives on Thomas Hobbes*, ed. G. A. J. Rogers and A. Ryan (Clarendon, 1988).

6. Leo Strauss, "On the Basis of Hobbes's Political Philosophy," in *What Is Political Philosophy?* (University of Chicago Press, 1988), 177.

7. Leo Strauss, *The Political Philosophy of Hobbes: Its Basis and Its Genesis* (University of Chicago Press, 1952), 168.

8. Michael Oakeshott, "Introduction to *Leviathan*," reprinted in *Rationalism in Politics and Other Essays*, new and expanded edition (Liberty, 1991), 227. For an even sharper articulation of this point, see Oakeshott, "Logos and Telos," in the same volume. On the one-sidedness of this aspect of Oakeshott's interpretation of Hobbes, see Patrick Riley, *Will and Political Legitimacy* (Harvard University Press, 1982), 44.

9. Val Plumwood, *Feminism and the Mastery of Nature* (Routledge, 1993), 70.

10. Peter Marshall, *Nature's Web: An Exploration of Ecological Thinking* (Simon and Schuster, 1992), 5.

11. Andrew Brennan, *Thinking about Nature* (University of Georgia Press, 1988), 185.

12. Michel Serres, *The Natural Contract* (University of Michigan Press, 1995), 45.

13. For their dispute, see Thomas Hobbes and René Descartes, "The Third Set of Objections with the Author's Reply," in *Philosophical Works of Descartes*, ed. E. S. Haldane and G. R. T. Ross (Cambridge University Press, 1911). Samantha Frost quite appropriately makes this contrast central to her analysis in *Lessons from a Materialist Thinker*.

14. *Leviathan*, chapter 46, 459.

15. Thomas Hobbes, *Elements of Philosophy, the first section, concerning Body*, in *The English Works of Thomas Hobbes*, volume 1, ed. Sir William Molesworth (London, 1839), chapter 6, 72. This is the English translation of Hobbes's *De Corpore* published during his lifetime. Hereafter it will be cited as *De Corpore*. See also *Leviathan*, chapter 1, 7.

16. The concept that allows Hobbes to move from nature to human nature is "endeavour" ("conatus" in his Latin works). See Richard Peters, *Hobbes* (Penguin, 1956), 91–92; John W. N. Watkins, *Hobbes's System of Ideas*, second edition (Gower, 1989), 87–88.

17. Frost, *Lessons From a Materialist Thinker*, 169. A full understanding of Hobbes's materialism and its implications for his political theory must take account of Frost's analysis in this important book.

18. Carolyn Merchant, *The Death of Nature: Women, Ecology, and the Scientific Revolution* (HarperCollins, 1989), 193; Freya Mathews, *The Ecological Self* (Barnes and Noble, 1991), 29.

19. Merchant, *Death of Nature*, 206; Mathews, *Ecological Self*, 29.

20. Mathews, *Ecological Self*, 29.

21. William Ophuls, *Requiem for Modern Politics: The Tragedy of the Enlightenment and the Challenge of the New Millennium* (Westview, 1997), 187–188.

22. In his writings of the 1970s, Ophuls often appealed to "Leviathan" as the way to address environmental challenges. *Requiem for Modern Politics* rejects such an appeal.

23. Ophuls tries to do so in *Plato's Revenge: Politics in the Age of Ecology* (MIT Press, 2011).

24. See John M. Meyer, "*Another* Inconvenient Truth," *Dissent* 53, no. 4 (2006): 95–96. More generally, see Mike Hulme, *Why We Disagree About Climate Change: Understanding Controversy, Inaction, and Opportunity* (Cambridge University Press, 2009).

25. Tom Sorell, "The Science in Hobbes's Politics," in *Perspectives on Thomas Hobbes*, ed. Rogers and Alan Ryan, 69. See also Watkins, *Hobbes's System of Ideas*; Peters, *Hobbes*; Thomas A. Spragens, *The Politics of Motion: The World of Thomas Hobbes* (University Press of Kentucky, 1973); Maurice M. Goldsmith, *Hobbes's Science of Politics* (Columbia University Press, 1966).

26. "The Assayer," in *Discoveries and Opinions of Galileo*, tr. Stillman Drake (Anchor, 1957), 237–238.

27. *Leviathan*, chapter 46, 456.

28. *Leviathan*, chapter 14.

29. *Leviathan*, chapter 15, 100.

30. "*Will*," Hobbes asserts, is "*the last appetite in deliberating*." To define "will" non-naturally, such that one could act *against* one's will, would be nonsensical; it would make "no action voluntary." *Leviathan*, chapter 6, 33.

31. *Leviathan*, chapter 14, 79.

32. *Leviathan*, chapter 13, 76.

33. *Leviathan*, chapter 17, 109.

34. On experimental science as a threatening, independent realm of power, see Shapin and Schaffer, *Leviathan and the Air-Pump*, 327.

35. *Leviathan*, chapter 17, 109.

36. *Leviathan*, chapter 19, 120. Hobbes *prefers* monarchical government, but because he equates politics with sovereignty itself he cannot incorporate this preference into his philosophical system.

37. *Leviathan*, chapter 15, 100.

38. See Edwin Arthur Burtt, *The Metaphysical Foundations of Modern Physical Science*, revised edition (Routledge & Kegan Paul, 1932); Alexandre Koyré,

"Galileo and Plato," in Koyré, *Metaphysics and Measurement: Essays in Scientific Revolution* (Harvard University Press, 1968), 37.

39. *Elements of Law*, chapter 2, #10, 26 (emphasis added). Also *De Corpore*, chapter 8, 101–119; *Leviathan*, chapter 1, 7.

40. Martin A. Bertman, *Hobbes: The Natural and the Artifacted Good* (Lang, 1981), 20. Also see Richard Tuck, "Optics and Sceptics: The Philosophical Foundations of Hobbes's Political Thought," in *Conscience and Casuistry in Early Modern Europe*, ed. Edmund Leites (Cambridge University Press, 1988), 243.

41. *Leviathan*, chapter 15, 100 (emphasis added).

42. *De Cive*, chapter 3, #31, 150.

43. For a thorough analysis of the causes of conflict in Hobbes's state of nature, see François Tricaud, "Hobbes's Conception of the State of Nature from 1640 to 1651: Evolution and Ambiguities," in *Perspectives on Thomas Hobbes*, ed. Rogers and Ryan.

44. *Leviathan*, chapter 7, 35.

45. *Leviathan*, chapter 13, 78.

46 Evidence of this contest can increasingly be found under the banner of "climate justice." Also see John M. Meyer, "Populism, paternalism and the state of environmentalism in the US," *Environmental Politics* 17 (April 2008): 228–232.

5

John Locke: "This Habitable Earth of Ours"

Zev Trachtenberg

Their many differences notwithstanding, environmentalists and their opponents can agree that no thinker has had a greater influence on the way we treat nature than John Locke. Environmentalists see in Locke's theory of property the justification for private appropriation of natural resources, and in his theory of government the justification for political efforts to limit state regulation of environmentally damaging activities. And indeed, defenders of property rights and opponents of environmental regulation frequently appeal to Locke in just these ways to support their positions.

In this chapter, therefore, I will take up Locke's account of property and the state, both to review and to assess this standard reading of his theory. But I also hope to do more. I hope to show that Locke's deepest significance for environmental political theory is that he understands human life as embedded in the environment. Conceptually, he starts from the fundamental imperative of organic survival. Survival, he recognizes, requires transforming the environment. Minimally, it involves displacing items from outside the body to inside the body. But distinctively human survival involves rearranging items in the environment so that natural processes yield more of what human beings want. Locke's account of labor emphasizes the transformations of the environment that human beings carry out as they go about the business of living. That process, whereby human beings inhabit their surroundings, transforms the raw environment into their habitat. I shall read Locke, therefore, as presenting a theory of habitation.[1]

For Locke, the Earth's suitability for habitation, its readiness to repay humans' efforts to transform it to fulfill their desires, is evidence of the moral rightness of that effort. The Earth is habitable and it is ours.[2] This belief is the moral core of Locke's account of the right of private property. For Locke, the rightness of humans' transformations of the environment, their conversion of their surroundings into habitat, is conveyed through his concept of property; basing property in labor shows that Locke understands property specifically as the result of humans' interactions with the natural world. Of course, for Locke property is the center of politics; the state is founded explicitly to protect property rights. In this way Locke places at the center of politics the human relationship with nature, i.e., the human mode of inhabiting the Earth.

In this chapter, then, I will approach some fundamental ideas in Locke's political theory as ideas about habitation. I will question the standard view that Locke's writings justify unrestrained exploitation of nature by human beings. I will argue instead that Locke's understanding of habitation suggests that his theory supports some normative limits on human activity in the environment. Nonetheless, I will conclude that, because his theory isn't sensitive to ecological considerations, it is mistaken to see Locke as a proto-environmentalist.

Background

John Locke was born in Somerset, England on August 29, 1632.[3] He attended Westminster School, and then Christ Church, Oxford, where he studied with the scientist Robert Boyle and eventually received a degree in medicine. His medical training led to an acquaintance with Anthony Ashley Cooper, later Earl of Shaftesbury; Locke joined Shaftsbury's household as his personal physician in 1666. However, Locke also assumed a variety of other duties for his politically active patron, assisting him with business, political, and personal affairs. Caught up in the turmoil surrounding the balance of power between the king and Parliament, Locke fled to Holland in 1682. He returned in 1689, in the wake of the "Glorious Revolution" that brought William and Mary to the throne and established the political dominance of Parliament. He served the new government until his retirement due to ill health in 1700. He died October 28, 1704.

Locke wrote on political and moral philosophy, epistemology, education, religion, and finance, and other topics. His major works were not published until after his return to England from Holland. His *Essay Concerning Human Understanding* (1690) is one of the seminal texts in the philosophical tradition of empiricism; in it he argues against the doctrine of innate knowledge, arguing instead that all knowledge is derived from experience.[4] He wrote a series of essays on religious toleration, most notable among them *A Letter Concerning Toleration* (1689), in which he established a basis for free expression of religious faith that became a foundation for liberal political theory. His *Two Treatises of Civil Government*

(1690), widely interpreted as a justification for the Glorious Revolution, are also important texts in the development of liberalism. The *Second Treatise* is undoubtedly the source for the most thematically relevant and historically influential of Locke's writings that concern the environment.[5] In that work he narrates the emergence of property and the creation of the state.

Locke's "Labor Theory," Natural Law, and the Origins of Property Rights

Locke's "labor theory" explains how an individual owner's property claims can have a moral justification. He begins with the pre-civil "state of nature," in which all of the Earth's goods are granted by God to all human beings in common—that is, nothing at all is privately owned. However, God grants the Earth to humanity for a purpose: to provide for our survival. In order for the goods of the Earth to fulfill that function, they must be consumed by individuals. But, in light of the original common ownership, how may one individual rightfully exclude another from consuming any particular item? This problem must be solved, or "man had starved, notwithstanding the plenty God had given him" (2T, §27).

Locke's solution rests on his "self-ownership" thesis.[6] He holds that there is an exception to the original condition of common ownership of the goods of the Earth: each person has an exclusive right to his or her own body. He appeals to that exclusive right to explain how individuals can obtain an exclusive right to what begins as a commonly owned item in nature. The key is his observation that people must physically transform nature in order to consume those items they need to survive: an apple must be picked from its tree before it can be eaten. The physical activity of the person—the labor of his or her body—is "mixed" with the item, marking it off as no longer common, but rather as exclusive, private property. Leaving aside the puzzles associated with the mixing metaphor,[7] let us simply note that Locke invests our relationships with certain external objects (our property) with the moral authority of our autonomous selfhood—our right over our own bodies. Note also that for Locke both the general entitlement to some property or other, as needed to support survival, the specific entitlement to one's own body, and hence to the items one appropriates through labor, stem directly from God. Therefore, Locke characterizes property as a natural right, justified in terms of natural law.[8]

Locke's account is particularly vivid with respect to items that are hunted or gathered from nature. But the relatively low-impact harvesting of readily available natural products is short of the fuller sense of habitation his theory provides. For he uses the labor theory to justify property rights in the habitat itself; beyond spontaneous products that can be foraged, agricultural labor grounds ownership of the transformed land. "As much land as a man tills, plants, improves, cultivates, and can use the product of, so much is his property."[9] (2T, §31)

Nonetheless, Locke imposes stringent moral limits, characterized in terms of natural law, on the right of property. Because God's purpose for the Earth is to support human survival, and goods that spoil can no longer fulfill that function, labor doesn't generate the right to more than one can consume before it spoils. Nor may one appropriate from the common stock without leaving sufficient goods (of sufficient quality) to support others' survival. These "provisos" of natural law apply both to consumable items and to land: one may not forage more wild fruit, or claim an amount of land that will produce more crops, than can be consumed.[10] But one may exchange the excess yield of one's labor with others for products they have produced. These products may be such that they persist for a long time without spoiling; the spoilage proviso doesn't preclude extensive holdings of imperishable property. Thus, Locke insists if someone "bartered away plums that would have rotted in a week, for nuts that would last good for his eating a whole year, he did not injury" (2T, §46).

In this way Locke introduces the idea of storing value—a function fulfilled by money, and one even more important than money's function as a medium of exchange that facilitates trade. Because money can be held indefinitely without violating the spoilage proviso, it makes possible a radically unequal distribution of goods, notwithstanding the equality of property implied by the original situation of common ownership. In particular, the system of exchange facilitated by money allows for the expansion of holdings in land: because owners can sell their harvests, they can legitimately own tracts of land that yield more than they themselves can consume. Thus, Locke's theory provides a natural-law justification for substantial inequality in the most significant form of property: agricultural land.[11]

The Lockean Argument Against Regulatory Takings

The expansion of holdings made possible by the system of exchange sets the stage for the transition from the state of nature to civil society, and for Locke's account of government. Locke observes that although the unequal distribution of property in the state of nature is justified by natural law, it is subject to a variety of "inconveniences" that render individuals' property rights fragile. Owners are fully entitled to their property, but they are not secure in their possession. Thus, they are motivated to establish, through the social contract, a civil authority whose purpose is precisely to secure their natural property rights, which Locke understands to encompass people's "lives liberties and estates" (2T, §123). For Locke, civil society has the task of enforcing a preexisting and conceptually independent moral order.[12]

We can now see how Locke's view can be used to justify opposition to environmental regulation. The state whose function is to guarantee its members' natural rights against other must respect those rights (2T, §135). The allied notions that property is a natural right and that the function of the state is precisely to protect natural rights jointly place property owners in an extremely strong position with respect to state action: any state action that interferes with the free exercise of property rights is illegitimate (2T, §138). In the United States, this moral vision, which limits government to make room for the exercise of property rights, is institutionalized and enforced by the Fifth Amendment to the Constitution. The "Takings Clause" in that amendment—"nor shall private property be taken for public use, without just compensation"—restricts the burdens the state may place on property rights to those that serve a public purpose, and requires that any owner so burdened be fairly compensated.

Many environmental regulations have been challenged as violations of the Takings Clause: by limiting what owners can do, the state has in effect taken some measure of their property, and must compensate them.[13] Because environmental regulations typically prevent land owners from engaging in otherwise permissible activities, much of the framework of law and regulation designed to protect the environment operates by placing limitations on the use of private property. In general, the requirement of compensation functions as a brake on efforts to regulate property use, since it can make those efforts simply too expensive for the state to enforce. Thus, the Takings Clause may be the most environmentally significant institutionalization of Locke's ideas.

Revisiting Locke's Views on Property and Environmental Protection

Locke's theory has undoubtedly been used to justify a strong vision of private property rights, at the expense of environmental protection. As was noted at the outset of this chapter, environmentalists and their opponents, who disagree on the value of Locke's influence, concur on its strength. Nonetheless, a case can be made that this agreement is based on an incomplete reading of Locke.[14] His actual historical influence notwithstanding, a fuller reading might suggest the outlines of a Lockean theory more sympathetic with certain environmentalist themes—while stopping short of suggesting that Locke would ally himself with environmentalism.

Therefore, let us revisit the labor theory of property. To focus exclusively (as many readers do) on the version Locke provides in chapter 5 of the *Second Treatise* is to miss that account's polemical context. That context is Locke's theory of legitimate civil authority—which is paired with a wholesale rebuttal of the alternative, important in Locke's day, offered by Sir Robert Filmer.[15] Filmer argued that the king had absolute authority over his domain and his subjects as a matter of inheritance from Adam, who was granted absolute dominion over the world and his children by God. Thus, on Filmer's "divine right" view, people are born into a condition of natural subjection to their monarch, rebellion against whom is illegitimate.[16]

In order to deny that monarchs have an absolute claim to the obedience of their subjects, Locke argues that God's grant of dominion to Adam was not to Adam personally and hence isn't an entitlement that can be passed along through his eldest heirs. Rather, Locke holds, God granted dominion to all of Adam's (and Eve's) descendants collectively—that is, to humanity as a whole. The famous "dominion" passage at Genesis 1:28, Locke argues, "is so far from proving Adam sole proprietor, that, on the contrary, it is a confirmation of the original community of all things amongst the sons of men" (1T, §40). But Locke's picture leaves open the following question: If humanity as a whole has a claim to all the goods of the Earth, how do individuals gain the right to exclusive use of any particular items? It might be thought that all people voluntarily agree to a distribution of items from the common stock.[17] But the implausibility of that proposal could be taken to show Locke's assumption that the Earth is held in common to be false, and to uphold Filmer's doctrine that dominion belonged to Adam personally.

With this context in mind, we can better understand the political significance of Locke's labor theory of property acquisition. It provides a plausible, indeed compelling explanation for property that supports Locke's claim that God gave the Earth to humanity in common in the face of the counterclaim that dominion was Adam's alone. In turn, the weakening of the notion that Adam had exclusive dominion helps to discredit Filmer's broader defense of divine right—precisely Locke's project in the *First Treatise*.

Acknowledging the polemical context of Locke's account of property forces us to acknowledge the dependence of Locke's justification of property rights on his theological commitments.[18] Thus, in denying the divine right of kings, Locke in no way intends to deny the moral basis of political authority in God's will. Rather, he intends to affirm the correct way to interpret God's will: as favoring a political order, based in voluntary agreement, that upholds natural right. In general, from a Lockean perspective, it isn't possible to understand the morality of the state's enforcement of natural right except by grasping that natural rights express the moral order that God built into Creation.[19]

More specifically, we can understand the moral character of the right of property only by reference to God's purpose for the physical world. That purpose is, as noted above, to provide for human survival: the world furnishes humanity's habitat. Locke argues that, because "God ... bid mankind increase and multiply," we can conclude that God himself gave all humans "a right to make use of the food and raiment, and other conveniences of life, the materials whereof he had so plentifully provided for them" (1T, §41). It is only because God grants all human beings dominion over the Earth and its foison, so that humanity can survive and flourish as a species, that anyone is able to have a right to any particular item, to provide for his or her particular survival as an individual. This appeal to God's moral intention explains the "provisos" that limit appropriation of property in the state of nature. Because allowing an item to spoil prevents it from fulfilling its moral function of supporting human existence, no one retains a property right in any item that is at the point of spoilage. Thus, an owner forfeits his or her right to goods that are about to spoil; they may be appropriated by others who will put them to use. "As much as any one can make use of to any advantage of life before it spoils, so much he may by his labour fix a property in: whatever is beyond this, is more than his share, and belongs to others." (2T, §31) Indeed, Locke argues that individual property rights are subordinated to the survival needs of people who lack property. Thus, Locke holds, "it would always be a sin, in any man of estate, to let his brother perish for want of affording him relief out of his plenty" (1T, §42).[20] The duty of charity, note, is not a matter of individual kindness, but a matter of respect for the function God assigns the natural world—the same function that justifies the right to private property itself.

Theorists who go back to Locke for arguments that the state may not regulate property have tended to discount or even reject his theological commitments.[21] They seem to acknowledge that focusing on his theological commitments in fact allows us to see past the standard reading to a Locke who doesn't advocate the unbridled assertion of individual property rights. Without God's grant of the Earth to humanity in common, there is simply no moral basis for individual property rights. Acknowledging that grant implies acknowledging that the right of property is not absolute, and opens the possibility that the state isn't forbidden to regulate it. Thus, even though Locke's theory has been deployed in opposition to interventionist environmental regulation, on a more complete reading it can be used as a source of arguments that favor environmental policy.

Lockean Sustainability

From the outset, we must plainly acknowledge that Locke is unabashedly anthropocentric; indeed, he may not have recognized a non-anthropocentric position as intelligible. He affirms repeatedly his moral axiom that God dedicated nonhuman creation to the purpose of supporting the life and survival of humanity; to say that Locke regards the natural world as humanity's habitat is to admit that he regards it as a store of resources for human exploitation.[22] Any contribution Lockean ideas might make to environmentalism would thus be to a frankly anthropocentric version. We can see how this kind of contribution might work by exploring a Lockean argument for sustainable development (which I will refer to as sustainability).

In perhaps its best-known statement, sustainability involves meeting "the needs of the present without compromising the ability of future generations to meet their own needs."[23] In the Lockean spirit, that is, sustainability takes as its fundamental goal the survival of human beings, and conceives of the natural world as a means for attaining that goal.[24] Let us examine three aspects of Locke's outlook that are particularly in keeping with the ethics of sustainability.

The first is the temporal scale of Locke's moral vision. Recall Locke's polemic against Filmer, in which Locke insists that God's grant of the Earth is not to Adam personally, but to all of Adam and Eve's descendants throughout time. The original moral warrant for using the Earth applies equally to *any* descendant, independent of temporal position; all descendants, at all times, have the same entitlement to survival, and hence to the means required for it (1T, §§29–31). Thus Locke argues that neither Adam nor Noah "had any private dominion, any property in the creatures, exclusive of his posterity, as they should successively grow up into need of them, and come to be able to make use of them" (1T, §39). Thus all people at all times are on an equal moral footing; people who live earlier in the history of Creation have no moral priority. The strong conclusion follows that activities in the present that will diminish the suitability of the Earth to support human life in the future are violations of natural law.

Observe two corollaries: On the one hand, this Lockean conclusion supports the positive injunction to maintain the natural environment in a condition that will allow it to continue to fulfill its function. That injunction is obviously at work in the "provisos," discussed above, that regulate initial appropriation from the common stock: appropriators may not let anything go to waste, and they must not foreclose the possibility of others gaining support for their lives from nature.[25] In particular, Locke's comment that appropriators leave "enough and as good" for others might be glossed as a demand that appropriation must not diminish the productivity of natural systems. Beyond the provisos, however, there is no reason to think that the injunction doesn't apply to any activity that can affect the Earth's productivity, including ongoing interactions with nature after it has been appropriated, indeed after the state of nature has given way to civil society.[26] On the other hand, recall that for Locke supporting human life isn't limited to providing for bare survival; he includes the provision of conveniences as part of the legitimate use of the Earth. That is, supporting human life means supporting a distinctively *human* life. The Lockean demand for sustainability would not be satisfied if the quality of future generations' lives were to be substantially compromised.[27]

A second argument that Locke's theory supports an ethic of sustainability can be drawn from several insights of James Tully's, which together suggest that the fundamental justification for property—God's intention that human beings survive—implies what is and is not subject to ownership. Because survival is obtained directly from the *products* of nature rather than their underlying *sources*, Locke's theory doesn't grant ownership of the productivity of nature itself. That remains God's, who merely allows people to benefit from it.[28] Tully thus interprets Locke to hold that God grants human beings *usufructory* rights to the Earth—rights to use the products of nature, but not absolute ownership of the underlying natural systems that ultimately provide for humanity's survival by generating those products.[29] For example, although the usufructory right to draw water from a river grants one an exclusive right to the water one draws for one's own use, it doesn't encompass the right to exclude others from drawing from the river (2T, §33). We can base this reading on

Locke's declaration that, "in respect of one another, men may be allowed to have propriety in their distinct portions of the creatures; yet in respect of God the maker of heaven and earth, who is sole lord and proprietor of the whole world, man's propriety in the creatures is nothing but that liberty to use them, which God has permitted" (1T, §39). I shall argue that in that "liberty to use" we can see, along with the notion of sustainability, the core of Locke's understanding of habitation.

But first, isn't the idea that Locke only provides for a usufructory right contradicted by his explicit declaration that people can own land? As Neal Wood argues, Locke's conception of property is bound to developments within the agricultural economy—to what he calls agrarian capitalism.[30] This system implies an understanding of land ownership according to which people not only have an exclusive right to the products that support their survival but also have the right to exclude others from the given parcel—that is, to deny them the right (as in the river example) to draw the means of their survival generated by that parcel's productivity. We can address this challenge by following Tully's discussion of Locke on labor.[31] Tully suggests that the morally significant fact about labor is not that something of the self, and hence of one's own, is "mixed" with a previously commonly held object, but rather that labor involves the transformation of something received from nature into *something new*. In other words, labor creates a qualitatively new kind of object. Objects in their natural state must be transformed by being made ready for consumption. (See 2T, §§37, 46.) That transformation by human beings is required for the objects given in nature to fulfill their function of supporting human survival. As Locke put it in a journal entry, "Nature furnishes us only with the material, for the most part rough and unfitted to our use; it requires labour, art and thought, to suit them to our occasions."[32] That is, Locke envisions humanity as a kind of partner with God in the creation of the set of objects that constitute food, clothing, and shelter.[33] The use of nature that God permits is for humanity to create a "second nature," which is its habitat proper.[34, 35]

According to Tully, the process of transformation from an object-in-nature into an object-in-the-human-world undergirds a property right because Locke associates that right with the causal efficacy the laborer exerts to make the transformation happen.[36] Thus, a person can gain a right to a part of underlying Creation (say, a parcel of land) only insofar as he or she transforms it, through labor, into a *field*, an entity in the "second nature" created by humanity. In so doing, the person harnesses the productive capacity of that parcel. This is what counts, for Locke, as the divinely intended form of habitation of the Earth: "God gave the world to men in common; but since he gave it them for their benefit ... it cannot be supposed he meant it should always remain common and uncultivated. He gave it to the use of the industrious." (2T, §34) And for Locke that process of habitation yields the exclusive right to the goods that result from it. Absent the person's labor, those goods would not have been forthcoming; hence Locke's observation that agricultural land yields many multiples more than land in its natural condition (2T, §42).

However, although Locke affirms that within the humanly fashioned habitat individuals have property rights that exclude other human beings, those rights are subordinate to God's ultimate ownership of the underlying Creation—the locus of the productivity which human beings are licensed to exploit. Let us use the river example to ground an analogy. Suppose that someone constructs a diversion channel to make water easier to obtain. Locke's theory countenances that person's exclusive and ongoing right to the water captured by that channel (subject, of course, to the provisos discussed above). But with respect to the river itself, the character of that right remains usufructory. By analogy, a field is like a diversion channel, used to capture the productivity of the land. One's ongoing right to the products yielded by this transformation of the original object of nature entails the right to exclude others not only from the products but also from the parcel of land; otherwise one's own access to the products would be lessened. But this doesn't yield absolute ownership of the land's productivity, construed as the right not to observe the land's divine purpose. For Locke, with respect to God, any individual's "right" to the benefits of the land's productivity is no more than the permission God has granted him or her as a human being to transform His Creation into human habitat.

It isn't hard to draw a link between usufructory rights and sustainability. For a usufructory right to have value over time, the underlying system that produces the relevant good must continue to function well enough to continue to produce it. Actions that degrade the productivity of the system are wrong precisely because they infringe on that usufructory right; the right to take fish from a body of water is infringed, for example, when the stock is overharvested, preventing the population from maintaining itself. It is no defense that the damaging actions are within the purview of an individual's property right. The right of property gives individuals the authority to exclude *one another* from their holdings. But there is no individual property right *with respect to* God; that they have permission to use Creation is in line with God's purpose, but it implies that individuals are obliged to act in ways that don't impede that purpose. Locke's theory suggests, in other words, that unsustainable practices are violations of natural law. The obligation to the future implicit in the usufructory character of property reinforces the notion that the parity of right Locke sees between Noah and his sons applies to all of humanity. Earlier generations have no greater claim on the goods of the Earth than later generations; hence they have an obligation to support their own survival in ways that don't foreclose the prospects of their descendants (1T, §39).

The usufructory character of property points toward the third way Locke can be used to lend support to sustainability: by way of a re-interpretation of his theory of the state. The system of individual appropriation envisioned by the standard reading of Locke leads, via the mechanism of the tragedy of the commons, to unsustainable harvests and eventual resource crashes—as in the overfishing case just mentioned. But if we take into account the role Locke assigns to the state, we can see that he would actually fully support a public management policy aimed at sustainable yield. The standard idea that Locke supports a minimal state dedicated solely to the protection of natural property rights misses two crucial points. On the one hand, it misconstrues Locke's conception of property, taking it to be absolute instead of usufructory; on the other, it ignores Locke's repeated assertions that the state must act to protect the common (or public) good (2T, §§89, 131, 134, 135, 142). Framing individual property as usufructory highlights the *interdependence* of property rights: each individual's ability to exercise his or her right relies on the condition of the underlying system that generates the goods in question. Protecting each individual's property thus requires the maintenance of the underlying system—in a word, requires that the Earth be used sustainably.

In particular, each individual's rights must be protected against unsustainable exercises by other individuals of their rights. Thus, Locke licenses the state to coordinate individuals' exercise of property rights, so that their aggregate affect isn't harmful. Though the state may not deprive anyone of his or her property, Locke acknowledges that "the prince, or senate, [has] power to make laws, for the *regulating* of property between the subjects one amongst another" (2T, §139; emphasis added). The state, that is, may regulate individuals so that they don't interfere with each other's rights, i.e., by coordinating their simultaneous actions. But Locke must think that this power may operate to restrain adverse impacts in the future as well as in the present. Because people across time have equal moral footing, the state may regulate individuals so that their actions don't interfere with the rights of people later in time.[37] Precisely in virtue of assigning the state the role of preserving property, that is, Locke's theory can be interpreted as assigning it the role of enforcing a policy of sustainability.

Limits of the Lockean Perspective

It is important not to overstate the case for revising our understanding of Locke; it would be a mistake to claim him as an early environmentalist. There are a number of features of his theory that limit its usefulness in advancing an environmentalist political program;[38] I will focus on the absence from Locke of what we might call ecological awareness.

There is, of course, an intimate relationship between environmentalism as a moral and political outlook and ecology as a scientific account of the natural world. But as deeply familiar as Locke was with the science of his day, the field of ecology was not available to him. As Brent Haddad suggests, Locke shows some awareness of the notion of ecosystem services.[39] But Locke most certainly did not understand the pervasiveness, complexity, scale, and (most important) the fragility of the range of organic and inorganic processes that connect the components of ecosystems.

The absence of ecological awareness explains a limitation in Locke's understanding of value. Locke famously declares that "*labour makes the far greatest part of the value* of things we enjoy in this world: and the ground which produces the materials, is scarce to be reckoned in, as any, or at most, but a very small part of it" (2T, §42; emphasis in original). But, as Haddad observes, Locke radically understates the contribution of ecosystem services to the production of value.[40] Against Locke's assertion that labor is responsible for 99% of a product's value (2T, §40), Haddad argues that "ecologists would reach different conclusions on relative effort involved in production. If based on energy fluxes, they might include the energy required for ... ecological processes that eventually result in the availability of an acorn on the forest floor. The human energy of gathering and transporting acorns out of the forest, which to Locke is sufficient to establish a property right, could be less than 1% of the total energy expended to generate, acquire, and deliver an acorn to one's home."[41] If Haddad is correct, it appears that human labor only produces value by, in effect, leveraging a vast amount of natural capital.

But, as we saw, Locke's theory of property allows an owner to exclude others from his or her field: unless land is scarce, the capture of the productivity of this parcel doesn't prevent others from capturing the productivity of the soil elsewhere. Locke assumes that the activities of the owners of different plots are distinct and independent, because the natural capacities that yield the goods needed for survival are localized: they are more or less tied to and contained in those distinct plots. From an ecological perspective, however, there might be subtle and unnoticed linkages between those (only apparently) distinct plots, in virtue of which activities on one can lead to the decline in the productivity of another. For example, clearing shrubbery from one plot to make more room for crops might destroy habitat for birds, resulting in a proliferation of insects and damage to crops on a plot some distance away. In the absence of ecological understanding, the harms suffered by the remote owner are not attributable to the original actions. They would count simply as bad fortune, and not as a trigger for the kind of regulation designed to protect sustainability we saw above that Locke's theory allows. In cases of the wholesale transformation of land forms arguably permitted under Locke's conception of property rights, the cascade of adverse impacts through interlocking ecosystems can be quite profound—but Locke's understanding of nature implies that his theory could not respond. In seeing land as privatized parcels, Locke fails to see it in ecological terms, and his theory is thus unable to fully accommodate environmentalists' concerns.

But to observe that Locke's account of property cannot fully express an environmentalist outlook reminds us of its historical importance in justifying a legal system that has favored property rights at the expense of environmental protection. That historical fact alone explains why environmental political theorists have engaged with his views and will continue to do so. But the value of that engagement is not, finally, exhausted by environmentalists' efforts to diagnose Locke's errors, or to redeem his theory either by revealing other readers' misinterpretations or by deploying his arguments to support their own policy positions. Beyond those projects is the more general lesson. We can take Locke's view as a model of a genuinely environmental political theory. His vision of politics emerges from what I have called his understanding of habitation—his grasp of the fact that human life involves the active transformation of the natural world into a humanized domain, marked both by a physical structure created by human action and by a moral structure that human action is obliged to observe. This view of habitation provides essential ingredients for robust political theorizing about the human place in the environment, and it explains why Locke's approach should serve as a model, even to those who disagree with his conclusions.

Acknowledgments

My thanks to John Cheek for research assistance with this paper, and to suggestions for revisions of an earlier draft by Peter Cannavò, Joe Lane, and Piers Stephens.

Notes

1. For another theory of habitation, see Peter Cannavò's discussion of Hannah Arendt in this volume. Cannavò sees Arendt's approach as less instrumentalizing of nature than Locke's.
2. The phrase in my title appears in Locke's *Two Treatises of Government*. I will cite the *First Treatise* and the *Second Treatise* as 1T and 2T, and will give the paragraph number rather than the page; the present citation, for example, is Locke 1T, §40.
3. Biographical details from R. Woolhouse, *Locke: A Biography* (Cambridge University Press, 2007). See also the introduction to *Two Treatises of Government*, ed. P. Laslett (Cambridge University Press, 1988).
4. See also Piers Stephens's remarks on Lockean empiricism and on John Stuart Mill's revision of it in this volume.
5. For discussions of how others of Locke's works bear on the environment, see K. M. Squadrito, "Locke's View of Dominion," *Environmental Ethics* 1, no. 3 (1979): 255–262, at 258ff.; P. Stephens, "Green Liberalisms: Nature, Agency and the Good," *Environmental Politics* 10, no. 3 (2001): 1–22, at 6ff.
6. Though the term isn't Locke's own, it expresses his meaning: "every man has a *property* in his own *person:* this no body has any right to but himself" (2T, §27). The self-ownership thesis is a central topic of discussion in Locke scholarship, particularly among readers who seek to insulate property rights from regulation by the state. See, for example, R. Nozick, *Anarchy, State, and Utopia* (Basic Books, 1974), 225; E. F. Paul, *Property Rights and Eminent Domain* (Transaction Books, 1987), 209.
7. Important discussions can be found in Nozick, *Anarchy, State, and Utopia*, 174ff.; J. Tully, *A Discourse on Property: John Locke and His Adversaries* (Cambridge University Press, 1980), 116ff.; J. Waldron, *The Right to Private Property* (Clarendon, 1998), 184ff.; G. Sreenivasan, *The Limits of Lockean Rights in Property* (Oxford University Press, 1995), 60ff. I will return to the question of how labor grounds the property right.
8. By contrast, for example, with Hume's treatment of property right as a matter of convention—see the chapter in this volume by Andrew Valls. As we shall see below, Locke's insistence that property has a basis in natural law is influenced by his polemical goal—not central to Hume's theory—of arguing against an absolutist conception of sovereignty.

9. In *John Locke and Agrarian Capitalism* (University of California Press, 1984), Neal Wood argues against the view—advanced by C. B. Macpherson in *The Political Theory of Possessive Individualism: Hobbes to Locke* (Oxford University Press, 1962)—that Locke is theorizing early industrial capitalism, holding instead that Locke is more specifically offering a theory of the "agrarian capitalism" that was emerging in the seventeenth century, incorporating a Baconian vision of improving nature through agricultural innovation (57ff.). Wood suggests that Locke was seen by his contemporaries and by eighteenth-century readers as "the classic theorist of landed society and the landholder" (113), but that his theory actually reflects the emergence of a novel, capitalistic organization of the agrarian economy.

10. The Lockean provisos are a central topic of scholarly discussion. See, for example, Macpherson, *The Political Theory of Possessive Individualism*, 199ff.; Nozick, *Anarchy, State, and Utopia*, 174ff.; Waldron, *The Right to Private Property*, 207ff.; Sreenivasan, *The Limits of Lockean Rights in Property*, 47ff., 122ff.

11. Macpherson, *The Political Theory of Possessive Individualism*, 208; Wood, *John Locke and Agrarian Capitalism*, 49.

12. Tully, *A Discourse on Property*, 154, 162.

13. J. M. Meyer, "Property, Environmentalism, and the Lockean Myth in America: The Challenge of Regulatory Takings," *Proteus* 15, no. 2. (1998): 51–55; R. A. Epstein, *Takings: Private Property and the Power of Eminent Domain* (Harvard University Press, 1985).

14. See, for example, Squadrito, "Locke's View of Dominion." See also K. Shrader-Frechette, "Locke and Limits on Land Ownership," in *Policy for Land: Law and Ethics*, ed. L. Caldwell and K. Shrader-Frechette (Rowman & Littlefield, 1993); R. P. Judge, "Restoring the Commons: Toward a New Interpretation of Locke's Theory Property," *Land Economics* 78, no. 3 (2002): 331–338; S. P. Liebell, "The Text and Context of 'Enough and as Good': John Locke as the Foundation of an Environmental Liberalism," *Polity* 43, no. 2 (2011): 210–241.

15. Tully, *A Discourse on Property*, 53–54.

16. Ibid., 55ff.

17. Waldron, *The Right to Private Property*, 149ff.

18. Judge, "Restoring the Commons," 332–33.

19. Tully, *A Discourse on Property*, 43, 45.

20. In a private communication, Piers Stephens pointed out that in other works, and in policy recommendations, Locke seems far less solicitous toward the poor.

21. See, for example, Epstein, *Takings*, 11; Paul, *Property Rights and Eminent Domain*, 206–207.

22. Özgüç Orhan, in this volume, argues against the reading of Aristotle as a source of this understanding of nature. Locke's version is no doubt more immediately influenced by his Christian commitments, but it seems likely that the more conventional reading of Aristotle could have entered into the natural-law tradition that Locke invokes through Aquinas. In any event, I am dubious that it is

possible to push Locke's theory in a non-anthropocentric direction, as Valls does with Hume's theory in this volume.

23. United Nations Environment Programme, *Report of the World Commission on Environment and Development: Our Common Future* (1987), chapter 2, §1.

24. There is a clear affinity between the Lockean-inspired position I will sketch here and the "liberal ethic of sustainability" that Piers Stephens describes in his chapter on Mill in this volume.

25. R. Attfield, *The Ethics of Environmental Concern*, second edition (University of Georgia Press, 1991), 107–110; B. M. Haddad, "Property Rights, Ecosystem Management, and John Locke's labor Theory of Ownership," *Ecological Economics* 46 (2003): 19–31, at 29.

26. It is a matter of scholarly debate as to whether the provisos still hold after the invention of money or the transition to civil society; see, for example, MacPherson, *The Political Theory of Possessive Individualism*, 203ff.; Tully, *A Discourse on Property*, 152ff.; Shrader-Frechette, "Locke and Limits on Land Ownership," 76ff.

27. It is currently argued that access to relatively undisturbed natural areas is in fact a contributor to quality of life. See, for example, R. S. Ulrich, "Biophilia, Biophobia, and Natural Landscapes," in *The Biophilia Hypothesis*, ed. S. R. Kellert and E. O. Wilson (Island, 1993), 100–102. Without claiming that Locke himself would view recreation in wilderness areas as central to a good human life, it doesn't seem unreasonable to extend his theory to encompass the non-use values nature provides to people.

28. Tully, *A Discourse on Property*, 119.

29. Ibid., 60.

30. Wood, *John Locke and Agrarian Capitalism*, 19.

31. Tully, *A Discourse on Property*, 166ff.

32. As quoted in Tully, *A Discourse on Property*, 121.

33. Locke's interest in agricultural methods is attested by Wood, *John Locke and Agrarian Capitalism*, 15ff., and is shown in a 1679 report, "Observations upon the Growth of and Culture of Vines and Olives," about farming techniques he observed in France, written for his patron Shaftesbury. Locke's notion of human-created habitat is not unlike Arendt's concept of the human artifice. (See Peter Cannavò's chapter on Arendt in this volume.)

34. C. J. Glacken, *Traces on the Rhodian Shore: Nature and Culture in Western Thought from Ancient Times to the End of the Eighteenth Century* (University of California Press, 1967), 145.

35. In my view, Locke thus anticipates the idea of hybridization that Timothy Luke discusses in his chapter on Marx in this volume.

36. Tully, *A Discourse on Property*, 120.

37. For an insightful discussion of the paradoxical fact that actions that are not individually harmful may cause harm when their effects are aggregated, see A. Kernohan, "Individual Acts and Accumulative Consequences," *Philosophical*

Studies 97, no. 3 (2000): 343–366. Also see W. S. K. Cameron's discussion of Martin Heidegger in this volume.

38. P. H. G. Stephens, "Picking at the Locke of Economic Reductionism," in *Environmental Futures*, ed. N. B. Fairweather et al. (Macmillan, 1999), 4–5.

39. Haddad, "Property Rights, Ecosystem Management, and John Locke's Labor Theory of Ownership," 25–26.

40. Ibid., 27.

41. Ibid., 27–28.

6

David Hume: Justice and the Environment

Andrew Valls

It is sometimes claimed that liberal political theory stands in tension with or is even incompatible with environmentalism. For example, Andrew Dobson suggests that "liberalism and ecologism finally part company" because ecologism raises deep questions about "the good life" that liberalism seeks to bracket and leave to individuals' private determination.[1] Yet, as Zev Trachtenberg and Piers Stephens show in their respective chapters on Locke and Mill in this volume, matters are not so clear. Trachtenberg argues that even John Locke, the great theorist of natural property rights, can be read in an environmentally friendly way, though Trachtenberg admits that his reading is unorthodox. Stephens similarly argues that although John Stuart Mill is an individualist, he isn't a possessive individualist, and that Mill's engagement with Romanticism imbues his liberalism with a deep appreciation of nature.

In this chapter I argue that David Hume's philosophy provides us with a theory that is more deeply compatible with environmental concerns than either Locke's or Mill's—or indeed that of any other canonical liberal thinker. Hume presents a classical liberal theory[2] that provides a basis for addressing issues of justice in three realms related to the environment: environmental justice among humans (intra-species justice), inter-species justice, and ecological justice (justice to ecosystems and their constituent parts). As I argue in the first section, Hume's theory of justice is explicitly situated in the natural environment, but is also highly conventionalist. His "laws of nature" that govern property evolve over time and are subject to revision by positive law, so there are no natural property rights (as in Locke's theory) that limit the state's ability to pursue an environmentally friendly policy that addresses concerns about intra-species environmental justice. In the second section I argue that Hume sees humans and nonhuman animals as sharing a fundamentally common nature. Though Hume denies that justice extends to nonhuman animals, he affirms that they are legitimate subjects of moral concern, and leaves open the possibility that justice can be extended to them. In the third section I discuss J. Baird Callicott's argument that Hume provides the philosophical basis for Aldo Leopold's Land Ethic. I try to show that Callicott's arguments are not persuasive, not only because they are not plausible interpretations of Hume's philosophy, but also because they make claims that are dubious on substantive grounds. Luckily, though, many of Leopold's conclusions can be supported without resort to the foundations that Callicott tries to provide them. For that reason, there is no necessary disagreement between Hume and Leopold, and indeed Hume's view of humans as embodied animals fits well with Leopold's vision of the biotic community and of ecological justice.

Environmental Justice

"For Hume," according to Ian Hacking, "in the beginning was the body."[3] Hacking is right, and Hume's foregrounding of the body, our physical natures, and our relation to our physical surroundings shapes much of his thought. Our embodiment means, for Hume, that we are surrounded by other human beings like ourselves, whose passions and feelings affect us through the mechanism of sympathy. As we will see, it also means that as embodied creatures—as animals—we have much in common with other animals. Our embodied nature and our relation to our physical environment also have important implications for Hume's theory of justice.

For Hume, the rules of justice are, first and foremost, rules that regulate property. But Hume's account of the development of those rules should be seen as a paradigm for a broader account of the origins of the norms that govern cooperation. Such norms, Hume argues, are not conclusions of reason and are not rules that are agreed upon through an explicit social contract. Rather, they are norms that have evolved to solve the problem of the distribution of goods. Hence, though Hume often calls the rules of justice "laws of nature," it must be emphasized that the ontological status (the sense in which they can be said to exist) of Hume's laws of nature is quite different from, say, that of Locke's. For Locke, the laws of nature are legislated by God and discovered by human reason. They precede the existence of government, and they limit what government may do. For Hume, since the laws of nature are evolved norms, founded not on reason but on convention, they lack the superior moral status that they enjoy in Locke's view. They are subject to revision by the state once it exists. Hence, for Hume property rights enjoy no special protection that would obstruct efforts by the state to regulate property rights in an attempt to protect the environment and to protect people from the negative environmental consequences of the actions of others.

Hume begins his account of property rights by noting the benefits of social cooperation, including increased force and power, the division of labor and specialization, and increased security and protection from "fortune and accidents" (T 485).[4] But "in order to form society, 'tis requisite not only that it be advantageous, but also that men be sensible of its advantages" (T 486). The latter condition, Hume suggests, would not necessarily obtain among those who have not already begun to cooperate. At this point, where other philosophers rely on reason and reflection, Hume gives the central role to nature and biology. "Most fortunately," there is another aspect of human nature that "may justly be regarded as the first and original principle of human society. This necessity is no other than that natural appetite betwixt the sexes, which unites them together, and preserves their union, till a new tye takes place in their concern for their common offspring." (T 486) Here we can see that Hume, as Annette Baier puts it, gives nature its due. Though justice, as we will see, is conventional, it has its origins in biological facts about human existence. As Baier explains, "It is only because of our way of procreating, of letting family lines continue, and the psychological preconditions and effects of that, that we are able to do any social creating. Hume's story of the genesis of the social artifice is centered on this key sociobiological fact about us."[5]

In addition to these features of human beings, Hume's account of the origins of property and justice relies on his account of what are now commonly called the "circumstances of justice." Here Hume argues that the very ideas of property and justice arise because of certain empirical facts about the human condition, and that if these facts were otherwise such notions might never have come about. The two dimensions of the human condition that Hume emphasizes are limited human generosity and limited goods. However, as Hume admits, even very generous humans might be inconsistently generous, and thus would still stand in need of some conventions to coordinate social interaction (T 487). The aspect of the circumstances of justice that does the real work in Hume's account, then, is our "outward circumstances," our relation to our environment and the natural world. Hume argues that if the things that we needed were so scarce that each individual's very survival depended on violating the rules of property, those rules would be impotent to regulate human behavior and would never have been thought of. By the same token, if nature spontaneously produced anything anyone might desire in great abundance, no rules determining what is mine and what is thine would be necessary. It is only because the material conditions lie somewhere between abundance and extreme scarcity most of the time, in most places where people live, that justice is both necessary and possible (T 486–495).

Hume's account of the circumstances of justice has important environmental implications. Rules of property are required, Hume says, only if a resource is scare, but if a resource is unlimited such rules are unnecessary. Hume's main examples of goods that are so abundant as to make justice superfluous are "air and water" (T 495). Of course, it shouldn't be surprising that Hume, writing in the eighteenth century, would have thought of air and water as unlimited resources. However, Hume's account implies that if air and water aren't unlimited resources then they, too, have to be regulated by rules of justice. (I will return to this issue at the end of this section.)

Hume assumes that there are obvious advantages to allowing individuals to appropriate, own, and transfer property, and in this respect his account is similar to Locke's theory of property. Hume's endorsement of private property is part of what makes him a recognizably classical liberal political theorist. However, in other respects Hume's defense of private property is markedly different from Locke's in ways that make Hume's endorsement of it much more qualified. In emphasizing that the rules of justice are conventional, Hume rejects any attempt to place property on the foundation of "nature" or "reason." In Hume's catalog of virtues, justice is an artificial virtue, not a natural one, meaning that in the absence of human conventions it would not be a virtue at all. Hume also rejects a contractarian conception of property whereby the rules of justice are explicitly agreed to. Rather, on Hume's account, the rules of justice evolve and develop: "Nor is the rule concerning the stability of possession the less deriv'd from human conventions, that it arises gradually, and acquires force by a slow progression, and by our repeated experience of the inconvenience of transgressing it." (T 490) The development of the institution of property, and of the rules of justice to govern it, is like the development of natural languages, which are "gradually establish'd by human convention without any promise" (T 490). Thus, while endorsing private property, Hume refuses to sanctify it.

What is of interest in Hume's account of the rules of justice is not their content, since they "follow the standard outlines of Roman law, which had been incorporated into Scottish jurisprudence of his day"[6]; it is how he describes the foundations of the institution of property and the rules that govern it. Consistent with the generally anti-rationalist cast of his thought,

Hume argues that the rules are based on the faculty of the mind that he calls "the imagination" (and, sometimes, "the fancy")—the tendency of our minds to associate certain ideas with one another. He argues that our ideas about cause and effect are products of the imagination and not of reason (T 69–179). He argues that, although our notions of property are guided by the imagination, that faculty is often unable to arrive at consistent, determinate results when it isn't clear what should belong to whom. "There are, no doubt, motives of public interest for most of the rules, which determine property," he writes, "but still I suspect, that these rules are principally fix'd by the imagination, or the more frivolous properties of our thought and conception." (T 504) To say that the rules of property are based on "the more frivolous properties of our thought" is hardly a ringing endorsement of expansive and entrenched property rights.

Indeed, Hume seems to delight in dwelling on examples of property claims that don't lend themselves to determinate or rational resolution. For example: "A wild boar, that falls into our snares, is deem'd to be in our possession, if it be impossible for him to escape. But what do we mean by impossible? How do we separate this impossibility from an improbability? And how distinguish that exactly from a probability?" (T 506) There is also the example of two messengers who go in search of a rumored empty city, which each hopes to claim as a colony. One throws a spear that lands within the city's gates before the other touches the gate with his hand. To whom does the colony belong? "For my part I find the dispute impossible to be decided," Hume writes, "and that because the whole question hangs upon the fancy, which in this case is not possess'd of any precise or determinate standard." (T 508n) Hume's point here is that the rules of justice are conventions, but they are conventions that often lack a rational basis. The need for some rules is clear to Hume, but the content of the rules is highly contingent. There will always be cases in which some considerations suggest one outcome to a property dispute and other considerations suggest the opposite result—in which "the reasons on both sides are so equally ballanc'd, that 'tis impossible for us to give any satisfactory decision. *Here then is the proper business of municipal laws, to fix what the principles of human nature have left undetermin'd*" (T 513n, emphasis added). I emphasize the last sentence because it reflects an important implication of Hume's conception of the laws of nature, which is that it leaves considerable room for the role of the state in regulating private property. Indeed, Hume affirms that, rather than constraining the state as the laws of nature do in Locke's theory, Hume's laws of nature are "changeable by human laws" (T 528). This makes sense in light of Hume's conventionalist account of property: if property rights are merely conventions, they enjoy no sacrosanct place in his moral or political theory. Though they precede government in Hume's account, once government comes into being it establishes positive law, which takes over the role of assigning property rights. Hume rejects the Lockean (or, perhaps more accurately, libertarian) view that the state exists only to enforce pre-existing property rights. Rather, Hume argues that the state may advance the common interests of its citizens and may modify property rights in doing so: "Thus bridges are built; harbours open'd; ramparts rais'd; canals form'd; fleets equip'd; and armies disciplin'd." (T 539)[7]

Hence, to the extent that strong conceptions of property rights have been a major obstacle to environmental regulation, Hume's theory of justice can—because it undermines such conceptions—be seen as eco-friendly, yet liberal. This suggests that, contrary to what is sometimes claimed, liberalism itself isn't necessarily antithetical to environmental concerns. This may or may not be true of particular conceptions of liberalism, but Hume's version, while recognizably liberal and granting a role for property rights, preserves the role of the state to modify property rights in the common interest. We can see this if we return briefly to the case of air and water (which, we saw above, Hume believed to be unlimited and therefore not fit subjects for rules of property). The implication of this, I suggested, is that if it turns out that air and water are not unlimited resources, then they become appropriate subjects for rules of property that the state may establish. We now know better than Hume did whether air and water are unlimited: they are not. We know that at least one aspect of air is a limited resource: the capacity of the atmosphere to absorb carbon and other greenhouse gases. In light of this, on a Humean view, it is entirely appropriate for the state (or a number of states acting together) to regulate the use of this dimension of the atmosphere. On a Humean view, those who would argue that such regulation oversteps the legitimate powers of a (liberal) state are mistaken. The state may establish rules of property in the case of limited resources, and it is now clear that air (contrary to what Hume thought) is such a resource. As Amartya Sen has pointed out, Hume's philosophy preserves a role for science and its findings in ethical theory, and so can take account of changing circumstances and changing understandings of the natural world.[8]

Inter-Species Justice

Hume's view places human beings squarely in the natural world, emphasizes the contingency and revisability of the rules of justice, and by doing so provides resources for environmentally friendly policies. But what of inter-species justice, the possibility of rules of justice applying across species boundaries? This topic has attracted the attention of a number of scholars[9] who ask whether norms of justice can and should be extended to nonhuman animals. What might a Humean approach to this issue be?

To answer this question, we must first consider the role of animals in Hume's overall philosophy, and then consider them in relation to his view of justice. The primary role that animals play in Hume's work is to support and confirm his conclusions about human nature. That is, Hume often sees the similarities between humans and animals, and his theory's ability to cover both cases, as supporting his view of human nature: "'Tis usual with anatomists to join their observations and experiments on human bodies to those on beasts, and from the agreement of these experiments to derive an additional argument for any particular hypothesis." (T 325) Hume, emphasizing the continuity and unity of animal (human and nonhuman) nature, depicts human mental and emotional life as being essentially the same as the mental and emotional life of many nonhuman animals. For example, he suggests that nonhuman animals have reason: "no truth appears to me more evident, than that beasts are endow'd with thought and reason as well as men" (T 176). He also suggests that the main passions in humans that he analyzes—pride, humility, love, hatred—also exist in the animal world (T 326, 397).

Perhaps most important, Hume argues that sympathy operates among nonhuman animals and between humans and other animals. Hume's account of sympathy is absolutely central to his account of humans' social nature and to his account of morality. It is the tendency of human beings to be affected by others, to share their feelings and their thoughts, that makes society and a shared morality possible. Hume also asks us to "observe the force of sympathy thro' the whole animal creation, and the easy communication of sentiments from one thinking being to another. In all creatures, that prey not upon others, and are not agitated with violent passions, there appears a remarkable desire of company, which associates them together without any advantages they can ever propose to reap from their union." (T 363; see also T 398) These features of Hume's thought provide further evidence that Hume's philosophy places human beings in the natural world, and casts them fundamentally as biological creatures. For Hume, as Tom Beauchamp observes, "Humans are as much a part of the natural realm as other animals. ... Like Darwin after him, Hume has a powerful way of demythologizing the idea that humans have some magical capacity that distances them as a species from the rest of creation."[10]

Anthony Pitson adds that Hume's view "represents a philosophical revolution in which the view of man as a unique creation in God's image is replaced with that of man as a natural object differing only in degree from other animals."[11]

The common nature shared by humans and nonhuman animals raises the question of the moral status of the latter in Hume's theory, and in particular the question of how they may stand in relation to justice. This issue has been the subject of some controversy, much of it focused on the following passage:

> Were there a species of creatures intermingled with men, which, though rational, were possessed of such inferior strength, both of body and mind, that they were incapable of all resistance, and could never, upon the highest provocation, make us feel the effects of their resentment; the necessary consequence, I think, is that we should be bound by the laws of humanity to give gentle usage to these creatures, but should not, properly speaking, lie under any restraint of justice with regard to them, nor could they possess any right or property, exclusive of such arbitrary lords. Our intercourse with them could not be called society, which supposes a degree of equality ... .This is plainly the situation of men, with regard to animals ... . (EM 190–191)

In this passage, Hume argues that relations of justice presume a degree of equality among participants. He is making the Hobbesian point that cooperative relations governed by mutually binding rules are unlikely to emerge between unequals, since that inequality would create little incentive for the more powerful party to bind him- or herself. Though there is some debate among Hume scholars about the meaning of this passage,[12] and in particular whether it describes the origins or the content of justice,[13] I think there are powerful reasons to conclude that Hume is here considering the origins, not the content, of justice.[14] The point is not that justice always presumes equality—that would imply that justice is suspended in any situation in which there are two unequal parties. Indeed, at the end of the discussion of the origins of justice in which this passage appears, Hume describes the "natural progress of human sentiments, and ... the gradual enlargement of our regards to justice" (EM 192). I want to suggest that, as such progress takes place, animals may come to be thought of as protected by norms of justice.

Such an argument must begin by noting that, although Hume denies that justice applies to nonhuman animals, he affirms that humans have duties to animals based on "humanity." What does this distinction between justice and humanity imply? Recall that for Hume justice is an artificial virtue, which means, among other things, that it is a matter of formal rules. The rules of justice determine property, and Hume argues that to have a stable normative and legal regime governing property the rules must be inflexible and consistently applied. This means that, although the whole system of rules is beneficial, particular applications of it may fail to achieve the greatest benefit to society. Hence, at one point Hume considers a property dispute between two individuals: "Here are two persons, who dispute for an estate; of whom one is rich, a fool, and a bachelor; the other poor, a man of sense, and has numerous family." (T 532) Hume admits that one's natural inclination may be to give the estate to the person for whom it would do the most good—presumably the poor, sensible family man. But this isn't an appropriate basis on which to settle the dispute, because a regime of property rights depends on rules that can be readily and impartially applied to produce predictable and determinate outcomes. The rule "in cases of dispute, grant property to the person to whom it does the most good" clearly doesn't fit the bill.

The point here is that to participate in a regime of rules determining property, one must be able to understand and act in accordance with fairly abstract rules. Hume thought that nonhuman animals lacked that capacity[15] and thus weren't capable of respecting the property rights of others or of possessing such rights themselves.

Here it is important to remember two other features of Hume's account of justice. First, for Hume the concept of justice is very narrow. It doesn't apply, as it does for John Rawls, to the basic structure of society—to the way all the institutions of society work together to distribute the benefits and burdens of social cooperation. Rather, justice applies only to property, so to say that justice doesn't extend to animals, on Hume's view, is only to say that animals cannot own property. This leaves open the question of whether, on a broader conception of justice, animals might enjoy some protection. Second, justice doesn't rank very high in Hume's catalog of virtues. Recall that, in his discussion of the circumstances of justice, justice comes about only because of scarce goods and limited human generosity. Under more favorable conditions, Hume says, justice would be replaced with "much nobler virtues, and more valuable blessings" (T 495). Elsewhere Hume calls justice "the cautious, jealous virtue" (EM 184).

Although Hume withholds the protection of justice from animals, he affirms that humans have duties toward animals based on humanity. Hume more or less equates "humanity" with "benevolence."[16] And in Hume's catalog of virtues, humanity enjoys a more exalted position than justice. According to Joyce Jenkins and Robert Shaver, one reason why "Hume prefers humanity to justice" is that justice is inflexible, whereas humanity allows us to attend to the needs of individuals on a case-by-case basis.[17] In light of Hume's view of the virtues, to say that something (such as cruelty to animals) isn't contrary to justice is not to endorse it. Though it is true, as Aaron Garrett states, that for Hume animals "cannot extract our benevolence as a right," it is a mistake to conclude, as Garrett does, that for Hume "there is no obligation between men and brutes," or that "the consanguinity of animal and human passion cannot be the basis of a moral duty."[18] This conclusion assumes that for Hume justice is the whole of morality, whereas in fact it is only a part—and not the most important part. As Baier reminds us, "since the artificial virtues are only a small subset of the virtues, the fact that animals have no obligations or rights would not mean that no moral wrongs can be done them. ... The duties of justice will not be owed to them, but all the natural virtues [including humanity or benevolence] will cover our treatment of animals."[19] Furthermore, there is no reason to think that the requirements of humanity are any lower or less demanding than those of justice.[20] In some cases they are likely to be more demanding, since humanity isn't constrained by the rules governing justice.

Thus, the fact that Hume places animals outside of justice doesn't mean that humans' treatment of them isn't outside morality; rather, as Pitson writes, "animals are, for Hume, legitimate objects of moral concern."[21] Though Hume is no animal-rights theorist, it is perfectly compatible with the passage from the *Enquiry* quoted above to say that animals are entitled to good treatment, and that our interactions with them are constrained by ethics. Moreover, those of us who affirm a broader conception of justice may, consistent with generally Humean philosophical commitments, extend our notion of justice to animals. This extension of justice to animals would thus be a case of Hume's "progress of sentiments." Indeed, Mary Wollstonecraft's call for the just, humane, and benevolent treatment of animals, discussed by Barbara Seeber in this volume, may be quite consistent with a Humean perspective.

Ecological Justice

If, on a Humean view, animals with whom we share enough in common to feel bonds of sympathy are entitled to moral consideration, what of nonsentient life, inanimate objects in the natural world, and whole ecosystems? Are they entitled to moral consideration in and of themselves. If they are, can Hume's philosophy underwrite such a view? The environmental ethicist J. Baird Callicott has argued, rather controversially, that the answer to these questions is "yes." In this section I examine Callicott's use of Hume to underwrite such a view of ecological justice.

Callicott[22] aims to situate Aldo Leopold's[23] Land Ethic in an intellectual tradition running from Hume and Adam Smith, through Charles Darwin, to Leopold. Leopold's *Sand County Almanac*, of course, is an essential text in environmental ethics, though, as Callicott notes, it has often been derided or dismissed by philosophers. Callicott attempts to reconstruct and defend Leopold's argument by placing it in the eminently respectable tradition that flows from Hume.

Leopold's Land Ethic makes two distinctive claims. The first is that humans should not see themselves as standing over nature, dominating it, but rather should see themselves as members of "the biotic community," along with "soils, waters, plants, [and] animals."[24] Leopold argues that throughout history the dominant conception of community, within which members are entitled to just treatment, has gradually expanded to embrace all human beings, and that the next step should be to extend such community membership beyond humanity to include not only animals but also other elements of the natural world. The second claim is that we must extend such moral consideration not only to individual members of the natural world but also to whole ecosystems. This is necessary, Leopold says, because ecological science tells us that living organisms are mutually dependent on one another within ecosystems, often in ways that we don't fully understand. It isn't enough to treat individual organisms with justice; we must extend moral consideration to whole ecosystems.

How does Callicott attempt to support Leopold's Land Ethic with Hume's philosophy? He makes several connections, some more plausible than others. First, Callicott is right that there is an intellectual lineage from Hume to Darwin to Leopold. Hume posited that our biological natures make us the social and passion-driven beings that we are, but he did not attempt to explain why. For that we need Darwin, whose theory of evolution explains how social cooperation and affective connection with others, particularly our children and kin, contribute to our species' survival.[25] And there are other resonances between Hume and Leopold. Hume's emphasis on humans' commonality with other animals certainly fits nicely with (though it doesn't necessarily entail) Leopold's image of a biotic community, of which humans are one set of members.

But Callicott sees more to the Hume-Leopold connection. He argues that Hume's moral theory substantiates Leopold's claim that ecosystems deserve moral consideration. Callicott's basic argument is as follows: Hume's theory of moral sentiments holds that human beings are not egoists, but rather have a natural concern for others. This concern for others extends to society as a whole. And this moral concern for society as a whole is, according to Callicott, analogous to Leopold's Land Ethic. Both, according to Callicott, are cases of ethical holism, the idea that we should have moral concern for, and perhaps moral obligations toward, wholes (such as societies or ecosystems) over and above whatever moral concern or obligation we have toward their individual members. Hence, Callicott interprets Hume's assertion that "we must adopt a more public affection, and allow, that the interests of society are not, even on their own account, entirely indifferent to us" (EM 219) as saying that we ought to have concern for society, independent of concern for its individual members. As Callicott's critics argue, there is little basis in Hume's work for this interpretation.[26] Callicott is right that Hume rejects psychological egoism and believes that humans naturally have concern for one another. But when Hume writes of "the interests of society" or "public interest" (T 500), there is no reason to think that he is endorsing some kind of holism, or that he has in mind anything beyond the interests of the individuals who make up society. Recall that for Hume the foundation of morals is sentiment, and that our concern for others is grounded on sympathy. Though we can extrapolate from sympathy with concrete others to considering the public interest at large, it is difficult to conceive, on Hume's view, how we can sympathize with, or take moral concern in, an abstraction such as society as a whole or, for that matter, an ecosystem, over and above its individual members. It is also difficult to see how, on a Humean view, we can extend moral considerability to inanimate objects such as soils and waters. Complex as these are, and as crucial as they turn out to be to the ecosystem, in and of themselves they simply are not the kind of things for which, on a Humean view, one can have an independent moral concern. It is difficult to imagine the progress of sentiments extending that far.

But if Callicott's critics are right (as I think they are) that Hume's philosophy doesn't support ethical holism and doesn't support extending moral concern to inanimate objects, does this mean that Leopold's Land Ethic is left unsupported? Not necessarily. One option is to look to philosophers other than Hume for theoretical support for the Land Ethic. But of course the difficulty with Callicott's argument is not merely that moral considerability for inanimate objects and ethical holism are alien to Hume's philosophy, but that these doctrines may be implausible on substantive grounds. And if they are simply implausible, whether this or that philosopher would support them becomes a secondary issue.

Fortunately, much of the Land Ethic can be supported without appeal to these highly debatable notions. And Hume is indeed helpful here, though not in all the ways that Callicott suggests. When Hume says that "the interests of society are not, even on their own account, entirely indifferent to us," he is making a point similar to one that Leopold makes many times: that we have interests that are not economic, that are not narrow *self*-interests. In view of our social nature and the ways we are moved through sympathy by the plight of others, the narrow conception of self-interest that is associated with more atomistic views of human nature are simply implausible. *Of course* we have interests beyond the economic, and interests in the interests of others—how could we not? Furthermore, as was suggested above, the findings of science are not, on Hume's view, irrelevant to ethics. If it is the case that the long-term well-being of humans and of nonhuman animals depends on our treatment of the natural world, then this may impose new moral obligations upon us.

Another aspect of Leopold's thought also takes us back to Hume. Throughout *A Sand County Almanac*, Leopold urges us to appreciate values he sees embodied in nature, especially "diversity and beauty."[27] As several of Callicott's critics have noted, these aesthetic considerations are not morally irrelevant from a Humean perspective.[28] If we value these aesthetic aspects of nature, they may provide a rationale for preserving it.

Given these considerations, we may not require the ethical holism that Callicott advances, and for which he appeals to Hume for support. Nor must we grant soil and water independent moral standing. Rather, we may be obligated to protect soil and water, and ecosystems as wholes, because life depends on them in complex ways, because they have the aesthetic appeal of beauty and diversity, and because animals that depend on or inhabit them deserve humane treatment. Leopold can support his main conclusions (though perhaps not every detail of his argument) without appealing to philosophically dubious notions. Consequently, there is no reason to look for support of those notions in Hume or elsewhere. And it isn't a shortcoming of Hume's thought that it isn't holistic in the way that Callicott suggests. Rather, the way Hume places humans squarely in the natural world, and emphasizes our commonality with nonhuman animals, combined with the appreciation of the complexity and interdependence of ecosystems that modern science provides, gives us plenty of grounds for taking seriously the ethics of our relation to the natural world.

Conclusion

The virtue of Hume's philosophy when it comes to environmental issues, I have suggested, is that he emphasizes the inescapably embodied nature of human beings, our dependence on the natural world, and our common nature with nonhuman animals. Hence, the sharp divide that is sometimes drawn between liberalism and environmental views isn't inevitable. Dobson suggests that liberalism "has distinguished sharply between the human and 'natural' realms," and that "ecologism, by contrast, insists that we are human *animals*, with all the implications that this brings in its train."[29] Hume joins ecologism in insisting that we are animals, and his philosophy, I have suggested, is shaped by this perspective. Our moral and political obligations should be informed by our physical and biological environment and by our best scientific understanding of how that environment operates. Hume is a recognizably liberal thinker—he endorses property rights, limited government, and a role for the market—yet his philosophy doesn't merely permit us, but encourages and even requires us to think about the ethics of our relations with nonhuman animals and the natural environment.

Acknowledgments

For helpful comments on a draft, I wish to thank the following kind individuals: Frederick Whelan, Angela Coventry, William Uzgalis, Allen Thompson, James Pontuso, Joseph Lane, and Peter Cannavò.

Notes

1. Andrew Dobson, *Green Political Thought*, fourth edition (Routledge, 2007), 153.

2. Hume is sometimes read as more of a conservative than a liberal. Although there are certainly conservative elements in his thought, I believe that his main moral, political, and economic doctrines place him squarely in the liberal tradition. I make this argument in my PhD dissertation, Hume and the Foundations of Liberalism (University of Pittsburgh, 1995).

3. Ian Hacking, "On Sympathy: With Other Creatures," *Tijdschrift voor Filosofie* 63 (2001): 685–717, at 696.

4. My discussion focuses mainly on Hume's account in *A Treatise of Human Nature* (second edition, ed. L. A. Selby-Bigge and P. H. Nidditch, Clarendon, 1978). I refer to it using T followed by a page number. I do, however, consider his *Enquiry Concerning the Principles of Morals* (third edition, ed. L. A. Selby-Bigge and P. H. Nidditch, Clarendon, 1975)—hereafter cited as EM—where that is appropriate.

5. Annette Baier, *The Cautious Jealous Virtue: Hume on Justice* (Harvard University Press, 2010), 138.

6. David Miller, *Philosophy and Ideology in Hume's Political Thought* (Clarendon, 1981), 68.

7. I admit that my brief remarks about Locke may be contestable, especially in light of Trachtenberg's revisionist (though persuasive) interpretation. Hence my comments could be interpreted as characterizing the standard textbook picture of Locke rather than as doing justice to Locke's full view.

8. Amartya Sen, "The Boundaries of Justice: David Hume and Our World," *The New Republic*, December 29, 2011: 23–26.

9. See, Brian Baxter, *A Theory of Ecological Justice* (Routledge, 2005); Martha C. Nussbaum, *Frontiers of Justice: Disability, Nationality, Species Membership* (Harvard University Press, 2006); David Schlosberg, *Defining Environmental Justice: Theories, Movements, and Nature* (Oxford University Press, 2007).

10. Tom L. Beauchamp, "Hume on the Nonhuman Animal," *Journal of Medicine and Philosophy* 24 (1999): 322–35, at 332.

11. Anthony Pitson, "The Nature of Humean Animals," *Hume Studies* 19, no. 2 (1993): 301–316, at 301.

12. See Arthur Kuflick, "Hume on Justice to Animals, Indians, and Women," *Hume Studies* 24 (1998): 53–70.

13. See Joyce Jenkins and Robert Shaver, "'Mr. Hobbes Could Have Said No More,'" in *Feminist Interpretations of David Hume*, ed. Anne Japp Jacobson (Pennsylvania State University Press, 2000).

14. Andrew Valls, "'A Lousy Empirical Scientist:' Reconsidering Hume's Racism," in *Race and Racism in Modern Philosophy*, ed. Valls (Cornell University Press, 2005).

15. Kuflick, "Hume on Justice to Animals, Indians, and Women."

16. Remy Debes, "Humanity, Sympathy, and the Puzzle of Hume's Second Enquiry," *British Journal for the History of Philosophy* 15, no.1 (2007): 27–57, at 29; Robert Shaver, "Hume on the Duties of Humanity," *Journal on the History of Philosophy* 30 (1992): 545–556, at 546.

17. Jenkins and Shaver, "'Mr. Hobbes Could Have Said No More,'" 138.

18. Aaron Garrett, "Anthropology: The 'Original' of Human Nature," in *The Cambridge Companion to the Scottish Enlightenment*, ed. Alexander Broadie (Cambridge University Press, 2003), 85.

19. Annette Baier, *Postures of the Mind: Essays on Mind and Morals* (University of Minnesota Press, 1985), 147, 149.

20. Shaver, "Hume on the Duties of Humanity," 550.

21 Tony Pitson, "Hume on Morals and Animals," *British Journal on the History of Philosophy* 11, no. 4 (2003): 639–655, at 639.

22. J. Baird Callicott, "Hume's Is/Ought Dichotomy and the Relation of Ecology to Leopold's Land Ethic," *Environmental Ethics* 4 (1982): 163–174; "The Con-

ceptual Foundations of the Land Ethic," in *Companion to* A Sound County Almanac: *Interpretive and Critical Essays*, ed. Callicott (University of Wisconsin Press, 1987); "Animal Liberation and Environmental Ethics: Back Together Again," *Between the Species* 4 (1988): 163–69; "Can a Theory of Moral Sentiments Support a Genuinely Normative Environmental Ethic?" *Inquiry* 35 (1992): 183–198.

23. Aldo Leopold, *A Sand County Almanac* (Oxford University Press, 1966), 237–264.

24. Ibid., 239.

25. See Darwin, *The Descent of Man, and Selection in Relation to Sex* (Murray, 1871).

26. See Alan Carter, "Humean Nature," *Environmental Values* 9 (2000): 3–37; James Fieser, "Callicott and the Metaphysical Basis of Ecocentric Morality," *Environmental Ethics* 15 (1993): 171–180; Y. S. Lo, "Non-Humean Holism, Un-Humean Holism," *Environmental Values* 10 (2001): 113–123; Ernest Partridge, "Ecological Morality and Nonmoral Sentiments," *Environmental Ethics* 18 (1996): 149–163; Gary Varner, "No Holism Without Pluralism," *Environmental Ethics* 13 (1991): 175–179; Jennifer Welchman, "Hume, Callicott, and the Land Ethic: Prospects and Problems," *Journal of Value Inquiry* 43 (2009): 201–220.

27. Leopold, *Sand County Almanac*, 249.

28. Carter, "Humean Nature," 26; Fieser, "Callicott and the Metaphysical Basis of Ecocentric Morality," 173; Partridge, "Ecological Morality and Nonmoral Sentiments," 149–163.

29. Dobson, *Green Political Thought*, 158.

7

Jean-Jacques Rousseau: The Disentangling of Green Paradoxes

Joseph H. Lane Jr.

Jean-Jacques Rousseau was a major political thinker of the European Enlightenment, even though (or perhaps because) he was, in Mark Hulliung's phrase, the first great "autocritic" of that Enlightenment.[1] He was born in Geneva in 1712. After many years as an itinerant music teacher, composer, and scribbler lurking on the fringes of French literary circles, he emerged as a major intellectual figure with the publication of *Discourse on the Arts and Sciences* (commonly called the *First Discourse*), which won the prestigious contest of the Academy of Dijon in 1751. That work was quickly followed by the *Discourse on the Origins of Inequality* (commonly called the *Second Discourse*) in 1754, an immensely influential essay that lost the Dijon prize but elicited lengthy rejoinders from nearly all of the major intellectual figures of the day. Rousseau then followed up these two foundational works with a remarkable number of major essays, novels, treatises, philosophical autobiographies, and other reflections that challenged both classical and contemporary thought and thus led Rousseau into numerous (and highly public) intellectual disputes over the two decades between his emergence as a major thinker and his death in 1778.

In this essay, I explore how Rousseau's works may be understood as reflections on many of the contemporary questions that are raised by current streams in environmentalist thought and suggest how his works might help us formulate our own answers to those questions. We cannot just mine Rousseau for direct advice. Rousseau did not foresee and could not perfectly predict our particular environmental issues, but he did provide a particularly penetrating account of their roots. His works, taken as a whole, provide an invaluable aid in understanding and mapping the many crises that "modernity" creates for human beings and the world(s) in which they live. Insofar as environmentalists understand themselves to be wrestling with the character and consequences of modernity, they should be particularly interested in Rousseau's critique of it. At the very least, they should be aware of the ways that Rousseau anticipated many of the foundational narratives of modern environmentalism even as he demarcated the limits of those narratives.

Rousseau confronted modernity directly as it emerged from the intellectual revolutions effected by his recent predecessors and his contemporaries—René Descartes, Francis Bacon, Thomas Hobbes, John Locke, Voltaire, and subsequent thinkers. There are of course many others who could be cited, but these figures together account for the three basic elements of modernity as Rousseau understood it: political governments that are at least formally grounded in the principles of political right as defined by Hobbes and Locke (liberalism), systems of production that are based on the application of Baconian natural science to the project of transforming the material of the natural world to provide for the satisfaction of human desires (technology and industrialism), and economic systems that employ markets to deliver the fruits of this production (the commodified goods and services that are produced by the application of instrumentalist reason to persons, animals and other resources of the Earth's ecosystems) to those who can pay for them (capitalism).

When we think about modernity in these terms, as many environmentalist writers do, we are thinking in Rousseau's categories and reciting Rousseau's narratives.[2] Tzevetan Todorov claims that Rousseau, "perhaps more than anyone else," "both discovered and invented our modernity."[3] Todorov suggests that "his adversaries" (and even his allies, I might add) should recognize that "we haven't yet freed ourselves from the myths in which he has entrapped us." When we understand our environmental problems as one of the essential problems, maybe *the most important* of the problems, created by modernity as defined above, we will see how Rousseau's efforts to explain and ultimately call into question the view of the world and the human condition advanced by modernity might relate to the environmentalist project of explaining and repairing the environmental damage done by those who have promoted this modern view of the world and the human condition.

Rousseau lived through the very first decades of what we have come to call modernity, and he recognized at the outset that the modern revolution in thought would lead to many intractable problems, including what we would call environmental degradation. He sketched these evils in only the broadest outlines, but many of his examples presage subsequent environmentalist narratives: He linked the rise of large-scale agriculture to the destruction of great forests (*Second Discourse*, henceforth cited as

SD, 3: 49), questioned the value of the damming of rivers, the razing of mountains, and the draining of swamps (*SD*, 3: 74, note *7), lamented the fact that even the most glorious alpine valleys were now marred by factories (*Reveries of the Solitary Walker*, henceforth *RSW*), Seventh Walk, 8: 66), warned of the "epidemic illnesses" that would result from "bad air" and the "corrupted foodstuffs" shipped in to feed growing cities (*SD*, 8: 76, note *7), and criticized those who only saw nature's biodiversity as a storehouse of resources for human purposes (*Botanical Fragments*, henceforth *BF*, 8: 250–252; *RSW*, Seventh Walk, 8: 64–65).[4]

Rousseau traced all these particular tragedies to his unique (if not unproblematic) understanding of humanity's "alienation from nature," and I argue that his thinking about the character, consequences, and prospective trajectories of this alienation may provide a deeper understanding of many of the political claims that are advanced to explain our environmental crises and to advocate for solutions to those crises.[5] I argue that the environmentalist concern for the preservation of "free" or "unchained" nature is Rousseauian in its origins and that most modern environmentalists draw deeply from Rousseau (although few acknowledge it). For this reason, Rousseau's deeply self-conscious political thought may help us to understand many of the conceptual and political difficulties that beset environmentalism. Rousseau famously declared "Man was/is born free and everywhere he is in chains." (*Social Contract*, henceforth *SC*, 4: 131) For Rousseau, humanity everywhere in chains is the inevitable result of our being slaves to "the petulant activity of our vanity" (*SD*, 3: 48). Rousseau is quite clear that it is this very "vanity" (Rousseau called it *amour-propre*) that brings us into continuous conflict with "Nature," a term that Rousseau pointedly uses in contradistinction to all developed human beings and human societies.

Obviously any claim about a quotation distinguished concept of "Nature" carries dozens of problematic assumptions (as many of the authors in this volume point out), but few would doubt that we have some ideas about what we mean when we use the word 'nature' to designate the organic processes of the biosphere in a certain (although always problematic) contradistinction to the human world. I argue that we cannot completely grasp the practical complexities of our invocations of this concept until we develop a proper understanding of how Rousseau understood, defined, and *created* the concept of "nature" in the normative sense (or senses) in which many of us, including almost all of those who would own the label "environmentalist," tend to use it today.

Rousseau's "Nature"

To provide an authoritative definition now may be presumptuous, but we must begin with at least a provisional understanding of how Rousseau (and we) understand this most quotidian concept.[6] As Rousseau himself suggests in beginning one of his most influential works, if "this word *nature* has too vague a sense," "[a]n attempt must be made to settle on its meaning" (*Emile*, I: 39).[7] In fact, Rousseau proceeds from the assumption that an accurate understanding of nature is the font from which all of his philosophic insights radiate. I argue that environmentalists, almost without exception, have followed him in both the formal or methodological sense of connecting their understandings of nature to their subsequent philosophies in what we might call a Rousseauian fashion and in adopting what are, substantially, Rousseauian visions of what "nature" *is*. Therefore, let us begin with some ideas about the broad outlines of Rousseau's understanding of "nature's" character and meaning.

For a starting point, I would suggest that a basic Rousseauian definition conceives of "nature" as a unitary and spontaneously self-ordering system of interrelationships that can maintain and sustain itself without conscious (whether divine or human) effort or direction. Thus, Rousseau's understanding of nature presupposes the germ of the idea that was once commonly referred to as a "balance of nature"; even if that phrase is now no longer widely accepted, it is consistent with a broader set of ideas that distinguish "nature" from human artifice by relying upon some combination of the concepts of "spontaneous organization," "sustainability," "stability," and "resilience" (all of which are commonly invoked in environmentalist thought). Andrew Dobson, for instance, re-formulates these aspects of Rousseau's understanding of "nature" into his "basic green principle" that we should preserve "the autonomous development of self-renewing systems."[8] "Nature," in this sense, is characterized by certain type of order and maintains that order (and thus itself) without external or conscious direction.

Any fair account of the Rousseauian definition of "nature" would have to account for Rousseau's most powerful normative judgment: "Nature is good." Rousseau's numerous formulations of this dictum vary from work to work, and each is invoked for specific purposes that must be inferred from their individual contexts, but his persistent commitment to the principle of nature's goodness is sustained and unmistakable: Nature "does everything for the best" (*Emile*, henceforth cited as *E*, II: 80). "Let us set down as an incontestable maxim that the first movements of nature are always right." (*E*, II: 92) "All the first movements of nature are good and right. They aim directly as possible toward our preservation and happiness." (*Dialogues* (*D*), 1: 9) "There is no original perversity in the human heart and the first movements of nature are always right." (*Letter to Beaumont* (*LB*), 9: 28) "The fundamental principle of all morals on which I have reasoned in all my writings ... is that man is a being that is naturally good." (*LB*, 9: 26) Rousseau, like modern environmentalists, privileges the movements, principles, and relationships of the "natural" world. Thus, when judging human actions he accords a special normative status to ideas, practices, beliefs, and institutions that are *in some sense* akin to nature, derived from nature, or consistent with nature.

Among environmentalists enshrining the same principle, Barry Commoner articulates his "Third Law of Ecology" as "Nature Knows Best." Commoner follows this law to what he sees as its most logical corollary: that "any major man-made change in a natural system is likely to be detrimental."[9] Rousseau anticipates this rule of thumb. He doesn't condemn all man-made systems, but he does think that they are all *at best* imitations of "nature" and only partial ones and *at worst* perversions of our nature that can only be dangerous to both our own happiness and the preservation of the natural systems on which we are dependent.

Rousseau's Historical Narrative: The Fall *from* Nature

Rousseau observed the emerging modern societies around him carefully and came to view his contemporaries as "deflected" from a natural path. It is true that Rousseau repeatedly holds out some possibility of our recovering our "true" course, but the fundamental Rousseauian narrative emphasizes that human beings are fallen creatures. The precise character of this deflection is discussed in a stunning passage from the *Dialogues*:

Picture an ideal world similar to ours, yet altogether different. Nature is there as on our earth, but its economy is more easily felt, its order more marked, its aspect more admirable. Forms are more elegant, colors more vivid, odors sweeter, all objects more interesting. All nature is so beautiful there that its contemplation, inflaming souls with love for such a touching tableau, inspires in them both the desire to contribute to this beautiful system and the fear of troubling its harmony; and from this comes an exquisite sensitivity which gives those endowed with it immediate enjoyment unknown to hearts that the same contemplations have not aroused. There as here, passions are the motive of all action, but they are livelier, more ardent, or merely simpler and purer, thereby assuming a totally different character. All the first movements of nature are good and right. They aim directly as possible toward our preservation and happiness. ... The inhabitants of the ideal world I am talking about have the fortune to be maintained by nature, to which they are more attached, in that happy perspective in which nature placed us all, and because of this alone their soul forever maintains its original character. (*D*, 1: 9)

In addition to characterizing "nature" as both sustainable and good, Rousseau insists that the "goodness" of nature is inextricably tied to its "original" character. For Rousseau, the nature of things is to be found in their origins, and we are led to conclude that change over time is generally to be viewed negatively. This insight is essential to understanding Rousseau's connection to modern environmentalist narratives and to appreciating the counter-progressive tendencies of many movements that have contested the aspirations of the Enlightenment.

In the *Second Discourse*, Rousseau offers an altered Eden story, a philosophical history of humanity that accounts for how we came to be alienated from nature and "insensitive" to its claims. That discourse contains the most explicit description of Rousseau's teaching that "nature made men happy and good," and it contains the most complete articulation of just how Rousseau uses the "goodness of nature" to make a moral judgment on human activities and passions, how he attaches his notion of goodness to the fundamental idea that nature may be defined by what is "original," durable, and self-sustaining, and how that which is "natural" in the "goodness of man" comes to be associated with the character of a "natural" (which is to say an "original") state of the world.[10]

The First Part of the *Second Discourse* offers an idealized picture of the "original" human animal, a creature that Rousseau describes as physiologically human and yet in no other way distinguishable from other animals. This portrait of the original human race is, for the most part, static and fixed. Although Rousseau alludes in the First Part to the motions within the "state of nature" that ultimately lead to its dissolution, he does so only to highlight the distinctive gap that separates the original (which is to say the "natural") human being from modern human beings. In fact, most of the discussion of "motion" in the First Part is couched in terms that suggest the improbability of the very motion that we know must have occurred: the movement from whatever human beings were originally to what they are today. Rousseau suggests that only "singular and fortuitous circumstances ... which could very well never happen" (*SD*, 3: 25) would have led human beings to make clothing and fixed dwellings. He argues that "it is impossible to conceive" how arts of metallurgy and agriculture first occurred to natural human beings (*SD*, 28). In many respects, the First Part tends to set out a state of nature as so durable, so well balanced, and so impervious to change that we should be surprised that it ever ended. Within this tableau, Rousseau reveals the human being as an ecologically embedded simple gatherer (not yet a hunter) who lives at peace with the planet and does not change the world through which he passes. This idealization of the primitive, ecologically safe human primogenitor is echoed in the writings of Paul Shepard and the deep ecologists, who see early human beings as the proper guide to an ecological existence. "One of the most remarkable intuitions in Western thought," Gary Snyder has proclaimed, "was Rousseau's Noble Savage: the idea that perhaps civilization has something to learn from the primitive."[11]

If the First Part of the *Second Discourse* is a portrait, the Second Part is a motion picture. It tells the story of how mankind changed from a peaceful, nomadic species of generally equal individuals firmly and physically embedded in the natural world into the tyrannical and environmentally destructive species that we find in the modern age.

While Rousseau presents his "pure state of nature" as a reasonably certain fact, the tone of Part Two of the *Second Discourse* is explicitly hypothetical. Rousseau offers possible explanations of how "two facts given as real are to be connected by a series of intermediate facts which are unknown or considered as such" (*SD*, 3: 42–43). It ought to be noted in this regard that a consideration of the "original state" of human beings in the world and discussion of the path by which humanity came to its present condition is a mode of argument adopted by many streams of environmental thought, including eco-feminism,[12] eco-Marxism,[13] the social ecology of Murray Bookchin,[15] and deep ecology.[15]

Indeed, any system of thought that argues that the human race is naturally, and ought to be, "at peace with all nature," but is now "ruining everything" in the vain hope of making itself "the sole master of the universe" (*SD*, 3: 75–76, note *7), must provide some account of how such a destructive misstep could occur in light of the fact that what is *wrong* with the human species cannot be inextricably part of who we are or of the natural world from which we emerged. Rousseau argues that natural man was entirely free of any systemic conflict with nonhuman nature because he lacked *the passions* that fuel the expansive desires that lead to the degradation of the natural world. The expansion of the scope of human desire by vanity, the passion that Rousseau terms *amour-propre*, ultimately leads to the technologies that have first expanded human desire, and then human capability, albeit at a tremendous cost to the natural world. In other words, Rousseau argues that human beings have become hostile to the world because they have developed desires that the world can never entirely fulfill and because no increase in our domination or production can ultimately make us happy. Thus, Rousseau implicates the expansion of human desires as the true cause of humanity's disproportionate impact on the natural world and also suggests an openness to the fundamental reform of human perceptions of our "needs" as the basis for a more environmentalist order. For Rousseau, there is nothing "given" about either the particular things that human beings want or the scope of human desire in general terms. Both are malleable expressions of humanity's acquired passion of *amour-propre*.

Amour-propre is related to but distinct from the simple love of one's own immediate living (*amour de soi*) that was present in man in the "pure state of nature" and is present in all other animals (*SD*, 3: 91–92, note *12). *Amour-propre* is at the root of the civilized man's love of his own well-being, broadly defined as what is good for himself, his reputation, and those persons and objects that he would place in the category of "his own."[16] This restless and malleable passion underlies Rousseau's account of humanity's transformation from a solitary being to a social one, and all of its consequences. "He who willed that man be sociable touched his finger to the axis of the universe. With this slight movement I see the face of earth change and the vocation of mankind decided."[17] For Rousseau, *amour-propre* explains how a creature who was originally and naturally a "physical being unproblematically embedded in physical nature" could make the astonishing transition into the "the tyrant of himself and nature" (*SD*, 3: 26).[18]

With *amour-propre* awakened, human beings are increasingly motivated to appropriate resources from the natural world. With metallurgy and agriculture, Rousseau argues, humans effected a series of changes that undermined their connection to nature, but Rousseau insists that this transformation was guided by neither biological need nor a conscious plan for human well-being so much as by *amour-propre*'s unnatural and insatiable quest for esteem that the self enjoys in the eyes of others.[19] But lest we think that the "fatal acquisition" of *amour-propre* is wholly tragic, Rousseau celebrates what he calls "the happiest and most durable epoch," an era in human development that was both "the best for man" and "the veritable prime of the world" (*SD*, 3: 48). The early hunter-gatherers of this period, living in families and the first villages, are presented as a "golden mean." Their self-consciousness, activated by the comparative promptings of *amour-propre*, provided an enhanced "sentiment of their own existence" *within* nature. The ugly side of *amour-propre* manifested itself even in these first societies, as they sometimes fought battles with neighboring villages or killed a neighbor over the love of a potential mate

(*SD*, 3: 49).²⁰ Nevertheless, the damage was small until agriculture necessitated more complex social units, metallurgy provided more deadly weapons, and technology facilitated greater control of the natural world.

When we recognize that it is the expansive desires of *amour-propre* that drive the transformation of human beings into the "tyrants" of others and of nature, "tyrants" driven by desires that nature cannot fulfill, we can understand why Rousseau was so critical of the emerging technologies of early modernity. His criticisms set the stage for deeper critiques of the more totalizing technologies that would follow.

It is telling that even though Rousseau relentlessly criticizes the application of the sciences to satisfying ever-expanding human needs in both the Second Part of the *Second Discourse* and (even more pointedly) in the *First Discourse*, he relies heavily on the experimental methods of modern natural sciences to explicate how we might know our origins through historical anthropology and to better understand what modern technology is doing to the world. This scientific critique of science is not a contradiction for Rousseau because the issue is not about how the human mind *works* but about what it is put to work *for*. The motivations are what matter. Insofar as Rousseau, or another "more natural" human being, engages in "contemplation" only "to contribute to this beautiful system" and not to destroy or exploit it, scientific inquiry is not unworthy of "the Aristotles and Plinys of our century" (quoting *D*, 1: 9 [cited at length above] and *SD*, 3: 13). Like many modern environmentalists, Rousseau uses modern natural science to criticize modern technology.

Unnatural but Good Lives

Having fallen from nature, developed *amour-propre*, and fortified its acquisitive impulses with the powerful tools of amoral utilitarian thought and ever-advancing modern technology, humanity, according to Rousseau, has fundamentally fallen from that "natural" original state in which sustainable lives were possible. Modern man posed, in Rousseau's way of thinking, an existential threat to both human happiness and the natural preconditions of human existence. But Rousseau doesn't think that modern human beings are doomed. They may not be able to lead *the* good life, and they certainly cannot return to a *natural* (in the sense of "original") life, but they may live *a* good life. What makes such lives "good," in Rousseau's understanding, is a connection with or a formal similarity to the lives that human beings lived before the fall into *amour-propre*. This similarity or connection draws on the concept of "unity" that is essential to Rousseau's romance of the pre-fall human creature, who is one both within himself and with the nature that surrounds him. Recovering or creating some simulacrum of that lost or imagined unity is the essential goal for a relatively naturalized, or re-naturalized, human existence. One might argue that Rousseau, like John Locke and Hannah Arendt (discussed in chapters 5 and 14 of this volume), presents a theory of human habitation, or re-habitation, of nature. Like Locke and Arendt, Rousseau sees tensions between our transformation of nature and our ongoing dependence on nature.

There are five basic variants of the "good life" in Rousseau's writings: the life of man in, or very nearly in, the state of nature (which we have discussed in our analysis of the *Second Discourse*); the life of the citizen (exemplified by the Spartans and the citizen of *The Social Contract*); the life of the "natural man in society" (exemplified by Emile); the life enjoyed by isolated pockets of mountain dwellers whose lives, even in modernity, somewhat resemble those of the human being of the golden age of the *Second Discourse*; and the life of the solitary walker (exemplified, with difficulty, by Rousseau himself).[21] These lives represent divergent thoughts on the avenues that remain open to us as human beings alienated from nature and struggling to reconcile our *amour-propre* with the fragile prospects for our own happiness and for a sustainable basis for living with our fellow human beings within our beleaguered natural order. Although Laurence Cooper and Arthur Melzer take very different approaches to recovering our natural unity, I follow them in arguing that Rousseau thought that all these "good lives" were equally worthy for human beings and ought not to be considered hierarchically.

A brief exploration of each of these four models will allow us to draw out how these models appear in various streams of environmentalism. Each is only part of Rousseau's prescriptive picture of the possibilities for post-state-of-nature humanity. So long as we remain focused on their common roots in Rousseau's account of the fall of humanity from nature, each allows us to better understand Rousseau's efforts to explain how we might restore the unity of the human soul and how Rousseau's thoughts on the alternative methods might inform the projects of ecological thinkers.

I have already suggested that, for Rousseau, the life of "savage man"—a creature that lives sustainably in, or very nearly in, the state of nature—is no longer an option. Rousseau does, however, offer a variant: "a savage made to inhabit cities" *(E*, III: 205). In *Emile*, Rousseau presents the testimony of a tutor named Jean-Jacques, who recounts how he educated a young man so that his *amour-propre* would be constructed in such a way as to always mirror the dictates of his simple "love of self" (*amour de soi*). Even the most casual reader is immediately struck by the great amount of artifice that is necessary to contain and restrict Emile's imagination, to shape and control his desires, and to channel and check his *amour-propre*. As his tutor notes, "One must use a great deal of art to prevent social man from being totally artificial." (*E*, IV: 317) Emile's life is one in which this tutor employs this art to channel *amour-propre* so that this conventional passion will reliably echo the small, quiet impulsion of nature. All of this is hidden from Emile's view because he can never sense that he is subservient to another lest his *amour-propre* be offended by his subordination. He has to think he is being governed by and living in accordance with nature even when the "voice of nature" is supplied by the tutor (*E*, I: 48 and 67, II: 83–84). Ultimately, Emile's sense of himself, although artificial in its origins, is largely consistent with what it would have been in the forever-lost "pure state of nature."

Among Rousseau's archetypes of possible good lives, the person who can most actively and truly see himself as part of a "whole" is the "Spartan citizen," the product of a society like that envisioned in *The Social Contract*. In fact, Rousseau's citizen sees himself *only* as part of the whole, and is willing to give himself for the whole because he believes in his heart of hearts that without the whole he is nothing (*SC*, 4: 139–141). Rousseau argues that such a person is, in a particularly important sense, no longer natural.[22] Teaching human beings to overlook themselves requires a thorough de-naturing that must be accomplished through a highly regulated education that teaches children to see themselves only as part of the whole. This fulfills a remarkable statement in *Emile*: "Good social institutions are those that best know how to denature man." (I: 39–40) This "artificial person" is a formal imitation of the natural unity of "natural man" in that the Spartan is never conflicted or confused by the contending passions of different types of "love of self" or different sources of duty.[23] It is in appeals to develop this sort of duty that Rousseau's vision of the *Social Contract* is echoed in Green philosophies that look to a more active state to impose a sense of duty that will transcend self-interest and ground our very sense of self in the land where we live.

The "good life" that Rousseau presents most sympathetically is that of the "solitary walker." Rousseau casts himself in this role, arguing that through his own direct and unmediated experience of the natural world the solitary walker aspires to the sense of "an outright union, with either nature or existence" that Arne Naess and other environmentalist thinkers have since celebrated as a "mature" sense of self. The solitary walker's sense of the world is characterized by a paradoxical dynamic between intuition and profound thought, a peculiar blend of the "high and low."[24] In the *Reveries of the Solitary Walker* and the *Confessions*, we see Rousseau himself struggling to reach this remarkable position. These works contain Rousseau's most beautiful nature writing and considerable evidence that he ought to be considered among the founders of that genre. Rousseau appears to offer an intuitive approach to knowing philosophical truths about the nature of man in the world that now figures very prominently in the writings of many deep ecologists as the most direct route to the discovery of man's proper place in the world. Like Henry David Thoreau's *Walden*, Edward Abbey's *Desert Solitaire*, and Aldo Leopold's *Sand County Almanac*, Rousseau's *Reveries* features a sojourner whose felt experience of nature confirms the ecological conception of the world and thus produces an integrated vision of the human-nature relationship.[25] The experience of knowing nature through such intuition is best exemplified in several astonishing passages from the *Reveries* in which Rousseau gives himself over to the rhythms of nature and allows his very being to settle into these motions. (See *RSW*, Fifth Walk, 8: 41–48.) "At such times his senses are possessed by a deep and delightful reverie, and in a blissful self-abandonment he loses himself in the immensity of this beautiful order, with which he feels himself at one." (Seventh Walk, 8: 59) Rousseau claims that his study of nature is the appropriate model for "anyone ... who only wants to study nature in order to discover ever new reasons for loving her" (Seventh Walk, 8: 63–64). Such reflections account for Rousseau's widespread acknowledgment as father of the Romantic movement.[26]

It is easy to see that there are points of connection between the "good life" represented by the solitary walker and the ideals expressed by environmentalist thinkers. For instance, we can easily see the conceptual connection to Snyder's insistence that "the real work" of ecology is to restore the unity within ourselves that made us self-sufficient as human beings and would enable us to again live sustainably in the world.[27] But we can make sense of these conceptual connections only if we recognize that the solitary walker is in one crucial respect like the citizen of the *Social Contract* and like Emile. None of these archetypes, not even the solitary walker, is a "natural human being" in the original and purest sense. Even in the case of the solitary walker, it is only the sublimation of Rousseau's *amour-propre* that enables him to "extend his being" to human and nonhuman others, thus making his experience of oneness with nature possible.[28]

Second, Rousseau, or at least his literary incarnation in the *Reveries* and the *Confessions*, is a construction and an ideal. Rousseau presents this constructed ideal of himself in intricate narratives that constantly demonstrate the limits that constrain the realization of this ideal.[29] Thus, we are forced to recognize that the life of the solitary walker is one that is necessarily limited to a very few persons who can participate fully in the experiential insight of the solitary walker only under very peculiar conditions, and only for limited periods of time.

I add a last possibility that is in many respects related to that offered in *Emile* and yet importantly distinct for our purposes, namely the peculiar celebration of life in mountain villages that emerges in both the *Letter to D'Alembert* and the epistolary novel *Julie, or the Nouvelle Heloise*. These portraits offer less perfect models than the citizen, Emile, and the solitary walker, but perhaps this incompleteness is necessary because they are more realistically drawn. Many of the details of the more natural lives to be found in the mountain villages must be adapted to the peculiar circumstances of particular places and cultures in a way that is less necessary in Rousseau's more theoretical accounts. Rousseau's allusions to the lives lived in places such as Neufchatel represent a certain fusion of both the post-state-of-nature Emile and those largely innocent human beings living on the very edge of leaving the state of nature in what the *Second Discourse* calls the "golden mean between the indolence of the primitive state and the petulant activity of our vanity" (*SD*, 3: 46–48). I would argue that, although the human way of life that Rousseau sketches in the "mountain village" is *not* a prescription for the restoration of unity within the human soul, there is yet a sense in which it may nevertheless hold out some possibility of a sustainable balance of human desires and the good of the natural whole.

Indeed, a number of environmentalist writers (among them Henry David Thoreau and Wendell Berry) have drawn inspiration from similar possibilities of situating human beings within aesthetically striking and culturally defining natural settings that bind them to the land and its preservation. Because the works of such writers have unmistakable echoes in environmentalist literature, it is important to reflect on why they fall somewhat short of the models in Rousseau's other works, and how they represent an unstable resolution that may yet be more attainable though less sustainable than the others that Rousseau offers. The model of village life was simply becoming less tenable, even in the eighteenth century. Rousseau lamented that the closing circles of modern society were bringing these pockets of mountain dwellers into the industrial age (*RSW*, Seventh Walk, 8: 65–66; *Letter to D'Alembert* 10: 295–296).

Even this brief survey of Rousseau's prescriptive writings demonstrates the radical divergence among Rousseau's alternative visions of human life. However, what these writing *share* is more important than what separates them. Each is offered as an alternative that may correct the damage done in the fall that is chronicled in the *Second Discourse*.

Conclusion

The glaring differences among Rousseau's many models for a better way of human life have led detractors to criticize his works as confused, self-contradictory, and ultimately incoherent. "Committed environmentalist thinkers," John Meyer noted in *Political Nature*, "have argued for and against democracy, for and against authoritarianism, for and against anarchism, for and against civil society, for and against religion."[30] The same can be—and has been—said about Rousseau. This is no accident. Rousseau's suggestions (and I think that is the right word for them) point in many disparate directions, but all of them (including the education of *Emile*, the small autonomous republics of the *Letter to D'Alembert*, the quasi-authoritarian state of the *Social Contract*, the return to nature of the *Reveries of the Solitary Walker*, and the natural deism of the "Profession of Faith of the Savoyard Vicar") aim to restore the "natural," which is to say "the original," unity of the human animal. This unity would consist of placing human desires (again?) within the bounds of human capacities. Only then will human beings live within the capacities of the planet.

All of Rousseau's suggestions, however, reinforce one very important point. Rousseau never assumes that we can wholly undo the damage that *amour-propre* has done to the human soul, nor does he suggest that we can expect a sustainable and ecological human way of life to emerge organically simply by undoing this historical development; he never argues that there is one particular form of human self-conception that is uniquely compatible with and necessarily productive of a more ecological form of being in the world. There is something "unnatural" about human beings as we now know them, and restoring human life (and human lives) to some naturally sustainable scale will require manipulating that which is most "unnatural" about human beings to serve a "natural" end. Recognizing that Rousseau is exploring a wide range of possible "manipulative strategies" allows us to recognize both something vitally important for understanding Rousseau *and* something vitally important for understanding environmentalism. We need to recognize that the paradoxes and contradictions that we find in Rousseau's works don't indicate that Rousseau was confused about the challenges and difficulties that confronted human beings at the dawn of the modern age. He understood what was likely to be dangerous, destructive, and unsustainable about human modernity quite well. However, he did not think that there was one perfect way to meet these challenges and thus correct our unsustainable behaviors. All the answers that he suggests draw on those very passions and technological impulses that lay at the heart of the problem itself, and each of them is a partial and incomplete solution. As Todorov put it in his elegant study of Rousseau, "Does this mean that he contradicts himself? I don't think so. If there is a contradiction, it is in the human condition; there is nothing contradictory in the act of observing and describing a contradiction."[31]

Nearly all environmentalists, I would argue, begin from a perspective derived from Rousseau. Yet in failing to recognize their kinship with Rousseau, environmentalists miss how they are trapped in the paradoxes that emerge most clearly in a synoptic reading of Rousseau's complex and multivariate thought. As a result of not fully grasping the point that Rousseau (and, in somewhat similar ways, Martin Heidegger, as W. S. K. Cameron discusses in this volume) understood so well, namely that all attempts to "re-naturalize" humans or bring human existence (back?) into consonance with nature draw on, and to some degree reinforce, the human capacities that have placed us at odds with "nature" in the first place, environmentalists fail to appreciate the real limits and contradictions that pervade their projects. Rousseau anticipated the wide range of environmentalist stances toward modernity and its consequent human crises, but he did not think that any perfect solution was to be found in centralized planning, naturalized religion, decentralized communities, or some atavistic return to the wild, each of which offered some amelioration of some aspects of *amour-propre*'s dangers while exacerbating others. Appreciating what Rousseau can teach us about environmentalism brings, among other things, a greater appreciation of the limits of our environmentalist projects and a better sense of the depth and pervasiveness of our difficulties.

Thus, reading Rousseau through the problems posed by contemporary environmentalist theory, and reading those problems through a synoptic account of the system of Rousseau's thought, ought to leave us impressed by the necessity of the "natural" as a point of critical reference by which we can criticize the world in which we find ourselves and simultaneously make us suspicious of totalizing narratives of environmentalism that insist that any particular practical approach to orienting human life, or nonhuman life, is ontologically grounded in nature. In chapter 4, John Meyer shows that we shouldn't simply derive a political orientation from some conception of nature. In one sense, Rousseau violates this dictum. Although he does derive his major *programmatic* approaches to addressing our environmental crises from a conception of nature, I have argued that he is well aware, and that he is teaching his readers, that the plurality and the contingency of these approaches reveal that each of them is both humanly constructed and inherently political. Rousseau also reminds us why we must remain open to the paradoxical (and dangerous) prospect of conflating the natural and the conventional if we are to regain those aspects of a more natural (or at least consistent with the preservation of nature) human existence that remain open to us. In this regard, the antipolitical, asocial path of personal transformation that we find in Rousseau's *Reveries, Confessions,* and *Dialogues* offers a very real advantage over his programmatic writings insofar as it is possible that a human individual might be able to grasp, and even embrace, both sides of our liminal existence in a way that is aware of both what nature offers and what our awareness always prevents us from enjoying.

As thinkers and theorists who investigate humanity's harmful impacts upon and tenuous connection with the natural processes of our world, we must live in this tension, the very tension that permeates and in many ways unites the various elements of Rousseau's work. This tension must be alive in our theorizing if our theories are to provide both a fruitful basis for creative suggestions about how we may live in a way closer to "the first impulses of nature" and the skepticism about human-constructed substitutes for "natural" reality that, if believed uncritically, would rob us of our evolved potentialities for moral freedom as well as of the tantalizing possibility that we may once more feel a real and meaningful connection to the nature within us.

In this respect, Rousseau can teach us to be aware of the tension between caring deeply for the particular nature around us as the necessary and indispensable setting for our own existence and being appropriately suspicious of totalizing narratives that posit "Nature" as a knowable and attainable normative standard for our behavior. Reading environmentalist thought through Rousseau may help us recognize how the theoretical problems that environmentalist theory seeks to answer are not nearly as new, or distinct, or special as we sometimes imagine them to be. It may help us situate our theorizing not only in the sense of grounding it in particular issues, threats, and conflicts that we face in our particular lives and communities but also in the sense of recognizing its continuities with other, older traditions of thought about the human condition. I would argue that doing so doesn't distract us from thinking about what is unique in the crises we face but in fact helps us recognize how we might better understand our unique crises by seeing them in the context of the problematic character of human self-consciousness, and the dreams of infinite power that our self-consciousness generates. In a world that is finite and delicately balanced, such dreams are both delusional and dangerous. No theorist understood better than Rousseau how to wake us to the real perils that we pose to ourselves as self-conscious creatures.

Acknowledgments

This chapter draws on two previous publications: "Reverie as Political Argument: Rousseau and the Experience of Convergence in Environmental Political Thought," *Review of Politics* 68 (summer 2006): 474–499, and "The Solitary Walker in the Political World: The Paradoxes of Rousseau and Deep Ecology," *Political Theory* 34 (February 2006): 62–94. Rebecca Clark's collaboration on the latter of those articles was essential to the development of many of these points, and I am sure that some of what I have written here reflects her authorship and her conversation. Comments and suggestions on earlier versions of this essay (and the larger work from which it is drawn) by Tim Luke, Kimberly Smith, Zev Trachtenberg, Alexandra Cook, and Peter Cannavò have been extremely helpful.

Notes

1. *The Autocritique of the Enlightenment: Rousseau and the Philosophes* (Harvard University Press, 1998).
2. Among many examples of similar definitions of "modernity" by environmentalist authors, I would cite George Sessions, "Spinoza and Jeffers on Man in Nature," *Inquiry* 20 (1977): 481–528; Robyn Eckersley, *The Green State* (MIT Press, 2004); Kirkpatrick Sale, *Dwellers in the Land: The Bioregional Vision* (Sierra Club Books, 1985), 15–23; Joel Jay Kassiola, "Questions to Ponder in Understanding the Modern Predicament," in *Explorations in Environmental Political Theory: Thinking about What We Value* (Sharpe, 2003), 182–183; Gilbert Lafreniere, *The Decline of Nature: Environmental History and the Western Worldview* (Academica, 2007), chapters 5 and 6.

3. Tzevetan Todorov, *Frail Happiness: An Essay on Rousseau*, tr. John T. Scott and Robert D. Zaretsky (Pennsylvania State University Press, 2001), 2.

4. All citations of Rousseau's works, unless otherwise noted, are to the authoritative and nearly complete English edition edited by Roger Masters and Christopher Kelly and published by the University Press of New England (twelve volumes, 1990–2006). Each citation gives the volume number and the page number. The only exception to my reliance on the Masters and Kelly edition of Rousseau's collected works is the citation of the Bloom translation of *Emile*.

5. Andrew Biro traces the trope of speaking of human "alienation from nature" to Rousseau and thence forward into modern thought in *Denaturalizing Ecological Politics: Alienation from Nature from Rousseau to the Frankfurt School and Beyond* (University of Toronto Press, 2005).

6. The problem of the meaning of "nature" in Rousseau's works haunts all attempts to make sense of Rousseau's corpus. "While Rousseau is notorious for the difficulties unifying his thought presents," Jonathan Marks writes, "the difficulty of finding a univocal conception of nature in his thought may be suspected of being more challenging than most such difficulties, at least if the paucity of treatments of this undeniably important problem in the vast literature on Rousseau is any indication of how challenging it is." (*Perfection and Harmony in the Thought of Jean-Jacques Rousseau*, Cambridge University Press, 2005, 111) Marks attempts to confront this problem directly in his work. Laurence Cooper offers a somewhat different reading in *Rousseau, Nature, and the Problem of the Good Life* (Pennsylvania State University Press, 1999). I will argue that both authors' perspectives offer valuable resources for thinking about how we can understand the "nature" problem in environmentalist literature by looking at the various vantages on "nature" in Rousseau's works.

7. Rousseau, *Emile, or On Education*, tr. Allan Bloom (Basic Books, 1979), emphasis in original.

8. *Green Political Thought, second edition* (Oxford University Press, 1995), 112. See also Robyn Eckersley's discussion of autopoiesis in *Environmentalism and Political Theory: Toward an Ecocentric Approach* (SUNY Press, 1992), 60–61.

9. See Barry Commoner, *The Closing Circle: Nature, Man, and Technology* (Knopf, 1971), 41–45, as cited in Sessions, "Spinoza and Jeffers on Man in Nature."

10. See Arthur Melzer, *Natural Goodness of Man: On the System of Rousseau's Thought* (University of Chicago Press, 1990), 15–17.

11. Gary Snyder, *Earth House Hold* (New Directions, 1957), 120.

12. See, for example, the introduction to Carolyn Merchant's book *The Death of Nature* (Harper & Row, 1980).

13. See, for example, Howard Parsons, *Marx and Engels on Ecology* (Greenwood, 1978); Donald Lee, "On the Marxian View of the Relationship between Man and Nature," *Environmental Ethics* 2 (1980): 3–16; James O'Connor, *Natural Causes: Essays in Ecological Marxism* (Guilford, 1998).

14. See, for example, Murray Bookchin, *The Ecology of Freedom: The Emergence and Dissolution of Hierarchy* (Cheshire Books, 1982).

15. See Paul Shepard, *Nature and Madness* (Sierra Club Books, 1982) and Chellis Glendinning, "Recovery from Western Civilization" and George Sessions, "Ecocentrism and the Anthropocentric Detour," both in *Deep Ecology for the 21st Century*, ed. George Sessions (Shambhala, 1995). Also consider Ken Wilber, *Up from Eden: A Transpersonal View of Human Evolution* (Shambhala, 1996). Although Wilber is probably not a "deep ecologist" in the strict sense, his account of the transpersonal maturing of humanity through history is certainly consistent with or similar to the thought of pioneering deep ecologist Arne Naess and his followers.

16. *Second Discourse*, 3: 47: "Each one began to look at the others and to want to be looked at himself, and public esteem had a value." See also Cooper, *Rousseau, Nature, and the Problem of the Good Life*, 154.

17. As quoted in Todorov, *Frail Happiness*, 8.

18. John T. Scott, "The Theodicy of the *Second Discourse*," 697. See also Biro, *Denaturalizing Ecological Politics*.

19. On the importance that environmentalist thinkers attach to the development of agriculture in marking the turn in human history, see Max Oelschlaeger, *The Idea of Wilderness: From Prehistory to the Age of Ecology* (Yale University Press, 1991), 24–53. Also see, William Ophuls, *Requiem for Modern Politics: The Tragedy of the Enlightenment and the Challenge of the New Millennium* (Westview, 1997), 20: "In sum, the Neolithic Transition [from hunter-gatherers to fixed agricultural communities with private property] was *the* decisive event in human history. The ecological and social forces unleashed by the agricultural revolution ignited a vicious struggle for economic survival, political hegemony, and military supremacy that launched humanity on a tragic trajectory toward civilization."

20. Tim Luke and others criticize deep ecologists for failing to explain their position on warfare among tribal peoples or on the potentially environmentally destructive practices of tribal religions. See Luke, "The Dreams of Deep Ecology," *Telos* 76 (June 1988): 65–92, at 75–76 and 87.

21. This typology of "good lives" in Rousseau is suggested in Melzer, *Natural Goodness of Man*. Three of these lives are explored somewhat more fully (excepting the cases of the "citizen" of the *Social Contract* and the mountain villagers of the *Letter to D'Alembert*) in Cooper, *Rousseau, Nature, and the Problem of the Good Life*. See also Todorov, *Frail Happiness*.

22. See Cooper, *Rousseau, Nature, and the Problem of the Good Life*, 52–53; Melzer, *Natural Goodness of Man*, 94–96.

23. On the distinction between "formal" and "substantive" nature in Rousseau, see Cooper, *Rousseau, Nature, and the Problem of the Good Life*, 183–187; Melzer, *Natural Goodness of Man*, 90.

24. Cooper, *Rousseau, Nature, and the Problem of the Good Life*, 172.

25. In fact, in his *Confessions*, Rousseau describes the composition of the *Second Discourse* as an intuition that he received in the wilderness (5: 326). Compare deep ecologists' accounts of "experiencing the wilderness":Bill Devall and George Sessions, *Deep Ecology* (Gibbs Smith, 1985), 7–9 and 109–113; Arne Naess, "The

Shallow and the Deep, Long-Range Ecology Movement: A Summary," *Inquiry* 16 (1973), no. 1, 95–100.

26. See the brief mentions of Rousseau on pages 481 and 497 of Sessions, "Spinoza and Jeffers on Man and Nature." Gilbert LaFreniere has traced Rousseau's influence on and through Romanticism into contemporary environmental thought in "Rousseau and the European Roots of Environmentalism," *Environmental History Review* 14, no. 4 (1990): 41–72.

27 Gary Snyder, *The Real Work: Interviews and Talks 1964–1979* (New Directions, 1980).

28. See Laurence D. Cooper, "Between *Eros* and Will to Power: Rousseau and 'the Desire to Extend Our Being,'" *American Political Science Review* 98, no. 1 (2004): 105–120.

29. Both Cooper and Melzer suggest that Rousseau presents these portraits in a way that draws attention to the constructed character of his own idealization and thus to the unlikelihood of its actual occurrence and the limits of our human possibilities. See Melzer, *Natural Goodness of Man*, 92: "One major purpose of Rousseau's voluminous autobiographical writings ... is to describe the character of this most unified and natural of civilized ways of life. They also describe the bizarre and unnatural conditions that were needed to create it." Compare Cooper, *Rousseau, Nature, and the Problem of the Good Life*, 193, note 7.

30. John M. Meyer, *Political Nature: Environmentalism and the Interpretation of Western Thought* (MIT Press, 2001), 139.

31. Todorov, *Frail Happiness*, 19.

8

Edmund Burke: The Nature of Politics

Harlan Wilson

The thought of Edmund Burke (1729–1797) provides a distinctive way of looking at the relationship between nature and politics and, by extension, at environmental issues today. This is the case even though Burke can hardly be considered an "environmentalist" or even a thinker for whom the relations between humans and nonhuman nature were of paramount importance.

One way to approach Burke's thought is to consider his explicit utterances about the relations between humans and nonhuman "nature," or, more generally, to ask what his conceptions of "nature" look like and how they inform human affairs. Another way, more abstract, is to ask what ideas about order and change, authority and power, community and freedom—ideas that can shape or affect conceptions of human relations with the rest of nature—are embedded in his political thought. In this chapter, I will try to show several dimensions of his political and economic thought as they relate both to his conception of nature and to his ideas about order, authority, power, freedom, and the like. I will also try to show tensions in and limitations of his political thought, specifically in his treatment of the relationship among nature, politics, and political economy.

Burke is widely considered the father of modern conservative thought. His ideas invite us to see whether, and how, conservatism and conservation can be linked other than etymologically. He was a British statesman of Irish origin who served in the House of Commons from 1765 to 1795. Despite his reputation as a founder of conservatism, his own reputation during his political life was as a reform-minded Whig, not a Tory. Evidence that he was indeed reform-minded included his attempts to rein in royal authority, his support for conciliation of (if not independence for) the American colonies, his defense of protest over continuing British oppression of Irish Catholics, his prosecution of the impeachment of Warren Hastings of the East India Company for willful destruction of Indian traditions and ways of life, and his advocacy of a gradual end to slavery and the West Indies slave trade. Initially, he wasn't even as hostile to the French uprisings of 1789 as he later would be. But as the French Revolution proceeded through its moderate Girondist stage and on to its Jacobin episode, Burke developed an animosity toward the revolution and the new French state that amounted to rage.[1] In his best-known work, *Reflections on the Revolution in France*, Burke enunciated most clearly the conservative principles for which he became famous, thus obscuring and, according to some of his contemporaries, betraying the reformism for which he was known in his own time.

Burke himself declared that theory must follow, rather than direct or transform, practice (1987, 151).[2] Still, this formulation obscures the sense in which Burke's political thought has a strong aesthetic element that is especially evident in his 1757 work *A Philosophical Inquiry into the Origin of Our Ideas of the Sublime and Beautiful*. Although Burke usually didn't invoke aesthetic conceptions of sublimity and beauty directly in his political writings, many of these works contain subtle aesthetic evaluations. (Stephen White states that "the term 'aesthetics' did not appear in English until about 1800,"[3] but it is widely and justly used to characterize Burke's thinking.) Beyond this, Burke frequently appealed to "nature" to support his political ideas, though the nature to which he appealed usually wasn't aesthetically charged.

In evaluating the significance of Burke's thought for its bearing on the relationship between nature and the political realm, we must first consider these aesthetic elements and relate them to the way in which Burke theorized social and political complexity. Then we can look more closely at his appeals to "nature" as a justificatory trope or standard that applies to political action.

Aesthetics

In the *Inquiry*, Burke identified two types of aesthetic responses to natural objects and their representations. His treatment is profoundly dualistic: The sublime and the beautiful are mutually exclusive. Objects partake of either one quality or the other. The sublime consists above all of terror—of that which inspires awe, and often horror or fear (such as the "gloomy forest and howling wilderness") (1826, 70). Sublimity is rough, unpredictable, and associated with astonishment and magnificence. Beauty, on the other hand, inspires affection and love and is associated with smoothness, lightness, and gracefulness, though not with symmetry.

Though Burke employed this distinction most often in regard to works of art (he seems to have had little use for "nature unrefined"), he often employed it in regard to natural objects.[4] For example:

> It is not the oak, the ash, or the elm, or any of the robust trees of the forest, which we consider as beautiful; they are awful and majestic; they inspire a sort of reverence. It is the delicate myrtle, it is the orange, it is the almond, it is the jasmine, it is the vine, which we look upon as vegetable beauties.

For Burke, sublimity doesn't entail proportion or symmetry. It emphasizes the jagged edges of terror and fear. But neither does beauty imply proportion: Burke criticized topiary horticulture for its violence toward nature and French formal gardens for their excessive regularity.

Burke also, on occasion, applied his aesthetic categories to judgments about social and political matters. For example, sublimity is more individualistic, beauty more social. Political life involves aspects of both sublimity and beauty—that is, fear and terror along with sociability and "loveliness." Sublimity implies hard-edged coercion; beauty implies affection and willing subordination. The political ruler is two-faced: shock and awe on one side, kindness and gentleness on the other.

In the *Reflections*, Burke takes aim at French formal gardens, connecting his aesthetic judgment with a critique of radical French political practice:

> The French builders, clearing away as mere rubbish whatever they found and, like their ornamental gardeners, forming everything into an exact level, propose to rest the whole local and general legislature on three bases of three different kinds: one geometrical, one arithmetical, and the third financial. ... [This] calls for no great legislative talents. Nothing more than an accurate land surveyor, with his chain, sight, and theodolite, is requisite for such a plan as this. In the old divisions of the country, various accidents at various times and the ebb and flow of various properties and jurisdictions settled their bounds. These bounds were not made upon any fixed system. (1987, 152)

Good gardening is a matter of allowing art and "nature" to cooperate through respect and nurture of what is given. That aesthetic sentiments such as beauty may be applied to politics is the clear portent of Burke's statement that "to make us love our country, our country ought to be lovely" (1987, 68). Indeed, he explicitly appealed to his colleagues not to "break up this beautiful order."[5] From this point of view, what was wrong with the French Revolution was that it was ugly or, perhaps, as White suggests, that it cultivated a kind of "false" or inappropriate sublimity. Though Burke certainly recognized a place for sublimity in politics and the state—for the emotions of pain, fear, majesty, reverence, and sometimes terror, associated with the state—he tended increasingly to see beauty rather than sublimity in the political realm.[6]

Burke's distinction is also gendered: sublimity is masculine, beauty feminine.[7] "The beauty of women is considerably owing to their weakness or delicacy." (1826, 165) Mary Wollstonecraft criticized Burke for applying aesthetic categories to both women and politics. But because Burke more and more came to think of the political realm as "beautiful" rather than sublime,[8] Wollstonecraft could attack Burke and his ideas as effeminate and as characterized by excess sensibility, as opposed to Reason—surely one of the great ironic reversals of literary criticism.[9]

Burke didn't consider that aesthetic judgments might be relative to circumstances. For example, as White comments, today an oak tree hardly evokes a traditional sense of the sublime.[10] Perhaps today some of us would call the rounded Appalachian Mountains or the Lake District of England "beautiful," and would think of the Alps or the High Sierra as "sublime" in Burke's terms. Others might contest those judgments. And though we might variously apply these aesthetic terms to human beings and their roles, many of us now question Burke's gender-based judgments and would contest the sharp, gendered dualism he asserts.

The aestheticizing of politics raises interesting questions for environmental political thought. What sorts of aesthetic judgments lie behind different policy or political priorities? Should wilderness protection be defended because the wild belongs to the domain of the sublime, whereas agrarian conservation invokes the beautiful? And for what sort of politics—affectionate, hard-edged, compromising, magnificent, or risk-taking—should environmental politics strive? Many environmental political theorists will say that sustainability and climate change are issues too urgent for human and planetary welfare to be held captive to subjective, contestable aesthetic judgments. Yet Burke's discussion at least inspires a worthwhile conversation that opens up some significant questions. What is the appropriate place of aesthetic judgments in environmental policy and politics? What are the natural, social, and political aesthetics of a planet worth inhabiting, and of the politics necessary to ensure the survival of such a planet?[11]

Complexity and Society

Another aspect of Burke's political outlook with a source in aesthetics and implications for green politics has to do with complexity. Burke nowhere defined "complexity," but the following characterization seems consistent with his usage. Conceptually, the elements of complexity might include size, differentiation, and interdependence of elements, and in addition a subjective element of "complication" or intricacy that defies human comprehension and control.[12]

Burke was one of the first political theorists, if not the first, to appeal explicitly to complexity both as a characterization of order and as a normative standard:

> Indeed in the gross and complicated mass of human passions and concerns the primitive rights of men undergo such a variety of refractions and reflections that it becomes absurd to talk of them as if they continued in the simplicity of their original direction. The nature of man is intricate; the objects of society are of the greatest possible complexity; and, therefore, no simple disposition or direction of power can be suitable either to man's nature or to the quality of his affairs. When I hear the simplicity of contrivance aimed at and boasted of in any new political constitutions, I am at no loss to decide that the artificers are grossly ignorant of their trade or totally negligent of their duty. (1987, 54)

For Burke, both human nature and institutions are highly complex. The human mind, in contemplating the interplay between human nature and institutions, must confront those complexities.

The idea of complexity cannot be easily assimilated to the sublime/beautiful binary, though I suppose one might say that a complex society was a thing of beauty to Burke. In any case, for Burke a "normal" political society is one that is so intricate that it can't be grasped or managed as a whole. Thus, the context for the passage just quoted is Burke's critique of what he regarded as simplistic notions of natural, "metaphysical" rights.

With regard to institutions, a healthy political society will have many different, interdependent parts. It is important to see that Burke didn't look at interdependence in a mechanistic way, but rather in relational terms. A society with complex interdependencies among its constituent institutions will be characterized by trust-based relationships, including political relationships. Because people trust one another, genuine authority relations, including personal authority, are possible. Because interdependence is essentially benign, societal complexity is not problematic, and there need be no overall management or superintendence of the whole.

For Burke, the error of overlooking complexity and regarding society as simple is fraught with consequences. The most common mistake is to reduce interdependent relations to a simple set of natural rights. Burke speaks of the dangers of "a simple view of the object, as it stands stripped of every relation, in all the nakedness and solitude of metaphysical abstraction" (1987, 7). Individual liberty, for example, must be viewed in terms of the context of human relations within which it has to be exercised. Burke held that if the habit were developed of regarding society as simple, society actually might become simple, at great cost to relationships of trust. Perhaps, just as creating artificial topiaries does violence to nonhuman nature, reduction to simplicity does violence to human nature and politics.[13]

Because, for Burke, interdependence consists ideally of trust (and authority) relations, complexity is experienced by members of an established social order as benign. As Michael Freeman has pointed out, Burke saw complexity not as bewildering but as protective. Circumstances may be complex, but in a healthy society individuals need not face the complexity alone, at once, or *in toto*.[14] No individual has to "cope" with a complexity that is essentially a buffer between oneself and primitiveness or savagery. One need not face all the consequences of social complexity alone.

Complexity also justifies the rule of elites. Only a few men are able to act politically; the others are the "thousands of great cattle, reposed beneath the shadow of the British oak, [who] chew the cud and are silent" (1987, 75). The opposite of a complex society, Burke argues, is one in which protective interdependences, the "decent drapery" of society, are torn off, generations become unlinked, and "men ... become little better than the flies of a summer" (1987, 67, 83). The complex order is maintained through the rule of those who are bred for positions of eminence and who protect the vulnerable.

There is a bit of mystification in Burke's appeal to complexity. His point of view is fundamentally aesthetic: Complexity is beautiful. What is missing in this discussion is any notion that social complexity itself might be deranged, that it could present obstacles to human thought and action. Burke, indeed, offers less a "theory" of complexity than an invocation—one that has been resorted to time and again by conservatives in order to stifle innovation. Burke's critique of simplicity is perhaps the first of many appeals to social complexity (including those of Hegel, Durkheim, Hayek, and many others) as an ideological reaction to the championing of "natural" simplicity by radicals such as Rousseau and Paine.

Burke's invocation of "complexity" leads to his famous transformation of the social-contract metaphor, in which he evokes a vision of interdependence and complexity over time as well as space. Parodying the Lockean and "new Whig" notions of contract, with their regrettable odor of popular sovereignty, Burke transforms the metaphor as follows:

> Society is indeed a contract. Subordinate contracts for objects of mere occasional interest may be dissolved at pleasure—but the state ought not to be considered

as nothing better than a partnership agreement in a trade of pepper and coffee, calico, or tobacco, or some other such low concern, to be taken up for a little temporary interest, and to be dissolved by the fancy of the parties. It is to be looked on with other reverence, because it is not a partnership in things subservient only to the gross animal existence of a temporary and perishable nature. It is a partnership in all science; a partnership in all art; a partnership in every virtue and in all perfection. As the ends of such a partnership cannot be obtained in many generations, it becomes a partnership not only between those who are living, but between those who are living, those who are dead, and those who are to be born. Each contract of each particular state is but a clause in the great primeval contract of eternal society, linking the lower with the higher natures, connecting the visible and invisible world, according to a fixed compact sanctioned by the inviolable oath which holds all physical and all moral natures, each in their appointed place. This law is not subject to the will of those who by an obligation above them, and infinitely superior, are bound to submit their will to that law. The municipal corporations of that universal kingdom are not morally at liberty at their pleasure, and on their speculations of a contingent improvement, wholly to separate and tear asunder the bands of their subordinate community and to dissolve it into an unsocial, uncivil, unconnected chaos of elementary principles. (1987, 85)

We are, Burke says, "life-renters," temporary possessors of our society and the land. Break those linkages and "men would become little better than the flies of a summer" (1987, 83–84); surely barbarism would result.

Burke's expression of intergenerational obligation is perhaps the most striking way in which his theory can support an environmental ethic. One has a duty, not only to one's living fellows, but also to one's ancestors and to posterity. In their treatments of John Locke, Karl Marx, and Hannah Arendt in this volume, Zev Trachtenberg, Timothy Luke, and Peter Cannavò, respectively, discuss how divergent elements of the conceptions of sustainability may be discerned and explored in thinkers who are commonly taken to be very different from one another and from current green thought. In Burke, we see one major strand of environmental sustainability: a commitment to that which "meets the needs of the present without compromising the ability of future generations to meet their own needs."[15] Here, Burke's approach seems superior to those of Thomas Paine and Jeremy Bentham, who had little sense of the complexities of intergenerational obligation. Though Burke didn't anticipate the analytical mode of treatment of this issue in environmental ethics, he did articulate the consequences of failing to consider intergenerational obligations in ways that could readily be extended to environmental contexts. Looking to Burke's embrace of complexity, one might go even further and assert that he envisioned a society working by "ecological" principles, but that seems a bit of a stretch.

The Authority of Nature

The "contract" passage cited in the preceding section displays Burke's idea of the subordination of human society to a "natural" moral order. Burke, in a tradition going back to Aristotle, sought to validate arguments and conventions by invoking "nature." What did Burke mean by the word 'nature'—and by 'Nature'?

First, Burke did *not* mean a pre-political or even a pre-social "state of nature" similar to that of Locke or Rousseau. "We are as much, at least, in a state of Nature in formed manhood as in immature and helpless infancy," wrote Burke in his 1791 *Appeal from the New to the Old Whigs*,[16] for humans are "naturally" interdependent creatures. And though he believed that nature is not of our making, Burke also maintained that "art is man's nature."[17] One might say, contrary to Rousseau, that for Burke civilization and artifice were "natural." Artifice doesn't obscure what makes us human; it *is* what makes us human.

Burke didn't simply appeal to a generic moral order of nature. He appealed to "natural law" often enough, it is true, in the traditional sense of a moral order that can be accessible to humans' knowledge and is the basic source of our obligations.[18] But in many passages he seems to go further and imply, or even state, that the very constitution of Nature provides a model of the proper functioning of political society, and that we are to follow the directions of Nature in shaping or preserving political and social arrangements.

In *Reflections* he writes of a "method of nature" that ought to be preserved in the conduct of the polity, and of the "happy effect of following nature." Here he is referring to the British constitution, which "preserves a unity in so great a diversity of its parts" (1987, 29). Nature, he writes, consists in a "reciprocal struggle of discordant powers" that "draws out the harmony of the universe" (1987, 31). Here, Burke suggests that a natural order—a meaningful, capitalized Nature—comprehends difference, plurality, and even conflict within a harmonious whole. Nature also teaches "moderation."

Political societies, regrettably, don't always follow the model of Nature. Burke equates the "unnatural" with the disorderly (1987, 34). Nature here is more than an invocation; it becomes a weapon of critique of the "unnatural." Further, there is a "natural aristocracy" consisting of the able and well-born (after all, society is natural).[19] Equality and egalitarianism, it seems, are "unnatural"—in sharp contrast with the egalitarian implications of harmony with nature suggested by Barbara Seeber's discussion of

Wollstonecraft in this volume. And indeed, Burke condemns the French revolutionary practices that were so prominently championed by Wollstonecraft and the resulting French state as "unnatural," just as he will go on to characterize departures from laissez-faire economics as "unnatural." Men can refuse to obey the "laws" of Nature, but Nature takes "her" revenge.[20]

Thus, Burke seems to suggest that political society is a model of complex order that should be followed in human practice. Society should mimic the universe. This anticipates the overenthusiastic ecological theorists who apply naturalistic inferences from the "complexity" depicted by ecological science to their preferred state of human interaction. Social order becomes part of, or an outgrowth from, "natural" order.[21]

In John Meyer's terms, Burke's invocation of nature appears "directive" rather than "constitutive"; that is, nature actually tells us what to do, rather than establish the context and constraints within which human beings must make choices. Readers of this volume will be aware, however, of a multiplicity of conceptions of nature, and of various justifications of political authority based on "nature," some much different from Burke's. Consider the contrasting conceptions of nature in the writings of Burke's contemporaries Rousseau and Hume, for example. Moreover, recent environmental political theory has thoroughly criticized such approaches.[22] Burke invoked nature as a discussion-stopper. To call a theory or practice a unnatural was intended to leave no further room for argument. Burke, after all, was one of the great masters of political rhetoric.

Precaution and Stewardship

From an environmentalist standpoint, perhaps the most valuable insight in Burke's writings, aside from his insistence on intergenerational obligations, can be found in his warnings about taking risks within fragile institutions and about the likelihood of unanticipated consequences in a complex social order. This perspective led Burke to something very close to what is now called the *precautionary principle*, i.e., that the policy presumption should be in favor of not risking harm, even in the absence of complete consensus on the certainty of harm.[23] The presumption, then, or the burden of proof, is on the risk-takers—those who would disturb the established order. Burkean caution about change, when extended to non-human natural processes, reveals the sense in which much environmental thought and practice is basically conservative. It is skeptical about the assumption of progress and the beneficence of risk. And, to a large extent, it is pragmatic in style and policy.

Applying the Burkean version of the precautionary principle is, however, complicated. Burke's precautionary traditionalism extends to the intellect, and that has problematic environmental implications. Consider what he says about "prejudice":

> We are generally men of untaught feelings. ... Instead of casting away all our old prejudices, we cherish them to a very considerable degree, and ... we cherish them because they are prejudices; and the longer they have lasted and the more generally they have prevailed, the more we cherish t them. We are afraid to put men to live and trade each on his own private stock of reason, because we suspect that this stock in each man is small, and that the individuals would do better to avail themselves of the general bank and capital of nations and of ages. (1987, 76)

Because obligations to future generations require the presumption of continuity, "prejudices" in favor of the present order of things are to be respected and are presumed to take precedence. Some environmental wisdom is no doubt contained in the prejudices of traditional communities, for example when stacked up against the rationalism of experts and technocrats.[24] On the other hand, a phenomenon such as anthropogenic global climate change cannot be ameliorated by relying on "prejudices" and folk wisdom or on mystifications and aesthetic judgments. In fact, as Scott Cameron suggests in his discussion of Martin Heidegger in this volume, long-standing prejudices in favor of anthropocentrism, productivism, consumption, and maximization of economic growth, not to mention myths about climate change, have actually perpetuated the environmental crisis. As Cameron, drawing on Heidegger, shows, green politics is not just about conserving our inheritance from the past but also about challenging problematic conventions.

In addition to precaution, two other Burkean notions are relevant here: *stewardship* and *trusteeship*. Stewardship is the notion that we are put on Earth by God to care for what exists. Though Burke didn't extend this idea very far into care for nonhuman nature, such a notion could be easily expanded to include environmental concern. And the notion of stewardship leads to that of trusteeship. For Burke, stewardship requires the maintenance of a political elite as well as a landed class entitled to deference. That deference is based on knowledge and character, and also on family reputation and status. This relates to Burke's famous defense of representation, according to which the representative is expected to act as a trustee of national interests rather than a delegate of particular ones.[25] Burke is sometimes depicted as a backward-looking defender of titled aristocracy, but in fact he was far more concerned with preserving a *political* class with linkages to the landed gentry. As Don Herzog points out, he was never completely sanguine about the titled aristocracy.[26] And, as we shall see, Burke's dominant political elite had primary responsibility for maintaining a recognizably "modern" (by eighteenth-century standards) capitalist economy, which in turn sustained that elite.

Nevertheless, property, specifically landed property, was a major element of stewardship and trusteeship for Burke. His defense of private property wasn't based on libertarian doctrine or Lockean natural-rights theory, but rather on the need for traditions and generational continuities that inherited property could help fulfill. Descendants of the great landed families would clearly benefit from wise trusteeship in the present. A country without a prominent and wealthy political class would be one in which "sophisters and calculators," as well as professors with only literary knowledge, would inevitably wield power, yielding in the end to the rule of the mob, as in France (Burke 1987, 26). This trusteeship was to be preserved through, among other arrangements, continued severe restrictions on the political franchise.

It is reasonable to draw from Burke a notion of preservation that depends on a notion of national heritage. From this point of view, rapid change in the land and in its naturally beautiful (and sublime) characteristics could be resisted on grounds of common national pride. It is easy to imagine Burke siding with conservationists against economists on this matter, with its aesthetic resonances. There are echoes of this outlook in twentieth-century green conservatism in Britain, with its reliance on the National Trust and on great landed estates as a means of conserving local spaces and places against the pressures of the multitudes. Burke thus has some commonalties with theorists, like Arendt, who emphasize the importance of place.

Clearly, Burke took seriously the meaning of the word 'conserve', the root of both 'conservation' and 'conservatism'. 'Conserve' is derived from a Latin word meaning "to save or preserve." This notion implies both stewardship and trusteeship. Slow reform preserves traditions and continuities.

To summarize, when it comes to environmental protection, Burkean theory supports approaches such as trusteeship and the precautionary principle. Yet for Burke those approaches would, in practice, mean trusting political elites and the ruling classes—the landed gentry, in particular—to conserve land and other resources. In Burkean theory there is none of the argument, suggested by Wollstonecraft (see chapter 9 below) and advanced explicitly by Frederick Douglass and W. E. B. Du Bois (see chapter 12 below), that inegalitarian arrangements lead to abuse of nature. Moreover, Burke would justify conservation on aesthetic, cultural, and political grounds more than on scientific or economic ones, perhaps dismissing the latter to a greater degree than present-day environmentalists would.

Theory and Practice

For Burke, theory follows practice. Or, perhaps, it *should* follow practice. (Burke wasn't always clear about which.) Theory is not to be based on abstract, *a priori* principles, but rather on human experience and accumulated wisdom:

> In old establishments various correctives have been found for their aberrations from theory. Indeed, they are the results of various necessities and expediencies. They are not often constructed after any theory; theories are rather drawn from them. (1987, 151)

Neither ideology nor natural-rights political philosophy should be the basis for political action. Indeed, Burke was suspicious of abstractions in politics from any source, including natural science. For one thing, scientific experimentation and public commentary were dangerous in politics. And science was too hard-headed, too unsentimental.[27] An environmentalism inspired by Burke would not be one in which scientists would be on top or even much on tap. Rather, it would be inspired by human experience—which, in Burke's case, amounts to elite experience. And, as has been noted, with regard to climate change, experiential narratives and knowledge can be misleading because they focus on weather events when the real issue is climate patterns.

Burke's approach to theory and practice involves an immersion in the pragmatic, not only in terms of political thought, but in terms of political education as well. Elite rule is secured through apprenticeships that develop a certain pragmatic wisdom akin to Aristotelian phronēsis. Foundations would be reinforced through the inclusion and nurturing of apprentices gradually learning to have a stake in the system.[28] Change would be incremental, slow, accepting of folkways, and insistent on not disturbing the authority of traditional elites.[29] But although Burke's approach is ethically pragmatic and reformist, it bears little resemblance to our conception of environmental policy today, inasmuch as Burke's approach would be based, not on technical expertise, but on lived experience and on deliberation by wise trustee-representatives charged to articulate the public interest.

Burke's view that theory follows (or should follow) practice is, of course, a mainstay of conservative principles, as is his invocation of complexity and trusteeship. Burke, not unlike present-day environmentalists, thought it arrogant and prideful of humans to think they can redesign entire complex systems according to a single theoretical plan. Yet Burke's approach, when extended to environmental politics, would leave little room for radical experimentation or innovation. It would valorize a sort of pragmatism, though not the kind of pragmatism that characterizes quantitative policy analysis or ecologically informed experimentation.[30]

Political Economy

Burke didn't have much to say about political economy—about markets and whatever involvement the state might have in them—until quite late in his life. "Thoughts and Details on Scarcity"[31] was written in 1795, less than two years before his death and four years after the publication of the *Reflections*, as a reaction to the controversy over the Speenhamland Act. Like Jeremy Bentham and Thomas Malthus, Burke was vigorously opposed to the Speenhamland program,[32] whose purpose was to provide relief to the poor. His opposition gave him an opportunity to develop principles of economic analysis. The principles he came up with were quite harsh and doctrinaire. Indeed, in "Scarcity" Burke seems to betray his own principles of historically and aesthetically inspired thinking, and becomes a rigid ideologue. Burkean political economy reveals a tension between two strands of conservatism, one free-market and libertarian and one traditional and paternalist.

The other context for the "Scarcity" is the French Revolution and its leveling tendencies. As the Revolution became more radical, Burke allowed himself to be convinced that the leveling spirit could, and would, spread to England if economic policy didn't discourage it. Burke's notions of political economy must be understood in terms of his fear of social disorder.

Burke's position in "Scarcity" is that free trade and markets should be sacrosanct. Little if any "interference" by the state in markets could be justified. Markets alone, not traditional notions such as "just price" and "just wage," should dictate prices. According to "the nature of things," labor is a commodity, nothing more. The employer is compensated for his risk and investment by surplus value. Those who are not direct participants in voluntary contracts must mind their own business. "Zealots of the sect of regulation" ought to stay out of the fray. This includes regulation of child labor. There must be no redistribution of wealth toward greater equality. If the poor suffer, they must remember their place. Justice is purely commutative, based on obeying the market.[33] The multitude should not be allowed to dictate policy in place of the laws of the market. Price controls would result in popular "phrenzy."[34] And so on. The harshness of Burke's rhetoric almost rivals that of Malthus or the Social Darwinists later on, and, at least according to Trachtenberg's discussion in this volume, would far surpass any economic inegalitarianism advanced by Locke.

Burke's manner of justification should be familiar from our earlier discussion: Nature justifies all. Thus "the nature of things" is that labor is a commodity. The necessities of labor are provided by nature.[35] Unlike Marx, who, as Luke argues in this volume, saw the market as creating a metabolic rift between society and nature, Burke sees the principles of markets as "natural." The poor shouldn't be given welfare when "divine providence has pleased to withhold" it.[36] Justice is commutative, not distributive; it means obeying the market and protecting property and contractual right.[37] Whereas Friedrich Hayek and Milton Friedman defend free-market economic ideas on grounds of liberty and efficiency, Burke's justification of *laissez-faire* principles involves neither.

Burke hinted at, without developing, a Hayekian argument that the state shouldn't intervene effectively in economic matters because it lacks the synoptic perspective necessary to master the complexities of interactions. A thousand nameless circumstances, Burke says, can't be dictated in advance.[38] But he doesn't really develop that point much. Was that because he recognized that the sort of ideal interdependences he romanticized in *Reflections* and elsewhere didn't resemble the grim realities of industrial factories and market relationships? Probably not. He did, like Hayek, worry about excessive state power and authority, and about government intervention subverting market principles. Ultimately, however, Burke's argument relied not so much on libertarian principle or on Lockean rights as on the need for social order. Economic (market) order is good because it stabilizes a society and provides incentives for deference. Though Hayek certainly insisted that complexity was stabilizing, he would never have justified deference, or divine guidance, in the manner of Burke—indeed, Burke's position was far more *laissez-faire* than Hayek's.[39]

Politically, as J. G. A. Pocock has pointed out, Burke held "commercial progress to be part of the science of human nature and perfectly compatible with hereditary monarchy and landed aristocracy."[40] C. B. Macpherson agrees with this point and expands on it, noting that the political economy Burke inhabited was already a recognizably capitalist one, in which many members of the landed gentry and of the aristocracy were major participants.[41] Without deference there could be no accumulation.

Burke's position, then, was that deference is both a foundation and a result of unregulated markets—a view clearly at odds with present-day libertarian thinking, which celebrates virtually unlimited, unregulated freedom as "choice." For Burke, market arrangements, which are inevitable and "natural," require order, docility, and deference. Social mobility is to be feared. Redistribution of wealth can only promote disorder. The alternative would be Jacobin-style leveling. It is difficult to avoid Macpherson's inference that Burke was justifying class rule—not implicitly, as is typical with bourgeois justifications, but explicitly and openly.[42]

About the Enclosure Acts—the legally forced enclosure of formerly common lands that turned hundreds of thousands of peasants into urban refugees—Burke had little to say, perhaps because a public position might complicate his pro-market stance. According to Francis Canavan, he generally favored enclosure so long as it was carried out "in a fair and legal way."[43] What Burke meant by that isn't clear. Russell Kirk comments that enclosures were a source of great power to Whig magistrates, even though they undermined the British yeomanry.[44] Perhaps one can say that Burke lacked the enthusiasm for the economic benefits of enclosure that Locke exhibited a century earlier. Yet one might have expected a defender of traditional stability to see in enclosure a profound disturbance of continuities of life. In the end, however, Burke fully accepted the new market order, seeing in it a basis for continued social stability.

It is difficult to see how Burke's way of thinking about political economy can inspire any sort of environmentalist perspective. Burke's defense of markets is primarily concerned neither with libertarian values nor with productive efficiency, so it cannot generate a case for either "free-market environmentalism" or "green capitalism." It seems to contradict the "earlier" Burke (who articulated conservative values that more readily support conservation, the precautionary principle, and national heritage arguments) and the Arendtian view that a market-oriented society can end up devouring the natural and built landscape. These contradictions, however, can be somewhat reconciled if we understand the political economy Burke was idealizing: an emerging capitalist society in which the "upper classes" and associated political elites have the dominant roles and the many defer to the few for the sake of social order.

Conclusion

Burke's writings, if we factor out the *laissez-faire* justification of social deference, contain ample support for strong conservationist values, and perhaps for a general defense of sustainability. Relevant points here include the aestheticizing of politics, ideas of complexity with which ecological ideas may be imbricated, appeals to Nature as a source of moral order, obligations to future generations akin to the precautionary principle, notions of stewardship and trusteeship, and cultivation of loyalties to specific places and spaces.

It is just as important to identify what might be left out of a Burkean approach to environmental protection. First, if one believes that democracy is either a means to environmental sustainability or part of its content, Burke is hardly reassuring. In contrast, for example, to the Arendtian politics laid out in chapter 14 below, Burke had no faith in democracy as a primary means toward a sustainable future. He asserted that the "swinish multitude" was incapable of democratic self-government, that "a perfect democracy is ... the most shameless thing in the world," and that "as it is the most shameless, it is also the most fearless" (1987, 82). He had little use for "coffeehouse" discussions of politics, either; he denied that popular discussion had epistemic authority.[45] Thus we have Burke's image of the faithful, loyal cattle-like multitude in silent repose (see above) versus the "little, shriveled, meager, hopping though loud and troublesome (locusts) of the hour" (1987, 75). Clearly the reinvigoration of democracy is not part of the agenda.

Burke would undoubtedly be unsympathetic with what is now called environmental justice. For Burke, as has been noted, justice was only commutative. Burke hated the very thought of state-sponsored redistribution (and hence "distributive justice"), to say nothing of changes in power structures. He would be highly unlikely to view environmental sustainability as implicating environmental justice or injustice. Accordingly, he would not challenge inequalities of class and status.

A number of authors have attempted to develop Burkean ideas into a theory of "green conservatism."[46] A Burkean green conservatism would attempt to cultivate an attitude of trusteeship and stewardship on the part of citizens. It would probably see social stability and moral order as bound up with conservative green principles. It would muddle through a modest regime of state regulation of private industry. Despite Burke's own free-market excesses, green conservatism would probably reject the kind of neo-Malthusian harshness associated with Garrett Hardin's ideas, though it might well insist on some form of authoritarian politics. It would be uncomfortable with the libertarian ideology that inspires Terry Anderson and Donald Leal's book *Free Market Environmentalism*, though perhaps not with "free" markets themselves. It would be open to green capitalism of the sort once advocated by Paul Hawken and would certainly insist on private property rights. Contrary to the recent American Tea Party movement, it would urge respect, if not reverence, for the state and its modest regulatory functions. Accordingly, it would reject the liberal individualism characteristic of what passes for American conservatism. It would be partial to mainstream environmental groups and advocates while rejecting the self-righteousness of radical enviro-activism. It would reject any form of eco-socialism or eco-anarchism, though it would retain some of the animus of socialists toward excessive liberal individualism. It would insist on national sovereignty and distrust global initiatives, perhaps at the cost of international global climate agreements. It would be respectful of place-based environmental initiatives and sensibilities, perhaps encouraging restrictive immigration policy. Its relation to natural science and its authority in environmental matters would be uncertain, but probably skeptical, rejecting positivist epistemologies and scientific authority in politics. It would have difficulty dealing with crisis conditions born of the dominant structural and economic forces in the modern world, which are anything but conservative. It would not be particularly sympathetic to democracy, either in terms of the formal organization of the state or in the form of grass-roots movements. Nor would it be likely to view environmental justice as central to a sustainable society.

Notes

1. Isaac Kramnick, *The Rage of Edmund Burke* (Basic Books, 1977).

2. Here and below, citations of Burke 1987 refer to *Reflections on the Revolution in France* (Hackett). Citations of Burke 1826 refer to *The Works of the Right Honorable Edmund Burke* (printed for F. C. and J. Rivington).

3. Stephen K. White, *Edmund Burke: Modernity, Politics, and Aesthetics* (Sage, 1994), 5.

4. Russell Kirk, *The Conservative Mind*, seventh edition (Regnery, 1985), 51.

5. Isaac Kramnick, *The Portable Edmund Burke* (Viking, 1999), 496.

6. White, *Edmund Burke*, 21, 75ff.

7. Kramnick, *The Rage of Edmund Burke*, 122ff.

8. White, *Edmund Burke*, 48ff.

9. Mary Wollstonecraft, *A Vindication of the Rights of Men and A Vindication of the Rights of Woman*, ed. Sylvana Tomaselli (Cambridge University Press, 1993), 1–64.

10. White, *Edmund Burke*, 90.

11. Walter Benjamin connected Fascism with the "introduction of aesthetics into political life, remarking that "all efforts to render politics aesthetic culminate in one thing: war." This connection, however, seems not quite applicable to Burke, and not merely for historical reasons. Burke didn't seek to "aestheticize politics" as an instrumentality of ruling, and certainly had no notion of investing individual "heroic" leaders with aesthetic qualities, as Nietzsche did and as the Nazis and Fascists later did. Nor was Burke a sort of forerunner of deep ecology who sought to infuse aesthetic values into practice in some direct way. Rather, he showed how politics is always already invested with qualities that appropriately invoke emotional attachments on the part of citizens and subjects.

12. Harlan Wilson, "Complexity in Political Theory," in *Organized Social Complexity*, ed. T. R. La Porte (Princeton University Press, 1975).

13. Ibid.

14. Michael Freeman, *Edmund Burke and the Critique of Political Radicalism* (Blackwell, 1980). See also Wilson, "Complexity in Political Theory."

15. World Commission on Environment and Development, *Our Common Future* (Oxford University Press, 1987), 8.

16. Kramnick, *The Portable Edmund Burke*, 496.

17. Ibid.

18. Peter J. Stanlis, *Edmund Burke and the Natural Law* (University of Michigan Press, 1958).

19. Kramnick, *The Portable Edmund Burke*, 496.

20. Freeman, *Edmund Burke and the Critique of Political Radicalism*, 24.

21. Ibid., 16ff, 135; William Ophuls and A. Stephen Boyan Jr., *Ecology and the Politics of Scarcity Revisited* (Freeman, 1992), 294ff.

22. John M. Meyer, *Political Nature: Environmentalism and the Interpretation of Western Thought* (MIT Press, 2003), 6–8.

23. Kerry H. Whiteside, *Precautionary Politics* (MIT Press, 2006).

24. Vandana Shiva, *Staying Alive: Women, Ecology and Development* (Zed Books, 1989).

25. Kramnick, *The Rage of Edmund Burke*, 155–157.

26. Don Herzog, *Poisoning the Minds of the Lower Orders* (Princeton University Press, 1998), 89.

27. Freeman, *Edmund Burke and the Critique of Political Radicalism*, 75.

28. Kramnick, *The Portable Edmund Burke*, 46.

29. Michael Oakeshott, *Rationalism in Politics* (Basic Books, 1962), 1–36.

30. For an experimentally driven approach to green governance, see John S. Dryzek, *Rational Ecology: Environment and Political Economy* (Blackwell, 1987).

31. Kramnick, *The Portable Edmund Burke*, 194–212.

32. See, for example, Karl Polanyi, *The Great Transformation* (Beacon, 1944), 128. See also Gertrude Himmelfarb, *The Idea of Poverty: England in the Early Industrial Age* (Knopf, 1983).

33. Kramnick, *The Rage of Edmund Burke*, 195ff.

34. Ibid., 207.

35. Ibid., 197.

36. As quoted in Kramnick, *The Rage of Edmund Burke*, 209.

37. Kramnick, *The Rage of Edmund Burke*, 203.

38. Kramnick, *The Portable Edmund Burke*, 197, 202.

39. Linda C. Raeder, "The Liberalism/Conservatism of Edmund Burke and F. A. Hayek: A Critical Comparison," *Humanitas* X, no. 1 (1997): 70–88; Friedrich A. von Hayek, "The Results of Human Actions but Not of Human Design," in Hayek, *New Studies in Philosophy, Politics, and Economics* (University of Chicago Press, 1978).

40. J. G. A. Pocock, introduction to *Reflections on the Revolution in France*, by Edmund Burke (Hackett, 1987), xv.

41. C. B. Macpherson, *Burke* (Hill and Wang, 1980), 5, 37.

42. Ibid.

43. Francis Canavan, S.J., *The Political Economy of Edmund Burke* (Fordham University Press, 1995), 118–119.

44. Kirk, *The Conservative Mind*, 21–22.

45. Herzog, *Poisoning the Minds of the Lower Orders*, 183–184.

46. John Gray, *Beyond the New Right* (Routledge, 1993); John R. E. Bliese, *The Greening of Conservative America* (Westview, 2001); Roger Scruton, "Conservatism," in *Political Theory and the Ecological Challenge*, ed. Andrew Dobson and Robyn Eckersley (Cambridge University Press, 2006); Ophuls and Boyan, *Ecology and the Politics of Scarcity Revisited*; Kirk, *The Conservative Mind*; John Barry, "Straw Dogs, Blind Horses and Post-Humanism: The Greening of Gray?" *Critical Review of International Social and Political Philosophy* 9, no. 2 (2006): 243–262; Roger Scruton, *Green Philosophy: How to Think Seriously About the Planet* (Atlantic Books, 2012).

9

Mary Wollstonecraft: "Systemiz[ing] Oppression"—Feminism, Nature, and Animals

Barbara K. Seeber

Mary Wollstonecraft (1759–1797) is a central figure in the history of feminist thought. Her texts, in a range of genres including educational treatise, political tract, novel, and travel narrative, analyze the subordination of women within patriarchy and advocate educational reform. Wollstonecraft, most famously in *A Vindication of the Rights of Woman* (1792), protests a "false system of education" that "consider[s] females rather as women than human creatures" and limits their learning to pleasing accomplishments (such as music) for the marriage market.[1] Wollstonecraft's two novels, *Mary, A Fiction* (1788) and *The Wrongs of Woman: or, Maria* (1798), dramatize the political analysis set out in the *Vindication of the Rights of Woman*: women are shown as economically dependent on men; rather than choosing partnerships based on friendship and mutual esteem, they are enslaved by ideas of romance that result in unhappy and abusive marriages; their lives lack purpose. Her heroines question received ideas about marriage and education, and their struggles speak to the need and possibility of social transformation. Wollstonecraft anchored her political discourse in women's rational capacity: women are not creatures of emotion and instinct; like men, they are "rational creatures" (5: 75).

Wollstonecraft's work, I argue, is important not only to the history of feminism, but also to the specific history of ecofeminism. It clearly articulates a connection between the human-nature dualism and other social hierarchies and thus anticipates one of the central insights of contemporary ecofeminism. Recognizing that the subordination of women within patriarchy is rooted in the ideology of women's proximity to the natural and physical realms, rather than the rational (masculine), Wollstonecraft interrogates the social construction of not only women's but also animals' nature. Her argument for gender equality also proposes better treatment of animals. Wollstonecraft develops a political critique rooted in the perceived interconnectedness of structures of domination based on gender, class, *and* species.

In the travel narrative *Letters Written during a Short Residence in Sweden, Norway, and Denmark* (1796), Wollstonecraft attempts to reimagine the relationships between humans and nature and between humans and animals as non-hierarchical. It is significant that for Wollstonecraft encounters with landscape are encounters with a fully animate nature and beings who are similar to humans in their ability to feel pleasure and pain. In this recognition of continuities between human and nonhuman animals, we can see connections between Wollstonecraft and David Hume's philosophy as explored by Andrew Valls in this collection. In Wollstonecraft, the crucial question of how humans view nature and animals is inextricably connected to power relations among humans. Her texts are important to our understanding of the history of environmentalism, ecofeminism, and animal rights, and the sometimes vexed relationship among them.

Environmentalism, in its broadest terms, is concerned with the relationship between humanity and nature. Karen J. Warren, drawing on Aldo Leopold's seminal 1949 essay "The Land Ethic," summarizes the key components of the environmental ethic: "humans are co-members of the ecological community; humans should love and respect the land; and, it is wrong to destroy the integrity, stability, and beauty of the biotic community." Warren herself advances an ecofeminist position. While sharing in the aforementioned environmentalist principles, ecofeminism articulates a pointed critique of environmental ethics for its "ethical absolutism" and "conceptual essentialism," and, most importantly, for failing to acknowledge the connection between the domination of nature and the domination of women.[2] The main elements of ecofeminism, as summarized by Mary Mellor in *Feminism and Ecology*, are a critique of the dualism in Western patriarchal society between humanity and nature (a dualism in which "humanity" becomes "men," and women are classed with nature and both are subordinated), a recognition of how this dualism promotes a material relationship between women and nature, a call for "a non-destructive connectedness" between humanity and nature, and a focus on "the centrality of women to creating that connectedness." The last point is contentious among ecofeminists: positing women's special role in healing humanity's relationship to nature can come close to "returning to the essentialist arguments that denied women's equality in the first place."[3] Indeed, Victoria Davison argues for the distinction between "ecofeminine" positions (claiming a biological connection between women and nature, and celebrating it) and social constructionist positions (historicizing the association of women and nature as patriarchal domination).⁴ I see Wollstonecraft as anticipating the latter school. Ecofeminism is united in its assertion that the dualism of humanity (man) and nature underpins systems of oppression based on not only gender but also on race and class. That is, groups socially constructed as closer to nature rather than culture (the privileged term) are subordinated, and their subordination, in turn, is legitimized as natural.

Ecofeminism also comments on patriarchal tendencies within mainstream environmentalism ethics. Discussions of animals within environmentalist ethics focus on species preservation and the wild and overlook the lives of individual animals and domesticated animals. That tendency reinforces a patriarchal logic that devalues the particular, the personal, and (by association) the female. Yet while ecofeminism has criticized environmental ethics for abstracting nature, it arguably suffers a similar limitation in its elision of animals. For example, when Warren speaks of "women–other human Others–nature interconnections" as central to the ecofeminist project,⁵ the place of animals within these interconnections is left unclear as animals are subsumed within the broad category of nature. Indeed, as Carol J. Adams asks, "Where are animals in ecofeminist theory and practice?"⁶ Critics such as Adams, Josephine Donovan, and Karen Davis draw on the combined insights of ecofeminism and animal-rights discourses to theorize the specific "historical association of women and animals."⁷ They argue that ecofeminism should include animals in its analysis, and that it should argue for social justice across species lines.

Although there are tensions between ecofeminism and animal rights (primarily because of the latter's individualistic and abstract notion of rights), there exists a strategic alliance between them, as well as historical connections between the feminist and animal-rights movements.⁸ In eighteenth-century and nineteenth-century texts by women, arguments about gender and species are often interconnected. We see this clearly in the writings of Mary Wollstonecraft. The inclusion of both wild and domesticated animals in her ethical framework is a significant component of her feminism. Moreover, her focus on the animal is an important part of her thinking about the environment: nature is not an abstract category, but a living presence.

In a 1990 article titled "Animal Rights and Feminist Theory," Josephine Donovan cited Wollstonecraft as one in "a long list of first-wave feminists who advocated vegetarian or animal welfare reform," and listed *Vindication of the Rights of Woman* and *Original Stories from Real Life* in the attendant footnote.⁹ Even so, though numerous studies have demonstrated the emergence of animal-rights arguments in the eighteenth century and the early nineteenth century, Wollstonecraft has been seen as holding to the traditional view of the human-animal divide. Mary Mellor argues that "in common with Enlightenment thinking of the time, she framed her claim for a common humanity in terms of the distinctiveness of human beings from 'brute nature.'" Rod Preece writes that "despite her insistence on kindness to animals, the gulf she describes between humans and animals is far greater than any we find expressed by the Romantic poets." Christine Kenyon-Jones sees Wollstonecraft's attitudes to animals as "political[ly] conservative": "human beings' place in the chain of being" as superior "is stressed time and time again." Similarly, David Perkins, while acknowledging that Wollstonecraft is "strongly in favor of kindness to animals," sees her ultimately as "quite traditional" since she "maintained" that animal "behaviour is merely instinctive."[10]

These assessments of Wollstonecraft's view of animals don't take into account the full range of her writings. When we look at her work as a whole, we can see that she contributes to the eighteenth-century case for the ethical treatment of animals. In fact, she was quoted by George Nicholson as support for his vegetarian argument in *On the Primeval Diet of Man* (1801).[11]

Eighteenth-century animal welfare and rights discourses center on animals' sentience and ability to feel pain. In these texts, animal suffering matters in and of itself, but also intersects with other forms of oppression. In *A Dissertation on the Duty of Mercy and Sin of Cruelty to Brute Animals* (1776), Humphrey Primatt protests human slavery alongside animal suffering: "the white man (notwithstanding the barbarity of custom and prejudice) can have no right … to enslave and tyrannize over a black man." Noting that "cruelty to animals … tends to render those who practice it, cruel towards their own species," Thomas Young, in his 1798 *Essay on Humanity to Animals*, situates animal welfare alongside other claims for social justice, "the sufferings of the prisoner," "the condition of the poor," and "the abolition of the slave trade."[12] There are many parallels between Wollstonecraft's writings and these texts. Indeed, animals' ability to feel pain is a recurrent idea in Wollstonecraft's writings. Yet an important difference between Wollstonecraft and her contemporaries lies in the inclusion of gender as a fundamental variable in her political analysis.

Wollstonecraft understood the connections between the social construction of women's emotional "nature" as separate from men's and the subjugation of women as part of nature. In this she anticipates the ecofeminist theorist Val Plumwood, who argues that "the human essence is often seen as lying in maximizing control over the natural sphere (both within and without) and in qualities such as rationality, freedom, and transcendence of the material sphere," and that "these qualities are also identified as masculine and hence the *oppositional* model of the human coincides or converges with a masculine model."[13] We see this very clearly in *A Vindication of the Rights of Woman*, which challenges gendered programs of education such as the one set out by Jean-Jacques Rousseau in *Emile or On Education*. Rousseau argues that man and woman "ought not to have the same education." The title character's female counterpart, Sophie, is raised only to become a wife and mother, as "the whole education of women ought to relate to men." For Rousseau, "it is part of the order of nature that the woman obey the man." Moreover, the "law ... of nature" demands women's circumscribed education and role in society: "The quest of abstract and speculative truths, principles, and axioms in the sciences, for everything that tends to generalize ideas, is not within the competence of women. All their studies ought to be related to practice. It is for them to apply the principles man has found, and to make the observations which lead man to the establishment of principles." Given that Rousseau repeatedly speaks of the importance of women's "docility,"[14] Wollstonecraft concludes that women are to be raised as "gentle, domestic brutes" (5: 89) and excluded from humanity: "they are treated as a kind of subordinate being, and not as part of the human species" (5: 73). Wollstonecraft astutely recognizes that Rousseau's political theory, in effect, reduces women to the category of the animal. Hence, the argument for co-education in *Vindication of the Rights of Woman* takes as its starting point a reiteration of the human-animal divide: "In what does man's pre-eminence over the brute creation consist? The answer is as clear as that a half is less than the whole; in Reason." (5: 81) Women, like men, are rational beings, not animals. Yet Wollstonecraft's invocation of this familiar human/animal divide is strategic; it is also not as clear-cut as has been suggested.[15] It is significant that Wollstonecraft compares women's social condition to that of domesticated animals. For instance: "Considering the length of time that women have been dependent, is it surprising that some of them hug their chains, and fawn like the spaniel? 'These dogs,' observes a naturalist, 'at first kept their ears erect; but custom has superseded nature, and a token of fear is become a beauty.'" (5: 152) Sharon Ruston argues that Wollstonecraft's knowledge of contemporary natural history "gave her additional evidence of the characteristics which were both natural and unnatural to women, and enabled her to argue that women should be given equal rights."[16] The animals in the *Vindication* tend to be pets, not animals in their habitat; Wollstonecraft posits a parallel between women and animals under patriarchy, and suggests that the shaping of animals into pets is connected to the naturalizing of female subservience.[17] In *Mary,* the heroine's mother, a model of the femininity Wollstonecraft satirizes throughout her work, is accessorized with pets: two dogs "shared her bed, and reclined on cushions near her all the day." The narrator is careful to distinguish between the fashionable pet-keeping and taking "pleasure in providing for the subsistence and comfort of a living creature" (1: 8). In *Letters Written during a Short Residence,* Wollstonecraft describes animals in their natural habitat. The animals in the *Letters* are not suffering; they are not objects of pity; and some evade her observation. The occasion and genre of the political tracts must be kept in mind before labeling Wollstonecraft's position on animals as conventional. If we shift the focus from the famous polemical works to other genres, a different Wollstonecraft begins to emerge.

Her early educational writings all emphasize compassion for animals. In *Thoughts on the Education of Daughters* (1787), she suggests that if children "were told stories" of animals and "led to take an interest in their welfare and occupations" they "would be tender to them; as it is, they think man the only thing of consequence in the creation" (4: 44). In *Original Stories from Real Life; With Conversations, Calculated to Regulate the Affections, and Form the Mind to Truth and Goodness* (1788), Mrs. Mason explains "Goodness" to her female pupils: "It is, first, to avoid hurting any thing; and then, to contrive to give as much pleasure as you can" (4: 368). This system of ethics includes nonhuman animals. The first three chapters are titled "The Treatment of Animals." In chapter 1, Mary and Caroline progress from running "eagerly after some insects to destroy them" (4: 367) to nursing wounded birds who had been shot at by an "idle boy" (4: 368). Kindness is owed to animals, Mrs. Mason explains, not only because they are part of God's Creation but also because of their sentience: "Look at it [a wounded bird]. ... Do you not see [that] it suffers as much, and more than you did when you had the small-pox, [when] you were so tenderly nursed" (4: 369). Animals also are attributed emotional lives; they are capable of "strong parental affection": "if you take away their young, it almost kills them" (4: 373). Though *Original Stories* doesn't challenge the chain of being (men are superior to animals just "as men are inferior to angels" [4: 371]), it fosters an ethical awareness. The reader is asked to imagine herself in the place of an animal.

As Sylvia Bowerbank argues, *Original Stories* "is designed to stimulate relational ways of thinking even as the child learns the facts of natural history," and "the animal is granted status as a feeling subject requiring ethical consideration."[18] Wollstonecraft's argument for ethical treatment is based not only on the principle of sentience but also on the similarities between children and animals.

The educational writings frequently suggest that relations between humans and animals ought to be governed by the same principle governing relations between adults and children. For example, in *Original Stories*, Mrs. Mason delivers this retort to Mary's statement that "worms are of little consequence in the world": "Yet ... God cares for them, and gives them every thing that is necessary to render their existence comfortable. You are often troublesome—I am stronger than you—yet I do not kill you" (4: 368). Though the comparisons between animals and children can be seen as inscribing human dominance (or, in its less violent version, stewardship of the animal world), they simultaneously destabilize the hierarchical power relations of the human-animal divide. If animals and children are comparable, then animals' ethical status surely is increased in significant ways. Alan Richardson comments that Wollstonecraft "reject[s] the 'arbitrary principle' of parental authority and the 'blind obedience' that renders children 'slavish' in character."[19] In *Lessons* (1798), a fragment on the education of infants and children published posthumously by William Godwin, a mother says the following to her child:

Oh! the poor puppy has tumbled off the stool. Run and stroke him. Put a little milk in a saucer to comfort him. ... You are wiser than the dog, you must help him. The dog will love you for it, and run after you. I feed you and take care of you: you love me and follow me for it. When the book fell down on your foot, it gave you great pain. The poor dog felt the same pain just now. (4: 473)

Though the child is "wiser than the dog," the ability to feel "the same pain" and "love" crosses species lines. Nor is the topic of kindness to animals relegated to Wollstonecraft's writings for children. In *Vindication of the Rights of Woman*, she argues that "humanity to animals should be particularly inculcated as a part of national education" (5: 243):

Habitual cruelty is first caught at school, where it is one of the rare sports of the boys to torment the miserable brutes that fall in their way. The transition, as they grow up, from barbarity to brutes to domestic tyranny over wives, children, and servants, is very easy. Justice, or even benevolence, will not be a powerful spring of action unless it extends to the whole creation; nay, I believe that it may be delivered as an axiom, that those who can see pain, unmoved, will soon learn to inflict it. (5: 244)

Wollstonecraft's fiction further explores the interconnections between gender, class, and species oppression. In *Mary*, the heroine's father is an avid hunter *and* a domestic tyrant: "He hunted in the morning, and after eating an immoderate dinner, generally fell asleep" (1: 7). Mary "was continually in dread lest he should frighten her mother to death" (1: 10); in anger, he "had a dog hung" (1: 11) and, in a turn of poetic justice, he meets his death by being thrown from his horse. Similarly, in *The Wrongs of Woman*, the heroine's brother, "from tormenting insects and animals, ... became the despot of his brothers, and still more of his sisters" (1: 124). The connection between the suffering of animals and domestic tyranny is a pattern in Wollstonecraft's work and appears to be grounded in the author's lived experience. In the *Memoirs of the Author of a Vindication of the Rights of Woman*, William Godwin describes his wife's childhood in a violent home:

The conduct [her father] held toward the members of his family, was of the same kind as that he observed towards animals. He was for the most part extravagantly fond of them; but, when he was displeased, and this frequently happened, and for very trivial reasons, his anger was alarming. ... In some instance of passion exercised by her father to one of his dogs, she was accustomed to speak of her emotions of abhorrence, as having risen to agony.[20]

Animal cruelty doesn't happen only from the top down; as Wollstonecraft explains in *Vindication of the Rights of Woman*, it also is perpetrated as a compensation by those who "are trodden under foot by the rich": they "domineer over ... [animals] to revenge the insults that they are obliged to bear from their superiors" (5: 244). And she condemns those of the upper class who "continually exclaim ... against the cruelty of the vulgar to the brute creation" while treating their own servants as less than human (6: 254). Here one might also note strong parallels with the connections drawn by Frederick Douglass and W. E. B. Du Bois between racial oppression and environmental abuse, as discussed by Kimberly Smith in this volume.

Animals repeatedly figure as tropes for the suffering of women across class lines in *The Wrongs of Woman*. Jemima, the laboring-class servant with whom the imprisoned upper-class Maria forms a friendship, describes her life as one of being "treated like a creature of another species" (1: 108). Illegitimate, orphaned, and poor, she endured a childhood of abuse: "It seemed indeed the privilege of their superior nature to kick me about, like the dog or cat. If I were attentive, I was called fawning, if refractory, an obstinate mule, and like a mule I received their censure on my loaded back." (1: 109) "I was the filching cat, the ravenous dog, the dumb brute, who must bear all." (1: 109–10) Maria, too, uses these tropes: "I could not sometimes help regretting an early marriage; and that, in my haste to escape from a temporary dependence, and expand my newly fledged wings, in an unknown sky, I had been caught in a trap, and caged for life." (1: 138) Both women describe themselves as hunted animals (1: 110, 112, 160, 165, 168, 179). Although Wollstonecraft protests the Game Laws that restrict shooting to the land-owning class in *Vindication of the Rights of Men* (1790), her depictions of rural sports in general are negative. *The Female Reader* (1789) includes passages from William Cowper's *The Task* that denounce hunting, and in *The Vindication of the Rights of Woman* she "inveigh[s] against ... ardour in hunting, shooting, and gaming" (5: 74). The hunting trope connects the plight of the working-class and upper-class woman, reflecting the novel's intent "to show the wrongs of different classes of women, equally oppressive, though, from the difference of education, necessarily various" (1: 84). These tropes open up a space in which the reader is encouraged to criticize not only the abuse of women across class lines but also the abuse of animals. Since cruelty to animals paves the way for the cruel treatment of humans, and since animals, like humans, are sentient beings (a point repeatedly made in the early educational writings and noted above), the treatment of animals is of ethical and political import in Wollstonecraft's writings. In *The Wrongs of Woman*, she connects the ideologies that oppress along gender, class, and species lines, and interrogates "perversions of the understanding, which systematize oppression" (1: 88). The role of the animal is crucial in the systemizing of oppression. It is because Jemima is "view[ed] ... as a creature of another species" (1: 111) that she is treated cruelly and excluded from moral consideration. In Wollstonecraft's fiction, animals, like women, are abused, but when we turn to her travel narrative, we encounter representations of animals who evade human control.

In *Letters Written during a Short Residence in Sweden, Norway, and Denmark*, Wollstonecraft moves beyond depicting animals' suffering at the hands of humans, and instead attempts to relate to them outside the socially constructed human-animal divide. *Letters*, composed during the summer of 1795 on a business trip to Scandinavia that Wollstonecraft took on behalf of her lover, Gilbert Imlay, crosses many generic boundaries and covers a wide range of topics, among them capital punishment, the treatment of servants, mortality, theater, education, trade, and prison reform. In 1797 Robert Southey, praising the text's nature descriptions, wrote that Wollstonecraft had "made [him] in love with a cold climate, and frost and snow, with a northern moonlight."[21] Several readings have focused on the ways in which Wollstonecraft's nature descriptions significantly rework eighteenth-century aesthetic theories. Elizabeth Bohls states that *Letters* is a "critique [of] disinterested contemplation by destroying the distance between a perceiver and a statically framed scene"; Jeanne Moskal explains that "the roles of affectionate mother and picturesque traveler do not conflict but combine"; Beth Dolan Kautz argues that the speaker "presents herself as a whole person moving through landscapes, rather than as the conventional disembodied and distanced aesthetic eye."[22] These readings illuminate how Wollstonecraft subverts the convention of the detached masculine viewer of an objectified feminine landscape, and a number of critics have extended this analysis to make a claim for the *Letters* as an ecofeminist text. Karen Hust suggests that Wollstonecraft rewrites the nature-culture dualism by entering into a "dialogue with nature": she "connects ... deeply to the land while maintaining the difference between them." Lila Marz Harper identifies ecological consciousness in Wollstonecraft's recording of the destruction of nature caused by mining, canal-building, and glue manufacturing. Sylvia Bowerbank calls *Letters* a "significant text in the history of ecological feminism" because Wollstonecraft, "in her observations on the Scandinavian environment, . . . comes to understand the ongoing reciprocal relationships between human settlements and nonhuman life, both animate and inanimate, that makes civilization possible."[23] Wollstonecraft's representation of the animal world is an important, and overlooked, aspect of the text's ecofeminist potential. The reflections on the natural world go beyond climate, frost, snow, and moonlight to include bears, seals, starfish, cows, goats, eagles, vultures, seagulls, foxes, hares, crows, bittern, and wild geese. Wollstonecraft situates herself in the landscape, and this disruption of subject-object relations has important ramifications for the human-nature *and* human-animal hierarchies. One passage describes her coming upon a natural spring of water:

A slow fever preyed on me every night, during my residence in Sweden, and after I arrived at Tonsberg. By chance I found a fine rivulet filtered through the rocks, and confined in a bason for the cattle. It tasted to me like a chalybeat; at any rate it was pure; and the good effect of the various waters which invalids are sent to drink, depends, I believe, more on the air, exercise and change of scene, than on their medicinal qualities. I therefore determined to turn my morning walks towards it, and seek for health from the nymph of the fountain; partaking of the beverage offered to the tenants of the shade. (6: 280–281)

Nature here is not a static object; rather, Wollstonecraft emphasizes reciprocity between the spring and herself, thus undermining the human-nature dualism. She shares this reciprocity with the animal world, "partaking" of the same water as the cows. In this scene, animals, human and nonhuman alike, are embodied beings situated in a shared ecological space.

The observer-object dualism is also subverted when Wollstonecraft records her sighting of starfish during a rowing expedition near Tonsberg and remarks on her failure to see any seals:

Sometimes, to take up my oar, once more, when the sea was calm, I was amused by disturbing the innumerable young starfish which floated just below the surface: I had never observed them before; for they have not a hard shell, like those which I have seen on the sea-shore. They look like thickened water, with a white edge; and four purple circles, of different forms, were in the middle, over an incredible number of fibers, or white lines. Touching them, the cloudy substance would turn or close, first on one side, then on the other, very gracefully; but when I took one of them up in the ladle with which I heaved the water out of the boat, it appeared only a colourless jelly.

I did not see any of the seals, numbers of which followed our boat when we landed in Sweden; for though I like to sport in the water, I should have had no desire to join in their gambols. (6: 281)

Harper comments that Wollstonecraft's "observation points to a major weakness in a study of nature that is limited to the results of measurement and collection. The glob of colorless jelly in Wollstonecraft's ladle bears no resemblance to the graceful moving creature in the water. Only subjective and immediate observation could provide such information."[24] Moreover, I argue, Wollstonecraft recognizes that animals have agency; they are subjects, not objects. They withhold something from her, and do so "very gracefully," which elevates the action above mere instinct. They are not an open book—they remain outside our full comprehension and defy assimilation by humans. Similarly, the seals don't present themselves for viewing; neither does a "wild" bear Wollstonecraft "wished to have seen" (6: 263). And although she again sees a commonality between her and animals (like the seals, she enjoys "sport in the water"), she doesn't reduce them to sameness, and she recognizes that the seals' "gambols" are "their[s]."

Wollstonecraft concludes the passage quoted above by anticipating an interruption to her reverie: "Enough, you will say, of inanimate nature, and of brutes, to use the lordly phrase of man; let me hear something of the inhabitants" (6: 281). Here she sets into dialogue two views on animals: one, the narrator's, sees animals as subjects and indeed counts them among the "inhabitants"; the other does not. The latter perspective maintains the human-animal divide, and is clearly marked as not only anthropocentric but also androcentric: it is the "lordly" view. Wollstonecraft understands the human-nature dualism as patriarchal. The interruption of the "you" attempts to cast a wedge between culture and nature, between humans and animals, and between men and women. And though Wollstonecraft connects the female speaker with nature and animals, she does so in a way that undercuts the "naturalizing" of the associated gender hierarchy. The passage emphasizes incompleteness: she has not captured the "essence" of the starfish or that of the seals. Both creatures escape her. By extension, the culture/nature, man/animal, man/woman dichotomies are flawed oppositions derived from subjective and defective characterizations of the self and its position. It is also important that the critical "you" is not an active participant, only an observer of Wollstonecraft's encounters with nature. Wollstonecraft challenges the humanity-nature dualism by emphasizing immersion in the natural environment as well as similarities between humans and animals. Wollstonecraft doesn't abstract nature; for her, to think about nature also means to be in nature.

The split between the "I" and "You" in *Letters* also manifests itself in the division between the main body of the text (the letters) and the appendix. The letters describe animals with interest, respect, and affection: "I like to see animals sporting, and sympathize in their pains and pleasures." (6: 259) In the appendix, on the other hand, nature and animals are reduced to a strictly instrumental function. The first note provides factual information on Norway's geography, political organization, military, and economy, and it includes animals among the resources: "Its natural products are wood, silver, copper, and iron, a little gold has been found, fish, marble, and the skins of several animals." And after detailing the profits accrued through copper and iron production, Wollstonecraft writes: "The exportation of salted and dried fish is very considerable. In the year 1786 the returns for its exportation amounted to 749,200 rix-dollars, £169,840." (6: 347) Though earlier she lamented the destruction of nature ("to commerce every thing must give way; profit and profit are the only speculations"—6: 343), here the cost is evaded. Trees become wood, and the "pains and pleasures" of animals are erased as they are reduced to their value as food and leather.

The internal contradiction between the main text and the appendix is reflected in other passages. Similarly, we encounter moments when Wollstonecraft seems to reiterate the conventional Enlightenment view that man, endowed with the power of "mind," is the "lord of the creation." Her disdain for the local residents in Letter One is framed as their closeness to the "brute creation" (6: 245). In Letter Sixteen, she records with disapproval the drunken revelers who, "though the evening was fresh, ... were stretched on the grass like weary cattle." Later that evening, she enters a local inn and is "almost driven back by the stench—a softer phrase would not have conveyed an idea of the hot vapour that issued from an apartment, in which some eight or ten people were sleeping, not to reckon the cats and dogs stretched on the floor"; when leaving in the morning, she "hastened through the apartment ... not wishing to associate the idea of a pigstye with that of a human dwelling" (6: 314). These moments, troubling in their class prejudice, are in stark contrast to Wollstonecraft's identification with animals examined above, or her fond musings about her daughter Fanny, "I never saw a calf bounding in a meadow, that did not remind me of my little frolicker. A calf you say." And although this statement of affection is again interrupted by the skeptical "you" (6: 299), it remains a gesture toward the blurring of the boundaries between species. These contradictions and moments of ambivalence tell us much about the ideological constraints within which Wollstonecraft lived and wrote.

Thomas Taylor's satirical *Vindication of the Rights of Brutes* (1792) mocks Wollstonecraft's political theory by claiming that her argument for the rights of women might as well extend to the rights of animals (something Taylor takes to be self-evidently, indeed naturally, ludicrous). The political struggle to include women in the category of the "human" was far from over at the end of the eighteenth century. Woman's position as a thinking, speaking, and writing subject was at stake, and the tensions in Wollstonecraft's work reflect this. Though Wollstonecraft's strategic emphasis on reason seems to make her an unlikely contributor to ecofeminism, we need to take into account the full range of her work. As I have shown in this chapter, Wollstonecraft anticipates one of ecofeminism's most central insights: the connection between human-nature dualism and social hierarchies. In *Speaking for Nature*, Bowerbank traces the beginnings of environmentalist and ecofeminist movements in texts by seventeenth-century and eighteenth-century women writers. Wollstonecraft is an important part of this history. She theorizes the legitimization of social hierarchies as rooted in the construction of the human-nature dualism, sees sentience as common to both humans and animals, and posits sentience, not reason, as the determinant of ethical treatment of animals. And in *Letters Written during a Short Residence*, noted since its publication for its attentiveness to landscape, she undermines the boundary between observer and object, that between humans and nature, and that between humans and animals. Though not all environmentalist theorists and not all ecofeminist theorists focus on the human-animal relationship, that relationship emerges as pivotal in Wollstonecraft's writings on nature precisely because the animalizing of women, children, and the poor is a specific manifestation of the ways in which human-nature dualism underpins social hierarchy.

Notes

1. Mary Wollstonecraft, *The Works of Mary Wollstonecraft*, ed. Marilyn Butler and Janet Todd, volume 5 (Pickering & Chatto, 1989), 73. All subsequent parenthetical citations are of Butler and Todd's seven-volume collection (Pickering and Chatto, 1989).

2. Karen J. Warren, *Ecofeminist Philosophy: A Western Perspective on What It Is and Why It Matters* (Rowman & Littlefield, 2000), 82, 88. Also see Ariel Salleh, "The Ecofeminism/Deep Ecology Debate: A Reply to Patriarchal Reason," *Environmental Ethics* 14, no. 3 (1992): 195–216.

3. Mary Mellor, *Feminism and Ecology* (New York University Press, 1997), 59–60, 70.

4. Victoria Davison, "Is Ecofeminism Feminist?" in *Ecological Feminism*, ed. Karen J. Warren (Routledge, 1994). Andrée Collard and Joyce Contrucci's *Rape of the Wild: Man's Violence against Animals and the Earth* (Indiana University Press, 1989) is an example of the first school; Val Plumwood's *Feminism and the Mastery of Nature* (Routledge, 1993) is an example of the second. Mellor's *Feminism and Ecology* provides a comprehensive overview of the differences and continuities between theorists who posit "affinity of women with the natural world" (45) and those who emphasize social constructionism.

5. Warren, *Ecofeminist Philosophy*, 2.

6. Carol J. Adams, "Ecofeminism and the Eating of Animals," *Hypatia* 6, no. 1 (1991): 125–145.

7. Carol J. Adams and Josephine Donovan, *Animals and Women: Feminist Theoretical Explorations* (Duke University Press, 1995), 4.

8. The notion of animal rights is also criticized by ecofeminists for emphasizing animals' similarity with humans. For detailed discussions see Susanne Kappeler, "Speciesism, Racism, Nationalism … or the Power of Scientific Subjectivity," in *Animals and Women*, ed. Adams and Donovan, and Deane Curtin, "Towards an Ecological Ethic of Care," *Hypatia* 6, no. 1 (1991): 60–74.

9. Josephine Donovan, "Animal Rights and Feminist Theory," *Signs* 15, no. 2 (1990): 350–375, at 359.

10. Mellor, *Feminism and Ecology*, 72; Rod Preece, *Awe for the Tiger, Love for the Lamb: A Chronicle of Sensibility to Animals* (University of British Columbia Press, 2002), 203; Christine Kenyon-Jones, *Kindred Brutes: Animals in Romantic-Period Writing* (Ashgate, 2001), 64, 63; David Perkins, *Romanticism and Animal Rights* (Cambridge University Press, 2003), 26.

11. George Nicholson's *On the Primeval Diet of Man,* ed. Rod Preece (Mellen, 1999).

12. Humphrey Primatt, *A Dissertation on the Duty of Mercy and Sin of Cruelty to Brute Animals* (1776), in *Animal Rights and Souls in the Eighteenth Century*, volume 3, ed. Aaron Garrett (Thoemmes, 2000), 11; Thomas Young, *An Essay on the Humanity to Animals* (1798), in *Animal Rights and Souls in the Eighteenth Century*, volume 5, ed. Aaron Garrett (Thoemmes, 2000), 3, 2. See also Richard Dean, *An Essay on the Future Life of Brutes* (1768), in *Animal Rights and Souls in the Eighteenth Century*, volume 2, ed. Aaron Garrett (Thoemmes, 2000). The emphasis on sentience and the interconnectedness of systems of oppression continues to be pivotal in contemporary discussions about animals. See, for example, Peter Singer, *Animal Liberation: A New Ethics for Our Treatment of Animals* (Random House, 1975).

13. Val Plumwood, "Nature, Self, and Gender: Feminism, Environmental Philosophy, and the Critique of Rationalism," *Hypatia* 6, no. 1 (1991): 17–18. Also see Plumwood, *Feminism and the Mastery of Nature*.

14. Jean-Jacques Rousseau, *Emile or On Education*, tr. Allan Bloom (Basic Books, 1979), 363, 365, 407, 358, 386, 370.

15. Darren Howard ("Necessary Fictions: The 'Swinish Multitude' and the Rights of Man," *Studies in Romanticism* 47, no. 2, 2008: 161–178) demonstrates that the category of the human was "unstable" (178) in the political discourse of the 1790s, including that of Wollstonecraft. Howard states that in *Vindication of the Rights of Men* and *Vindication of the Rights of Woman* Wollstonecraft "bases her argument for universal equality on a concept of the human as universally rational at the same time [as] she relentlessly explores facets of human irrationality" (178) with the hope for a more rational human future. He doesn't argue for Wollstonecraft's interest in promoting animal welfare and rights, as I do.

16. Sharon Ruston, "Natural Rights and Natural History in Anna Barbauld and Mary Wollstonecraft," in *Literature and Science*, ed. Sharon Ruston (Brewer, 2008), 70.

17. Wollstonecraft's political tracts do admit ambivalence about animal souls. For example, in a footnote in *Vindication of the Rights of Men* (5: 31) Wollstonecraft qualifies the absoluteness of the human-animal distinction: "I do not now mean to discuss the intricate subject of their [animals'] mortality; reason may, perhaps, be given to them in the next stage of existence, if they are to mount in the scale of life, like men, by the medium of death."

18. Sylvia Bowerbank, *Speaking for Nature: Women and Ecologies of Early Modern England* (Johns Hopkins University Press, 2004), 152, 149.

19. Alan Richardson, "Mary Wollstonecraft on Education," in *The Cambridge Companion to Mary Wollstonecraft*, ed. Claudia L. Johnson (Cambridge University Press, 2002), 37.

20. William Godwin, *Memoirs of the Author of a Vindication of the Rights of Woman*, ed. Pamela Clemit and Gina Luria Walker (Broadview, 2001), 46.

21. Richard Holmes, introduction to Mary Wollstonecraft's *A Short Residence in Sweden, Norway and Denmark* and William Godwin's *Memoirs of the Author of the Rights of Woman* (Penguin, 1987), 17.

22. Elizabeth A. Bohls, *Women Travel Writers and the Language of Aesthetics, 1716–1818* (Cambridge University Press, 1995), 151; Jeanne Moskal, "The Picturesque and the Affectionate in Wollstonecraft's *Letters from Norway*," *Modern Language Quarterly* 52, no. 3 (1991): 263–294, at 269; Beth Dolan Kautz, "Mary Wollstonecraft's Salutary Picturesque: Curing Melancholia in the Landscape," *European Romantic Review* 13, no. 1 (2002): 35–48, at 42.

23. Karen Hust, "In Suspect Terrain: Mary Wollstonecraft Confronts Mother Nature in *Letters from Norway*," *Women's Studies* 25, no. 5 (1996): 483–505, at 498, 497; Lila Marz Harper, *Solitary Travelers: Nineteenth-Century Women's Travel Narratives and the Scientific Vocation* (Fairleigh Dickinson University Press, 2001); Sylvia Bowerbank, "The Bastille of Nature: Mary Wollstonecraft and Ecological Feminism," in *Mary Wollstonecraft's Journey to Scandinavia: Essays*, ed. Anka Ryall and Catherine Sandbach-Dahlström (Almquist & Wiksell, 2003), 181; Bowerbank, *Speaking for Nature*, 211.

24. Harper, *Solitary Travelers*, 45.

10

John Stuart Mill: The Greening of the Liberal Heritage

Piers H. G. Stephens

John Stuart Mill (1806–1873) is one of the greatest of liberal thinkers. Perhaps most famous for his classic defense of individual freedom *On Liberty* (1859), Mill fundamentally rethought utilitarian moral philosophy in *Utilitarianism* (1861), gave early voice to sexual egalitarianism in *The Subjection of Women* (1869), and produced the Victorian era's most influential work of economics: *Principles of Political Economy* (1848). In this chapter, I examine Mill's theoretical accounts of utilitarianism, human agency, liberty, and economic development. I maintain that his liberalism contains many of the priorities that green thinkers support, and that it offers a morally grounded vision of a sustainable society that remains attractive today.

I argue that the tendency of greens to *necessarily* link the anthropocentric bias of economic instrumentalism—the reduction of nature to primarily an instrument or resource for economic development and accumulation—with liberal individualism is misplaced: it is not individualism *per se* that should be the target but, as C. B. Macpherson put it, *possessive* individualism, of which Mill cannot be accused. Since I agree with Macpherson in seeing John Locke as a primary exemplar of possessive individualism and have argued elsewhere that Locke's position is antienvironmentalist in ways that Mill's is not,[1] I must confess to significant disagreement with my friend and fellow Locke scholar Zev Trachtenberg's treatment of Locke in this volume. Virtuous though his scholarship is, I believe he significantly underplays Locke's economically expansionist emphases and transformative dynamics, and I disagree with his treatment of Locke's provisos and of the religious dimension of his thought. Further details would take us too far afield from the topic at hand, but I regard the differences between Lockean possessive liberalism and Millian expressive liberalism as essential to identifying a liberal politics that can deliver environmentalist priorities. This chapter also hints at the ongoing debate over the compatibility of green politics' normative core—sustainability incorporating some version of respect for and protection of external nature—with certain types of liberalism.[2]

Grasping Mill's thought begins with understanding his intensive Benthamite utilitarian education under his father, James Mill, and his subsequent reaction against it. The basic story is simple: Brought up in an intellectual testing ground that had given him potent expertise in history, mathematics, political economy, classical languages, and philosophy by the start of his teens, at age 20 Mill suffered severe depression and a near breakdown, which he attributed to the imbalance between the excessive analytic emphasis in his education as against the paucity of emotional stimulation. Though still broadly loyal to utilitarianism, he found himself "stranded at the commencement of my voyage, with a well equipped ship and a rudder, but no sail" for "to know that a feeling would make me happy if I had it, did not give me the feeling."[3] Mill's slow recovery brought a transformation of perspective, motivating him to develop a many-sided and sophisticated philosophical system that incorporated and integrated much that had been absent from his Benthamite beginnings. Most immediately significant was his fundamental rethinking of utilitarian moral philosophy and its accounts of happiness and agency.

Utilitarianism, Romantic Nature, and Liberal Agency

Mill's psychological recovery was inspired by his reading of William Wordsworth, whose poems he found "addressed themselves powerfully to one of the strongest of my pleasurable susceptibilities, the love of rural objects and of natural scenery" in such a way as to express "not mere outward beauty, but states of feeling, and of thought colored by feeling, under the excitement of beauty." Mill found Wordsworth's poetry to thus "be the very culture of the feelings, which I was in quest of," a profound reassurance that "there was real permanent happiness in tranquil contemplation."[4] Mill's engagement with Romantic thought, a school his father's Benthamite utilitarianism had repudiated, went further, drawing influences from Coleridge and Goethe; it was from Goethe that he took a self-conscious emphasis on "many-sidedness," a notion that influenced his entire intellectual development but especially his conception of truth. His encounter with Romanticism also brought Mill back to reflect on Plato and the classical heritage, adding an extra ingredient for still broader synthesis. His new recognition that only those who "have their minds fixed on some object other than their own happiness" and who, "aiming thus at something else[,] find happiness by the way" are happy pushed Mill toward the indirect reliance on rules found in his reformulated utilitarian moral theory. There was also a correlative shift in Mill's thought toward a concern with character and virtues: "cultivation of the feelings became one of the cardinal points in my ethical and philosophical creed" with "maintenance of a due balance among the faculties" being "of primary importance."[5] Thus both a deontological style engagement with rules and a virtue-orientated concern for culture find their way into aspects of Mill's utilitarianism.

Though these biographical details help us understand the stimulus to Mill's reformulation, the philosophical significance of his new utilitarianism runs deeper for our purposes. Central to this reformulation was his introduction of a qualitative conception of pleasures, replacing Bentham's quantitative felicific calculus with a distinction between higher and lower pleasures that owed much to the Aristotelian *eudaimonia* discussed by Özgüç Orhan in this volume, especially in its emphasis on states of character and striving toward improvement of one's higher capacities. Mill wanted to eliminate from Bentham's utilitarianism the problem of antisocial but perhaps intense pleasures (e.g., those of the sadist) and the fixation with quantification that had drawn Charles Dickens's satirical ire in *Hard Times* (1854). Mill's solution was to appeal to an account of human capacities and a criterion of the experienced competent judge to give primacy to the higher pleasures: "It is better to be a human being dissatisfied than a pig satisfied; better to be Socrates dissatisfied than a fool satisfied. And if the fool, or the pig, are of a different opinion, it is because they only know their own side of the question. The other party to the comparison knows both sides."[6]

This emphasis on higher pleasures, especially intellectual pleasures engaged with the quest for truth, linked in turn to Mill's belief in social progress and his principles of liberty. In Mill's view, the "one social element which is ... predominant, and almost paramount, among the agents of the social progression" is "the state of the speculative faculties of mankind." Since this is "the main determining cause of the social progress," it must be encouraged in social policy, although relatively few people are fundamentally motivated by truth-seeking.[7] Primary among these encouragements is support for individual liberty in the quest for truth, which in turn mandates the arguments for maximal freedom of speech, enquiry, social experiment, and diversity of life advanced in *On Liberty*. That work's familiar arguments—that censoring opinions may deprive society of full or partial truths and of the better understanding vouchsafed to it by the open clash of debate, that geniuses need an atmosphere of freedom in which to operate, that the plurality of life options offered by a society based on individual liberty encourages greater human improvement than a highly regulated one—thus connect back to Mill's revised utilitarianism and his doctrines of human virtue and progress, but would not fit with Bentham's model.

Mill's revision of utilitarianism thus drew on Romantic and Greek influences to enrich Benthamite accounts of human capacities, breadth, and flourishing. As we shall see, it also utilized a new notion of moral agency. Before moving to that, however, we must note an important conceptual crossover between certain forms of anarchism, green political thought, and liberalism. Andrew Belsey notes that Presocratic nature, the all-embracing notion of *kosmos*, embodies conceptions of order, morality, harmony, and beauty immanent in the natural world, processively unfolding in organic spontaneous development. He adds that the linkage of *kosmos* with the anarchist ideal of free human development has survived as a thread of resistance in anti-authoritarian writings throughout the Western philosophical tradition.[8] Since *kosmos* is all-embracing, this tradition of thought points to the harmonious developmental principles of nature not merely as *outside* but also as *inside* the human. It is a tradition that celebrates *thymos* (spiritedness), and one that warns against the dangers of alienation through an excessive "civilization" that may divorce the individual from their inherent tendency of growth. According to Charles Frankel, the essence of this tradition is "nature as a principle of development," and this tradition tells us that "there is something under the human skin with its own vitality, something not wholly malleable, not susceptible to Skinnerian conditioning except at the price of destroying spontaneity, talent, zest, vitality." This notion of nature celebrates the natural as a sphere that transcends all powers of human rule and artifice, and insists that "no social plans ... can annul the random and unpredictable, that it is the inner vitality of human beings that counts for most, and that society should *provide the environment likely to safeguard this vitality*" (my emphasis).[9] This thematic philosophical linkage is shared by anarchism, green politics, and liberalism, each of which can be seen as a perspective from which all attempts to control and dominate, all claims to totalizing knowledge or authority, are to be regarded as suspicious and ripe for challenge. An awareness of both the importance of *thymos* and the difficulty involved in encapsulating it in any formal political system can thus be seen as a shared underlying theme of both green political discourse and certain forms of liberalism. As we shall see, this theme is found abundantly in Mill.

In keeping with this emphasis, Mill's synthesis of utilitarian, Romantic, and Greek thought avoids reductive, atomistic, or economistic models of the self while providing a set of guidelines for flourishing human agency and its ability to create a space in which the experience of nature may be granted a morally significant role. Mill is engaged in a rethinking and a broadening of the liberal empiricist approach to agency. Essentially, this approach, drawn from Locke and Bentham, saw individual human agency as based on knowledge drawn from multiple individual sensory experiences and later reflections upon the associations of these experiences, with negative or painful experiences subsequently avoided and positive ones desired again. The best recent account of Mill's revision of this approach is given by Robert Devigne.[10]

On Devigne's account, Mill started by recognizing that the egoist, calculative model of the self, associated with Benthamite utilitarianism and with negative conceptions of liberty as the mere absence of external coercion, was inadequate, for "if our understanding of liberty is restricted to what others cannot do to the individual by the exercise of their wills, society will ignore the task of cultivating self-mastery and thus truly free individuals."[11] The Benthamite view upheld associationism—the belief that all mental and moral feelings are created through experienced associations, which are internalized by connection to our pleasures and pains—but the price of this, Romantic critics charged, was to make the mind passive in relation to the external world and also to interpret even non-egoistic actions as self-interested. The problem was that if all complex phenomena emerge from simple particular ideas gained in personal sensation or reflection, and if these ideas are internalized according to their effectiveness in maximizing our pleasures and minimizing our pain, then even apparently non-egoistic motives, such as moral sympathy, turn out to be egoistic, because they always can be traced back to personal pleasure.

Mill's solution to these problems was to emphasize the mind's active role in transforming experiential particulars into general ideas that are qualitatively different from their antecedents, a process that Mill calls "mental chemistry"; his scheme thus claims that "when a complex feeling is generated out of elements very numerous and various ... the resulting feeling always seems ... very unlike any one of the elements composing it, [and] very unlike the sum of those elements."[12] Mill's "mental chemistry" thus attempts to resolve the problem that no truly non-egoist ethics was available on traditional associationist grounds, because the new complex feelings may become general ideas that are qualitatively different from, and essentially prior to, their antecedent simple parts. As such, impartial and non-egoist feelings can, with proper application, emerge from egoistic ones and supplant them, the key to which was self-mastery through self-development. Mill thus sought a higher synthesis whereby a revised empiricist individualism could produce both a superior variant of free agency and a better moral relationship to the social collectivity. In this regard, according to Devigne, "Mill wants nothing less than to combine the cultivation of human faculties and the fostering of higher modes of individualism with the pursuit of the common good as understood in an overarching of justice and more extended forms of social unity."[13] In doing so, Mill establishes a model of the self that is strongly relational and complex rather than mechanically egoistic.

Two further points should be made here to draw out the implications of Mill's account. The first is that this naturalistic account of the self helps correct certain recent criticisms of Mill that paint him as an anti-nature dualist, largely because of a single essay, *Nature*, that was actually aimed against religiously conservative forms of ethical naturalism that saw a divinely ordered nature as providing moral guidelines for human society.[14] In fact, even in *Nature* Mill shows more sensitivity to some naturalist claims than one might think after reading such criticisms. Comparing the development of character to gardening, he declares himself "happy to admit the fact" that human nature contains the "germs of all ... virtues," but maintains that these must be cultivated. It is "through such fostering, commenced early" that "the most elevated sentiments of which humanity is capable become a second nature, stronger than the first, and *not so much subduing the original nature as merging it into itself*" (emphasis added).[15] Building on his model of the self, Mill thus incorporates a slightly Aristotelian notion of "higher nature" to give naturalistic support to his utilitarian ethics while rejecting ethical naturalism as a mode of establishing ethical standards.

As with the Aristotelian model discussed by Orhan in this volume, however, it is the intellectual "elevated sentiments" that require most active cultivation in order to promote self-mastery, which in turn gains concreteness through good habits. As Devigne puts it, Mill "views human nature as not wholly determinate of human actions, but not irrelevant to it either," and thus espouses a position that emphasizes self-mastery, and in which "ethics are based on fostering habits that overcome our natural instincts, but that virtues reflect an assessment of the ways humanity can possess either base or noble ends and are not mere conventions."[16]

Though Mill doesn't defend any notion of intrinsic value in nature, he is no anti-nature dualist, the aforementioned interpretations of the

Nature essay notwithstanding. Nor is he, on my reading, a possessive individualist of the Lockean stripe, emphasizing the economic use-values of nature. Rather, as Wendy Donner asserts, Mill's view "offers a middle way between the anti-environmentalist Lockean perspective that maintains that nature is only a collection of natural resources and the radical environmentalist tradition that claims untouched nature has intrinsic value."[17] This middle way is evident in his views on inner (i.e., human) nature and the cultivation of character. For Mill, self-mastery and harmonizing reason with the passions should be sought through the intelligent use of associations, and natural vitality and energy should be channeled rather than squashed in the process. Natural vitality, thymotic energy, must not be crushed by a repressive education if a full, spontaneous, balanced person is to be the result.

Moving toward our second consequence of Mill's model of agency, we can see similarities between Mill's emphases on vitality and balance of the faculties and green demands for an integrated model of rationality that incorporates the passions. Mill's agency model also shares the ethos of spontaneity and organicism, and here John Zvesper's work on liberalism is illuminating. Zvesper invokes *thymos* as a liberal value— a bridge between natural desire and reasoning artifice that checks both the soullessness of bureaucratic calculation on one side and excesses of passionate private interest on the other. For the naturalistic liberal, it is neither "calculating reason" nor "raw desires" but "courageous, spirited speech and deeds" that "constitute the essence of politics."[18] There is thus the strong claim of linking rationality and feeling, reason and nature. Assaulting formalistic conceptions of liberalism that employ economistic, non-naturalistic, or disembodied views of human agency, Zvesper maintains in Millian fashion that the mediating thymotic element in education is crucial, for it is the "self-righteous resistance to domination" which "leads humans, even young ones ... to insist on their own equality and freedom." According to Zvesper, it is this—the "natural political spiritedness of human beings"—that is "at the heart of the classical liberal recognition of natural equality and liberty."[19] From this perspective, a link opens up between the central values of Mill's liberalism and green political theory, and I now turn to *On Liberty*. Since I hold that Mill's primary concerns were social and ethical rather than egoistic and economistic, it seems proper to note immediately that, in my view, the interpretation of *On Liberty*'s doctrines as necessarily supporting the unregulated market are quite mistaken. Mill is surely sufficiently explicit in his limited treatment of the question of state action on economic affairs in the last chapter: "these are questions which, though closely connected with the subject of this Essay, *do not, in strictness, belong to it* ... cases in which the reasons against interference *do not turn upon the principle of liberty*" (my emphases).[20] Whatever one may think of Mill's economics, *On Liberty* is no defense of possessive individualism. Rather, as Devigne writes, it shows Mill as "a romantic-expressive liberal" who holds that "the best life is distinctive and authentic, something every individual can discover for himself."[21]

One illustration of this is Mill's pervasive use of metaphors and analogies in which natural tendencies of growth are opposed to the mechanical, the stifling, the artifactual. In his chapter on individuality, Mill complains that there is "only too great a tendency in the best beliefs and practices to degenerate into the mechanical" and asserts that without continuous originality such beliefs would become "dead matter" that "would not resist the smallest shock from anything really alive." Diversity of conditions for existence is required, Mill maintains, for different people "require different conditions for their spiritual development" and "can no more exist healthily in the same moral, than all the variety of plants can in the same physical, atmosphere and climate." Excessive moralism of public opinion represses natural spontaneity, he complains, setting up an ideal of character which is "to desire nothing strongly"; such conventionality tends "to maim by compression, like the Chinese lady's foot, every part of human nature which stands out prominently."[22] Time and again this thymotic association of individual nature with spiritedness and the self's tendency of growth is used as the touchstone of Mill's argument. "Human nature," he insists, "is not a machine to be built after a model, and set to do exactly the work prescribed for it, but a tree, which requires to grow and develop itself on all sides, according to the tendency of the inward forces which make it a living thing." The invocation of (in Frankel's words) "nature as a principle of development" could scarcely be clearer, and it is complemented by the insistence on a balance of reason and the passions: "desires and impulses are as much a part of a human being as beliefs and restraints: and strong impulses are only perilous when not properly balanced; when one set of aims and inclinations is developed into strength, while others, which ought to co-exist with them, remain weak and inactive."[23] This is a liberalism grounded in a conception of the growing, active, integrated being with multiple faculties and capacities to develop, not the bourgeois calculator.

In fact, the importance of natural energy and spiritedness features throughout Mill's writings. *Active* virtue, Bernard Semmel convincingly argues, is a theme central to all of Mill's thought,[24] while a similar dynamism features in Mill's vision of "progress"; as noted, Mill's focus is on *moral* progress, for which natural energy is essential, not merely on economic advancement. Indeed, though he championed ideals of modern improvement against the Rousseau-inspired veneration of simplicity (eloquently discussed by Joseph Lane in this volume), Mill was strongly aware of over-refinement's corrupting features and capacity to cause imbalances. It was no accident that, in illustrating the many-sidedness of truth in *On Liberty*, Mill tacitly linked back to his own synthesis of Romanticism with empiricism by observing the "salutary shock" with which the eighteenth century saw "the paradoxes of Rousseau explode like bombshells in the midst, dislodging the compact mass of one-sided opinion, and forcing its elements to recombine in a better form and with additional ingredients."[25] Conventionality's fetters on free self-development are a major theme of *The Subjection of Women*. In the 1836 essay *Civilisation*, Mill laments the educated classes' decline of energy, reviles the passive consumerism of the wealthy, and attacks the manner in which the self-reliant craftsman is being driven out of business by the capitalist con man. "Success in so crowded a field," Mill complained, "depends not upon what a person is but upon what he seems: mere marketable qualities become the object instead of substantial ones, and a man's labor and capital are expended less in *doing* anything, than in persuading other people that he has done it."[26] Surface appearances replace real human worth, vitality, and knowledge. In his complaints against dead dogmas and the moral laziness of the affluent, as Ian Cook has observed, he even took this so far as to hold that while economic development may begin by stimulating intellectual development, beyond a certain point it ends by impeding it.[27] Once we recognize this view alongside Mill's championing of intellectual development, we can see how Mill could advance *moral* and not merely prudential arguments for the "stationary state"—a sustainable zero-growth economy—he advocated in *Principles of Political Economy* (1848).

Mill's Liberal Ethics of Sustainability

Though Mill did not support any notion of intrinsic value in nature, elements of his thought may still be compatible with environmentalists' desired outcomes.[28] Significantly, Mill's account of the stationary state is informed by his wider view of human flourishing. For Mill, as Dale Miller puts it, "evaluations of economic systems are based more on what sorts of *people* they tend to produce than how many widgets they turn out," and, in keeping with Mill's modified utilitarianism, a truly "happy life, one rich in the 'higher pleasures,' requires only a modest amount of material wealth."[29] Most present-day environmentalists probably would find this attractive, though many present-day greens probably would find Mill's Malthusian emphasis on population pressures rather than consumption problematic. That caveat aside, Mill's interwoven ideas about the stationary state, wealth, and human fulfilment are even more compatible with current environmental thought than is generally recognized.

John Parham notes that Mill, from the time of his first reflections on economics, found the abstraction of conventional political economy—its focus solely on the acquisition and consumption of wealth—unsatisfactory because of his awareness that these wealth-related activities were always subject to change both by physical laws and by human social forces. Indeed, even the latter part of the full title of Mill's 1848 work, *The Principles of Political Economy, With Some of Their Applications to Social Philosophy*, indicates awareness of wider social forces and concerns.[30] Closer examination of the full work proves still more revealing.

In the first chapter of Book I, Mill argues that wealth originates from nature in two senses: nature supplies raw materials and sources of power. Accordingly, the "matter of the globe is not an inert recipient of forms and properties impressed by human hands; it has active energies by which it cooperates with, and may even be used as a substitute for, labor." Maintaining that "it will be seen hereafter how much of the economy of society depends on the limited quantity in which some of the most important natural agents exist," Mill concludes the first chapter by speculating about possible limitations in land, water, air, coal, metallic ores, and even fish stocks.[31] This sets up his claim in chapter 12 of book I that the tendency to overlook natural limits is "not only an error, but the most serious one to be found in the whole field of political economy," for the "question is more important and fundamental than any other," involving "the whole subject of the causes of poverty, in a rich and industrious community."[32] As Parham explains, Mill thus opens his whole investigation with, and gives a central role to, the embeddedness of political economy within the finite economy of terrestrial nature. Moreover, although Mill generally favors a larger scale of operations for industry, he makes an exception for agriculture. In chapter 9 of Book I, he sympathetically analyzes small-scale peasant proprietor agriculture, citing various examples from Western Europe, and in chapter 6 of Book II he refers approvingly to Wordsworth's praise for the Lake District's small peasant proprietors.

"No other existing state of agricultural economy," Mill concludes, "has so beneficial an effect on the industry, the intelligence, the frugality and prudence of the population, nor tends on the whole so much to discourage an improvident increase in their numbers; and that no other, therefore, is on the whole so favorable, in the present state of their education, both to their moral and their physical welfare."[33] This approval, as Donald Winch has recently shown, appears to have roots in Mill's 1831 meeting with Wordsworth in the Lake District, an event that "had both passing and permanent significance to Mill's development," with the permanent importance lying in precisely this area, where "Mill exceeds Wordsworth in his enthusiasm."[34]

In later years Mill fused this support for peasant agriculture into advocating a form of localized collective co-operationism that he called socialism, and Parham goes so far as to say that "Mill's socialism broadly corresponds to the emphasis on sustainable, decentralized governance in contemporary ecological social philosophy."[35] It also connects to Mill's hope that a more egalitarian distribution of wealth might create "a much larger body of persons than at present, not only exempt from the coarser toils, but with sufficient leisure, both physical and mental, from mechanical details, to cultivate freely the graces of life."[36] Mill's hope was that the rising movement of workers' cooperative ventures competing in the market would develop the spirit of initiative and self-improvement among those workers while reducing wealth differentials, for in cooperatives the fruits of commercial success were more evenly shared, so progress and individuality could be fostered with far less poverty and drudgery. He thus connects quantitative issues of production and distribution to quality-of-life concerns.

In his highly significant announcement of the stationary state, Mill calls for limits on the growth of population and capital:

There is room in the world, no doubt, and even in old countries, for a great increase of population, supposing the arts of life to go on improving, and capital to increase. But even if innocuous, I confess I see very little reason for desiring it. The density of population necessary to enable mankind to obtain, in the greatest degree, all the advantages both of co-operation and of social intercourse, has, in all the most populous countries, been attained. A population may be too crowded, though all be amply supplied with food and raiment. It is not good for man to be kept perforce at all times in the presence of his species. A world from which solitude is extirpated, is a very poor ideal. Solitude, in the sense of being often alone, is essential to any depth of meditation or of character; and solitude in the presence of natural beauty and grandeur, is the cradle of thoughts and aspirations which are not only good for the individual, but which society could ill do without.

Nor is there much satisfaction in contemplating the world with nothing left to the spontaneous activity of nature; with every rood of land brought into cultivation, which is capable of growing food for human beings; every flowery waste or natural pasture ploughed up, all quadrupeds or birds which are not domesticated for man's use exterminated as his rivals for food, every hedgerow or superfluous tree rooted out, and scarcely a place left where a wild shrub or flower could grow without being eradicated as a weed in the name of improved agriculture. If the earth must lose that great portion of its pleasantness which it owes to things that the unlimited increase of wealth and population would extirpate from it, for the mere purpose of enabling it to support a larger, but not a better or a happier population, I sincerely hope, for the sake of posterity, that they will be content to be stationary, long before necessity compel them to it.[37]

Mill then insists that stationary economic growth doesn't mean stationary human improvement, as there "would be as much scope as ever for all kinds of mental culture, and moral and social progress" and "as much room for improving the Art of Living, and much more likelihood of its being improved, when minds ceased to be engrossed by the art of getting on."[38] Parham regards this portrait of the stationary state as following from Mill's subordination of political economy both to natural economy and to social organization, and as subordinating established dogmas about eventual scarcity to a Romantically influenced "conception of 'quality of life' that transcends the merely economic and resonates with contemporary social ecology."[39] This, however, doesn't tell us anything about *why* "the world with nothing left to the spontaneous activity of nature" might leave us dissatisfied, and for Mill the answer cannot lie in nature's intrinsic value in any externally locational sense. Donner suggests one possible option. She argues that "Mill connects moral and emotional development with opportunities to experience natural beauty which tend to elevate feelings and cultivate imagination." She suggests, I think rightly, that an "authentic, appreciative and knowledgeable encounter with the environment is a spur to some of the most uplifting, regenerative, and contemplative states of awareness, so much so that in Mill's mind they are the basis for what Romantics experience as transcendental and mystical forms of tranquility, bliss and awe."[40] But Donner's observations here are suggestive rather than assertive, partly because, as she herself argues, Mill's appreciation of Wordsworth's poetry did not translate into support for the transcendental mysticism in his philosophy. Though I agree with Donner that Mill repudiates transcendental claims about nature experience, I suggest that evidence may exist to tie Wordsworthian nature reverence more tightly to Mill's invocation of the value of a world retaining "the spontaneous activity of nature."

There is evidence that Mill wished to articulate Romantic ideas in non-mystical ways. Thomas Carlyle was, for Mill, a successor to Wordsworth as a Romantic influence. Writing to him in March of 1834, nearly seven years after his mental crisis and at a time when his new philosophical synthesis was taking shape, Mill made a significant declaration: "if I have any *vocation*, I think it is exactly this, to translate the mysticism of others into the language of Argument."[41] A Millian defense of Wordsworthian nature experience in terms of its effects on human character would fit precisely with this vocation, as well as fitting with the tendency to recast Romantic insights into empiricist terms that we saw with Mill's revision of associationism. Winch asserts that, in regard to Romantic nature raptures, "Mill was prepared to share the raptures, while giving ... the mystical metaphysics a more solid basis of his own construction," one that "consorted better with his utilitarian ethics" and with "his interest in the natural and moral sciences."[42] Moreover, both Mill's and Wordsworth's accounts of nature experience are individualist: Mill doesn't speak of hiking in groups as elevating, but rather of "solitude in the presence of natural beauty and grandeur" as being "the cradle of thoughts and aspirations ... which society could ill do without." Mill was an avid walker and an amateur botanist, frequently inspired by nature,[43] and thus a man who, like Rousseau and Wordsworth before him, enjoyed reveries as a solitary wanderer. Indeed, in view of the emphasis on developing autonomy in Mill's political theory, it might even be the case that nature inspires precisely through its dynamism and otherness—the associations one gains from it are always in flux and can thus inspire complementary dynamism and novelty more easily so long as other human company doesn't keep one in habitual thinking patterns.

Circumstantial evidence from Mill's political career also gives some support to the idea that he regarded protection of nature as having utilitarian merit. On April 25, 1866, Mill used his status as a Member of Parliament to support protection of the newly created common for the public at Hainault Forest, and to complain to the Home Secretary that "the timber on the fifty acres of recreation ground granted by Parliament in 1862 for the use of the Metropolitan public is being cut down, thereby destroying the forestal appearance of the spot, which the intention of the Legislature was to keep uninclosed and preserved in its natural wildness."[44] Nor was this an isolated instance: his biographer Nicholas Capaldi notes that in later years Mill "was responsible for the preservation both of Epping Forest and the elm trees in Piccadilly."[45] Three interventions on environmental protection issues may seem relatively little, but

Mill was a Member of Parliament only from 1866 to 1868. His activities arguably indicate significant interest by the standards of the time, and all these actions would be consistent with a view of nature experience as significantly uplifting.

Summing up, Mill's liberalism offers a remarkably congenial fit with contemporary environmental values. His emphasis on breadth of human development and capacities rather than purely material, economic growth looks compatible with environmentalism's bent toward "alternative hedonism" and with the skepticism toward specialization found in the recent writings of Juliet Schor.[46] His revised utilitarianism, with its emphasis on indirect fulfillment, spiritedness, and the balance of personality, offers space for integration of ideas from environmental virtue ethics[47] today just as it drew on Romanticism at its inception. Mill's liberalism is naturalistic and incorporates a relational account of the self that fits well with articulating environmental values, as well as finding room for validating the inspirations often drawn from nature experience. Perhaps most striking, if I am right that Mill's support for nature preservation was linked to his Romantic sympathies and his encouragement of the imagination and individuality, his account may offer the start of an argument that a sustainable society will be not merely necessary or fulfilling, but in some senses also freer and more diverse—a more truly *liberal* society—than what we have now.

Acknowledgments

I would like to thank Joe Lane, Peter Cannavò, and three anonymous MIT Press referees for their helpful comments on earlier drafts.

Notes

1. See Piers H. G. Stephens, "Plural Pluralisms: Towards a More Liberal Green Political Theory," in *Contemporary Political Studies*, ed. Iain Hampsher-Monk and Jeffrey Stanyer (UK Political Studies Association, 1996); Stephens, "Picking at the Locke of Economic Reductionism," in *Environmental Futures*, ed. N. Ben Fairweather et al. (Macmillan, 1999); Stephens, "Green Liberalisms: Nature, Agency, and the Good," *Environmental Politics* 10, no. 3 (2001): 1–22. For my attempt to capture some of the more attractive aspects of private property theory in a sketched non-Lockean green liberal framework, see Stephens, "Plumwood, Property, Selfhood and Sustainability," *Ethics and the Environment* 14, no. 2 (2009), 57–73.

2. See Stephens, "Plural Pluralisms"; Stephens, "Green Liberalisms"; Marcel Wissenburg, *Green Liberalism: The Free and the Green Society* (UCL Press, 1998); Marcel Wissenburg and John Barry eds. *Sustained Liberal Democracy: Ecologi-*

cal Challenges and Opportunities (Palgrave, 2001); Marius de Geus, *The End of Over-consumption: Towards a Lifestyle of Moderation and Self-restraint* (International Books, 2003); Andrew Dobson, *Citizenship and the Environment* (Oxford University Press, 2003); Simon Hailwood, *How to Be a Green Liberal: Nature, Value and Liberal Philosophy* (Chesham, Acumen, 2004); John M. Meyer, *Political Nature: Environmentalism and the Interpretation of Western Thought* (MIT Press, 2001); John M. Meyer, "Green Liberalism and Beyond," *Organization and Environment* 18.1 (2005): 116–20.

3. John Stuart Mill, *Autobiography of John Stuart Mill* (Signet Classics, 1964), 110.

4. Ibid., 115–116.

5. Ibid., 110, 112–123.

6. John Stuart Mill, *Utilitarianism, On Liberty, and Considerations on Representative Government*, ed. H. B. Acton (Everyman, 1984), 10.

7. John Stuart Mill, *A System of Logic*, in *Collected Works of John Stuart Mill*, volume 8, ed. J. M. Robson (University of Toronto Press, 1974), 926.

8. Andrew Belsey, "Chaos and Order, Environment and Anarchy," in *Philosophy and the Natural Environment*, ed. Robin Attfield and Andrew Belsey (Cambridge University Press, 1994), 157–160.

9. Charles Frankel, "The Rights of Nature," in *When Values Conflict*, ed. Laurence H. Tribe, Corinne S. Shelling, and John Voss (Ballinger, 1976), 104, 107.

10. Robert Devigne, *Reforming Liberalism: J. S. Mill's Use of Ancient, Religious, Liberal, and Romantic Moralities* (Yale University Press, 2006).

11. Ibid., 15.

12. John Stuart Mill, "Comments on James Mill's *Analysis of the Human Mind*," in *Collected Works of John Stuart Mill*, volume 31, ed. J. M. Robson (University of Toronto Press, 1989), 239.

13. Devigne, *Reforming Liberalism*, 15, 27.

14. See, for instance, Hailwood, *How to Be a Green Liberal*, 65–66; Robert E. Goodin, *Green Political Theory* (Polity, 1992), 47–49.

15. John Stuart Mill, "Nature," in *Three Essays on Religion* (Holt, 1884), 53.

16. Devigne, *Reforming Liberalism*, 53–54.

17. Wendy Donner and Richard Fumerton, *Mill* (Wiley-Blackwell, 2009), 126.

18. John Zvesper, *Nature and Liberty* (Routledge, 1993), 97.

19. Ibid., 135.

20. Mill, *Utilitarianism, On Liberty, and Considerations on Representative Government*, 178.

21. Devigne, *Reforming Liberalism*, 76.

22. Mill, *Utilitarianism, On Liberty, and Considerations on Representative Government*, 132, 136, 138.

23. Mill, *Utilitarianism, On Liberty, and Considerations on Representative Government*, 127.

24. Bernard Semmel, *John Stuart Mill and the Pursuit of Virtue* (Yale University Press, 1984).

25. Mill, *Utilitarianism, On Liberty, and Considerations on Representative Government*, 114–115.

26 John Stuart Mill, "Civilization," in *Collected Works of John Stuart Mill*, volume 10, ed. J. M. Robson (University of Toronto Press, 1977), 133.

27. Ian Cook, *Reading Mill: Studies in Political Theory* (Macmillan, 1998), 53.

28. The possibility that a sufficiently broad, enlightened anthropocentric ethic could yield similar results to ecocentrism has been debated at least since Bryan Norton's *Toward Unity Among Environmentalists* (Oxford University Press, 1991).

29. Dale Miller, *J. S. Mill: Moral, Social, and Political Thought* (Polity, 2010), 170.

30. John Parham, "What Is (Ecological) 'Nature'? John Stuart Mill and the Victorian Perspective," in *Culture, Creativity and Environment: New Environmentalist Criticism*, ed. Fiona Becket and Terry Gifford (Rodopi, 2007), 42–44.

31. John Stuart Mill, *The Principles of Political Economy* (Little & Brown, 1848), 30, 34–36.

32. Ibid., 213–214.

33. Ibid., 349.

34. Donald Winch, "Thinking Green, Nineteenth-Century style: John Stuart Mill and John Ruskin," in *Markets in Historical Context: Ideas and Politics in the Modern World*, ed. Mark Bevir and Frank Trentmann (Cambridge University Press, 2004), 113–114.

35. Parham, "What Is (Ecological) 'Nature'?" 46–47.

36. Mill, *The Principles of Political Economy*, 316.

37. Ibid., 316–317.

38. Ibid., 317.

39. Parham, "What is (Ecological) 'Nature'?" 43.

40. Donner and Fumerton, *Mill*, 133–134.

41. Nicholas Capaldi, *John Stuart Mill: A Biography* (Cambridge University Press, 2004), 94–95.

42. Winch, "Thinking Green, Nineteenth-Century Style," 112.

43. Richard Reeves, *John Stuart Mill: Victorian Firebrand* (Atlantic Books, 2007), 33.

44. John Stuart Mill, Public & Parliamentary Speeches, 1850–1868, in *Collected Works of John Stuart Mill*, volume 28, ed. J. M. Robson (University of Toronto Press, 1988), 74.

45. Capaldi, *John Stuart Mill*, 325.

46. Juliet Schor, *Plenitude: The New Economics of True Wealth* (Penguin, 2010).

47. See, for example, Ronald Sandler and Philip Cafaro, eds., *Environmental Virtue Ethics* (Rowman & Littlefield, 2005).

11
Karl Marx: Critique of Political Economy as Environmental Political Theory

Timothy W. Luke

Karl Marx (1818–1883) remains one of the most influential revolutionary thinkers, political philosophers, and social scientists of the nineteenth century. During his lifetime, he became a preeminent theorist of political economy as well as a committed revolutionary in working-class movements seeking to create a socialist, and then communist, way of life. Born in Trier, he was educated in Bonn and Berlin. His political activities in Prussia, France, and Belgium troubled the authorities enough that he was compelled to spend the rest of his life as an exile in England. Remembered mostly for his ground-breaking study of political economy *Capital* (1867), he also co-authored *The Manifesto of the Communist Party* with his friend and benefactor Friedrich Engels in 1848. These writings on historical materialism, in turn, became inspirational texts for many socialist and communist labor unions, political parties, and revolutionary movements from the 1860s to the present. Although only a few Marxist-Leninist peoples' democracies survive (ironically, the People's Republic of China, with its dynamic mixed-market economy, is now the most recognized example of "working Marxism"), Marx's thought still is essential in any consideration of environmental political theory today.

Environmental political theorists often dismiss Marx as little more than an anthropocentric celebrant of industrial society's dominion over Nature. This domination supposedly serves humanity's aspirations to plunder the Earth and satisfy the unchecked desires of either bourgeois elites or the toiling peasant and proletarian masses. While such critics point to the outrageous ecological ravages inflicted by decades of Stalinist forced industrialization in the former Soviet Union, China, Poland, Romania, Bulgaria, and other communist states, those misbegotten undertakings cannot be attributed to Marx. Indeed many have been intent upon discrediting Marxian ideas since 1848,[1] and these misreadings continue on many fronts to undercut his critique of capitalist political economy. Yet when Marx is read carefully, it is clear that he would not endorse the wasteful plundering of Nature at all costs to benefit humanity.

In fact, Marx exhibits great respect for Nature. Humanity and Nature, for Marx, always are one. Each one's survival is fully implicated in the other. Moreover, Marx shows how the dynamics of profit seeking under capitalism violate and degrade both human beings and natural ecologies in the pursuit of monetary gain and material excess. By following Marx's nuanced conception of social and material relations between humans and nonhuman nature, environmental political theory can avoid "the kind of technical and ethical dualism exhibited by mainstream environmentalism,"[2] a dualism that often either favors humanity over nature or puts ecology before people. Instead, environmental theorists can understand how the exploitation of humanity and of nature are bound up with one another.

Marx and Nature

William Leiss accurately asserts that Marx has "the most profound insight into the complex issues surrounding the idea of mastery over nature to be found anywhere in nineteenth-century social thought."[3] For Marx, human life is "Nature," and natural history should not be divided from human history. All of society begins "from these natural bases and their modification in the course of history through the action of men."[4] This linkage is the core of Marxian historical materialist criticism. Indeed, it is the key nexus of his social theory, political philosophy, and moral economy for realizing a communist society. For Marx and Engels, the actions of humanity toward Nature must always involve caring for the Earth.

Even as labor is exploited and abused by capital, and markets make some of Nature's bounty more available to humanity, the rational entrepreneur should be a good steward of the land. As *Capital* maintains, "Even a whole society, a nation or even all simultaneously existing societies together, are not the owners of the globe. They are only its possessors, its usufructuaries, and like *boni patres familias* they must hand it down to succeeding generations in an improved condition."[5]

The ongoing squabbles over Marx's supposedly unreflective anthropocentrism, absolute technophilism, or crass economism basically center upon how far, and under what conditions, "an improved condition" of Nature by Society could extend to all as a truly equitable and emancipatory common future.[6] Who should advance what changes for whom under which concrete conditions of economic improvement is the crucial political question, and Marx pitches his response as a critical counterpoint to Adam Smith.[7]

Marx would be the first to acknowledge how few capitalist entrepreneurs are truly rational, and how modern market exchange abuses everything it engages. Still, he also is quite clear about his ultimate starting points: Humanity is Nature, Nature is Humanity, so the emancipation of people and nature should go hand in hand. Therefore, any anthropocentrism in his project also is ecocentrism, and ecocentrism would also be anthropocentrism owing to the unity of Humanity and Nature. They are one and the same. As a result, the ecological ties of Humanity and Nature are, and should be, linked together through circuits of beneficial social usufruct, as Jean-Jacques Rousseau supports—rather than conceived in terms of conquest for individual plunder, as John Locke enables[8]—if societies are to realize the goals of Marx's environmental political thought.

One can assess Marx's view of the environment by reconsidering his insights into humanity and history in *The Eighteenth Brumaire of Louis Bonaparte*, where he observes that "men make their own history, but they do not make it just as they please; they do not make it under circumstances chosen by themselves, but under circumstances directly found, given and transmitted from the past."[9] The circumstantial conditions of significance for Nature today are those encountered by humans in their anarchic competition in global, national, and local markets. Here, they struggle against social and material scarcities to produce private, and social, abundance (albeit never equitably distributed or enjoyed) of beneficial products, or commodities, while containing noxious by-products that Marx would see as harmful to humans and nature.

The imperative of capitalist globalization, as Marx asserts in *Wage Labor and Capital*, continuously "compels capital to intensify the productive forces of labour," since intense global competition gives "capital no rest" as it "continually whispers in its ear: 'Go on! Go on!'"[10] Marx saw that as competition drives capitalist exchange to advance, the collective social mechanisms of human economies' exchanges with Nature put the Earth's ecologies under tremendous pressures to be maximally productive. Success comes at the cost of super-exploiting accrued natural capital stocks to the point of robbing from both the past and the future. Long-time accumulations of soil nutrients, fresh water, fossil fuels, or available energy are quickly exhausted, at the same time the possible current recharge rates for the future are disrupted or destroyed to rob rapid returns from the Earth,[11] to the detriment of future generations.

Far too often, serious environmental criticism to defend "Nature" tends only to assess the discrete ecological effects of various disconnected cultural, economic, and social processes as separate silos of degradation that need to be tallied up continuously to gauge their "environmental impact." To truly disclose what is happening today, however, Marx would have environmental political theorists stay focused on Justus von Liebig's studies of agroeconomic metabolism (see below) by reevaluating the complex hybridities of Nature/Society at multiple sites, which intermix the natural and the social, like the "built environments," "natural history," or "political ecology" of all public, private, and pristine ecologies.[12]

These unstable amalgams of Nature/Society are what constitute the stocks, services, and systems that sustain and/or degrade overall levels of health and environmental quality for both human and nonhumans. They manifest themselves in highly commercialized patterns of urban settlement, industrial ecology, and natural economy; such patterns are never neatly divisible into orderly material outcomes.[13] Marx's very holistic perspective takes full advantage of a continuous overview of everything as the most effective way to discover solutions for environmental problems.

Since Nature is Humanity and Humanity Nature, one should also detach Marx's thinking about economic and technological collectivization from the abusive adaptation of collectivist ideas in twentieth-century Marxism-Leninism. Bruno Latour offers a concept of collectivism more akin to Marx's original intent. Latour utilizes "the word 'collective' to describe any association of humans and nonhumans."[14] Seen in this manner, collectives are flexible, varied mediations of these dynamic associations, which can be regarded as "the environments" populated by people and things as the planet is "modified by the actions of men" in modernity. These hybrid assemblies of subjects and objects, living and nonliving beings, humans and nonhumans, agents and structures, actors and artifacts, or places, systems, and things are not unlike how Latour appraises them: as "simultaneously real, like nature, narrated like discourse, and collective, like society."[15]

Marx's materialist conception of history sees these hybrid assemblies, such as the goods and services of humanly fabricated commodities in the means and relations of production, as the most determinate force in society. These complex relations are responsible for shaping the consciousness of men as well as constituting the cores of productive activity that control and utilize the creation of wealth in the production of spaces for Humanity and Nature.[16]

Commodification as Control

Marx's care about the environment highlights the ravages of capitalist commodification as the high toll paid by Humanity for control over Nature. Such control is realized through the bourgeoisie's control over the proletariat in capitalist production. Like John Locke or Hannah Arendt,[17] Marx focuses upon the economic and social interactions in the productive process, but he highlights how these interactions distort each human being's relationships with Nature, other humans in society, and their own inner psychic life, alienating human beings and their labor from Nature, society, and themselves.[18] Marx regarded the commodity form as a relentlessly destructive force. Wherever the commodity form takes hold in everyday life, it aims to extract more profitable output of exchange value for less input of time, labor, energy, and materiel. Commodification increasingly invades all social relations; Marx's political project is based upon resisting and overcoming its destructive machinations.

Commodification proceeds through a kind of mystification that Marx called *commodity fetishism*. When trapped in the thickets of monetized operation, and alienated from the labor that produced them, the origins and the existence of all socially produced artifacts become mystified. Commodities seem to have "absolutely no connection with their physical properties and with the material relations arising therefrom."[19] Instead, people perceive their value solely in terms of market exchange, creating a kind of mystical quality in these objects: "[T]here is a definite social relation between men, that assumes, in their eyes, the fantastic form of a relation between things. In order, therefore to find an analogy, we must have recourse to the mist-enveloped regions of the religious world. In that world the productions of the human brain appear as independent beings endowed with life, and entering into relation both with one another and the human race. So it is in the world of commodities with the products of men's hands."[20]

As Marx asserts in the preface to *A Contribution to the Critique of Political Economy*, "it is not the consciousness of men that determines their being, but, on the contrary, their social being that determines their consciousness," he is mapping a precise impact of "the economy" upon "the environment."[21] His critique of the commodity form and its mystifying aspects under capitalist conditions of production dissects the conditions under which human labor is extracted and embedded within complex systems and material things to create value. That analysis, then, also amounts to an exacting examination of who dominates whom in commanding and controlling the legal and technical processes of economic commodification and mystification that shape the course of history. Through this analysis, Marx examines how Nature is degraded as its sites and services pay excessively for who benefits in the ever-mutable modifications of human and nonhuman beings associating together as both Nature and Culture. There is much for environmental political theorists to learn here.

As that assemblage of systems for producing, circulating, consuming, and accumulating commodities, the world market is where environmental political theorists should be probing the coupled complex systems of political economy and the environment and the mystifying phenomenon of commodity fetishism. The networks concentrate value via collectives of exchange as well as construct the conditions of human exploitation and natural despoliation. "By an exchange," Marx argues, as human beings, "we equate as values our different products, [and] by that very act, we also equate, as human labour, the different kinds of labour expended up on them. We are not aware of this, nevertheless, we do it." Marx extends this claim: "When therefore, Galiani says: Value is a relation between persons ... he ought to have added: a relation between persons expressed as relations between things."[22]

Value, as a relation between people mediated by relations between things, ensnares all products in the techniques of control and freedom, whose mystifying social hieroglyphics of exploitation lie awaiting their decoders. That decoding can then reveal the utility of value, value as labor, the labor in objects, object as product, and the product itself all as material expressions of human and nonhuman labor, artificial and natural resources, contemporary and historical developments, which are all needed to relate persons and things in these systematic assemblies of activity and thought with value.[23] Through Marx's analytical efforts amid the economy and society, then, "we try to decipher the hieroglyphic, to get behind the secret of our own social products."[24] The commodification of Nature, embodying the corrupted energies of unchecked accumulation without end, crystallizes human sapience and sentience as environments within works of labor, whether it is gold ore, skyscrapers, unrefined oil, computers, harvested wheat, steel or suburban housing. Alienated will, intelligence, and energy are concentrated by industry, distributed in markets, and graded by exchange as something mystical, enigmatic, transcendent, or ordinary, apparent, normal, in commodities.

Marx's sense of capitalist political economy relies heavily on what he saw as "the metabolic rift" in capitalism's unchecked exploitation of

Nature as human society consumes natural resources, violating nature's metabolic processes, and creating products and wastes. Following Locke, the imperatives of capital accumulation treat natural resources as inexhaustible stocks of assets for this "metabolic interaction" between Society and Nature. Marx, however, respected the findings of agronomic soil chemistry that account for such energy and material exchanges. These cycles had been studied thoroughly by Liebig in his surveys of English agriculture during the 1850s and the 1860s. Liebig's "Law of the Minimum" asserts that growth is constrained by the scarcest factor needed for production. He saw the growing concentration of land ownership in England, the overuse of farm plots, and the depopulation of rural areas as a nexus where imported artificial inputs had to be injected to compensate for degraded biochemical factors that ordinary natural resource recharge rates could not supply. Hence, the new extractive capitalist global economy was designed, in part, to fuel rapid urbanization in Great Britain with imported natural materiel. As Marx learned from Liebig's research, stocks of food, fiber, and minerals were destructively mined at sites from all over the Earth's countryside in systems of production and consumption to serve major urban markets in Britain or elsewhere.[25]

Marx saw that "man *lives* on nature" to the degree Nature can be regarded as humanity's body "with which he must remain in continuous interchange,"[26] an interchange that is "complex, dynamic,"[27] in order to survive. On the one hand, a sustainable metabolic exchange is to some extent "prescribed by the natural laws of life itself."[28] Yet these prescriptions also are entirely contingent, historical, and mutable to the extent they are "bound up with the social relations of the time,"[29] as when colonial exploitation allows the powerful to flout Liebig's laws by abusing other peoples and ecologies to generate commodities. Marx argues that the metabolic exchanges of humanity with Nature should serve as "the regulative law of social production."[30] However, the pressures of overshoot in continuous competition for perpetual profit push aside the regulative boundaries intrinsic to the natural laws of life. These pressures generate massive material machinal formations that can only survive by consuming even more super-exploited external inputs to service the means of commercial exchange.

Martin Heidegger observes that Humanity treats Nature as its "standing reserve" of wealth.[31] More concretely, Marx argues that the social relations of market exchange in capitalist globalization force agricultural producers to mine dirt for its nutrients. Capital accumulation lowers "the agricultural population to an ever decreasing minimum and confronts it with an ever growing industrial population crammed together in large towns; in this way it produces conditions that provoke an irreparable rift in the interdependent process of social metabolism, a metabolism prescribed by the natural laws of life itself. The result of this is a squandering of the vitality of the soil, which is carried by trade far beyond the bounds of a single country."[32]

We replace the slow, organic replacement of soil with artificial inputs drawn from coal, oil, gas, or other mineral sources. And, to maintain productivity, human energy, animal power, and biofuel stocks must be replaced by more powerful sources of energy, such as coal, oil, or natural gas. Greater scales of such production require more "material for labour at the most varied stages of elaboration, as well as ancillary materials. As the scale of production grows, and productive power of labor grows through cooperation, division of labour, machinery, etc., so does the mass of raw materials, ancillaries, etc. that go into the daily reproduction process."[33] The huge demand for new energy sources and other mineral substitutes leads to rapacious raids on untouched mountaintops, offshore deposits, subterranean shale beds, and hitherto undeveloped regions. More and more production at many points scattered around the world impels companies and entrepreneurs to exploit the easy, then the tough, and soon the almost inaccessible stocks of new material, labor, and fuel. As Paul Sweezy asserts, in terms completely consistent with Marx's analysis, "caught up in this process of restless innovation and expansion, the system rides roughshod over even its own beneficiaries if they get in the way or fall by the roadside. As far as the natural environment is concerned, capitalism perceives it not as something to be cherished and enjoyed but as a means to the paramount ends of profit-making and still more capital accumulation."[34]

Capitalism thus disrupts the pre-existing energy and material flows of the planet. The production and transportation of immense harvests of commodities and stocks of imported nutrients, and the flows of hydrocarbon energy needed to sustain these circuits of unsustainably intense production, wound Nature and Humanity. As pollutants, wastes, and excesses systematically degrade the material metabolisms interlinking humanity and nature, disaster by design takes shape.[35]

In the short run, today's green capitalists might appear to be making amends by tending to these circuits of natural renewal, but Marx would argue that such efforts are minor and fleeting. Capital *per se* always "disturbs the metabolic interaction between man and the earth, i.e. it prevents the return to the soil of its constituent elements consumed by man in the form of food and clothing; hence, it hinders the operation of the eternal natural condition for the last ing fertility of the soil."[36] Overcoming such capitalist irrationalities would have to become part and parcel of the attainment of a socialist society.

Political Economy as Environment

Marx represents commodities as volatile mysterious entities through which real human relations of labor utilization between owner and worker, men and women as well as humanity and Nature hybridize things and thoughts in objectified, mystified social relations. Thus, humans consciously and unconsciously create and then degrade environments with their economy. The environment is shaped by the commodities humans produce, because states, peoples, and companies transfer intellectual and material properties to "dead matter" as "living" agencies, as Marx's notions about commodity fetishism suggest.

Today's vital materialists, such as Jane Bennett, struggle to clarify these outcomes by characterizing them as "vibrant matter,"[37] but stopping with this obvious elementary recognition is insufficient. That is, such theories ignore the far more variable and contradictory historicized material vibrations of who and what is at work to whose benefit and at what cost beyond the evident vibrations in such environmental assemblages. Marx's perspective would decode the "who, whom" at play in the destructive animus of exchange under conditions of commodity fetishism.[38] In fact, Marx's works should remind contemporary green thinkers that the dynamics of social and economic classes must be understood historically and politically if we are to articulate a comprehensive environmentalist perspective. They cannot be dismissed as vibrating social and political materialities detached from any eco-political concern. As Marx and Engels note in the Communist Manifesto,

Constant revolutionising of production, uninterrupted disturbance of all social conditions, everlasting uncertainty and agitation distinguish the bourgeois epoch from all earlier ones. All fixed, fast-frozen relations, with their train of ancient and venerable prejudices and opinions are swept away, all new-formed ones become antiquated before they can ossify. All that is solid melts into air, all that is holy is profaned, and man is at last compelled to face with sober senses, his real conditions of life, and his relations with his kind.[39]

Commodification volatilizes, liquidates, fluidizes matter and spirit, but the products and by-products of these disruptive political economies become "our environment"—the liquid modernity, material flow, and volatile rush of excess.

Historicizing Materialism in Action

Locke's labor theory of value is quite clear. His liberalism holds that property accrues to those who will mix their labor with the raw materials of Nature, but he omits how extensively, in producing this mix of matter with work, "men not only act on nature but also on one another." "In order to produce," Marx writes, "they enter into definite connections and relations with one another and only within these social connections and relations does their action on nature, does production, take place."[40] Here "the environment" forms in the containments, surveillance, boundaries, and structure of political economy. Capital is a powerful social relation of production, and all its shapes and substances are "creations of labour, products of labour, *accumulated labour*."[41] Environments, then, integrate alienated, and now commodified, individual work into the working collectives of Nature and Society at the nexus of capital/labor accumulation and, ultimately, into the heavily worked matter that capitalists and proletarians fabricate. Such environments of "alienated labor," therefore, presume the inhabitation of them by the "alienated man," or "estranged labor, of estranged life, of *estranged* man."[42]

Though many Marxists would regard such alienated labor as "dead labor," congealed into machinery and other products or artifacts, it carries many material vibrations of the more displaced, referred, or transmitted currents of "undead labor," such as the technological momentum, commodity demand, market equilibrium, and embedded exchange—all typically labeled as "market forces"—that break down barriers to appropriation. Furthermore, as these energies accumulate in, for, and as capital, environmental assemblages unfold their collectives of human and nonhuman interaction. It is "accumulated, past, materialised labor over direct, living labor that turns accumulated labor into capital." Capital "does not consist in accumulated labor serving living labor as a means of new production. It consists in living labor serving accumulated labor as a means of maintaining and multiplying the exchange value of the latter."[43]

Environments are hybrid formations of more enduring human works and nonhuman natural settings. Capital will openly degrade life in the commodification process enveloping humans and things, and this process should be a crucial focus for environmental political theory. Amalgams of living capital and undead labor reshape natural and social forces, coevolving as economy and alienation, or estrangement, amid the forces of commodification.

As Marx explains alienation, estranged human labor becomes embedded within things, and thereby from, the human beings who invested their time, energy, and skill in those things:

> The worker puts his life into the object; but now his life no longer belongs to him but to the object. Hence, the greater this activity, the greater is the worker's lack of objects. Whatever the product, of his labour is, he is not. Therefore the greater this product, the less is he himself. The *alienation* of the worker in his product means not only that his labor becomes an object, an *external* existence, but that it exists *outside him*, independently, as something alien to him, and that it becomes a power of its own confronting him; it means that the life which he has conferred on the object confronts him as something hostile and alien.[44]

Properties of human agency are transferred, in part, to nonhuman sites, systems, and structures. The environment's vitality and concreteness also suffuse human conduct and cognition with the charmed energies of estranged intelligence and mystified commodity relations in this political economy. And, with every fetishized commodity circulating in the capitalist marketplace, the environment awakes, evolves, and unsettles human and nonhuman beings with its hybridities.

These flows are environmental inasmuch as commodities constitute the sites, structures, and services that sustain human beings regardless of their irrational and rational properties:

> As plants, animals, minerals, air, light, etc., in theory form a part of human consciousness, partly as objects of natural science, partly as objects of art ... so they also form in practice a part of human life and human activity. Man lives physically only by these products of nature; they may appear in the form of food, heat, clothing, housing, etc. The universality of man appears in practice in the universality which makes the whole of nature his *inorganic* body: (1) as a direct means of life, and (2) as the matter, object, and instrument of his life activity. Nature is the *inorganic* body of man, that is, nature insofar as it is not the human body. Man *lives* by nature. This means that nature is his body with which he must remain in perpetual process in order not to die.[45]

To the extent that Nature constitutes "man's inorganic body" in which all of humanity and nonhumanity remain perpetually engaged, political ecology must study all the direct bases of human life, which are the matter, objects, and instruments of all human life activity, as environmental constructs. Multiple environments—the built environment, the yet-to-be-built environment, and the never-built environment, for example—emerge in the forms of economic organization and interpretation through which human societies transform Nature into "humanity's inorganic body" as food, heat, clothing, housing, and so on.

The antinomies of class conflict between labor and capital mediate other struggles conducted along the shears between nature and society, between environment and economy, and between ecology and technology. As is true of Rousseau, this is where Marx finds most poor subjects dominated by a few rich subjects as well as all human subjects becoming more subservient to nonhuman objects. Technics are not only tools forged to reach certain instrumental goals; they are regimes of empowerment and disempowerment that environmentally bias behavior, predetermine practices, and transmute thought in ideologies of control. Commodities collectivize being, but human being is disrupted destructively in the collectives of commodification that accumulate in vast built environments.

Within today's global capitalist mode of production, the collectivities of Nature and humanity at work appear now almost exclusively fused in commodified forms. If the totality of all human relationships constitutes the environment, it now "presents itself as 'an immense accumulation of commodities.'"[46] Furthermore, this second Nature of "the environment" serves as a regime for the domination of people through the ecology and economy, creating the overall social product. As Marx suggests, the social product of labor transforms each person's work and Nature itself "into a being *alien* to him, into a *means* to his *individual existence*. It estranges man's own body from him, as it does external nature and his spiritual essence, his *human* being."[47] Nature becomes the hard hostile crust of different environments. This processed world concretely expresses a new co-evolutionary order, which Arendt would cast as "the human condition,"[48] that corporate capital, state power and consumer culture jointly constitute Nature as "near" and "far" "environments," as part of their own operations in the transnational actualization of rational economies. This sense of collectivization as environmentalization is suggested in *Capital* when Marx asserts that "technology reveals the active relation of man to nature, the direct process of the production of his life, and thereby it also lays bare the process of the production of the social relations of his life and of the mental conceptions that flow from these relations."[49] Marx's observations here should anchor any contemporary critique of political economy and the environment.

Enterprise and Ecology?

Present-day environmentalists would do well to return to Marx's *Eighteenth Brumaire*. In today's peculiar circumstances, it is clear that men and women make their own environments. Nonetheless, they make those environments, not under circumstances chosen by thems, but under circumstances directly encountered, given and transmitted from past. Many of today's capitalist entrepreneurs, therefore, are working to leverage the current generation's environmental overshoot as the foundation for their working business plans by opening "clean energy" firms, creating carbon-credit exchanges, and developing new smart infrastructure to cope with the greenhouse gassing, soil depletion, and ecosystem degradation of the past.

As production becomes more social, fully global, and quite technified, "capital now sets the worker to work, not with a manual tool, but with a machine which itself handles the tools."[50] Capital sets the laborers to work within the systems of systems, services of services, and stocks of stocks that "the environment" becomes to those caught up within today's clean, green and lean transnational capitalism. Any ecology can morph into a reified site or a vast natural machine to harvest energies (wind, solar, tidal, biomass, etc.), exploit materials (industrial waste, obsolete commodities, consumer trash, rare minerals, etc.), or divert services (CO_2 capture, soil regeneration, solar reflectivity, plant pollination, etc.). Assigning economic values, money prices, and aggregate goals to "the environment" *qua* Nature recasts it as an improvable, evolving agroindustrial infrastructure. Today's rapid evolution of "green capitalism" into "clean capitalism" is but another articulation of the "lean capitalism" at the heart of late globalism's ongoing economic rationalization.[51]

Humanity lives by Nature, but Nature increasingly lives by Humanity. Marx argues that political power and ethical choice can direct these trends toward more humane and sustainable outcomes if capitalism's abuses of Humanity and Nature end. Whether particular species do or do not go extinct, however the atmosphere changes, wherever or how much the seas rise, whenever the cryosphere melts, and whichever ecosystems collapse is now a much more fully human endeavor. "Nature is the *inorganic* body of man," and its original nonhuman bodies of inorganic material help sustain humanity "in perpetual process"[52] to live more fully (as well as often more unstably) amid the artifices of "environments." Sustaining the biosphere's perpetual process of self-renewal in order for humanity not to die is essential, but then so too now are "the matter, object, and instrument of human life" integral elements of the planetary environment. Bitter new dialectics develop here. Species extinctions, greenhouse gassing, biome degradation, and ecosystem overshoot are decisive indicators of how "the universality of man appears in practice in the universality which makes the whole of nature his *inorganic* body."[53]

Through mining, building, farming, shipping, engineering, and manufacturing, global business concerns and small local firms are continuously reorganizing the Earth as "terrestrial infrastructure," and this infrastructure now demands more rational management in accord with the economy's immanent machinic regularities. This spatiality often seems unfixed with regard to its localities, stabilities, or properties.[54] The manifolds of environmental space appear as machinic mediations of practices in place and in process, like the oil rigs, pipelines, oil refineries, tankers, and gas stations that fuel the spaces of automobility as well as the earthliness of greenhouse gassing. In this respect, Michel de Certeau would observe, commodification compels producers and consumers in the world economy and planetary ecology to take "into consideration vectors or direction, velocities, and time variables. Thus space is composed of intersections of mobile elements. It is in a sense activated by the ensemble of movements deployed within it. Space occurs as the effect produced by the operations that orient it, situate it, temporalize it, and make it function in a polyvalent unity of conflictual programs or contractual proximities."[55]

In asserting that "the global environment" exists *per se*, and that it can be defined, assigned reliable metrics, and then managed within society as stocks of environmental capital, big business (assisted by green research groups) implicitly concedes that the industrial revolution has fully become one with the ongoing reengineering of the planet's evolution. The deanimating, deruralizing, deagrarianizing, deindustrializing, dehumanizing, and decentering of the productive lifeworlds in more traditional historic forms of civilization proceed as human settlements make way, on another level, for more petroleum-powered Nature/Society hybrid machinic ensembles in which two billion cars coexist with seven billion people.

Marx foresaw how, instead of once rich and rewarding human civilization, more poor and punishing collectives of commercial commodification assemble more flexible ensembles of artificial and natural systems, coexisting in chaotic, turbulent, complex networks of green capitalism.[56] The extraordinary condition of nearly full urbanization, which seemed only "a horizon, an illuminating virtuality"[57] a generation ago, is now fully colonizing the Earth with hyper-urban sprawl. On this reassembled Earth, ecological "overshoot"[58] leads to a planet of slums or a world of dumps intermixed with bioengineered forests, privatized seed strains, cultivated wildlife, and the carbon-credited-and-debited atmosphere.

When all that is solid melts its toxicities into the thin air of angst without end, Marx believes, the agony of accumulation, production, consumption still can come full cycle around the world into a more humane and natural mode of free equitable being under communism. Without Marx's intellectual project, it would be more difficult to grasp—either as finely or as fully—the critique of political economy and the environment under today's conditions of global capitalist production. Marx's environmental political thinking sharpens the vision of those opposing Nature's end. This commitment to the continuous critique of commodification is what must be done by environmental political thinkers, because, like the runaway radioactive emissions of Fukushima Daiichi, Chernobyl, or Three Mile Island before them, capitalist commodification's toxic byproducts are everywhere. Creating the political will, power, and order to end those toxic effects, and then live beyond them, is decisively important.

Acknowledgments

Portions of this chapter were presented at the annual meetings of the Western Political Science Association and the Global Studies Association in 2011.

Notes

1. Francis Fukuyama, "The End of History?" *The National Interest* 16 (1989): 3–18.
2. Paul Burkett, *Marx and Nature: A Red and Green Perspective* (Palgrave Macmillan, 1999), 18.
3. William Leiss, *The Domination of Nature* (McGill–Queen's University Press, 1994), 85.
4. Karl Marx and Friedrich Engels, "The German Ideology" (1846), in *The Marx-Engels Reader*, ed. Robert C. Tucker, second edition (Norton, 1978), 150.
5. Karl Marx, *Capital: A Critique of Political Economy*, volume III (International Publishers, 1967), 776.
6. World Commission on Environmental Development, *Our Common Future* (Oxford University Press, 1987).
7. Robert L. Heilbroner, ed., *The Essential Adam Smith* (Norton, 1987).
8. For a different view of Locke, see Zev Trachtenberg's chapter in this volume.
9. Karl Marx, "The Eighteenth Brumaire of Louis Bonaparte" (1852), in *The Marx-Engels Reader*, second edition, ed. Robert C. Tucker (Norton, 1978), 595.
10. Karl Marx, "Wage Labour and Capital" (1847), in The Marx-Engels Reader, second edition, ed. R. Tucker (Norton, 1978), 213.
11. Karl Marx, *Capital: A Critique of Political Economy*, volume I, tr. Ben Fowkes (Penguin, 1976), chapter 15.

12. Timothy Luke, *Ecocritique: Contesting the Politics of Nature, Economy, and Culture* (University of Minnesota Press, 1997). On Liebig's influence on Marx, see, especially, John Bellamy Foster, Marx's Ecology: Materialism and Nature (Monthly Review Press, 2000).

13. Georg Lukacs, *History and Class Consciousness: Studies in Marxist Dialectics*, tr. Rodney Livingstone (MIT Press, 1971).

14. Bruno Latour, *We Have Never Been Modern* (Harvester Wheatsheaf, 1993), 4.

15. Ibid., 6.

16. Henri Lefebvre, *The Production of Space* (Blackwell, 1991).

17. See chapters 5 and 14 in this volume.

18. Karl Marx, "Economic and Philosophic Manuscripts of 1844," in *The Marx-Engels Reader*, second edition, ed. Robert C. Tucker (Norton, 1978). See also Joseph Schumpeter, *Capitalism, Socialism and Democracy* (Allen and Unwin, 1943).

19. Marx, *Capital*, volume I, 72.

20. Ibid.

21. Karl Marx, "Preface to *A Contribution to the Critique of Political Economy*," in *The Marx-Engels Reader*, second edition, ed. Tucker (Norton, 1978), 4.

22. Marx, *Capital:*, volume I, tr. Moore and Aveling, 74.

23. John Bellamy Foster, Brett Clark, and Richard York, *The Ecological Rift: Capitalism's War on the Planet* (Monthly Review Press, 2010).

24. Karl Marx, *Capital*, volume I, in *The Marx-Engels Reader*, second edition, ed. Tucker (Norton, 1978), 322.

25. Justus von Liebig, *Familiar Letters on Chemistry* (Chemical Society, 1844).

26. Karl Marx, *Economic and Philosophic Manuscripts of 1844* (International Publishers, 1964), 112.

27. Foster, Marx's Ecology, 158. The concept of "metabolic rift" as used in this chapter derives from John Bellamy Foster, "Marx's Theory of Metabolic Rift: Classical Foundations for Environmental Sociology," American Journal of Sociology 105, no. 2 (September 1999): 366–405.

28. Karl Marx, *Capital: A Critique of Political Economy*, volume III, tr. David Fernbach (Penguin, 1981), 949–950.

29. Karl Marx, *The Poverty of Philosophy*, third edition (Foreign Languages Press, 1977), 158.

30. Marx, *Capital*, volume I, tr. Fowkes, 638.

31. Martin Heidegger, "The Question Concerning Technology," in *Basic Writings: Martin Heidegger*, revised edition, ed. David Farrell Krell (HarperCollins, 2008).

32. Marx, *Capital*, volume III, tr. Fernbach, 949.

33. Karl Marx, *Capital: A Critique of Political Economy*, volume II, tr. David Fernbach (Penguin, 1978), 218–219.

34. Paul Sweezy, "Capitalism and the Environment," *Monthly Review* 56, no. 5 (2004): 87.

35. Foster, Clark, and York, *Ecological Rift*.

36. Marx, *Capital*, volume I, tr. Fowkes, 637.

37. See Jane Bennett, *Vibrant Matter: A Political Ecology of Things* (Duke University Press, 2010).

38. Henri Lefebvre, *The Urban Revolution* (University of Minnesota Press, 2003).

39. Karl Marx and Friedrich Engels, "Manifesto of the Communist Party" (1848), in *The Marx-Engels Reader*, second edition, ed. Tucker (Norton, 1978), 476.

40. Marx, "Wage Labour and Capital," in *The Marx-Engels Reader*, 207.

41. Ibid.

42. Marx, "Economic and Philosophic Manuscripts," in *The Marx-Engels Reader*, 79.

43. Marx, "Wage Labour," 208–209.

44. Marx, "Economic and Philosophic Manuscripts," in *The Marx-Engels Reader*, second edition, ed. Tucker (Norton, 1978), 72.

45. Karl Marx, "Economic and Philosophic Manuscripts of 1844," in *Karl Marx: Selected Writings*, ed. Lawrence H. Simon (Hackett, 1944), 63.

46. Marx, Capital, volume I, in *The Marx-Engels Reader*, 302–303.

47. Marx, "Economic and Philosophic Manuscripts," in *The Marx-Engels Reader*, 77.

48. See Hannah Arendt, *The Human Condition* (University of Chicago Press, 1958).

49. Marx, *Capital*, volume I, tr. Fowkes, 493, n.4.

50. Ibid., 509.

51. Timothy W. Luke, *Capitalism, Democracy and Ecology: Departing from Marx* (University of Illinois Press, 1999).

52. Marx, "Economic and Philosophic Manuscripts of 1844," in *Karl Marx: Selected Writings*, 63.

53. Ibid.

54. On the devouring placelessness of consumer capitalism, see also Cannavò's chapter on Arendt in this volume.

55. Michel de Certeau, *The Practice of Everyday Life* (University of California Press, 1984), 117.

56. Hans-Joachim Schellnhuber and Herman Held, "How Fragile Is the Earth System?" in *Managing the Earth: The Lineacre Lectures 2001*, ed. James C. Briden and Thomas E. Downing (Oxford University Press, 2002).

57. Lefebvre, *The Urban Revolution*, 17.

58. William Catton Jr., *Overshoot: The Ecological Basis of Revolutionary Chance* (University of Illinois Press, 1980).

12

W. E. B. Du Bois: Racial Inequality and Alienation from Nature

Kimberly K. Smith

Like the other theorists in this collection, William Edward Burghardt Du Bois (1868–1963) is not usually considered an environmentalist. But in fact he was deeply engaged in the nineteenth-century and twentieth-century conversations about progressive agricultural reform, the back-to-the-land movement, and wilderness preservation. Those conversations informed his critique of American race relations and his defense of social and political equality for blacks, helping to form his background assumptions about the proper relationship between humans and the natural world. An underappreciated element of his philosophy concerned the impact of racial oppression on environmental stewardship and on a community's ability to establish meaningful relationships with the land, making him an important forerunner of the contemporary environmental justice movement. This chapter explores that theme in his writings, focusing in his analysis of the effect of oppression on agricultural stewardship and the urban environment, his critique of the wilderness preservation movement, and his understanding of the relationship between land sovereignty and racial identity.

Du Bois has been called "the premier architect of civil rights activists in the United States."[1] He was one of the founders of the National Association for the Advancement of Colored People, an editor of the NAACP's journal *The Crisis*, and a leading spokesperson for pan-Africanism. Indeed, his career as an activist almost overshadows his contributions to twentieth-century political thought. He wrote sixteen books on sociology, history, politics, and race relations, and several novels, but his most influential work remains his 1903 collection of essays titled *The Souls of Black Folk*. These essays introduce the main themes of his body of scholarship: the nature of racial identity, the tensions and contradictions between democratic ideals and the racial basis of social organization, and the corrosive effect of racial prejudice on social and economic life. It was in *The Souls of Black Folk* that Du Bois predicted that "the problem of twentieth century" would be "the problem of the color line."[2]

Despite his extraordinary influence on our understanding of racial identity, racism, and democracy, Du Bois is often relegated to the margins of Western political thought in general and liberal thought in particular. Undoubtedly this marginal status is due in part to the relatively recent emergence of race as a major category of Western political thought. But it is also due in part to Du Bois's style of philosophical reasoning, which is practical, concrete, and problem-driven. Although he engages many of the same themes discussed by theorists in this collection (particularly property, oppression, and alienation), his political thought grows out of his experience with a specific set of interrelated problems facing a unique and particular community: the United States at the beginning of the twentieth century. He generalized from that case but resisted the urge to abstraction. For this reason, his style resonates strongly with the place-based prose of the American nature writers who were publishing during the same period. Du Bois's writings, in fact, exhibit a very strong sense of place; even in his most academic work, he pays careful attention to the material reality in which humans find themselves (in both senses of the phrase).[3] So the natural environment—the physical landscape itself, in all its historical, spiritual, social, and biological complexity—is more present in his writings than it is in most of the other works of political theory discussed in this collection. For Du Bois, the land is central to the social, political, economic, and spiritual problems faced by African-Americans, who had been forced by a peculiarly modern theory and practice of race into a peculiarly modern condition of alienation from themselves, their community, and the natural world.

Du Bois is thus not only an important political theorist but also an important voice in the great American conversation about humanity and nature. His long career overlapped with the careers of John Muir, Gifford Pinchot, Lewis Mumford, Jane Jacobs, Aldo Leopold, and Rachel Carson, and he was subject to many of the same intellectual influences that informed their work. Indeed, the civil rights and conservation movements were interrelated aspects of the cultural sea change that opened the twentieth century: the emergence of modern industrial society. Broadly speaking, both movements were in part efforts to preserve non-instrumental values, to defend the view that human beings and/or the natural world they are part of are not mere resources to be exploited but have objective value in themselves.[4] This resistance to the dominance of instrumental values is prominent in Du Bois's work, but he goes beyond this general theme, exploring in depth how racial inequality and oppression affected how black Americans and white Americans worked, owned, and made homes on the land. Drawing on a rich tradition of black environmental thought,[5] he argues that racial injustice impaired environmental stewardship, distorted black Americans' moral and spiritual relationship to the natural environment, and had an equally destructive impact on white Americans' relationship to nature. In developing these arguments, Du Bois made a significant contribution to twentieth-century environmental thought, and particularly to the political tradition that culminates in the contemporary environmental justice movement.

Race and Stewardship

It shouldn't surprise us that environmental stewardship was a central concern in black political thought. Abolitionism was, among other things, an agricultural reform movement, and the political tradition it generated continued for many decades to focus on the status of black farmers and the problem of black landlessness. Du Bois's writings share that focus. It is significant that the second essay in *Souls of Black Folk*, "The Dawn of Freedom," concerns the Freedman's Bureau, the North's abortive attempt to rectify the chief injustice of slavery by giving freed slaves their own land—to create, under government auspices, a "peasant proprietorship" of the abandoned lands of the South. According to Du Bois, the effort failed not because it misconceived either the problem (landlessness) or the solution (property ownership), but because it ran into intractable resistance. The Freedman's Bureau was dissolved in 1872, thus ending the first attempt to establish black Americans as a secure land-owning class. The dream of "forty acres and a mule"—"the righteous and reasonable ambition to become a landholder, which the nation had all but categorically promised the freedmen"—was destined (in most cases) to disappointment.[6] But the ambition didn't die, and the civil rights movement, under Du Bois's leadership, would continue to understand the "problem of the color line" as rooted not just in civil inequality but also in landlessness or, more broadly, homelessness. It is a central insight of this tradition that slavery and racial oppression worked to alienate black Americans from the American landscape.

The theme of alienation from the land appears frequently in Du Bois's writings. One of the earliest and most striking examples can be found in the concluding passage of "The Dawn of Freedom":

I have seen a land right merry with the sun, where children sing, and rolling hills lie like passioned women wanton with the harvest. And there in the King's Highway sat and sits a figure veiled and bowed, by which the traveller's footsteps hasten as they go.[7]

It is a common trope in Western letters, this contrast between the beauty of the pastoral landscape and the ugliness of injustice. But for Du Bois it is much more than a commonplace; it captures a fundamental dynamic. Racial oppression was, not just figuratively but literally, destroying the pastoral beauty of the southern landscape. Du Bois develops one dimension of this point in the seventh essay in *Souls*, "Of the Black Belt." Here he describes "the crimson soil of Georgia stretching away bare and monotonous." The land is dotted with "straggling, unlovely villages." Attentive as always to detail and difference, Du Bois notes the transition from the "bare red clay and pines of Northern Georgia" to the "rich rolling land, luxuriant, and here and there well tilled" around Macon (the land, he notes, that was seized against strong resistance from the native Creek Indians).[8] But the Black Belt in general, the rich Georgia soil that became the southeastern center of plantation slavery, now seems "forlorn and forsaken." The reason, we soon learn, is that most of the land is farmed by tenants with insecure leases and crippling rents, "and so the land is uncared-for and poor."[9] Under slavery, the rich land was already "partially devitalized by careless and exhaustive culture."[10] Forty years later, the environmental degradation was even worse. Poverty and debt made it impossible for the tenant farmers to practice more careful stewardship, rotate their crops, or tend gardens. And even if they could, they had few incentives to do so: It wasn't their land. In short, the failure to settle blacks permanently on the land, followed by decades of racial discrimination, was making barren the rich rolling hills of the South.

Du Bois didn't spell out the social and economic forces creating this scarred and degraded landscape in great detail. He didn't have to. By 1903, the impact of racial oppression on agricultural stewardship was well understood by black theorists, from T. Thomas Fortune to Booker T. Washington.[11] Indeed, the topic was already well developed as early as 1873, when Frederick Douglass took it up as the theme of his address to the Tennessee Colored Agricultural and Mechanical Association. This speech is an important precursor to Du Bois's essay; it gives insight into the intellectual tradition on which Du Bois was drawing thirty years later, and so helps to explain much that is left to inference in *Souls*. Moreover, the speech was given only a year after the demise of the Freedman's Bureau, which gives it not only a special poignance but a special historic significance: It may be taken as an implicit commentary on the Bureau's project, and so an important source for later black theorists' reflection on the problem of black landlessness.

Douglass opens the speech with what initially sounds like a standard paean to agriculture. The virtue of farming is a commonplace in nineteenth-century American rhetoric, but Douglass gives this familiar topic a racial slant. He praises black farmers for setting a "noble example" of industriousness and progress toward "civilization, culture and refinement," and reminds them that "in color, form, and features, we are related to the first successful tillers of the soil; to the people who taught the world agriculture." He underscores the point: "While the Briton and Gallic faces wandered like beasts of prey in the forests, the people of Egypt and Ethiopia rejoiced in well cultivated fields and abundance of corn." Unfortunately, he notes, prejudice has "driven the Negroes in great numbers from the country into the large cities, and into menial positions, where they easily learn to imitate the vices and follies of the least exemplary whites." Douglass encourages blacks to resist this trend and to view agriculture as "a refuge for the oppressed."[12] He then presses his main point: "emancipation ... was not only a triumph of justice, but a triumph of agricultural industry." After all, "what possible motive had the slave for a careful, successful cultivation of the soil? What concern could he have for increasing the wealth of the master, or for improving and beautifying the land?" Douglass reasons that wealthy masters were less likely to work in the fields with the slave, so wealth served to increase the distance and break down any sympathy between master and slave. Therefore, "it was in the interest of the slave to make the rich man poor and the poor man poorer." Even worse, under slavery the soil itself "was cursed with a burning sense of injustice." Slavery fostered anger and hatred in the slave, and "fields could not be lovingly planted nor faithfully cultivated in its presence." Farm animals were mistreated too: "The ox and the mule shared the general feeling of indifference to rights naturally engendered by a state of slavery. The master blamed the overseer; the overseer the slave, and the slave the horses, oxen and mules, and violence and brutality fell upon the animals as a consequence." Happily, liberty and justice would bring "respectability of labor" and a concern for the "general welfare" that promised to lead to a prosperous agriculture.[13]

Douglass's speech sums up an environmental critique of slavery first developed by Federalist critics of southern slave agriculture (notably Hector St. John de Crèvecouer, in *Letters from an American Farmer*[14]) and taken up later by the abolitionists. It is particularly prominent in the fugitive slave narratives, which are replete with descriptions of landscapes scarred by poor agricultural stewardship, the work of indolent masters and resentful slaves. These descriptions would be echoed by Du Bois and other critics of southern peonage. According to this critique, an unjust agricultural labor system (race slavery and peonage) explains the poor environmental stewardship in the South. In the absence of secure property rights, farmers have no economic incentive to care for the soil's fertility. Exploited agricultural workers feel no common interest with owners in the continuing productivity of the soil, nor are they psychologically disposed to be careful, responsible stewards or to respect farm animals. Secure property rights are therefore necessary to create economic and emotional incentives for good stewardship, and an equitable labor system creates a respect for labor that encourages good, careful farming.

The continuing insecurity of black rural land owners throughout Reconstruction and into the Jim Crow era ensured that this critique would resonate with black theorists well into the twentieth century. Not only did Du Bois draw upon this critique, as has already been noted above; he was the first to describe the same dynamic at work in northern cities. His first major work of sociology, *The Philadelphia Negro*, explores how economic forces combine with racial prejudice to create racially segregated urban ghettoes. Racial segregation, he notes, prevents wealthy blacks from moving into better neighborhoods, limits their employment options, and raises the price of housing for African-Americans by limiting its supply. These factors reduce the incentives for black homeowners to invest in their properties or neighborhoods (which receive very little public funding to begin with). The environmental consequences are easy to see: Most black urban neighborhoods suffered from substandard housing and a dangerous, unhealthy physical environment.[15] Sadly, the persistence of racial segregation in housing in the United States has given this analysis continuing relevance. Urban and rural blacks, facing the same racial prejudice, experience the same inability to establish themselves securely on the land. Racism undermines their capacity to create a home for themselves through the ordinary acts of land stewardship.

Race and Natural Beauty

The impact of racial prejudice on blacks' relationship to the land was not merely economic, however. Du Bois was equally concerned with how racism could affect a community's moral and spiritual relationship with the natural world. Indeed, the relationship between politics and aesthetics—a central concern for romantic philosophers such as Rousseau and especially Burke[16]—is also a major focus of Du Bois's thought. That nature held moral, spiritual, and aesthetic value was, for Du Bois, a claim needing no defense. He wrote about the natural world frequently and with an eloquence that John Muir might have envied. Consider his description of Bar Harbor, Maine:

> There the mountains hurl themselves against the stars and at their feet lie black and leaden seas. Above float clouds—white, gray, and inken, while the clear, impalpable air springs and sparkles like new wine. Last night we floated on the calm bosom of the sea in the southernmost haven of Mount Desert. The water flamed and sparkled. The sun had gone, but above the crooked back of cumulus clouds, dark and pink with radiance, and on the other sky aloft to the eastward piled the gorgeous-curtained mists of evening.[17]

At the urging of many elite New Englanders, this landscape became one of the first national parks (established in 1919). But preserving such wildernesses is not Du Bois's cause, and this essay ("Of Beauty and Death," from his 1920 collection *Darkwater*) explains why. He poses the question: "Why do not those who are scarred in the world's battle and hurt by its hardness travel to these places of beauty and drown themselves in the utter joy of life?"[18] In other words, why don't his fellow African-Americans follow John Muir's example—the example urged by so many wilderness enthusiasts—and seek freedom and happiness in the vast and glorious American wilderness? His answer is devastatingly succinct:

> Did you ever see a "Jim-Crow" waiting-room? . . . To buy a ticket is torture; you stand and stand and wait and wait until every white person at the "other window" is waited on. Then the tired agent yells across, because all the tickets and money are over there.
> "What d'ye want? What? Where?"
>   The agent browbeats and contradicts you, hurries and confuses the ignorant, gives many persons the wrong change, compels some to purchase their tickets on the train at a higher price, and sends you and me out on the platform, burning with indignation and hatred![19]

Twentieth-century bureaucracy aggravated by a large dose of racism makes the business of getting to the "great outdoors" intolerable. Du Bois doesn't deny that "there is nothing more beautiful in the universe than sunset and moonlight on Montego Bay in far Jamaica." But neither is there "a more disgraceful denial of human brotherhood than the 'Jim-Crow' car of the southern United States." He reminds wilderness enthusiasts that both things "belong to this our world, and neither can be denied."[20]

The "wilderness experience" depended on a growing industrial economy, with railroad access and leisure time that were unfairly distributed in a racist society, but that was not the only way racism interfered with

Americans' appreciation of natural beauty. Its deeper effects are the subject of one of Du Bois's most widely anthologized essays, "The Criteria of Negro Art." Most anthologized versions, unfortunately, leave out the beginning of the essay, which makes its relevance to the conservation movement clear. Du Bois begins with a description of the beauty and peacefulness of a Scottish lake: "You could glimpse the deer wandering in unbroken forests, you could hear the soft ripple of romance on the waters." But his pleasure was disrupted by a group of American tourists: "They poured upon the little pleasure boat. ... They all tried to get everywhere first. They pushed other people out of the way." They "struck a note not evil but wrong." He continued, "Their hearts had no conception of the beauty which pervaded this holy place."[21] That genteel complaint about ugly bourgeois Americans might have been written by Henry James. But Du Bois's diagnosis is surprising: white Americans' insensitivity to natural beauty, he reasons, is a result of racial oppression. Racism, he argues, has distorted American art. Both white and black artists are limited by the prevailing racial ideology. They cannot write from authentic experience, because no one wants stories that reveal the dignity of blacks or the "pitiful human degradation" of many whites. "In other words, the white public today demands from its artist, literary and pictorial, racial pre-judgment which deliberately distorts truth and justice." By depriving themselves of a vital, authentic art, white Americans deprive themselves of the resources to develop a sensitive appreciation for the complex beauty of the real world.[22] They can tolerate only an imaginary, picture-postcard version of nature from which all traces of human suffering and oppression have been erased. As a result, they hardly know how to see, much less respond to, an actual landscape.

This argument, of course, resonates with a major theme in American environmental thought: that developing a proper appreciation for the value of nature involves learning to see what is actually there. Nature writers instruct us that close observation and description, informed by a scientific understanding of ecology, is indispensable to forging an ethically and aesthetically rewarding relationship to nature. For Du Bois, however, close observation and description of the social world is equally necessary in appreciating the natural landscape. This was for him a chief advantage held by black American artists—those seventh sons and daughters, "gifted with second-sight," who could, with great effort, see beyond the racial ideology to a world more true and more real.[23] If Americans are to learn how to appreciate natural beauty, it seems, they should look not just to John Muir and Henry David Thoreau but also to Jean Toomer, James

Weldon Johnson, and Zora Neale Hurston. Who can see the southern landscape as merely pretty after reading Toomer's searing *Cane*, or Johnson's description of a lynching in *Autobiography of an Ex-Colored Man*, or Hurston's rich descriptions of the lives of the black rural community in *Their Eyes Were Watching God*? Such works give the landscape its deeper, richer meaning as the site of great beauty but also great suffering and sacrifice.

Nature and Race Consciousness

Connecting to the landscape, however, involves more than simply seeing it properly. Du Bois understood humans to be not just passive spectators of the landscape but creatively engaged with it. His comments on gardening, although few and scattered, offer important insights into how this creative interaction with nature shapes and is shaped by racial identity.

Gardening was as popular a topic among black theorists (as it was for almost everyone else) around the turn of the twentieth century. Alexander Crummell, Booker T. Washington, and George Carver all insisted on the importance of gardening to racial development. Du Bois, too, took up the theme in a five-part essay on "The Problem of Housing the Negro," published in 1901. One of his concerns in this piece is the lack of beauty in black homes. He notes that "it is manifest that the sense of harmony and beauty receives its first training at home." Sadly, he laments, southern districts are "bare, dull, unlovely places," and an unlovely home produces "minds without ... adequate appreciation of the beautiful world in which they live."[24] Racial oppression was, of course, a primary cause of this lack of natural beauty in the South, since (Du Bois reasoned) it led to poor stewardship. One response to this situation, he suggested, was greater attention to ornamental gardening by black homeowners. But his aim was not simply to beautify the landscape. For Du Bois, the purpose of gardening was to make the landscape meaningful to its black inhabitants.

Black homes and gardens, according to Du Bois, should embody the ideals of life peculiar to the race: "A real home is a way of thinking, a habit of doing ...an insight into the beauty of things." The homemaker's function is therefore primarily spiritual: to "interpret life and the world" to the family.[25] In Du Bois's view, slavery had destroyed slaves' home lives, depriving them of an important means of expressing and passing on to their children spiritual ideals. It had therefore left generations of blacks spiritually bereft, undermining an important basis of selfhood. Rebuilding the black home meant expressing blacks' own ideals of life. Under this view, domestic activities such as gardening should be means to develop and teach to the family black ideals of life, including "their interpretation of sunshine and rain and human hearts."[26] Gardening was a means to express and reinforce a distinct racial identity, and to give a distinctly African-American meaning to the landscape. Thus, gardening was a way for a people to express its aesthetic and spiritual ideals, and therefore to give meaning to the land. Conversely, racial oppression, by interfering with African-Americans' free, creative interaction with the land, could result in landscapes that lacked meaning and would be experienced as chaotic and frightening. Moreover, to the extent that racial oppression undermines a group's creative interaction with the natural world, it can lead to degraded, alienating environments devoid of meaning.

Land Sovereignty

The landscape described by Du Bois in the seventh and eighth essays in *The Souls of Black Folks*, "In the Black Belt" and "Of the Quest of the Golden Fleece," is indeed degraded, alienating, and devoid of meaning. The Black Belt is supposed to be the heart of the Cotton Kingdom, but, Du Bois asks pointedly, "where is the King?"[27] He finds here only struggling, debt-ridden tenant farmers, abandoned mansions, dilapidated overcrowded cabins, and little hope or expectation of improvement. This is fruit of the infamous racial peonage system that spread through the South after Reconstruction, a dramatic failure created by racist labor practices that kept black farmers in virtual slavery, compounded by an economy dangerously dependent on a single cash crop.

But there is a utopian element in political thought as in environmental thought, and in his 1911 novel *The Quest of the Silver Fleece* Du Bois reimagines the South as it might be.[28] Here he brings together his analysis of the economic and political forces leading to environmental degradation, the connection between race consciousness and cultivating the land, and an alternative perspective on wilderness preservation, bringing all these ideas to bear on the question of how a racially oppressed community can make a home for themselves on the land through political and economic organization. The novel thus explores the interconnections among political and economic forces, racial identity, and the land itself—the common ground that defines, limits, and empowers the community.

The Quest of the Silver Fleece follows Zora, an African-American girl born in a swamp near a poor black community in rural Georgia. The community is plagued by all the problems described in Du Bois's essays on the Black Belt: poverty, an economy controlled by a "cotton trust" for the benefit of the wealthy, and pervasive racism that made it impossible for black farmers to prosper. On the edge of this community lies the swamp, the novel's central image. The swamp is Nature in its romantic guise—wild and savage, a dark, "sinister and sullen" place of "strange power," but also a source of identity and cultural vitality. Although located in the United States, the swamp represents not only Nature but also the black community's African cultural heritage—and it is a deeply ambivalent heritage. The swamp is home to the witch Elspeth, a powerful figure who nonetheless prostitutes her daughters to the wealthy white land owners (a reference perhaps to both Africa's exploitation by Europeans and white Americans' exploitation of black slaves.) The swamp is undoubtedly a problem for the black community. But it is also, as we will see, an important resource.

Zora herself is one of Elspeth's daughters. Du Bois describes her as "a heathen hoyden," and when we first encounter her she is dancing in the firelight to "wondrous savage music," glowing "with vigor and life." But under the tutelage of her schoolteacher, Zora's savagery diminishes; she becomes "a revelation of grace and womanliness." Without losing her energy and spirit, she develops into "a brilliant, sumptuous womanhood; proud, conquering, full-blooded, and deep bosomed—a passionate mother of men." She also begins to speak "better English," drifting into "an upper world of dress and language and deportment." She eventually leaves her people to continue her education in politics and economics in the North. But, disillusioned by the cynical, self-serving brand of democracy practiced in Washington, she eventually returns to Georgia, intent on improving the economic and social condition of the black farmers. Her return to Georgia is a conscious reclaiming of her racial identity, her sense of solidarity with her people. Having experienced the larger world, she now sees her people "with new eyes," sensing a "vast unorganized power in this mass."[29] But in order to improve their condition, she concludes, "we must have land—our own farm with our own tenants." This would be "the beginning of a free community."[30] In fact, what she has in mind is much more ambitious, "a bold regeneration of the land." After tricking the white land owner into selling her the swamp, she convinces the farmers to clear it and to establish a democratically operated collective farm. Once their model farm is developed, complete with "agencies to make life better" (a hospital, a cooperative store, a cotton gin, and saw-mill), they will turn it over to a board of trustees who will in turn lease the land to small farmers. The trustees will operate not for profit but for "the public good."[31] Everyone will work the land, everyone will receive the product of it. Thus the swamp undergoes a transformation akin to Zora's: from a wild and savage place to a thriving communal cotton plantation.

One might see here a parallel to Plato's *Republic*, with the trustees serving as the community's "guardians." But, as Sheryl Breen points out in this volume, Plato's guardians are not only prohibited from owning land; they are not supposed to engage in agricultural labor at all. Plato's ideal republic is not, in fact, strongly connected to any place.[32] Du Bois, in contrast, implies that the trustees *will* engage in productive labor. The connection between the land and every member of the community is critical to his theory. That connection, and the community's common management of the land, is the basis for their race consciousness, their sense of identity with and connection to the community. In other words, for Du Bois devotion to the common good is a product of engagement by both elites and average citizens with the common labor of working the land.

And the physical characteristics of the land are also important to Du Bois's theory. The ideal community in *The Quest of the Silver Fleece* is built not just anywhere, but on a swamp, and part of the community's task is to preserve that ecological foundation. To be sure, Du Bois is not making a simple case for wilderness preservation here. The southern landscape doesn't need preserving as it is; it needs repair or restoration. In order to provide the basis for a well-ordered human community, the land itself must be regenerated—transformed through human labor into higher cultural forms. Nevertheless, the swamp doesn't wholly disappear in his account; its vital energy persists in the fertility of the soil, and in Zora's memory. Indeed, for Du Bois the point of transforming the wilderness *is* to preserve it, to maintain its vital energy, and to make that energy more widely available to the community. Much of what is valuable in wilderness—its fertility and natural beauty—is still present after its transformation, in the fertility of the soil, and in cultural representations of the swamp (the community's collective memory of this original wilderness.) But in Du Bois's view, if one of the goals of wilderness preservation is to forge a closer tie between wilderness and human culture, then some sort of transformation may be necessary to make what is valuable about wilderness *accessible* to the human community.[33]

African-Americans—who, although providing much of the labor of transforming the wilderness, had been subject to segregation and exclusion throughout their tenure on the American continent—couldn't take access to nature's gifts for granted. The swamp, after all, is owned by the white landlord; the community has to buy it in order to secure access to it. And the swamp holds many dark, troubling memories for Zora as for other members of the black community. For this reason, too, they can't fully embrace the swamp until it is transformed through their intentional labor into a place more suitable for human habitation.

Ultimately, however, Du Bois's solution to the black community's alienation from nature is not merely cultural, a matter of forging a spiritual and historical connection to the land. It is also, equally, political and economic: Black people must take possession of the land collectively, through socialist forms of ownership. Their economy should be governed by the public good—the flourishing of the human community with the land, rather than by the unending quest for profit, for individual material and social advantage. This conception of land sovereignty is Du Bois's ultimate solution to the alienation from the land worked by racial oppression. And it requires not only the reclaiming of one's history and sense of solidarity with the common people, but also wide-ranging cultural, political, and economic reform.

Conclusion

Reading the American landscape through the lens of race reveals a Nature very different from the sublime American wildernesses described by John Muir. Du Bois's America is a fallen world in need of spiritual regeneration, its natural beauty defaced by a legacy of injustice. His analytic framework focuses our attention not simply on the spiritual and aesthetic value of pristine nature but also on the interconnections between justice, racial identity, and the physical landscape. Who, he asks, enjoys the American wilderness, and under what social conditions? Who works these pastoral landscapes, and what are their lives like? Do they feel a connection to the land, and if so, what is the basis of that connection—historical, economic, spiritual? What is the role of art in shaping how a community interprets the landscape, and how does racial injustice affect that artistic production? Du Bois's environmental problematic thus raises a set of questions about the relationships between economic oppression, political inequality, racial identity, and the state of the natural environment—questions that have been raised more recently by the environmental justice movement.[34] Such questions will only become more important as the study of environmental thought expands to examine racial and ethnic groups marginalized or oppressed by Western colonialism.

In addition, and of equal value to environmental theory, Du Bois illustrates a mode of theorizing rooted in a specific time and place, in a particular group's experience with the landscape. Even his broad generalizations about the impacts of slavery on the land are carefully qualified, attentive to the differences attributable to region, ecology, level of urbanization, and the specific class and ethnic composition of a community. Theorists inevitably work with abstractions, of course. But environmental theory in particular is challenged to develop categories and models that highlight the relevance of ecological differences and the particularities of place and time. Du Bois's approach to theorizing, grounded in a particular community history, in particular modes of production, and in a particular social organization, offers a valuable model for explaining the dynamic interactions between social and ecological processes.

Notes

1. David Levering Lewis, *W. E. B. Du Bois, 1868–1920: Biography of a Race*, volume I (Holt, 1993), 4.

2. W. E. B. Du Bois, *The Souls of Black Folk* (1903) (Penguin, 1989), 5.

3. For another discussion of place, see Peter Cannavò's chapter on Hannah Arendt in this volume.

4. The rise of instrumentalism in political thought is discussed in this volume by Özgüç Orhan, Piers Stephens, and Tim Luke.

5. For a discussion of this tradition, see Kimberly K. Smith, *African-American Environmental Thought: Foundations* (University Press of Kansas, 2007).

6. Du Bois, *The Souls of Black Folk*, 27–28.

7. Ibid., 35.

8. Ibid. 93.

9. Ibid., 91, 96.

10. Ibid., 113.

11. See Smith, *African-American Environmental Thought*, 77–87.

12. Frederick Douglass, "Address before the Tennessee Colored Agricultural and Mechanical Association" (1873), in *African-American Social and Political Thought*, ed. Howard Brotz (Transaction, 1992).

13. Ibid., 291, 296–297. See also Barbara Seeber's discussion, in this volume, of Mary Wollstonecraft's similar insights into the relationship between oppression and environmental abuse.

14. J. Hector St. John de Crevecoeur, *Letters from an American Farmer* [1781] (Penguin, 1963).

15. W. E. B. Du Bois, *The Philadelphia Negro* (1899) (Blom, 1967), 295–96, 284.

16. See Harlan Wilson's chapter on Burke" and Joseph Lane's chapter on Rousseau in this volume.

17. W. E. B. Du Bois, *Darkwater* (1920) (Humanity Books, 2003), 227.
18. Ibid., 229.
19. Ibid., 229.
20. Ibid., 231.
21. W. E. B. Du Bois, "Criteria of Negro Art" (1926), in *Writings of W. E. B. Du Bois*, ed. Nathan Huggins (Library of America, 1986), 994.
22. Ibid., 1001.
23. Du Bois, *The Souls of Black Folk*, 5.
24. W. E. B. Du Bois, "The Problem of Housing the Negro, Part III" (1901), in *Writings by W. E. B. Du Bois in Periodicals Edited by Others*, volume I, ed. Herbert Aptheker (Kraus-Thomson, 1982), 120.
25. W. E. B. Du Bois, "The Work of Negro Women in Society" (1902), in *Writings by W. E. B. Du Bois in Periodicals Edited by Others*, volume I, 141.
26. W. E. B. Du Bois, "The Development of a People" (1904), in *Writings by W. E. B. Du Bois in Periodicals Edited by Others*, volume I, 212.
27. Du Bois, *The Souls of Black Folk*, 96.
28. W. E. B. Du Bois, *The Quest of the Silver Fleece* (1911) (Oxford University Press, 2007).
29. Ibid., 194.
30. Ibid., 198.
31. Ibid., 221.
32. See Breen's chapter on Plato in this volume.
33. On the interaction between founding and change on the one hand and preservation and stability on the other, and the significance of this interaction for human habitation of the world, see Cannavò's chapter on Arendt in this volume.
34. See Robert D. Bullard, ed., *Confronting Environmental Racism: Voices from the Grassroots* (South End, 1983); Bullard, ed., *The Quest for Environmental Justice: Human Rights and the Politics of Pollution* (Sierra Club Books, 2005); Dorceta E. Taylor, "Can the Environmental Movement Attract and Maintain the Support of Minorities?," in *Race and the Incidence of Environmental Hazards*, ed. Bunyan Bryant and Paul Mohai (Westview, 1992); David Schlosberg, *Environmental Justice and the New Pluralism: The Challenge of Difference* (Oxford University Press, 1999); Schlosberg, *Defining Environmental Justice* (Oxford University Press, 2007); Kristin Shrader-Frechette, *Environmental Justice: Creating Equality, Reclaiming Democracy* (Oxford University Press, 2005); Bron Taylor, ed., *Ecological Resistance Movements: The Global Emergence of Radical and Popular Environmentalism* (SUNY Press, 1995).

13

Martin Heidegger: Individual and Collective Responsibility

W. S. K. Cameron

Virtually alone among major twentieth-century philosophers, Martin Heidegger examined the human-nature relationship and diagnosed an insidious disease. Fortunately its symptoms—properly appreciated—also portended the "saving power," a fever through which healthier relations could reemerge. Heidegger's prognosis remained vague, but his diagnosis was undeniably compelling. Though he rarely addressed political questions directly, Heidegger's discussion of the human-nature nexus would seem an essential guide to green political theory.

Or maybe not. In 1933, Heidegger was promoted to Rector of the University of Freiburg. Ten days later, Heidegger joined the National Socialist Party; his inaugural address ended with a call that the German people (*Volk*) "will itself" and "fulfill its spiritual mission"; and in a 1935 speech he explicitly praised National Socialism's "inner truth and greatness." As Rector he cooperated in, even if he initially resisted, the "harmonization" of government institutions with Nazi policy; and although he resigned from the rectorship after only a year, he seems to have been motivated more by frustration at his lack of influence than from dissatisfaction with, let alone resistance to, the regime. After World War II, Heidegger refused to acknowledge, much less apologize for, what he privately admitted was his "great stupidity."[1] He thus appears to be the last thinker one should consult on any question, least of all a matter political theory.[2]

Why, then, consider Heidegger here? Not to defend his worst decisions: some were indefensible, and any defense would require a more nuanced historical look than I can indulge. Yet Heidegger provides invaluable insights into the possibilities and limits of insight and action—which together form the ground of the political—and his reflections on the environment are prescient and profound. We simply cannot afford to overlook this major, if sometimes misguided, thinker.

I'll begin with Heidegger's early work from the 1920s. His theoretical focus shifted in the 1930s and the 1940s; and after the war, he directly addressed environmental problems. Yet his theoretical reorientation, as we'll see, leads to a political dead end. I contend that his earlier account provides a more fruitful contribution to green political theory by resolving an important present-day question: How can creative *individual* action contribute to significant structural and political change?

Heidegger's Phenomenological Approach to Ontology

Heidegger doesn't address political theory directly. His life's aim, as articulated in his monumental work *Being and Time*, first published in 1927, was to "raise anew *the question of the meaning of being*" (Heidegger 1962, BT 19 / SZ 1).[3] He dismissed ethical and political questions as comparatively trivial. Yet his ontology implies instructive insights for ethics and politics—not least, by undermining the individualistic and voluntaristic assumptions of Western philosophy in general and liberal political theory in particular. To appreciate this, we must begin where Heidegger did: with a phenomenological approach to the meaning of being. Phenomenology, as developed by Heidegger's mentor Edmund Husserl, focuses on things as they appear to consciousness while bracketing questions about their mind-independent existence. Yet for Heidegger phenomenology uncovers the limits of consciousness and of every attempt to attain knowledge through disciplined method. How?

Heidegger begins with the "ontological being"—the "being for whom being is an issue"—i.e., human being. Naming our mode of being Dasein (literally "being there"), Heidegger forestalls our assuming that we know what he means by avoiding such familiar terms as "subjectivity" and "consciousness." Indeed the modern focus on consciousness was, as Hans-Georg Gadamer put it, a "distorting mirror,"[4] because our best efforts to attend phenomena sharply and self-consciously actually occlude awareness of the *context* of those phenomena. Consider the experience of a theater. We arrive aware of the setting, the décor, and the beautiful, interesting, or odd folk around us. Yet when the lights dim, darkness envelops all and the stage lights focus our attention so we entirely forget those beside us, let alone those farther away. They are there, of course, and they may obtrude into awareness by whispering, coughing, or letting a cell phone ring, but we resent those distractions, since only as the world around us disappears can we truly see the drama unfolding on stage before us. Following René Descartes, modern philosophers had all assumed that a well-chosen method would reveal truth; Heidegger showed that an attentive focus on some things actually obscures our awareness of others.

The finitude of our awareness creates a second, related problem: We cannot grasp *all* particulars, i.e., the whole world, at once. On reflection it is obvious that no one could comprehend her own house, let alone her neighborhood, simultaneously in all its detail. Moreover we cannot secure fixed and final knowledge of how all those particulars are scientifically related. We can examine and correct beliefs about how some particulars are related, but the process of doing so presumes other assumptions that are not questioned at the same time. Each of those assumptions can be studied and corrected on the basis of still other assumptions, but after several such moves we can no longer be sure that our newest insights are consistent with our older ones. Heidegger's emphatically postmodern conclusion is that no method can render knowledge free of doubt either in whole or in part.

Heidegger thus repudiates the core of modern philosophy.[5] Modern philosophers thought it scandalous that we could not demonstrate the existence of the external world; to Heidegger, the scandal was, rather, "that *such proofs are expected and attempted again and again*" (BT 247, 249 / SZ 203, 205). On his view, we attend particular phenomena—the computer at my fingertips, the voices in the hall—only by directing our attention *within* a worldly context too primordial and too extensive to be determinately thematized, let alone secured. Indeed the assumptions that constitute this worldly context can be revealed and corrected only indirectly, when we turn from rare moments of hyper-consciousness to the character of our experience "proximally and for the most part" (BT 68–69, 149–150 / SZ 42–43, 113–114).

Heidegger's refusal to characterize Dasein as "human consciousness" reflects a key post-modern insight: We are much less consciously aware of the world than we typically presume. Consider how many miles you have driven without noticing the world passing by. Humans are more pragmatically and much less theoretically oriented than familiar descriptions, either ancient or modern, suggest. Proximally, and for the most part, we are vaguely aware of our immediate plans and barely aware of the "ready-to-hand" network of tools with which we accomplish our goals. This is not problematic; we are generally more effective that way. Indeed, we distort experience by explicitly attending to such nouns as "goals," "networks," and "tools." A closet is not primarily an architecturally describable space, though I can describe it thus; it is somewhere I hurriedly hang things until I need them. When I open the door of my closet, its arrangement emerges, and what I seek probably stands out. But our attitude is pragmatic, not theoretical. The closet, the clothing stored there, the arrangement of the clothing, and the shirt I seek exist in complex relationships. Yet I never reflect on these relationships; when I look into my closet, everything other than the shirt I seek is a distraction.

In his justly famous phenomenological analysis of the carpenter's hammer, Heidegger demonstrates that our most basic experience of objects is not as theoretically and self-consciously "present-at-hand" but rather as environmentally available, or "ready-to-hand." The carpenter doesn't reflect on his hammer, but reaches for something that will drive a nail to secure a hook. The hammer comes out; the carpenter swings; the hammer goes back—no problem, and virtually no explicit thought. What provokes consternation and explicit awareness is not the hammer's availability, but its frustrating *un*-availability when, for instance, a gap in the carpenter's belt reveals that he left his hammer elsewhere, or when, as he swings, the head flies off and he must fix his tool or find a substitute to finish the job (BT/SZ, sections 15 and 16). "Proximally and for the most part," we are only vaguely aware of our tools and world—and we function effectively just because we need not explicitly think. A driver, a musician, or an athlete learning new skills concentrates hard—and performs less effectively than he will years hence, when he will have internalized pragmatic routines so effectively that he need not think.

Learning can demand concentration, but we typically absorb the relationships that structure our world by growing up among them. Heidegger thus characterizes Dasein as "thrown" and "projecting" (BT 174, 184, 185 / SZ 135, 145). Dasein is thrown to a physical environment, a historical period, a language, and a socioeconomic class, to gender, ethnic, and familial roles, and to a particular body, none of which it chooses and some of which it finds uncomfortable, though it inhabits them all as deeply familiar. Borrowing a theological category, though one emptied of theological content, Heidegger describes Dasein as lost, even fallen, in *das Man*, the "they" (BT 219–224 / SZ 175–180). Its awareness is vague, average, and unexamined (BT 21–33 / SZ 2–13), the product of "curiosity," "ambiguity," and the "idle talk" of neighbors (BT/SZ, sections 35–37). Usually Dasein does *not* think for itself, but thinks as *they* do, complacently describing its world in platitudes "everyone knows."

Yet if Dasein is originally lost, it can achieve a more adequate, "authentic" understanding (BT 275–278 / SZ 232–235). Indeed it must do so, for Dasein is not just thrown, but thrown to a mode of being that "projects"; that is, it makes plans to cope with its world. Dasein discovers that its taken-for-granted maps sometimes run it aground on the shoals of actual experience. It can respond with denial, simply ignoring experience—for example, I may cover for my alcoholic spouse, buy something to make myself happy, or hope trickle-down economics will work *this* time. But experience may undeniably reveal the superficiality or inconsistency of our familiar, idle, ambiguous everyday talk, forcing Dasein to replace faulty presuppositions with more adequate ones. Recall the carpenter who "knows" where the hammer is until a look reveals that it is gone or broken. Thus Heidegger's view, though emphatically postmodern, doesn't preclude the possibility of insight. But every such insight is finite. Provoked by experience, Dasein overturns inadequate presuppositions—yet each gain presumes other, as yet unexamined and potentially problematic ideas. The Cartesian aspiration of modern philosophy—to secure all our presuppositions as knowledge—cannot be consummated. Dasein sees through a glass darkly—but as finite Dasein, it will never see Truth face to face.[6]

Heidegger's Explicit Work on Nature

Shortly after the publication of *Being and Time*, Heidegger shifted his theoretical emphasis and addressed environmental concerns explicitly.[7] He deemphasized Dasein in favor of the ultimate Ground that both makes Dasein possible and recognizes itself in Dasein's self-awareness.[8] Yet his most decisive theoretical development was already intimated in *Being and Time*. G. W. F. Hegel had argued that Dasein was historical because it was thrown to a particular world and thus inherited a worldview in the light of which all its concerns appeared. Heidegger added that Dasein was temporal in a second, heretofore unnoticed sense. Philosophers study objects as "present-at-hand," accessible *now* for examination and description. But underneath its superficial fascination with what is immediately *present* lies Dasein's fundamentally *futural* orientation—its pragmatic concern "What *will I make* of this?" Any answer to that question, furthermore, will take its orientation from Dasein's *past*—the possibilities it inherited and the consequences of former decisions ("What *has been* done with this?"). Heidegger thus revealed that Being appears in time—that is, under one of three modes of temporality: past, present, and future (BT/SZ, sections 65 and 66). Objects not only exist in a historically particular interpretive context, but also appear to our examination in temporally modulated ways.

In later work Heidegger radicalizes this insight. Not only is Dasein historical; Being itself has a history. How so? Heidegger starts from Friedrich

Nietzsche's assertion that the death of God removes any supra-worldly touchstone for truth. On Nietzsche's view, our supposed search for transcendent truth is in fact motivated by more worldly concerns—the struggle for survival and our quest for power among humans and over nature. In short, what we have called "reason" embodies a will to power. Heidegger accepts Nietzsche's description as true of Western philosophy so far, but recoils from concluding that thinking *necessarily* distorts objects in the funhouse mirror of Dasein's interests and values. He thus pursues two themes: diagnosing the ways the will to power currently enframes our perceptions so powerfully and self-reinforcingly that we cannot imagine any other perspective, and searching ever earlier in the tradition for a point before Being was understood as what resists our will.[9] Heidegger's work bears fruit in his essays on technology, as he shows how our fascination with power has led to a deepening environmental crisis and the threat of nuclear annihilation while we struggle like the sorcerer's apprentice to control the forces we have unleashed. Heidegger's failure to identify or elaborate any alternative, as we will see, renders this work, for all its suggestiveness, politically problematic. But at least the problem he is struggling with is clear: once we have become obsessed with making ourselves the "lords and masters of nature" (Descartes), *willing* to resist this temptation only serves—like whiskey gulped to cure a hangover—to magnify rather than manage our problems.

Before turning to Heidegger's political insights, I will summarize his interest in the environment as involving three areas or themes.[10] *Ontologically*, he distinguishes more and less fundamental modes of experience, arguing that we have ignored the former and fastened on the latter. In *Being and Time*, the environing network of relations that tacitly guides us is more fundamental than the particular objects we investigate thematically. But the later Heidegger argues that the way things appear is determined even more fundamentally by our epoch in the history of being. Epochs embody the presuppositions in the light of which everything else appears. These presuppositions rarely become conscious except when (as now) their limits emerge, suggesting the possibility of a new era.

This leads Heidegger to a new *methodological* focus. The aspiration to control was always the goal of the scientific method—and this method is the latest, most effective form of the general Western tendency to trap and investigate beings as present-at-hand. Physics "sets nature up to reveal itself as a coherence of forces calculable in advance."[11] Heidegger doesn't question science's effectiveness—it works very well—but he questions whether science actually captures the world in its breadth and depth. In fact, science ignores much: Measure me all you like, but do you thereby capture *me*? *Pace* its boosters, science cannot capture nature as such. Or rather, it captures nature as mathematically predictable, but ignores all that cannot be reduced to predictive relations.

To be sure, predictability brings benefits, for the predictable can be technologically subjected. Yet Heidegger's third theme is that this *technological* focus—the secret aspiration of Western metaphysics as will to power—distorts our perception of nature. We presume we are capturing the flower when we discover its genome—but poets, mystics and painters have revealed other aspects, so the scientific story cannot be the whole story, and is not obviously the most significant story. Discovering a plant's medical uses reveals more about us than about it: we see not the plant as such, but the plant as useful for us. Yet the most toxic effect of "enframing" the world as useable "stock" is to discredit every other mode of revealing. We fire cannonballs more predictably, we invent successively more efficient machines, and soon "efficiency experts" appear to direct the deployment of *human* "resources."[12] Attempting to master nature technologically, we find ourselves subjected as objects of scientific studies and techniques of control. Technology solves some problems at the cost of others that we fix only by causing still other unanticipated consequences. Consider an all-too-familiar example: we introduce a species or a pesticide to control one environmental problem, then find ourselves facing a cascade of other, more severe problems. Technology has unleashed ever more power—and now threatens to overcome us.

The Fruits of Heidegger's Analysis for Environmental Political Theory

Those mining Heidegger for environmental insights typically turn to the later ruminations that address nature directly. Heidegger's environmental reflections warrant study, but, as I have argued elsewhere, his late work so emphasizes our thrownness to an especially dark epoch of Being that it is hard to know what to do with his insights.[13] Heidegger virtually concedes that these writings suggest futility: in a late interview, he suggests that "only a god can save us" now.[14] His worry is justified, for if the disease is our compulsive quest for control, striving to control that compulsion appears just to be another symptom. Heidegger thus questions the practical point of philosophy and abandons philosophy for "thought"—an expectant, quasi-mystical waiting for a new epoch in the history of Being.

Yet isn't waiting also something we will? We face a forced choice: we will do *something*—act or wait—willy nilly. I thus return to Heidegger's earlier work as offering a more nuanced perspective on how finite thought and action can recognize and redress our problematic presuppositions. Given colossal environmental crises, we cannot forgo action; our challenge is discerning how to act *well*.

As an example of the early Heidegger's fruitfulness for political theory, consider recent arguments against any individual obligation to minimize the generation of greenhouse gases.[15] I will focus on one advanced by Walter Sinnott-Armstrong. Sinnott-Armstrong concedes the reality, the significance, and the severe consequences of anthropogenic global warming, especially for the young and vulnerable poor; he then asks whether that justifies an individual obligation to forgo simple pleasures such as a Sunday drive undertaken only for the pleasures of the view and the satisfying roar of a borrowed gas-guzzler.[16] Questioning his pre-critical intuition that driving would be wrong, Sinnott-Armstrong seeks a moral principle to ground it. And since no general principle he considers survives close examination, he concludes that individuals have no such moral obligation. Refraining from wasteful driving may be praiseworthy, and we should advocate laws that limit carbon emissions. But in advance of such laws, one has no private obligation to forgo simple pleasures even if they foreseeably contribute to global catastrophe.

I will not address his arguments in detail here, but Sinnott-Armstrong's main conclusions follow from apparently incontestable empirical and moral assumptions. First, my drive will have no measurable effect on atmospheric carbon. And since my drive "is neither necessary nor sufficient for global warming [in general]" (289) and "my exhaust on that Sunday does not cause any climate change [effect—e.g. a storm or a flood] at all" (291), I bear no blame. Of course *global warming* causes harm, yet I'm culpable only if *my drive* does so, and my drive is too trivial to harm any determinate individual (291, 293–294, 302). One drive doesn't constitute a broader, harm-causing habit, and any influence on others from my drive is very limited, so I will not undermine anyone's commitment to environmental advocacy. Sinnott-Armstrong concludes that "global warming is such a large problem that it is not individuals who cause it or who need to fix it," but he also argues against those who in despair might be tempted to just keep their hands clean by living simply and withdrawing from political and economic life. Instead, he argues, we must act collectively to effect policy change.

In my view, Sinnott-Armstrong's initial intuition that we have an individual obligation is correct, but he is then befuddled by his tendency to consider acts and individuals in isolation from the social context and the political effects of their decisions. Heidegger's early work exposes this common short-sightedness.

Sinnott-Armstrong's conclusion follows from his insistence that the decision to drive is an *individual* act (not a habit) with *individual* significance (I enjoy it, but influence no others) that creates a negligible (and thus no?) *individual* effect (drought or hurricane) on the climate. Added together, millions of individual decisions *can* cause corporate effects that should be regulated corporately, but my act alone is physically and socially insignificant. And it is hard to deny Sinnott-Armstrong's assumptions. When rare acts have negligible consequences, it is unreasonably perfectionistic to condemn them.

The problem lies in Sinnott-Armstrong's move from this plausible view to denying any *general* obligation to minimize such acts. Against this, Derek Parfit insists that when we know the physical consequences of individual acts will add up, we are responsible for contributing to their overall effect.[17] Heidegger would agree, but more importantly, he adds insights into the way *individual* acts gain *social* significance—and thus offers a rich view of the role that individuals and groups can play in envisioning, motivating, and effecting broad political change.

How would Heidegger contest Sinnott-Armstrong's traditional liberal individualism? On Mill's classic formula, actions are licit unless they harm others.[18] Heidegger, in contrast, anticipates the communitarian view of the self as socially constituted. Recall that Dasein "knows" its familiar, taken-for-granted world through the vague, ambiguous, idle talk of its era. Dasein thinks uncritically as *they* do, so nonconformity is threatening, and truly radical thought potentially incomprehensible. In this context, no neat distinction among my thoughts, comments, and acts is possible; rather, we influence one another mutually all the time.

But if our effects on and thus our responsibility for others' thoughts and actions is very diffuse, our responsibility doesn't disappear. On the contrary, one of Heidegger's virtues is to show we are not just stuck in a communal tradition; for Heidegger, the evolution of views is not merely possible but inevitable and unsuppressible.[19] Just because Dasein's understanding is finite, it is regularly surprised or disappointed by unexpected outcomes. Denial is possible, but often such surprises breed new insights confirmed by experience. As more people question the gap between expectations and experience, new views spread in the same way that old ones did, and Dasein's social context evolves so that views once wildly heretical (e.g., that women are equal to men) eventually become so commonplace that earlier views seem absurd. Thus Dasein is responsible not only for harming individuals in determinable ways,[20] or contributing to cumulative effects harmful to others,[21] but also for its role in reinforcing or questioning its taken-for-granted milieu.

What does this mean more concretely? Would-be reformers face tremendous inertia. People had to be taught to participate in a throwaway society,[22] and they will withdraw their participation only reluctantly if conceptual and motivational innovations overcome the disincentive of inconvenience. Here individuals and small groups have important roles to play: as academics exploring the implications of ideas; as preachers, pundits, and politicians reframing and refocusing debates; as teachers introducing emerging ideas; as musicians and storytellers making those ideas compelling; or as experimental communities living out their consequences.

Moreover, Dasein's primordial focus is not theoretical, but practical, and coping with the world provides constant feedback. Dasein's own experiences and others' responses inevitably reinforce or problematize its expectations. For this reason, not only talk but *all* action is socially meaningful even—and sometimes especially—when Dasein doesn't intentionally communicate. Typically Dasein chooses default paths because earlier Dasein has made them seem obvious, and thus its responsibility is somewhat mitigated. But because it *could* have chosen otherwise, Dasein is responsible nonetheless. The saying that "people get the government they deserve" is fair warning in a democracy in which laws are often shaped by the intentions of a few and the inattention and inaction of countless others. The legitimate condemnation of inaction is also the point of Pastor Martin Niemöller's rueful reflection after World War II: "First they came for the communists, and I didn't speak out because I wasn't a communist ... ."[23]

Sinnott-Armstrong may be right that individual action to reduce one's carbon footprint makes a vanishingly insignificant difference to the atmosphere. Yet to atomize action as unique and only individually significant belies its normal structure as socially meaningful—especially to those who know us well, but even to casual observers. Forgoing a pleasure drive prevents the emission of a tiny but real amount of carbon; however, its more important effect might be social: to problematize other everyday acts, such as using a car for short errands. Of course the effect may be larger when I communicate my intentions, but I need not mount a soapbox; even passing references tell my listeners I take this seriously enough to do something about it and suggest, by example, that perhaps my listeners should do the same. Action is (to borrow a military analogy) a "force multiplier": ideas affect us more powerfully when people back them with deeds.

And deeds are significant even when others don't know our motives. Seeing the odd cyclist riding to work may not wake many from complacency; however, that cyclist embodies the fact that cars are optional, and as more people join in cycling to work they can demand reasonable accommodations in public places and at workplaces. Businesses provide covered parking for cars; why not for bikes? Could lockers and showers replace spaces no longer needed for parking? As people demand bike paths and ride in numbers sufficient to command motorists' attention, the stress and danger of bicycling decline to the point where it can offer a new, healthier model of normal daily travel. Just as our unsustainable carbon emissions can and should suffer "death by a thousand cuts" as more people choose transportation alternatives, so too the tacit assumptions that hid the problem will falter as they appear first optional and then problematic. This is not to say by any means that individual action is sufficient: huge numbers of people must change their behavior, so collective political action is necessary. But while we await political success, acting well encourages a new mindfulness in us and in others. Individual actions appear quixotic only if we remove them from the historical trajectory within which they can and do mark the beginning of, or contribute to, much larger social changes.

It may appear that I'm highlighting the ethical, but not the political implications of Heidegger's view. On the contrary, my point is to link individual action with consequences at a collective or structural level, a link often obscured by the disciplinary boundary between philosophy and political theory. We human beings can recognize the collective patterns and structures of individual actions and contribute to preserving or preventing them. New forms of self-expression or self-discipline can appear pointless in view of the limited power and influence of any one individual. But even small actions contribute constructive and destructive interference to standing patterns of action. And because of our diffuse but real influence on others, they can, in addition, become models for others who want to break up persistent patterns and replace them with new ones.

Conclusion

Heidegger's late reflections on technology and the environment are poignant, yet his earlier synthesis is far more helpful politically. By revealing both the limits and the possibilities of human insight and action, Heidegger discredits the allegedly unbridgeable gap between individual action and significant social change. To be sure, this barely gets us started on the challenges we face: Heidegger identifies inertial influences that we must yet overcome. But that first step is important; it validates the political potential of the individual thought and action that is our most accessible avenue of social change. The environment is as close to us as the air we breathe—and, owing to our numbers, we affect it as measurably as it affects us. To mitigate our more toxic effects, many of us—especially those in rich countries—must change our daily behavior. Among other insights for green political theory, Heidegger shows why for Dasein, in the words of the old slogan, the personal really is political.

Notes

1. Heinrich Wiegand Petzet, *Auf Einen Stern Zugehen. Begegnungen und Gesprache mit Martin Heidegger, 1929 bis 1976* (Societäts Verlag, 1983), 53.

2. As a prominent philosopher in a nation that valued philosophy, Heidegger was well known. He did not confront the regime directly, but aspired, he claimed, to coopt it for higher ends—the renewal of the German university, the country, and perhaps the West. Insofar as he thought this possible, he was hardly the first philosopher to believe that his ideas should guide events, nor was he the first or the only prominent German to underestimate Hitler's brutal effectiveness in subjugating the country to far darker ends. Heidegger always presented himself as well-intentioned but ineffective. The discovery of East German Stasi records, however, stained this self-portrait. The debate is too complex to address here. For criticism of Heidegger, see Victor Farias, *Heidegger and Nazism*, ed. Joseph Margolis and Tom Rockmore (Temple University Press, 1991); Hugo Ott, *Martin Heidegger: A Political Life* (Basic Books, 1993); Emmanuel Faye, *Heidegger: The Introduction of Nazism into Philosophy in Light of the Unpublished Seminars of 1933–1935* (Yale University Press, 2011). For a defense of his thought, if not of Heidegger himself, see Julian Young, *Heidegger, Philosophy, Nazism* (Cambridge University Press, 1988). I agree that Heidegger's work *could* be taken in ways sympathetic to Nazism, as Heidegger's own words and actions showed, yet his work did not *require* this interpretation--indeed, by associating his own work with Nazism, Heidegger betrayed his best insights. As will be discussed later in this chapter, Heidegger rightly and consistently appealed to then-current ideas—but he was not bound to deploy the particular ones he chose.

3. Martin Heidegger, *Being and Time*, tr. John Macquarrie and Edward Robinson (Harper and Row, [1927; seventh German edition, 1953] 1962). Since translations have recently multiplied, I have supplemented references to my English edition with pagination from the original, *Sein und Zeit*, thus: BT XXX / SZ YYY.

4. Hans-Georg Gadamer, *Truth and Method*, revised second edition, ed. J. Cumming and G. Burden (Crossroad Press, 1991), 276–277.

5. Yet Heidegger is no skeptic. Though final demonstration is impossible, certainty *is* possible in restricted areas. Euclid accepts unproven but apparently incontestable axioms, but if they are true then every theorem deduced follows with

certainty. More broadly, Heidegger assumes our capacity to grasp truth. Modern philosophy presumed that we knew only what we could definitively *demonstrate* that we know—but on that account, I could never conclude that my spouse of 24 years loved me. Heidegger, in contrast, denies the possibility of definitive demonstration, but not our claim to know as such, nor our ability to back claims with good reasons.

6. Heidegger would thus affirm the line from Bruno Latour by which Timothy Luke characterizes Marx in chapter 11 above: Dasein faces ensembles of living and nonliving beings that "are simultaneously real, like nature, narrated like discourse, and collective, like society" (Bruno Latour, *We Have Never Been Modern*, Harvester Wheatsheaf, [1991] 1993, 6). We cannot apprehend either nature or society directly—which is not to deny its presence and reality, but only to insist that we access it through a web of taken-for-granted linguistic and cultural interpretations. With Marx, Heidegger agrees that we falsely hypostatize human-human and human-nature relations that are in fact fluid and contestable. He rejects Marx's confidence that we could apprehend, much less eliminate, the irrationality of those relationships. But Heidegger insists that we can resist their false substantialization and naturalization.

7. This theoretical shift responded to misunderstandings of terms such as 'guilt', 'care', 'authenticity', and 'Being-toward-death'. Heidegger was wrongly linked to the existentialists. This was no minor error, as Heidegger had challenged, not emphasized, the modern self-creating subject associated with existentialism. In addition, Heidegger's shift was sparked by doubts about the practical point of philosophy after his 1933–34 rectorship and his struggle with Nietzsche's argument that reason embodied a will to power.

8. Importantly, this Ground is not God. For Heidegger, "gods" too are beings produced by this ultimate Ground or Nature as uncreated self-presentation. He has left his Christian roots behind.

9. This abstract language about Being could be put far more concretely: Rocks are real because when I push them they resist me.

10. I owe this trifold summary to David E. Cooper's excellent article "Heidegger on Nature" (*Environmental Values* 14, 2005: 339–351).

11. Martin Heidegger, "The Question Concerning Technology," in *The Question Concerning Technology and Other Essays*, tr. William Levitt (Harper and Row, 1977), 21.

12. Martin Heidegger, "The Age of the World Picture," in *The Question Concerning Technology and Other Essays*, tr. Levitt (Harper and Row, 1977), 118–127.

13. W. S. K. Cameron, "Seeing through Technology: Martin Heidegger, Hans-Georg Gadamer, and the Role of Hermeneutic Experience," in *Between Description and Interpretation: The Hermeneutic Turn in Phenomenology*, ed. Andrzej Wiercinski (Hermeneutic Press, 2005).

14. Martin Heidegger, "'Only a God Can Save Us': The *Spiegel* Interview (1966)," tr. William J. Richardson, in *Heidegger: The Man and the Thinker*, ed. Thomas Sheehan (Transaction, 1981), 57.

15. For an exchange based largely on Garrett Hardin's article "The Tragedy of the Commons" (*Science* 162, 1968: 1243–1248), see Baylor Johnson, "Ethical Obligations in a Tragedy of the Commons," *Environmental Values* 12, no. 3 (2003): 271–287; Marion Hourdequin, "Climate, Collective Action and Individual Ethical Obligations," *Environmental Values* 19, no. 4 (2010): 443–464; Johnson, "The Possibility of a Joint Communique: My Response to Hourdequin," *Environmental Values* 20, no. 2 (2011): 147–156; Hourdequin, "Climate Change and Individual Responsibility: A Reply to Johnson," *Environmental Values* 20, no. 2 (2011): 157–162.

16. Walter Sinnott-Armstrong, "It's Not My Fault: Global Warming and Individual Moral Obligations," in *Perspectives on Climate Change: Science, Economics, Politics, Ethics*, volume 5, ed. Walter Sinnott-Armstrong and Richard B. Howarth (JAI, 2006). The parenthetical page references in the next paragraph are to this article.

17. Derek Parfit, "Five Mistakes in Moral Mathematics," in *Reasons and Persons* (Oxford University Press, 1986).

18. John Stuart Mill, *On Liberty* (Hackett, 1978), 12.

19. Heidegger's student Gadamer develops this theme in *Truth and Method*. I cannot defend the claims of inevitability and unsuppressibility here, but I have done so elsewhere, using Sabina Lovibond's structurally similar view. See Sabina Lovibond, *Realism and Imagination in Ethics* (University of Minnesota Press, 1983); W. S. K. Cameron, "The Genesis and Justification of Feminist Standpoint Theory in Hegel and Lukacs," *Dialogue and Universalism* 15 (2005): 19–41.

20. Sinnott-Armstrong, "It's Not My Fault."

21. Parfit, "Five Mistakes in Moral Mathematics."

22. Heather Rogers, "The Conquest of Garbage," *International Socialist Review* (http://www.isreview.org/issues/53/garbage.shtml).

23. Originally a conservative nationalist Lutheran pastor, Niemöller supported Hitler until Hitler attacked the church's autonomy. Eight years in concentration camps taught him the costs of his initial inaction. "What would have happened," he later asked, "if in the year 1933 or 1934 ... 14,000 Protestant pastors and all Protestant communities in Germany had defended the truth until their deaths?" For many variants of the "First they came for the communists" quotation, see http://www.history.ucsb.edu/faculty/marcuse/niem.htm. In the next chapter, Peter Cannavò illuminates Hannah Arendt's category of "action"—the words and deeds that constitute and modify the complicated web of relationships between people of diverse perspectives. Arendt clearly learned much from her teacher, the early Heidegger, though their emphases varied widely. Heidegger, always wary of the West's intellectualist and voluntarist assumptions about persons, emphasized Dasein's foggy and passive reception of the interpretations it inherits, a tendency that only grows in his later work. Arendt, darkly alive to the moral calamities that fatalism had so recently wrought and of its convenience for totalitarian leaders, highlights the permanent possibility (if also the unpredictability) of new initiatives. In both thinkers the two insights are connected; in this chapter, I have played up the latter in Heidegger because it is so easy to ignore.

14

Hannah Arendt: Place, World, and Earthly Nature

Peter F. Cannavò

Hannah Arendt (1906–1975), a German Jew who fled the Holocaust and became a citizen of the United States, was one of the most important political theorists of the twentieth century. Commentators have largely focused on her concepts of the public and private spheres and of the realm of the social, on her theory of political action, on her agonistic politics, on her analysis of totalitarianism, and on her views on the relationship between politics and morality.[1] However, she has received scant recognition for her insights into humanity's relationship with its natural and built environments.[2] Both newcomers to Arendt and scholars of her work are likely to be unaware of these insights.

I argue that Arendt's writings in *The Human Condition* (1958)[3] and *Between Past and Future* (1968)[4] establish her as an important theorist of the environmental concept of "place," even though she doesn't explicitly use this term. Moreover, in her treatment of place Arendt anticipates contemporary writings that highlight the complexity and ambivalence of humanity's relationship with nature. We not only exist as part of the natural world and depend on its stability, but we must also struggle with and transform nature.[5] Arendt sees a stable, coherent geography and an enduring relationship with one's physical surroundings—both built and natural—as critical in making the world a reliable human home. At the same time, though, she is attentive to the complexities involved in our habitation of the Earth. We must simultaneously embrace and transcend our membership in earthly nature. We must preserve nature but also resist it. Arendt shows our relationship with the natural world to embrace the poles of both care and violence. Moreover, she strikingly anticipates environmentalists' call for a sustainable society and their concerns about unbridled consumerism and unregulated development.

Work and Action: Creating a Human Home on Earth

In *The Human Condition*, Arendt explores how the conditions for human life on Earth foster three basic activities: labor, work, and action. For Arendt, habitation of the Earth is the most fundamental condition of human existence. The Earth "is the very quintessence of the human condition" (2), and "earthly existence bestows the basic conditions of "birth and death, natality and mortality" (8).

The activity most related to humanity's basic biological existence is *labor*. Labor is the activity of attending to bodily needs, such as the need for food. Concerned with life-sustaining consumption rather than creation (118–126), labor produces goods to consume, but not lasting objects. Yet human beings seek to modify their earthly existence. Initially, Arendt describes nature as something to be battled and overcome. Nature is characterized by relentless cycles of birth, growth, and decay, without clear beginnings or endings. Organisms pursue sustenance and reproduction but are ultimately destroyed by other creatures or natural forces. Nature lacks permanence; it consumes its creations. Life is "a process that everywhere uses up durability, wears it down, makes it disappear" (96), and human beings are in a "constant, unending fight against the processes of growth and decay" (100). Labor doesn't resist these cycles; rather, it participates in them (7–8, 79–93). To create enduring objects and culture, human beings must overcome nature and their mere biological existence through two higher-order activities: work and action.

Work is the activity through which human beings create enduring physical objects from pre-given plans or designs. Work fashions objects that can resist natural decay and furnish a durable, built world—the "human artifice" (136).[6] "Man, in so far as he is *Homo faber*, instrumentalizes" the material world; "during the work process, everything is judged in terms of suitability and usefulness for the desired end, and for nothing else," and "the end justifies the violence done to nature to win the material, as the wood justifies killing the tree and the table justifies destroying the wood" (153–154, 156). Work depends on nature for materials, yet in altering the world and resisting natural processes it opposes nature's given arrangements. Work is "destructive" of nature as given; it can entail "killing a life process, as in the case of the tree which must be destroyed in order to provide wood, or interrupting one of nature's slower processes, as in the case of iron, stone, or marble torn out of the womb of the earth" (100, 139). Thus, "human productivity was by definition bound to result in a Promethean revolt because it could erect a man-made world only after destroying part of God-created nature" (139).

Action is the activity of words and deeds transpiring directly between persons (7). Action reflects human plurality, as it involves interaction among persons with diverse perspectives. Words and deeds constitute a shared, complex, lasting social reality, "the 'web' of human relationships" (183). Each individual's actions and life story shape this web and are in turn shaped by it (184). The web of relationships defines individuals' and communities' interactions, characters, purposes, and identities. Action thus constitutes both individuals and their common life. Action is fundamentally political (22–28, 196–198) and finds quintessential expression in deliberation over collective principles and ends.[7]

Unlike labor, action is not tied to physical sustenance and natural necessity. Unlike work, action doesn't simply execute pre-given plans. Moreover, action is not concerned with managing economic needs or relations or harnessing and consuming resources—activities that Arendt consigns to "the social."[8] Instead, action initiates new beginnings, through speech and deed, in the web of human relationships. Yet action doesn't fulfill a predetermined goal or subordinate itself to further ends; with action, means and ends are one. For Arendt, the realm of action is thus the realm of freedom (177). But this freedom has limits: One can initiate action, but one cannot control its outcome. Its outcome is determined collectively, as action reverberates through the web of relationships and engages with others' words and deeds (183–184, 191–192, 232–234).

Together, action and work resist nature's impermanence and create the human artifice. Words and deeds accord meaning to work's creations: "Without being talked about ... the world would ... [be] a heap of unrelated things" (204). Work, in turn, fashions the material objects that embody and preserve the social reality generated by action (95).[9] Action and work create the lasting meanings and objects that "constitute the conditions under which" human beings "can be at home on earth" (134). Arendt's concept of the human artifice thus involves what Zev Trachtenberg, in his chapter on John Locke in this volume, calls a theory of *habitation*: the idea that "human life involves the active transformation of the natural world into a humanized domain (i.e. a domain that has a physical structure created by human action) and a moral structure that human action is obliged to observe." As Trachtenberg says in regard to Locke, Arendt's theory of habitation suggests "normative limits on human activity in the environment."[10]

Importantly, Arendt distinguishes between *earthly nature* and *the world* (i.e., the built artifice).[11] Human beings participate in earthly nature through labor and its life-sustaining activities. However, through work and action, we also create and inhabit the human artifice.

Arendt's emphasis on the ultimate uncontrollability of action, on human plurality, and on the importance of political deliberation should dispel any ideas that this worldly home is free of conflict, difference, uncertainty, or change. To be at home in the world is not to have a static, quiescent existence, but to find just enough familiarity, stability, coherence, and meaning to confidently undertake long-term ends and projects and to fashion coherent, enduring individual and collective life stories rather than constantly negotiate a hostile, destructive environment.[12] Reliance on a worldly home enables us to do more than survive—that is, to do more than simply labor within nature's cycles.

Arendt's Human Artifice as a World of Places

Arendt discusses the human artifice in spatial terms, implying that distinct, enduring places are essential to being at home in the world.[13] The world created by work and action "relates and separates men at the same time," she says. It "gathers us together and yet prevents our falling over each other" (52–53). Social relationships are spatially organized through arrangements of things and places: "To live together in the world means essentially that a world of things is between those who have it in common, as a table is located between those who sit around it" (52–53). The world is *public*, a collective creation and a collective experience.[14]

Existing "between" individuals, the human artifice gives relationships spatial coherence and legibility.[15] A table is more than a useful surface. It can be a shared place around which individuals mutually orient themselves. Think of a table at which a group regularly meets, perhaps with each person at his or her usual spot. Gatherings at the table, and in the room in which it sits, maintain and refresh relationships and shared aims and values and even help sustain individuals' identities. People may change seats, the participants or their aims may change, and the table itself may be moved around the room, but still the table and the room provide continuity for the participants.

The table and other things of the human artifice, or world, thus create, on top of our natural context, a new set of conditions that shape human life (9). Consequently, in fashioning and refashioning the human artifice, we are fashioning and refashioning ourselves and our individual and collective identities.

Places as Founded, Not Found
Arendt suggests that raw nature cannot provide human beings with a coherent set of places. Because it consumes all its creations, nature cannot sustain enduring locations. Only the built artifice can: "The things of the world," Arendt says, "have the function of stabilizing human life" (137). People must therefore *build* a world and *found* places.[16]

Arendt certainly overemphasizes nature's destructiveness, for even though living things grow, change, and die, natural geography and topography may persist for thousands or millions of years. Yet her remarks usefully suggest how the natural world doesn't have entirely stable, predefined locales, at least not from a human perspective. Elements of the landscape seem to blend into one another, and organisms and natural forces traverse and alter landscapes and ecosystems. Though nature is not without stability, the dynamic character of the biosphere means that the natural landscape is in some measure ever in flux. Anne Chapman underscores this:

In most cases, of course, the rate of change is far longer than the human lifespan. … However, in some environments dramatic changes may happen over short periods of time. For example, the river channels in the tidal sands of Morecambe Bay, in North West England, can move significantly over just a few years. Recent movement of a river channel away from the north side of the bay has led to the growth of salt marsh grasses where there was previously sand.[17]

Is the north side of the bay then still the same place? Nature doesn't settle this question. We must, as human beings trying to make sense of our surroundings, pick out elements of continuity in the north side of the bay if we wish to designate it as a more or less coherent, enduring place. Stable places *qua* places are human constructs. Human beings must create or define coherent, enduring locales for themselves.[18]

Place-founding is most obvious with built structures and settlements. In this case, of physical construction, place-founding is most akin to work. But, as Arendt's discussion of work and action suggests, the creation of places involves not only physical effort but also descriptive words, including identification of distinctive features and boundaries. Identification and description are more like action than work. Recall that without action we have Arendt's "heap of unrelated things." We cannot have a recognized place without describing and delineating it.

Moreover, though Arendt herself doesn't acknowledge this directly, places can be created entirely through action without physically altering the landscape. Even "natural" places are, in some measure, human constructs, founded through description. To designate certain areas as wetlands, for example, researchers must decide on the general characteristics of wetlands and determine the locations and the boundaries of particular wetlands.[19] This does *not* mean that a moist, vegetated terrain doesn't exist prior to our naming and describing it.[20] Nor does it suggest that other animals don't have their own geographical perceptions and distinctions.[21] Yet, as was noted above, nature doesn't present human beings or other perceiving organisms with neat boundaries or sharply delineate itself into distinct ecosystems or terrains. To make sense of the natural world, we must interpret it and map it, drawing boundaries. At that point, natural locales are brought into the human world. According to Chapman, "all natural, non-human-created things that can appear in public (i.e. be experienced by different people, from a plurality of perspectives) have the potential to be part of our world and we make them part of our world by paying attention to them."[22] Thus, Arendt says, "whatever touches or enters into a sustained relationship with human life immediately assumes the character of a condition of human existence" (9). Indeed, Arendt notes that individual animals or plants, when actually recognized or marked out as individuals, can be included in our world (98).

However, anyone's description of a place is shaped by their particular perspective. The description or delineation of particular places, built or natural, is thus frequently contested[23]; for example, definitions and identifications of wetlands are politically quite contentious. As with other forms of Arendtian action, the description, delineation, and naming of places are all enacted in the web of human relationships and subject to challenge and amendment by other actors, who are oriented to the very same locations through different spatial perspectives, social relationships, and positions of power.

Yet a shared spatial environment, and minimal agreement that a recognizable place indeed exists there, create possibilities for collective deliberation. "Deliberative speech," Dana Villa notes in discussing Arendtian action and politics, "must be anchored in a shared world" that is the object of some minimum agreement, and "where such an agreement dissolves or is shattered, it is no longer possible to view the same thing from a variety of perspectives." A shared world doesn't mean a univocal perspective on the landscape, but it is in fact "a palpable 'in-between' [i.e.

a shared world] that makes plurality—a genuine diversity of perspectives on the same phenomenon—possible."[24]

The Mutual Constitution of Identity and Place

In founding places and creating the human artifice, individuals and communities also fashion identities: "men, their ever-changing nature notwithstanding, can retrieve their sameness, that is, their identity, by being related to the same chair and the same table" (137). Again, Arendt suggests a view of the human artifice not only in terms of things but also in terms of places. Arendt's table creates a common location for those around it, a place that helps define not only their relationships but also their identities.

How do places shape identities?[25] Individuals interact with places through various activities: residence, work, play, travel, shopping, worship, spiritual or aesthetic appreciation, and so on. These interactions shape mental and bodily dispositions, biographies, goals, possibilities, constraints, social relationships, daily routines, worldviews, and affiliations. When things and places, like Arendt's chair and table, are relatively stable, this helps stabilize human identities. However, because different persons approach the same place through different perspectives and interactions, that very same place may foster a variety of different identities.

Moreover, as with the conference table and Morecambe Bay, the stability of places, and hence that of identities, is never absolute. Places themselves change under social and ecological influences. As things and places change, they change those who interact with them. Over time, the world and its inhabitants constitute one another in an endless, open-ended process,[26] just as Arendtian action is itself open-ended. Places and identities are always "unfinished."[27] Yet, as was noted above, even if some elements of a place change, that place can still provide continuity for those interacting with it over time.

Founding as a Collective Project

Arendt's human artifice is thus a shared, public spatial environment, shared by individuals with different perspectives. As with Arendtian action, place-founding happens in a web of human relationships. How an act of founding turns out depends on how others respond. Place-founding is a collective activity, requiring some collective assent. I cannot unilaterally designate my street a cow pasture. There must be some agreement, however minimal, on the character of a place.

Granted, one could achieve such agreement despotically. History is replete with authoritarian place-founding by governments, land owners, and businesses. Yet such place-founding doesn't qualify as action in the true Arendtian sense, but is more akin to work, whereby a powerful actor forcibly reshapes the world according to a pre-given plan (220–230). To be truer to action, place-founding should involve democratic deliberation wherein parties offer up competing conceptions of a place but seek a collective, ever-evolving vision.

The Preservation of Places
Places are always in flux, but the concept of place also entails some stability. In resisting nature's cycles, human beings seek to create a useful, secure, meaningful, and *enduring* world, as seen with Arendt's chair and table, and ground their identities in such a world. We need to avoid perpetual change or instability, and we need to maintain historical or cultural artifacts and living, sustaining aspects of the social or ecological environment. Founding must be accompanied by *preservation*.[28] Chapman notes that the world "should be stable, not in the sense of never changing, but in the sense of lasting," and that "this may require some change, but it will be change that preserves what is significant, and that continues the story of the past into the future in a meaningful way."[29]

Preservation doesn't simply follow founding.[30] The proper relationship between the two is complex and ongoing. This interaction is revealed through Arendt's treatment of humanity's relationship with the Earth in *The Human Condition* and through her discussion of care and cultivation in *Between Past and Future*. In these discussions, we see not only Arendt's conception of place but also her view of the complex importance of earthly nature for humanity.

Earthly Nature: Struggle and Preservation
In *The Human Condition*, Arendt ultimately departs from her initially negative view of nature and expresses reservations about the violent instrumentalization of nature enacted through work. She suggests a preservationist attitude toward both earthly nature and the human artifice.

Arendt worries that *Homo faber*'s instrumentalism will escape from "limited and productive" bounds and commandeer our whole relationship with both earthly nature and the human artifice (157). Anticipating environmentalist critiques of crude anthropocentrism,[31] she warns of a "generalization of the fabrication experience in which usefulness and utility are established as the ultimate standards for life and the world of men"

(157), resulting in a "limitless devaluation of everything given, [a] process of growing meaninglessness in which every end is transformed into a means" (157). Arendt, whose own theory of habitation clearly departs from Locke's view of nature as largely a bank of resources, sees such instrumentalism as "degrad[ing] nature" and robbing it of its "independent dignity" (156).

According to Arendt, Earth and nature "clearly came into being without the help of man and have an existence independent of the human world" (156). Moreover, because existence on Earth is "the very quintessence of the human condition" (2), the Earth confers meaning on humanity. Though the "human artifice ... separates human existence from all mere animal environment," "life itself is outside this artificial world, and through life man remains related to all other living organisms" (2). Considering the prospect of space travel, Arendt says that it would involve a "repudiation of an Earth who was Mother of all living creatures" (2) and would represent "the most radical change in the human condition we can imagine" (10). Human beings "would have to live under man-made conditions, radically different from those the earth offers. ... Neither labor nor work nor action nor, indeed, thought as we know it would then make sense any longer." (10)

How can Arendt celebrate humanity's struggle against earthly nature and yet see nature as imbued with dignity and as a source of meaning? We may resolve this apparent contradiction through the distinction—also emphasized by Anne Chapman and by Paul Ott—between earthly nature and the human artifice. By building an artificial, enduring world of created things and meanings, we partially remove ourselves from nature, yet still remain part of nature in virtue of our biological existence. By stepping partly outside earthly nature rather than being entirely immersed in an unmediated relationship with natural processes, we make nature something objective to us. "Only we who have erected the objectivity of a world of our own from what nature gives us, who have built it into the environment of nature so that we are protected from her, can look upon nature as something 'objective'. Without a world between men and nature, there is eternal movement, but no objectivity."[32] (137)

At a partial remove, and objectified, nature shifts from a realm of "eternal movement" without stability or coherence to a larger, partly external, legible context for human endeavor. Nature thus provides both a material setting for humanity and an external set of processes for us to struggle against. For Arendt, it is our effort to overcome natural processes and fashion an enduring world that gives creative activity much of its purpose and significance. Human beings define themselves against, or in contrast to, the rest of nature. Earthly nature offers a larger, meaningful context and carries an "independent dignity" in virtue of its status as something from which human beings seek, but never quite obtain, full autonomy. We carve out our own built world, but one still physically and ecologically within, and dependent upon, nature.[33] Were we to abandon Earth and live encapsulated in life-support technology, human existence would lose an important external referent and source of purpose and seem ungrounded and subjective. For Arendt, space travel symbolizes the emptiness of a fully technological, denatured existence, one of self-referential human activity without clear need or purpose.

Yet meaningful struggle is not the only Arendtian support for nature preservation. Here Arendt's notion of place returns to the discussion. Most obviously, the stability and integrity of the human artifice would ultimately rest upon a stable, well-functioning biosphere.[34] Moreover, as was noted above, human beings bring the natural landscape into the enduring, meaningful world of things that provides our home and shapes our identities. Care for the human artifice would thus include care for its more natural elements,[35] including "natural" places such as rivers, mountains, forests, or wilderness. In view of these considerations, Arendtian place-founding must be tempered by a preservationism that considers the ability of earthly nature as a whole, as well as individual "natural" and built places, to absorb change without being effaced or ruined. Thus Arendt anticipates later green notions of sustainability.

Culture, Care, and Balancing Founding and Preservation

There must therefore be an ongoing balance between founding and preservation, a balance that Arendt suggests in discussing care and cultivation.[36] In *Between Past and Future*, Arendt considers the Latin origins of the word 'culture'. The word, she writes, "derives from *colere*—to cultivate, to take care, tend and preserve—and it relates primarily to the intercourse of man with nature in the sense of cultivating and tending nature until it becomes fit for human habitation. As such, it indicates an attitude of loving care and stands in sharp contrast to all efforts to subject nature to the domination of man."[37]

One might say that care allows the original qualities of a place to endure and flourish and provide a stable context, whereas cultivation enables new possibilities to smoothly unfold. Care allows continuity with the past that enables human life to be a coherent story, or narrative.[38] Cultivation facilitates incremental change and adaptation. By contrast, domineering, aggressive action abruptly destroys and replaces the existing environment and thus erases context. In short, Arendt urges the "building, preserving, and caring for a world that can survive us and remain a place fit to live in for those who come after us"[39]—the violence toward nature of individual acts of work must be subordinated to an overall attitude of care. Arendt presages the Brundtland Commission's famous characterization, three decades later, of sustainable development as "meet[ing] the needs of the present without compromising the ability of future generations to meet their own needs."[40]

Preservation and Action
Like founding, preservation of places and of earthly nature is a public, collective enterprise. The world is public, and its preservation happens in the web of human relationships. For example, one cannot unilaterally preserve a place, even one's own private property, if others are transforming the surrounding environment.

Preservation exists in a complex, ambiguous relationship with action. Action involves initiating, through words and deeds, a new, open-ended set of interactions in the web of human relationships. From this standpoint, action is characterized by founding—of places and other aspects of the world. Preservation, by contrast, seems to freeze action—for example, through laws that accord permanent protected status to a place. One might, in fact, class preservation with labor, in that it involves ongoing efforts to maintain the life of a place against decay or degradation, much as eating maintains the human body.

On the other hand, preservation is also pursued through public words and deeds in a more deliberative sense, as when activists affirm the ecological and cultural significance of a place and initiate or contribute to a debate over its protection. Admittedly, the end result of such activism is often permanent preservation, which narrows the scope of Arendtian politics with regard to protected parcels of land. Yet this is not necessarily a problem for Arendtian politics or action. Deliberation may be ongoing at a larger scale, and debates and decisions over degrees of founding and preservation in particular places may feed into larger, continuing discussions about the social and ecological character of, say, a metropolitan area or a watershed.[41] Moreover, an act of preservation doesn't persist automatically and without future action. A decision to preserve a place ultimately depends on whether it is validated through the deliberative action of succeeding generations.[42]

In the end, though, preservation does act as a kind of restraint on action. It limits the initiation of new ends, values, and meanings, and it limits associated acts of change in the landscape. However, it can also be argued that preservation underwrites the persistence of the world that makes action itself possible. For example, Bonnie Honig emphasizes the open-ended character of Arendtian politics but nevertheless remarks on the need to "address environmental issues, so that [we] might prevent or at least delay the destruction of the earth beneath [our] feet and preserve the most palpable condition of worldliness we have."[43] Thus, sustainability is absolutely necessary to Arendt's conception of habitation.[44]

Yet, as with an overemphasis on founding, an overemphasis on preservation is problematic. People dynamically interact with places, altering or refounding them in response to changing conditions. An overemphasis on preservation would radically curtail the freedom to initiate new beginnings that is the hallmark of Arendtian action. Human activity would be limited to carrying out a pre-ordained plan of sustaining and reproducing the existing world.

Alienation from Earth and World

In large part, *The Human Condition* concerns a generalized crisis of alienation from both Earth and world—that is, from nature and human artifice. Villa calls this a crisis of "homelessness, a lack of place."[45] To a significant degree, Arendt, in line with her concerns about rampant instrumentalization, blames this homelessness on utilitarian, consumerist values associated with modernity and capitalism. Consumerism radically devalues the physical environment and the meanings accorded to it by action, reducing both nature and the built world to "mere means" (156) for transient satisfaction and then disposal. We come to "look upon … every tree as potential wood" (158). This situation threatens "permanence, stability, and durability" (125–126). It "harbors the grave danger that eventually no object of the world will be safe from consumption and annihilation through consumption" (133). Arendt thus notes that "if … we were truly nothing but members of a consumers' society" we "would no longer live in a world at all but simply be driven by a process in whose ever-recurring cycles things appear and disappear, manifest themselves and vanish" (132–134). She warns that we face the dissolution of a meaningful, enduring human artifice. The result is a world that "has lost its power to gather [individuals] together, to relate and to separate them"

(52–53). In such a world, individuals would be "deprived of an 'objective' relationship with them [i.e. one another] that comes from being related to and separated from them through the intermediary of a common world of things" (58).[46]

From an environmental standpoint, Arendt's remarks are quite prescient. Writing more than ten years before the full emergence of modern environmentalism and its critique of consumerism, she suggests that a consumption-oriented economy has instrumentalized and devoured the natural and built worlds. Her warning of a world lacking in "permanence, stability, and durability" and unable to gather individuals and relate them to one another sheds light especially on the contemporary problem of unregulated development and sprawl.[47] From an Arendtian standpoint, sprawl is inimical to our successful habitation of the world. It involves an assault on preservation, durability, and a sense of place. Wilderness, farms, urban downtowns, village centers, and historic structures are physically erased—indeed, consumed—or economically marginalized by homogeneous, automobile-dependent, dispersed housing tracts and ugly, disposable, placeless shopping malls and big-box stores. Sprawl also privatizes the landscape, replacing mixed-used, pedestrian-friendly communities and their street life with subdivisions, office parks, retail centers, and high-speed roads.[48] The result is an alienating built environment that lacks historical depth, provides little sense of connection, and impoverishes public life.

Conclusion: Pursuing a Complex Relationship with Nature

Arendt, through her threefold scheme of labor, work, and action, envisions a complex relationship between humanity and nature that manages to embrace our biological dependence on and entrapment within ecological necessities; our transformation of our environment through instrumentalization, resource extraction, and even violence; and, ultimately, our capacity to limit such instrumentalization through care and sustainable cultivation. Arendt doesn't shy away from humanity's need to transform the physical environment in order to successfully inhabit the Earth. Yet she rejects Lockean instrumentalism. Unlike the conception of habitation that Trachtenberg associates with Locke, Arendt would limit our transformation of nature for reasons that go far beyond sustainable resource use. For Arendt, resource consumption is largely in the realm of labor. Her privileging of work and action over labor suggests that our relationship with nature must involve the creation of enduring meaning and development of a sense of place in the world, rather than just continued access to resources. Arendt thus warns against the rampant instrumentalization and consumption of both earthly nature and the built human artifice. Arendt's concepts of care and cultivation with regard to place, the human artifice, and earthly nature itself suggest that founding and change must be tempered by preservation and stability so that human beings don't undermine the natural and built foundations of a coherent, meaningful landscape. Her concept of action also suggests that the politics of nature and of place, while attentive to the need of sustaining the natural and built environment and the ecological conditions on which politics itself depends, nevertheless ought to be deliberative and open-ended.

What would an Arendtian green politics look like? Recall that Arendtian action, which can be involved in the creation and maintenance of places, happens in the context of human plurality and competing perspectives, some oriented more toward founding and others more toward preservation. For action to be unconstrained and to truly reflect human plurality, negotiation over places and other environmental matters should proceed democratically, the contesting parties situated fairly equally in terms of power. Such deliberation, including deliberation over the character of particular places, could happen within an overall commitment to preservation of larger-scale environmental features such as basic ecological processes, the integrity of ecosystems, and the cultural and natural heritage of a region. How such features should be defined would itself be a subject of deliberation, perhaps involving some agreement on more fundamental, "constitutional" guiding principles. The ideal is an inclusive, ongoing *conversation* at temporal and spatial scales large and small— what Villa calls a "shared enterprise," a "partnership, in argument and conversation."[49] In the United States, such a deliberative environmental politics of place has been approximated by movements for environmental justice and collaborative conservation and by efforts at regional government, particularly in the Portland, Oregon metropolitan area.[50]

An integrated balance of change and stasis, mobility and rootedness, and founding and preservation is, together with democratic governance of the landscape, essential for creating an enduring, yet vital and flourishing world. Arendt's concepts of work, action, and the human artifice, in conjunction with her affirmation of the Earth's dignity, her celebration of care and cultivation, and her critiques of consumerism and of alienation from Earth and world, teach the importance of place and of a balanced approach to both earthly nature and the built environment.

Notes

1. See, respectively, Seyla Benhabib, *The Reluctant Modernism of Hannah Arendt* (Sage, 1996); Hanna Fenichel Pitkin, *The Attack of the Blob: Hannah Arendt's Concept of the Social* (University of Chicago Press, 1998); Pitkin, "Justice: On Relating Private and Public," *Political Theory* 9, no. 3 (1981): 327–352; Dana Villa, *Arendt and Heidegger: The Fate of the Political* (Princeton University Press, 1996); Bonnie Honig, *Political Theory and the Displacement of Politics* (Cornell University Press, 1993); Margaret Canovan, *Hannah Arendt: A Reinterpretation of Her Political Thought* (Cambridge University Press, 1992); George Kateb, *Hannah Arendt: Politics, Conscience, Evil* (Rowman and Allanheld, 1983).

2. For exceptions, see Anne Chapman, "The Ways That Nature Matters: The World and the Earth in the Thought of Hannah Arendt," *Environmental Values* 16, no. 4 (2007): 433–445; David Macauley, "Out of Place and Outer Space: Hannah Arendt and Earth Alienation: An Historical and Critical Perspective," *Capitalism, Nature, Socialism* 3, no. 4 (1992): 19–45; Daniel Kemmis, *Community and the Politics of Place* (University of Oklahoma Press, 1990); Kerry H. Whiteside, "Hannah Arendt and Ecological Politics," *Environmental Ethics* 16, no. 4 (Winter 1994): 339–358; Kerry H. Whiteside, "Worldliness and Respect for Nature: An Ecological Application of Hannah Arendt's Conception of Culture," *Environmental Values* 7, no. 1 (1998): 25–40; Paul Ott, "World and Earth: Hannah Arendt and the Human Relationship to Nature," *Ethics, Place & Environment* 12, no. 1 (2009): 1–16; Kenneth Frampton, "The Status of Man and the Status of His Objects: A Reading of *The Human Condition*," in *Modern Architecture and the Critical Present*, ed. Kenneth Frampton (St. Martin's Press, 1982). Villa acknowledges Arendt as a critic of placelessness (*Arendt and Heidegger*, 171). Douglas Torgerson (*The Promise of Green Politics: Environmentalism and the Public Sphere*, Duke University Press, 1999) draws on Arendt's conception of action and political deliberation for its own sake to model what he calls a "green public sphere" in opposition to the instrumentalism of industrial society, but doesn't delve into Arendt's view of humanity's relationship with nature.

3. Hannah Arendt, *The Human Condition* (University of Chicago Press, 1958). Henceforth, page numbers in parentheses refer to this work.

4. Hannah Arendt, *Between Past and Future: Eight Exercises in Political Thought* (Penguin, 1977).

5. See Peter F. Cannavò, *The Working Landscape: Founding, Preservation, and the Politics of Place* (MIT Press, 2007). On the complexity of humanity's relationship with nature, see William Cronon, ed., *Uncommon Ground: Rethinking the Human Place in Nature* (Norton, 1995).

6. Arendt's distinction between labor and work is a bit problematic. Some life-sustaining activities that she deems "labor," such as agriculture, also effect enduring change in the environment. (See also Paul Ott, "World and Earth: Hannah Arendt and the Human Relationship to Nature," *Ethics, Place and Environment* 12, no. 1, 2009: 1-16.) Nevertheless, Arendt's account of work and labor usefully distinguishes between producing short-lived goods for consumption and produc-

ing enduring things to furnish a built world. On agriculture considered as labor rather than work, see Arendt, *The Human Condition*, 138–139.

7. See also Villa, *Arendt and Heidegger*, 32–33.

8. Arendt, *The Human Condition*, 38–49.

9. See also Benhabib, *Reluctant Modernism*, 108.

10. See chapter 5 in this volume. Also see chapter 12, in which Kimberly Smith discusses W. E. B. Du Bois's conception of human transformation and habitation of the Earth.

11. On this distinction, see Ott, "World and Earth" and Chapman, "The Ways That Nature Matters."

12. Cannavò, *The Working Landscape*, 6.

13. Whiteside says that the "fabricated world cuts across natural cycles to give a feeling of permanence, location, and belonging" ("Hannah Arendt," 353). Frampton makes similar points in "The Status of Man."

14. Chapman, "The Ways That Nature Matters," 435.

15. "This world of things in which we have interest," Pitkin writes, "is a tangible in-between (*inter-esse*)" ("Justice," 342).

16. On the founding and preservation of places, see Cannavò, *The Working Landscape*.

17. Chapman, "The Ways That Nature Matters," 440.

18. Martin Heidegger makes a similar point. See "Building Dwelling Thinking" in *Basic Writings*, ed. David Farrell Krell (Harper Collins, 1977).

19. For a similar point, see Robert David Sack, *Homo Geographicus: A Framework for Action, Awareness, and Moral Concern* (Johns Hopkins University Press, 1997), 66, 80.

20. Macauley correctly notes that Arendt overlooks how particular locales in nature, such as forests or rivers, already have a certain structure or coherence. See Macauley, "Out of Place," 44.

21. See Mick Smith's review of Cannavò, *The Working Landscape* (*Environmental Ethics* 31, no. 1, 2009: 97–100).

22. Chapman, "The Ways That Nature Matters," 437.

23. See also David Harvey, *Justice, Nature, and the Geography of Difference* (Blackwell, 1996), 309–310, 316, 322.

24. Villa, *Arendt and Heidegger*, 34.

25. The following paragraphs draw upon page 33 of Cannavò, *The Working Landscape*.

26. See Sack, *Homo Geographicus*, 2, 34.

27. Doreen Massey, "Spaces of Politics," in *Human Geography Today*, ed. Doreen Massey, John Allen, and Philip Sarre (Polity, 1999).

28. Cannavò, *The Working Landscape*, 41.

29. Chapman, "The Ways That Nature Matters," 435–436.

30. On the interaction of founding and preservation, see also Iris Marion Young, *Intersecting Voices: Dilemmas of Gender, Political Philosophy, and Policy* (Princeton University Press, 1997), 134–164.

31. See also Whiteside, "Hannah Arendt" and "Worldliness."

32. See also Ott, "World and Earth," 5–6; Villa, *Arendt and Heidegger*, 27–28.

33. For a similar view, see Robert Goodin, *Green Political Theory* (Polity, 1992).

34. Chapman, "The Ways That Nature Matters," 437–438.

35. See Whiteside, "Worldliness."

36. This paragraph draws on Whiteside, "Worldliness," and Cannavò, *The Working Landscape*, 44.

37. Arendt, *Between Past and Future*, 211–212.

38. See also Young, *Intersecting Voices*, 153.

39. Arendt, *Between Past and Future*, 95.

40. World Commission on Environment and Development, *Our Common Future* (Oxford University Press, 1987), 43.

41. On preservationist discourse as action, see also Ott, "World and Earth," 16.

42. I am indebted to W. S. K. Cameron for this insight.

43. Honig, *Political Theory*, 118.

44. See also Trachtenberg's discussion of the relationship between habitation and sustainability in chapter 5 of this volume.

45. Villa, *Arendt and Heidegger*, 171. According to Macauley ("Out of Place," 25), for Arendt, Earth and world alienation mean "a loss of roots and a common, shared sense of place, a realm of meaningful pursuits secured by tradition against the forces of change."

46. She was not alone in seeing an opposition between instrumental and place-based values. See Smith's chapter on Du Bois in this volume. Also, Arendt's opposition to a consumption-oriented society reflects Aristotle and the civic republican tradition, both of which saw material accumulation and market-oriented values as threatening to civic virtue.

47. See also Frampton, "The Status of Man."

48. See Cannavò, *The Working Landscape*.

49. Villa, *Arendt and Heidegger*, 34.

50. See Cannavò, *The Working Landscape* and William A. Shutkin, *The Land That Could Be: Environmentalism and Democracy in the Twenty-First Century* (MIT Press, 2000). For an approach to environmental political deliberation that draws on Arendt's notion of action, see Torgerson, *The Promise of Green Politics*.

15
Confucius: How Non-Western Political Theory Contributes to Understanding the Environmental Crisis

Joel Jay Kassiola

[I]n all or most societies throughout history there has been some thinking or theorizing about politics, about the right and wrong ways, and the proper and improper ways of conducting public life in a community. Yet, as least as far as the practice in the United States is concerned, the teaching of political theory has been confined almost exclusively to the so-called Western "canon," that is, the tradition of political thought stretching from Socrates to Marx or Nietzsche. No doubt, this is an immensely rich tradition and college students should be exposed to it and learn about its subtle nuances. However, in our age of rapid globalization, confinement to this canon is no longer adequate or justifiable. In our time, when the winds of trade spread not only goods but also ideas and cultural legacies around the globe, confinement to the Western tradition amounts to a parochial self-enclosure incompatible with university studies.

Fred Dallmayr, preface to *Comparative Political Theory: An Introduction*[1]

There is mounting evidence which suggests that the claims of universality made by modern western political philosophy are being questioned by other cultures, or at least by the significant representatives of these cultures. Indeed, in the West itself the claims of modern western philosophy are being questioned by those who challenge the assumptions underlying modernity. Such critical inquiry makes the comparative study of political philosophies both opportune and intellectually satisfying.

Anthony J. Parel, "The Comparative Study of Political Philosophy"[2]

The crux of the matter is that when we study political thought in a comparative perspective, we study above all the nature of politics, long before we claim to study the thought and practices of a region, or state, or culture, or religion. That is the crucial point about how to approach comparative political thought. Experts as we may be in some area or local phenomenon, it is a mistake to cut ourselves off from the larger purview of what is the type of thought-practice we are investigating. That is to say, rather than seeing ourselves just as scholars of India, or the UK, or Chile, or Islam, we are investigators of human political conduct and discourse who then rely on particular case studies.

Michael Freeden and Andrew Vincent, "Introduction: The Study of Comparative Thought," in *Comparative Political Thought: Theorizing Practices*[3]

Why Non-Western Political Theory and Confucianism Now?

In the previous chapters, my fellow contributors draw upon the Western political theory canon for insights into the contemporary environmental crisis. So why is there a chapter on an ancient Chinese philosopher who is neither Western nor typically associated with environmental scholarship?

In this chapter, I intend to demonstrate the need for and the value of non-Western political thought in understanding and responding more effectively to the environmental crisis. To accomplish this goal, I suggest, by way of illustration, examination of a major non-Western theoretical tradition: Confucianism. I will discuss the two-and-a-half-millennia-old, yet continuously evolving, tradition of commentary on Confucian thought, and how this Chinese tradition can advance environmental political thinking today. Again, Confucianism is meant in part as an illustration. A wealth of theoretical traditions exists beyond the horizons of Western thought, including the political philosophies of the Islamic world, South Asia, East Asia, Africa, and Latin America.[4]

It is my contention that such an expansion and diversification of the political philosophy canon beyond our mostly exclusive attention to Western political theory (valuable as the Western tradition may be, *pace* Dallmayr's statement quoted in the epigraph) can help yield a more comprehensive and efficacious environmental thought and a similarly more comprehensive and efficacious environmental policy. This is imperative as humanity attempts to make social changes to cope with existing and new environmental challenges. The editors of a recent series in comparative political thought describe their series' mandate in unmistakable transformative language: "The aim of the series overall is to change the landscape of political theory by encouraging deeper comparative reflection on the structure and character of the discipline and to arrive at a richer understanding of the nature of the political."[5] To my mind, these sentiments capture well the profound promise of non-Western political theory in general, and as we shall see, of non-Western environmental political theory in particular. In view of the scant attention to non-Western sources in environmental political theory, I hope that this chapter will stimulate other comparative political theorists to supplement the canonical Western sources on environmentalism. The chapter provides a bridge between the analyses of Western political theorists' environmental insights and a more wide-ranging, cosmopolitan, environmental political theory encompassing non-Western thinkers. The editors of this volume conclude that "these essays suggest the need for a broader dialogue, one that goes beyond Western political theory and embraces discourses from an entire planet now threatened by humanity's claims, productions, actions, and reactions." I hope this call for a more globally inclusive environmental political theory proves prescient.

I would go even farther. I envision within environmental political theory—young as this field is—a new subfield of non-Western or comparative environmental political thought that utilizes the entire world's intellectual resources and traditions in addressing today's global environmental challenges. Such a subfield need not, however, remain isolated from environmental political theory in general. Instead, it should inform a much more cosmopolitan perspective in environmental political theory as a whole. The original Ancient "theorists" were wanderers and observers who tried to account for the diversity of human cultures, thoughts, and ideas. I would suggest that environmental political theory, like political theory more generally, should return to these roots. This chapter is merely a prototype of what such a new subfield and its manner of inquiry might consist of and of the enlightenment it might provide.

But *why* consult non-Western philosophical sources? If environmental political theorists can provide trenchant analyses and compelling social prescriptions concerning the current environmental crisis, as my colleagues in this volume do, then widening the range of intellectual resources and insights beyond the Western canon will prove fundamentally useful in generating an enhanced and more effective environmental political theory. This is especially true with regard to ancient philosophers, such as Confucius.

Confucius's thought and the succeeding tradition of scholarship offer a powerful counterpoint to what many environmentalists consider a—if not the—root cause of the current environmental crisis: the globally hegemonic worldview of modernity and its values (embodied today in the doctrine of neoliberalism). Readers of Özgüç Orhan's chapter in this volume will notice that in providing a counterpoint to modernity, Confucius plays a role analogous to that of Aristotle.

However, Confucius and the Confucian tradition offer insights of their own, especially regarding the separation from and dominance humanity's over nonhuman nature (or what this volume's editors term "hard anthropocentrism," to distinguish it from more ecologically oriented forms of anthropocentrism; see their conclusion below). Moreover, Confucius's profound insight into the value of the past for the present—"Keeping past teachings alive and understanding the present" (*Analects*, 2.11)[6]—directly conflicts with modernity's intellectually myopic "contempocentric"[7] preoccupation, or Peter Euben's "Presentism," as the editors note in their introduction. Therefore, it becomes an instructive alternative teaching for today.

This is not to say that points of convergence do not exist between the Confucian view and the Western canon. In fact, such convergences (or, perhaps, parallels) are important for Western readers trying to understand non-Western thought for the first time. An important parallel, for example, exists between Confucius's view and what Tim Luke, in chapter 11, calls Karl Marx's "insights into humanity and history in *The Eighteenth Brumaire of Louis Bonaparte*." Luke quotes Marx: "Men make their own history, but they do not make it just as they please; they do not make it under circumstances chosen by themselves, but under circumstances directly found, given and transmitted from the past." Yet Confucianism can also provide an important system of distinctive ideas with the potential to create an alternative worldview to hegemonic Western modernity. These ideas have been undertheorized in the past 40 years of the environmental movement, a major error of omission in that movement.

The founders of comparative political theory, like the editors and contributors quoted in the epigraphs above, argue that their innovative approach seeks to criticize the modern social order and its underlying philosophy and to offer desirable alternatives to them. For example, Anthony Parel notes that "Gandhi's point is that modernity, with its consumerism, its technology, its disregard for the eco-structure of nature, its inequality, its violence and its atheism, exerts 'a baleful power and influence' not just on India but on humankind as a whole." Parel asserts that "comparative political philosophy can give us a neutralizing antidote to the 'baleful power or influence' of uncontested modern western political philosophy."[8] To put it even more strongly, if modernity is a main cause of the environmental crisis, with anthropocentrism at the core of Western modernity (indeed, at the very foundation of Western civilization dating back to Genesis[9]), then we require another critical vision to achieve the transformation of modernity and avert environmental disaster. Non-Western political theory can thus be a rich source of critical ideas that work against the dominant strain of Western modernity that has taken over the globe. Comparison of Western and non-Western perspectives across time and space may also expose presuppositions that are uncritically accepted or taken for granted in the modern Western view of humanity, politics, and society, particularly concerning the relationship between nature and humanity. Indeed, this comparative analytical process may improve one's understanding of one's own philosophy as well as that of other intellectual traditions.

Confucius's Time (551–479 BCE) and Society

Confucius's global philosophical importance has long been recognized by Western thinkers. Karl Jaspers considered him a "paradigmatic individual" along with Socrates, Buddha, and Jesus.[10] Ralph Waldo Emerson proclaimed him "the George Washington of the world of thought."[11] Immanuel Kant labeled him "the Chinese Socrates."[12]

The most relevant aspect of Confucius's life and thought for environmental political thinking is his role as a social "bell clapper." Confucius sounded the alarm for a societal transformation amid a violent and morally decadent society in crisis. The basis for this view of his social role derives from the one book we have of his thoughts: *Lunyu* (also known as *The Analects*, i.e. "selected sayings"), which consists of notes taken by his students, not unlike the teachings of some Western political philosophers). One translator, Simon Leys, offers the extraordinary observation that "no book in the cultural history of the world has exerted, over a longer period of time, a greater influence over a larger number of people than this slim little volume."[13]

The important passage on Confucius's role as a "bell clapper" is as follows:

After emerging from the audience [with the Master] the border official remarked: "you disciples, why should you be concerned about your Master's loss of office? The world has been without the Way [*Tao*] for a long time now, and Heaven [*T'ien*] intends to use your Master like a wooden clapper for a bell [to awaken the people]." (Confucius, *Analects*, 3.24)[14]

The translator Edward Slingerland says of this passage that "the border official's point is thus that Heaven has deliberately caused Confucius to lose his official position [in the State of Lu] so that he might wander throughout the realm spreading the teachings of the Way and waking up the fallen world."[15]

I want to emphasize this crucial "bell clapper" role of sounding the alarm and "waking up the fallen world" of Confucius's time and place. I see a strong analogy between Confucius's alarm-sounding role for his unstable Chinese society in the fifth century BCE and our own "fallen world" with its alarming environmental problems.

The Chinese society that was the social context of Confucius's thought was known as the Eastern or Later Chou Dynasty (751–222 BCE).[16] It was characterized by social corruption, upheaval, a crisis in values, and violence caused by venal and decadent kings and their courts. At the time of Confucius's death, in 479 BCE, China was on its way to full-blown civil war with the onset of the period known as "The Warring States" (480–222 BCE). This era of violent conflict eventually brought an end to Confucius's beloved Chou Dynasty, which had reigned for more than 800 years.[17]

We can find important correlates between Confucius's tumultuous time and place and fifth-century-BCE Athens, where Western political theory was born. As Sheryl Breen notes in this volume, fifth-century-BCE Greece was plagued by war and social turmoil, decline, and transformation; Athens, the home of Socrates and Plato, saw military defeat and the collapse of its democracy. Similar to Confucius's times, these dysfunctional and disharmonious social conditions life helped foster the rise of Western philosophy as a whole and political philosophy in particular. Indeed, this striking convergence in the relationship between societal disruption and the creation of political philosophy in the lives of Confucius and of Socrates and Plato is worth further exploration.

There are also parallels between Confucius's era and modern, Western globalized consumer society. We are currently burdened by value crises, increasing political violence and warfare within and between states, international and domestic terrorism, and rampant corruption among political leaders. These crises (involving social unrest, value disharmony and conflict, political and sexual scandals, and decadent luxurious consumption) in both developed and developing nations resemble Confucius's chaotic time. Furthermore, today's disorganized and violent global society recalls Thomas Hobbes's anarchical state of nature, with its "war of all against all," and Hobbes's historical era, which was beset by religious violence and which compelled Hobbes to seek a unified sovereignty theory aimed at the pursuit of peace.[18] Most relevant for this chapter, today's globalized world, marked by both violence and interdependence, faces lethal threats to its stability in the form of environmental challenges such as climate change, inadequate and polluted water supplies, dwindling energy resources, desertification, and habitat and biodiversity loss.[19]

To draw one more parallel, our global society's environmental, moral, political, and social decline echoes the problems highlighted by Jean-Jacques Rousseau in the first major critique of modernity, discussed in this volume by Joseph Lane. Interestingly, both Confucius and Rousseau may be termed "Golden Age decline theorists." Both see a past Golden Age in which goodness and political ideals reigned only to eventually deteriorate to a state of social decay and distress. For Confucius, such a social ideal, which he hoped to reconstruct, lay in earlier Chinese history, in the legendary era of the Sage Kings, Yao and Shun, in the third millennium BCE, and in the more recent Western or Earlier Chou society (1111–722 BCE). For Rousseau, as Lane discusses, the ideal was "unchained" or "free" nature before it was ruined by civilization and modernity.

Whether our present declining global order (for example, the ongoing failure to achieve an effective agreement to address climate change) will meet its own violent demise—either from military conflict, as happened to Confucius's Chou Dynasty, or from anthropogenic environmental catastrophe—remains to be seen. It is to be hoped that drawing inspiration and wisdom from Confucian thought will illuminate paths to a more sustainable and desirable society. To that end, I propose that if we follow Confucius's example of sounding the alarm to his troubled society and urge transformation as well as moral improvement, we will be able to avert environmental disaster and build a more morally righteous and satisfying life in a sustainable postmodern social order. Insights from the seminal non-Western intellectual tradition of Chinese Confucianism may also enable us to achieve a deeper understanding of the Western tradition and its relevance to the environmental crisis.

In the remainder of this chapter, I turn from Confucius himself to Neo-Confucianism, a school of later Confucians that began in the eleventh century CE during the Sung Dynasty (960–1279 CE). Neo-Confucian teaching offers a cosmoanthropic theory to address the place of humanity within the universe. Cosmology is foundational to the Neo-Confucian worldview, whereas Confucius himself was mostly concerned with ethics and religion.[20]

Neo-Confucian cosmology has a unique vision of relationships and interactions among Heaven, humanity, and the Earth (nonhuman nature). With Heaven forming a unity between humankind and the Earth, Neo-Confucianism challenges many canonical Western ideas about the nature-human relation presented in the previous chapters of this book.[21] Neo-Confucian cosmology can thus inspire a new ecological sensibility and sounder value judgments and policy regarding the health of the environment and its relation to humanity. We can secure lessons about our connection to the world to replace alienation from, and deter exploitation of, nonhuman nature.

Neo-Confucian Cosmology and Its Environmental Significance

A Confucian green theory can provide an example of how environmental political theorists might consult non-Western thinkers in order to envision a sustainable and just alternative to our modern social order. This theory may be drawn from the Neo-Confucian "continuity of being" cosmology or "anthropocosmic" theory of the eleventh century CE (Sung Dynasty), as labeled by the Confucian scholar Tu Wei-ming.[22] Another Confucian scholar has termed this Neo-Confucian cosmology, which is founded upon a triad of Heaven (*T'ien*), humanity, and the Earth, "cosmoanthropism."[23]

The progression of expressive names for Neo-Confucian cosmology demonstrates how Confucian theory overcomes the anthropocentrism of modernity: Tu's term, "anthropocosmic," places humanity first, at the center of the universe with the highest value; the second neologistic name, "cosmoanthropism" places the cosmos first and presents humanity merely as part of the larger cosmos with no superior cosmic status implied. The term's creator, Young-chan Ro, calls for a "cosmological anthropology rather than an anthropological cosmology; human beings must be understood in light of the universe rather than the human rationality or *logos* being imposed on the universe. Ecology based on anthropological cosmology will become anthropological ecology, which is but another form of anthropocentrism."[24] Neo-Confucian cosmology included such topics as the material force of the universe (*ch'i*), positive and negative cosmic forces or elements (*yin* and *yang*), and the unity of nature and humanity.[25] In contrast to the Earth-bound, anthropocentric Western view, the major significance of the Neo-Confucian cosmoanthropic theory for today's environmentalism is that we must define ecological issues on Earth from a "cosmocentric" perspective of the universe. This is similar to Aristotle's concept of *kosmos*, discussed in this volume by Özgüç Orhan. Orhan presents *kosmos* as an ordered reality consisting of the totality of things. Both Aristotelian *kosmos* and Neo-Confucian cosmoanthropic cosmology share with contemporary ecology an emphasis on the interrelationships of the universe's components and a contrast with modernity's mechanistic universe. Neo-Confucian cosmology also differs significantly from the Western, Judeo-Christian creation myth.

The Confucian scholar Tu, in his essay "The Continuity of Being: Chinese Visions of Nature," refutes the commonly accepted view that the fundamental difference between Western and Chinese cosmologies rests on the Chinese lack of a creation myth.[26] Tu's refutation of this view involves an important argument for the contribution of Confucianism and Neo-Confucianism to environmental political thought and policy: "The real issue is not the presence or absence of creation myths, but the underlying assumption of the cosmos: whether it is continuous or discontinuous with the creator. ... It is not a creation myth as such but the Judeo-Christian version of it that is absent in the Chinese mythology."[27]

It is this belief in the continuity and inter-connection between Heaven and nature that distinguishes Neo-Confucian cosmology from the Judeo-Christian construction of the creation of the Earth and humanity and from the Western conception of the relationship between creator and creation. The Western worldview features a discontinuous, transcendental God; in the Genesis account, a divine being creates the world *ex nihilo*—from nothing—and thereby establishes a fundamental dualism (God distant from the Earth) at the foundation of Western thought. This is reinforced by Plato's influential dualism regarding two worlds: the imperfect world of appearance and the invisible, ideal world of Forms or Ideas (see chapter 1). And with John Locke, we saw a natural world created by and separate from God and given to human beings for instrumental, material use (see chapter 5). We are thus presented with contrasting conceptions of the universe: its one-time creation by an external and disconnected divine source (Western dualism) versus its existence in an ongoing and endless process of creation, a process that entails a more unified cosmology (Neo-Confucianism). As Tu articulates the Neo-Confucian view, "there is no temporal beginning to specify, no closure is ever contemplated."[28]

The cosmoanthropic triad of Heaven, humanity, and the Earth, which is essential to Neo-Confucian cosmology, is explained in an important work of Classical Confucianism known as *The Doctrine of the Mean*:

Only those who are absolutely sincere [*ch'eng*] can fully develop their nature. If they can fully develop their nature, they can then fully develop the nature of others. If they can fully develop the nature of others, then can then fully develop the nature of things. If they can fully develop the nature of things, they can assist in the transforming and nourishing of Heaven and Earth, then can thus form a trinity with Heaven and Earth.[29]

The translator Wing-Tsit Chan says of this passage that "the important point is the ultimate trinity with Heaven and Earth. It is of course another way of saying the unity of man and Heaven or Nature, a doctrine which eventually assumed the greatest importance in Neo-Confucianism."[30]

In Neo-Confucian thought, Heaven is not imagined as a place but is thought of as "the source of normativity in the universe."[31] Heaven infuses humanity and the Earth with their essence, creating a triad of relationships among all three; this triad forms the unity or inter-connectedness of all the cosmological components of the universe. This triadic unity, in turn, structures a set of bilateral relationships between Heaven and humanity, between Heaven and Earth, and (most important for environmentalism) between humanity and the Earth. According to Tu, "to say that the cosmos is a continuum and that all of its components are internally connected is also to say that it is an organismic unity holistically integrated at each level of complexity."[32] In contrast with the Western dualist cosmology based upon anthropocentrism and the consequent subordination of nature, Neo-Confucian thought avoids the separation and supposed superiority of humanity with regard to the Earth.

The following passage from the Neo-Confucian Chang Tsai (1020–1077 CE) describes the Neo-Confucian cosmological triad and challenges Western assumptions:

> Heaven is my father and Earth is my mother, and even such a small creature as I finds an intimate place in their midst. Therefore that which fills the universe I regard as my body and that which directs the universe I consider as my nature. All people are my brothers and sisters, and all things are my companions.[33]

This cosmology, with its paternal Heaven and maternal Earth, makes all humans "children of the universe," connected to all "things" in the universe as "companions."

The sixteenth-century Neo-Confucian Wang Yang-ming (1472–1529) expands upon this essential Neo-Confucianist teaching as follows.

> Master Wang said: the great man regards Heaven and Earth and the myriad of things as one body. He regards the world as one family and the country as one person. As to those who make a cleavage between objects and distinguish between the self and others, they are small men. That the great man can regard Heaven, Earth and the myriad of things as one body is not because he deliberately wants to do so, but because it is nature to the humane nature of his mind that he do so. … Everything from ruler, minister, husband, wife, and friends to mountains, rivers, spiritual beings, birds, animals, and plants should be truly loved in order to realize my humanity that forms one body with them, and then my clear character will be completely manifested, and I really form one body with Heaven, Earth and the myriad of things.[34]

What is important to emphasize here about Neo-Confucian cosmology and its significance for environmental thought and policy is that it engenders respect, even reverence, for the Earth as a related creation of Heaven, as well as for all the "myriad things" on Earth as our companions.

Respect for one's ancestors and the duty of filial piety (*xiao*), which Confucius emphasized throughout the *Analects*, are fundamental to Chinese civilization and to Neo-Confucian cosmology. On the essential nature and importance of Confucian filial duty, Slingerland comments that "the virtue of being a dutiful and respectful son or daughter is considered by Confucians to be the key to other virtues developed in later life."[35] A filial relationship between Heaven and Earth, on the one hand, and between Heaven and all of the Earth's inhabitants and ecosystemic components, on the other, is thus envisioned by the Neo-Confucians Chang Tsai and Wang Yang-ming.

I consider the environmental implications of the Neo-Confucian tripartite cosmoanthropic vision to be profound. We are bound by filial duty to honor, respect, and take care of our cosmic mother, the Earth, and are united with all of nature because we regard the universe as our body and all things within it as our "companions." Thus, there is a sharp contrast between the Neo-Confucian order of the cosmos, and the West's anthropocentric domination, exploitation, and even stewardship of the Earth according to human interests.[36]

As Wang notes, Neo-Confucians espouse unity not only with fellow humans, birds, animals, and plants but (perhaps surprisingly to the Westerner) even "tiles and stones." Wang writes about an identification between humans, birds, animals, and plants that shows one body is formed among living entities, then adds a cryptic remark: "Yet even when he [humanity] sees tiles and stones shattered and crushed he cannot but help but feeling regret. This shows that his humanity forms one body with tiles and stones. ... Such a mind is rooted in his Heavenly-endowed nature."[37] The Neo-Confucian cosmology, therefore, ontologically unites the range of beings from stones to Heaven, including humankind and all other living creations as well as the "myriad things" in between.

What unifies all the seemingly disparate elements of the grand cosmic unity of Heaven, Earth, humanity, animals, plans, stones, tiles, and so on is the rich Chinese metaphysical concept of *ch'i*.[38] According to Tu, "The continuous presence of *ch'i* in all modalities of being makes everything flow together as the unfolding of a single process. Nothing, not even an almighty creator, is external to the process. ... The motif of wholeness is directly derived from the idea of continuity as all-encompassing."[39] Here Tu raises an interesting question: "Our main concern is to understand how the idea of the undifferentiated *ch'i* serves as the basis for a unified cosmological theory. We want to know in what sense the least intelligent being, such as a rock, and the highest manifestation of spirituality, such as Heaven, both consist of *ch'i*."[40]

The concept of ontological continuity throughout the universe explains how a rock and Heaven, and everything in between, can share the same substantial nature, *ch'i*, and are parts of a grand cosmic continuum called the "the great transformation" (*tu-hua*).[41] All-encompassing nature is the "concrete manifestation of the great transformation,"[42] or the universal continuity of being. Tu informs his readers that "nature is vital force (*ch'i*) in display" and is characterized by "union rather than disunion, integrity rather disintegration, and synthesis rather than separation."[43] The all-encompassing *ch'i* that constitutes all things in the universe creates the continuity of being.

Chang Tsai says that this unifying process of *ch'i* being all things in the universe forms "the Great Harmony."[44] Tu explains the Great Harmony as the integration ("intermingling") of the vital forces of the universe (*ch'i*) that take on concrete forms of "mountains, rivers, rocks, trees, animals, and human beings" as forms of *ch'i*.[45] This is how stones, Heaven, human beings, and all of nonhuman nature are connected: through their composition of *ch'i* and its components of *yin* and *yang*. By applying this interconnected vision of the universe, we can better comprehend Chang Tsai's famous statement about the universe as a human body and "all things its companions." Tu, concluding his account, calls this Neo-Confucian concept of "the continuity of being" "the general Chinese world view."[46]

Tu summarizes his presentation of the Chinese vision of nature as follows: "The image of the human that emerges here, far from the lord of the creation [as the Western cosmology drawn from Genesis and modernity hold] is the filial son and daughter of the universe. Filial piety connotes a profound feeling, an all-pervasive care for the world around us."[47]

From a Neo-Confucian perspective, the culturally dominant Western conception of humanity as separate from and superior to nature is an impossibility, although the analyses of canonical Western political thinkers in this volume show that this hegemonic doctrine is not a monolith and that non-anthropocentric exceptions, some even ecocentric, do exist within the Western political canon. For example, as is discussed in chapters 6 and 9, both David Hume and Mary Wollstonecraft see important continuities between human beings and other animals and see in such continuities a basis for moral obligations toward nonhuman animals. Moreover, we should take note of the editors' caution, in their concluding essay, about "incomplete or distorted readings of the canonical texts," and should not oversimplify our characterizations of two and a half millennia of Western political theory.

Conclusion

This brief presentation of Confucianism and the central Neo-Confucian cosmological vision of cosmoanthropic triad of Heaven, humanity, and the Earth has only touched upon the richness of detail within just one example of non-Western philosophy. Despite its brevity, I hope this chapter suggests a compelling alternative to the globally dominant Western viewpoint of nature and humans' relation to it and illuminates how this alternative can greatly contribute to environmental political theory. I join with the book's editors in urging additional efforts to show the environmental relevance and power of non-Western philosophical sources. Let us explore sources in addition to traditional Western political thought, including East Asian, South Asian, African, Latin American, and Islamic thought.[48]

Studying Confucianism and its 2,500-year commentarial tradition may help us to create another path for our placeless and wayward society—to rediscover the Way, as Confucians would put it. I propose that non-Western philosophy can generate innovative insights into the human political condition, and that it should constitute a new subfield within environmental political theory. Other worldviews can assist our response to the greatest challenge of the twenty-first century: How can we create an environmentally sustainable social order to protect the planet, humanity, and all the "myriad things" on Earth that are our "companions"?

Notes

1. Fred Dallmayr, ed., *Comparative Political Theory: An Introduction* (Palgrave Macmillan, 2010).

2. Anthony J. Parel, "The Comparative Study of Political Philosophy," in *Comparative Political Philosophy: Studies under the Upas Tree*, ed. Anthony J. Parel and Ronald C. Keith (Lexington Books, 2003), 11.

3. Michael Freeden and Andrew Vincent, eds., *Comparative Political Thought: Theorizing Practices* (Routledge, 2013), 2.

4. The work of Gandhi provides another excellent example of the valuable contribution offered by this global political literature. An analyst of this Indian political thinker and leader concludes a study of his thought as follows: "Throughout Gandhi had modern Western political philosophy in mind. But the basic analysis is understood with the aid of ideas taken from Indian moral philosophy. The outcome is an original theory of politics, many elements of which have applicability outside his own political tradition." Anthony J. Parel, "Mahatma Gandhi's Critique of Modernity," in *Comparative Political Philosophy*, ed. Parel and Keith, 181. On Gandhi's significance for environmental political theory, see Farah Godrej, "Ascetics, Warriors, and a Gandhian Ecological Citizenship," *Political Theory* 40, no. 4 (2012): 437–465. For a more general work on comparative political theory, see Farah Godrej, *Cosmopolitan Political Thought: Method, Practice, Discipline* (Oxford University Press, 2011).

5. Michael Freeden and Andrew Vincent, "Routledge Studies in Comparative Political Thought, Series Description," in *Comparative Political Thought*, ed. Freeden and Vincent.

6. Confucius, *Analects with Selections from Traditional Commentaries*, tr. Edward Slingerland (Hackett, 2003), 11. Conventional notation for the *Analects* is by book and chapter; for example, 2.11 means book 2, chapter 11. Hereafter, references to the *Analects* will follow this standard notational convention, though I also cite page numbers for the Slingerland translation..

7. On this concept and this word, see James Gustave Speth, *The Bridge at the Edge of the World: Capitalism, the Environment, and Crossing from Crisis to Sustainability* (Yale University Press, 2008), xvii.

8. Parel, "Comparative Study of Political Philosophy," 27–28.

9. See William Leiss, *The Domination of Nature* (Beacon, 1974). See also Lynn White, "The Historical Roots of Our Ecological Crisis," *Science* 155 (March 1967): 1203–1207.

10. Karl Jaspers, *Socrates, Buddha, Confucius, Jesus: The Paradigmatic Individual* (Harcourt, Brace & World, 1962), 41–63. "The four paradigmatic individuals," Jaspers writes on page 3, "have exerted a historical influence of incomparable scope and depth. ... When it comes to broad, enduring influence over many hundreds of years, they are so far above all others that they must be singled out if we are to form a clear view of the world's history."

11. C. Alexander Simpkins and Annellen Simpkins, *Simple Confucianism: A Guide to Living Virtuously* (Tuttle, 2000), ix.

12. Robert B. Lauden, "What Does Heaven Say? Christian Wolff and Western Impressions of Confucian Ethics," in *Confucius and the Analects: New Essays*, ed. Bryan W. Van Norden (Oxford University Press, 2002), 89, note 20.

13. Simon Leys, as quoted in Slingerland, *Analects*, xxv.

14. Slingerland, *Analects*, 27. The first bracketed phrase is included in the translation by Wing-Tsit Chan in *A Source Book in Chinese Philosophy*, tr. and ed. Wing-Tsit Chan (Princeton University Press, 1963), 25.

15. Slingerland, *Analects*, 27–28.

16. Information on the dates of Chinese dynasties was obtained from the "Chronology of Dynasties" on page xv of Chan's *Source Book in Chinese Philosophy*.

17. For a description of the "Age of Confucius," see Slingerland, *Analects*, xx–xxv.

18. See John Meyer's discussion of Hobbes in this volume.

19. For a recent description of eight such global environmental challenges threatening current global society, see chapter 1 of Speth, *The Bridge at the Edge of the World*, ominously titled "Looking into the Abyss."

20. See Chan, *A Source Book in Chinese Philosophy*.

21. Chan (ibid., 14) lists the topics uniquely raised by Neo-Confucianism, including the unity of nature and humanity.

22. This characterization of the Neo-Confucian cosmology and the label "anthropocosmic" are borrowed from Tu Wei-ming's important essay "The Continuity of Being: Chinese Visions of Nature," in *Confucian Thought: Selfhood*

as Creative Transformation, ed. Tu Wei-ming (SUNY Press, 1985). For more on on this cosmology, see Tu, *Centrality and Commonality: An Essay on Confucian Religiousness* (SUNY Press, 1989), especially chapter 4; Tu, *Humanity and Self-Cultivation: Essays in Confucian Thought* (Cheng and Tsui, 1998); Tu, *Way, Learning and Politics: Essays on the Confucian Intellectual* (SUNY Press, 1993), especially chapter 8.

23. See Young-chan Ro, "Ecological Implications of Yi Yulgok's Cosmology," in *Confucianism and Ecology: The Interrelationship of Heaven, Earth, and Humanity*, ed. Mary Evelyn Tucker and John Berthong (Harvard University Center for the Study of World Religions, 1998), 186. The term quoted here is first used on p. 171 of that work.

24. Young-chan Ro, "Ecological Implications of Yi Yulgok's Cosmology," 184.

25. Ibid., 184.

26. Tu, "The Continuity of Being," 35.

27. Ibid., 35–36.

28. Ibid., 39.

29. For a translation of *The Doctrine of the Mean*, see Chan, *A Source Book in Chinese Philosophy*.

30. Chan, *A Source Book in Chinese Philosophy*, 108.

31. Slingerland, *Analects*, 239.

32. Tu, "The Continuity of Being," 39.

33. Chang Tsai, *The Western Inscription*, in Chan, *A Source Book in Chinese Philosophy*, 497.

34. Wang Yang-ming, *Inquiry on the Great Learning*, in Chan, *A Source Book in Chinese Philosophy*, 659, 661.

35. Slingerland, *Analects*, 238. Slingerland goes on to cite several passages in the *Analects* where this foundational Confucian value is expressed: 1.2, 2.5, 2.7–2.8, and 19.18.

36. For the historical development of "hard" anthropocentrism, see Leiss, *The Domination of Nature*.

37. Wang, *Inquiry on the Great Learning*, in Chan, *A Source Book in Chinese Philosophy*, 660.

38. On this Neo-Confucian concept, see "Chang Tsai's Philosophy of Material Force" in Chan, *A Source Book in Chinese Philosophy*, where *ch'i* is translated as "material force." In addition, Chan provides a brief explanation of *ch'i* before the eleventh-century-CE Neo-Confucian movement began: "[C]h'i denotes the psychophysiological power associated with blood and breath. As such it is translated as 'vital force' or 'vital power.' ... " (784)

39. Tu, "Continuity of Being," 38.

40. Ibid., 38.

41. Ibid., 38.

42. Ibid., 40.

43. Ibid., 40–41.

44. See Chang Tsai, *Correcting Youthful Ignorance*, in Chan, *A Source Book in Chinese Philosophy*, 500.

45. Tu, "The Continuity of Being," 41.

46. Ibid., 43.

47. Ibid., 45.

48. For examples of such comparative political theory, although not specifically focused on the environment, see the three volumes cited in the epigraphs above.

Conclusion: The Western Political Theory Canon, Nature, and a Broader Dialogue

Peter F. Cannavò and Joseph H. Lane Jr.

As the essays in this volume demonstrate, the political theory canon offers a wealth of practical and theoretical insights into the relationship between humanity or, somewhat more specifically, political society and the natural world. In his discussion of Confucius, Joel Kassiola argues that the Western political theory tradition has problematic recurring themes that revolve around the concept of humanity's separation from and superiority to the rest of nature. Certainly, these essays give some credence to what we would term the "hard anthropocentric" aspects of the Western theoretical tradition. Plato's attempt to imagine a ruling class removed from direct physical engagement with the land, Niccolò Machiavelli's insistence on a recurrent contest between human *virtù* and nature as *fortuna*, Thomas Hobbes's reconceptualization of nature as a "dead" machine, John Locke's view that God granted humanity dominion over the Earth, and Hannah Arendt's accounts of nature as a devouring, destructive force all suggest this theme.

At the same time, as the essays demonstrate, Western political theory also presents us with much more complexity than one might initially think. At various points, Western thought not only contests hard anthropocentrism, but in some cases even offers up surprising twists on ecocentrism and in other cases provides useful insights for contemporary environmental politics and for green theorists and actors. Aristotle's teleological view of nature is in tension with his anthropocentrism; Machiavelli offers useful warnings for green advocates of decentralization; Hobbes may be read as offering a constitutive approach to nature and politics; Locke's work provides the basis for conservationist readings of our obligations to the Earth and other human beings; Rousseau offers a critique of the Enlightenment that provides a distinctively modern basis for environmentalist arguments against liberal modernity; Wollstonecraft provides insights into the interconnection between the domination of other human beings and the domination of nature; Mill shares important affinities with romanticism and with critiques of crude utilitarian approaches to nature; Marx provides a very perceptive critique of capitalism's commodifying, unsustainable relationship with nature; Du Bois analyzes how racial oppression impacts one's ability to form a meaningful connection with the natural world; Arendt provides valuable insights into how humanity's relationship with nature ought to involve care and a connection with place.

Thus, broad generalizations about or condemnations of the Western tradition are likely to be grounded in incomplete or distorted readings of the canonical texts. That some of those readings have become entrenched and widely accepted is no reason for us to close the book on any of these deep and perceptive authors. For this reason, many of the essays in this volume emphasize what we stand to gain by moving away from the most conventional readings of particular authors. The theorists profiled here often posited greener tendencies alongside their more domineering, instrumentalizing attitudes toward nature.

For example, Aristotle declares in the *Politics* that "plants exist for the sake of animals and that the other animals exist for the sake of human beings ... both for use and sustenance" (Book I, Chapter 8, 1256b 16–21). Yet Özgüç Orhan points out that Aristotle also sees significant kinship between human beings and other animals and thus argues that Aristotle actually counsels *against* the unlimited exploitation of nature.

David Hume doesn't extend justice to nonhuman animals; Andrew Valls observes that Hume sees us as having duties of benevolence toward animals and regards benevolence as a more exalted virtue than justice. Locke may be an "unabashedly anthropocentric" (in Zev Trachtenberg's words) champion of property rights; however, Trachtenberg also argues that Locke anticipates contemporary notions of sustainability and supports conservationist policies, and that he grants humans usufruct rights to nature but not rights over nature's fundamental ecological systems and relationships.

Mary Wollstonecraft presents the rationality of women and men as marking out a common humanity in contradistinction to other animals, yet Barbara Seeber cautions against such a standard anthropocentric reading. Wollstonecraft urges kind treatment of to animals and sees them as having traits in common with children. She also connects cruelty to animals with tyrannical behavior toward other human beings. Moreover, her descriptions of Scandinavia show a naturalist's appreciation of landscape, climate, and wildlife, lament human degradation of the natural environment, see agency in wild animals, and convey her personal immersion in nature rather than perpetuate anthropocentric, patriarchal conventions of the disembodied observer.

Conventional readings of Mill's essay "Nature" see Mill as urging the conquest and pacification of nonhuman nature and of humanity's own natural instincts, but Piers Stephens counters that the essay is mainly an attack on conservative, religiously oriented ethical naturalism, and that Mill, both here and in his other writings, urges us to retain and build on our own natural spiritedness. Moreover, as Stephens points out, Mill suggests ecological limits on economic expansion and appreciates natural beauty and wildness for their contributions to the cultivation of character.

What these essays suggest is, perhaps, something universal to humanity's relationship with nature: the unresolved and unresolvable ambivalence of trying to get our living out of nature by changing, controlling, and even killing it, *while at the same time* recognizing ourselves as part of, dependent upon, and in kinship with nature. Drawing from John Meyer's essay on Hobbes, we might say that the constitutive relationship between nature and politics entails an ongoing tension between the desire to craft a separate human realm (including a distinctive realm of the political) and the fact that our membership in the natural world creates an ecological context and ecological limits for politics. Similarly, as Peter Cannavò notes in his essay on Arendt, we try to overcome natural cycles, transcend them, and protect ourselves from them, and yet we still rely on nature for a fundamental sense of meaning. To fully "emancipate" ourselves from earthly nature—if that were even possible—would be to relegate humanity to a pointless, self-referential existence. Similarly, as Joseph Lane points out in his essay, Rousseau insists that although the most "natural" human existence is characterized by a certain blindness to nature's motions and beauties, "enlightened" human beings may be re-grounded in nature by a newly reconstructed, albeit mediated, relationship to it. Through minute attention to and appreciation of the motions of nature, we may reclaim some semblance of our lost "natural" existence.

The ambivalent interaction between human beings and nature was already evident in Aristotle's writing. However, with the rise of modernity, which is marked by humanity's increasing ability to transform nature and by the increasing predominance of views that subordinate Earth to humanity, that relationship arguably becomes even more fraught.

Political theorists, in grappling with the character of political society, have therefore had to confront the supremely complex relationship between humanity and the rest of nature, even though their insights have received insufficient attention from commentators. The thinkers discussed in this volume, who arguably have merited canonical status because of their particular insights into politics, may have had especial understanding into the implications of the human relationship with nature. The subtlety, the complexity, and indeed the ambivalence of their perspectives on humanity and nature testify to the depth of their insights.

Nevertheless, we must take seriously the calls by Kassiola and other comparative political theorists for an outside intervention into Western political theory. W. S. K. Cameron's essay on Martin Heidegger provides another opening for looking beyond the Western tradition. Cameron, in keeping with the rather unconventional readings in these essays, contests environmentalists' reliance on Heidegger's later "green" essays, such as "The Question Concerning Technology." Cameron argues that Heidegger's later works, while offering a powerful critique of hard anthropocentrism, provide little in the way of guidance for escaping our ecological predicament. For such guidance, Cameron turns back to *Being and Time* and draws on Heidegger's argument that Dasein, our mode of being, exists in a social context that imposes limits. However, Cameron notes, coming up against those very limits can reveal new horizons of thought and action: "Just because Dasein's understanding is finite, it is regularly surprised or disappointed by unexpected outcomes. Denial is possible, but often such surprises breed new insights confirmed by experience." Heidegger, Cameron says, shows that "the evolution of views is not merely possible but inevitable and unsuppressible." Because it is so jarring, the environmental crisis can open up such surprises and insights. Thinking beyond our social context can involve engaging with other traditions. This is the call issued by comparative political theory.

In the United States, comparative political theory, like environmental political theory, is a relatively new subfield in the academic discipline of political theory. Comparative political theorists approach familiar questions with new categories, traditions, and perspectives that can both instruct Western political theory and yield novel insights. The Confucian tradition, as Kassiola tells us, foregrounds a much more harmonious relationship with nature than does mainstream Western thought. However, one may see Confucianism as insufficiently attentive to humanity's inevitable tensions with nature. One might also object to the overtly religious aspects of Confucian cosmology (though there also are strong theistic elements in Locke's account) or to Confucianism's anti-democratic or anti-individualist implications. Nevertheless, Confucianism can be an important voice in the unavoidable and increasingly urgent discussion about the character and the future of humanity's relationship with nature. Moreover, Confucianism is fundamental to the culture of the world's most populous country, a nation with one of the largest environmental footprints. A serious engagement with Confucianism's green aspects by the West may give a green Confucianism greater visibility in China itself.

Comparative political theory also leads us beyond well-known thinkers to a global wealth of political and philosophical traditions that have, like the Western tradition, sought to better understand humanity's relationship with nature. Environmental thought and discourse, which has already recognized insights from the religious, cultural, and political traditions of indigenous peoples, would do well to study these traditions.[1] Such study would, in turn, enrich comparative political theory itself.

Not only does this volume reveal the complexity of our relationship with nature; it also highlights how traditional political categories and ideological distinctions obscure insights into the environment offered by writers across the political spectrum. Today environmentalism is generally identified with the political left, and conservatives, especially in the United States, have increasingly opposed environmental policies on principle. However, Harlan Wilson's essay shows Edmund Burke, the founder of modern conservatism, to have been a complex figure whose emphasis on the complexity and fragility of the social order led him to anticipate both a more modern focus on sustainability and the precautionary principle. Wilson's account of Burke thus challenges the divide between greens and conservatives.[2] Similarly, Kimberly Smith's essay on W. E. B. Du Bois challenges another political and ideological tension: that between environmentalists concerned about preservation of the natural world and activists concerned about racial and economic justice.[3] It is widely believed that this divide was finally bridged with the rise of the environmental justice movement in the 1980s. However, Smith's essay reveals another, much earlier bridge by highlighting how Du Bois theorized a strong connection between racism and mistreatment of the natural world. And Wollstonecraft, as Seeber documents, also connected environmental values and social justice.

In short, the essays in this volume not only illuminate insights into our relationship with nature provided by canonical political theorists; they also challenge a good deal of conventional wisdom to the effect that Western political theory has addressed the natural world in a neat, tidy, and consistent way. We have tried to take seriously the idea that Western thought is an assemblage of discordant parts and incomplete thoughts. Many of the thinkers who have contributed to this assemblage have participated in laying the groundwork for our environmental crises, but they also provide resources for re-thinking and reforming the world they have helped to make. Reading the Western philosophical tradition in our time helps us both to understand how we got here and to consider what we might do now.

At the same time, following Kassiola, these essays suggest the need for a broader dialogue, one that goes beyond Western political theory and embraces discourses from an entire planet now threatened by humanity's claims, productions, actions, and reactions. Obviously, such a call for a wider discussion suggests the need for another volume, one going well beyond the Western tradition. We invite interested scholars to grace us with such a sequel.

Notes

1. Here we echo a similar call made by Fred Dallmayr in *Return to Nature? An Ecological Counterhistory* (University Press of Kentucky, 2011)—especially on pages 141–153, where Dallmayr provides an overview of the ecological insights of Classical Indian, Buddhist, and Chinese thought. Dallmayr, in the bulk of his book, focuses on Western thought and, in parallel to our volume, traces a kind of philosophical counterhistory that offers a "green" corrective to the Western tradition's more dominant hard anthropocentrism.

2. Some conservative activists have begun urging a "greener" outlook. See, for example, Rod Dreher, *Crunchy Cons: The New Conservative Counterculture and Its Return to Roots* (Random House, 2006). Dreher himself cites Burke. See also Paul Foote, "Why Environmentalism is a Conservative Concern," *The Guardian*, November 11, 2010; John R. E. Bliese, *The Greening of Conservative America* (Westview, 2001); Roger Scruton, "Conservatism," in *Political Theory and the Ecological Challenge*, ed. Andrew Dobson and Robyn Eckersley (Cambridge University Press, 2006); Roger Scruton, *Green Philosophy: How to Think Seriously About the Planet* (Atlantic Books, 2012).

3. On this divide, see Robert Gottlieb, *Forcing the Spring: The Transformation of the American Environmental Movement* (Island, 2005).

Authors

Sheryl D. Breen is a professor of political science at the University of Minnesota at Morris.
W. S. K. Cameron is a professor of philosophy at Loyola Marymount University.
Peter F. Cannavò is a professor of government and environmental studies at Hamilton College.
Joel Jay Kassiola is a professor of political science at San Francisco State University.
Joseph H. Lane Jr. is a professor of political science at Emory & Henry College.
Timothy W. Luke is a professor of political science at Virginia Polytechnic Institute and State University.
John M. Meyer is a professor of politics and environmental studies at Humboldt State University.
Özgüç Orhan is a professor of political science at Fatih University in Istanbul.
Barbara K. Seeber is an associate professor of English at Brock University.
Francisco Seijo is a professor of political science at C. V. Starr-Middlebury College Schools Abroad, New York University, Fundacion IES, and the University of Southern California's programs in Madrid.
Kimberly K. Smith is a professor of environmental studies and political science at Carleton College.
Piers H. G. Stephens is a professor of philosophy at the University of Georgia.
Zev Trachtenberg is a professor of philosophy at the University of Oklahoma.
Andrew Valls is a professor of political science in the School of Public Policy at Oregon State University.
Harlan Wilson is a professor of politics at Oberlin College.

Index

Abbey, Edward, 144
Adams, Carol J., 175
Adams, Madonna, 39
Adorno, Theodor, 5, 6
Aesthetics
    Aristotle and, 48, 51
    Burke and, 154–158, 163, 164
    Du Bois and, 228–231, 235
    Mill and, 190, 192, 199–201
    as rationale for preservation, 129
    Wollstonecraft and, 181, 182
Agency, human, 20, 189–202, 239–250
Agriculture, 1
    Arendt on, 254–256, 263–266
    capitalism and, 211, 212
    environmental knowledge and, 35–37
    gardening, 17, 20, 155, 156, 231, 232
    Lockean labor theory and, 101, 102, 108, 109
    Marx and agroeconomics, 208–212
    in Mill, 198, 199
    in Plato, 29–41
    racial oppression and, 223–238
    as relationship between humans and natural world, 30
    in Rousseau, 134, 135, 140, 141
Alexander, Don, 77
Alienation, 6
    in Arendt, 264–266
    capitalism and, 209–211
    Du Bois on, 19, 20, 223–236
    kosmos and, 192
    of labor, 2, 209–215, 234, 235
    Marx on, 209–216
    Rousseauian, 135–142
Amour-propre, 135–147
Analects (Confucius), 273, 275, 280
Anderson, Terry, 169
Animals
    anthropocentrism and, 45, 51, 52
    Aristotle on, 49, 51, 53, 55
    compared to children, 179
    cruelty to, 18, 176, 179–181
    Douglass on, 227
    ecofeminism and, 175
    humans as, 16, 53, 117, 118, 130
    Hume on, 117, 118, 126, 130
    justice toward, 117, 122–126, 175, 288
    as sentient beings, 18, 55, 176–181, 185
    sympathy toward, 118
    Wollstonecraft on, 173–186
An Inconvenient Truth (Gore), 88
Anthropocentrism
    Aristotle and, 14, 45, 51–54, 288
    ecocentrism vs., 207
    humanism and, 65
    Marx and, 205, 206
    Western political theory and, 287–290
    Wollstonecraft and, 183, 184, 288, 289
Appeal from the New to the Old Whigs (Burke), 160

Arendt, Hannah, 11, 16, 21, 47, 115, 163, 216, 253–266, 287–289
Aristotle, 6, 14, 22, 45–59, 191, 273, 278, 288
Artifice, human, 21, 90–92, 115, 136, 254–266
Associationism, 193, 201
Attfield, Robin, 2, 3

Bacon, Francis, 10, 47
Baier, Annette, 119, 126
Ball, Terence, 4
Barry, John, 3, 4
Being and Time (Heidegger), 20, 240–243, 290
Belsey, Andrew, 192
Bennett, Jane, 3–5, 213
Bentham, Jeremy, 18, 159, 165, 190–193
Benton, Ted, 3–5
Berg, Peter, 2
Berry, Wendell, 2
Between Past and Future (Arendt), 253, 260–263
Bioregionalism, 2, 14, 70, 77
Biro, Andrew, 3–6
Bohls, Elizabeth, 182
Bookchin, Murray, 2, 6, 139
Botanical Fragments (Rousseau), 135
Bowerbank, Sylvia, 179, 182, 185
Breen, Sheryl D., 13, 14, 19, 29–45, 234, 276
Brennan, Andrew, 86
Bullard, Robert, 2
Burke, Edmund, 17, 154–169, 291

Cafaro, Philip, 4
Callicott, J. Baird, 30, 118, 127–129
Cameron, W. S. K. "Scott," 20, 162, 239–250, 290
Canavan, Francis, 167
Cannavò, Peter, 4, 15, 16, 21, 159, 253–266, 289
Capaldi, Nicholas, 201
Capital (Marx), 205, 206, 216
Capitalism
 and agriculture, 211, 212
 and alienation from nature, 209–211
 Burkean political economy and, 167
 "green," 19, 167–169, 212–218
 modernity and, 123
 sustainability and, 217
Carbon emissions, 212, 217, 218, 246–249
Carson, Rachel, 1, 6
Chaloupka, Bill, 3
Chan, Wing-Tsit, 279–281
Chang Tsai, 280
Chaos theory, 69
Chapman, Anne, 257–261
Citizenship, 1–7
 ecological, 58
 Hobbesian, 89
 Machiavellian decentralization and, 70, 74, 76
 in Plato's *Republic*, 32–42
 property rights and, 32–42, 58, 122
 in Rousseau's *Social Contract*, 142–145
Civilisation (Mill), 197
Clark, Rebecca, 5
Class, social
 in Marx, 215, 216
 in Plato's *Republic*, 30–42
Clements, Frederic, 69
Climate change, anthropogenic, 1, 20, 88, 94, 95, 156, 162, 164, 169, 246, 247, 277
Collectives and collectivity, 199, 208, 216, 239–250, 259–264
Commodification, 184, 209–219, 288
Commodity fetishism, 209–215
Commoner, Barry, 1, 2, 6, 137
Communalism, 33, 34
Communism, 205, 206, 218, 219
Complexity
 in Arendt, 21, 253
 in Burke, 17, 154–161, 166
 and phenomenology, 242
 Rousseau and, 17
Confucius and Confucianism, 11, 12, 21, 22, 271–283, 287–291. *See also* Neo-Confucianism
Conservation, 16, 17, 168, 169, 224, 230, 287. *See also* Preservation

Conservatism
  Burkean, 153–169
  green, 17, 168, 169, 291
  political, 16–18, 176
  religious, 196
Consumption, 21, 33, 167, 197, 276
  Arendt on, 253–255, 264–266
  of resources, 207, 210–212
Cook, Ian, 197
Cosmoanthropism, 278, 279, 282
Critias (Plato), 39, 40
Crito (Plato), 38
Cronon, William, 3

Dallmayr, Fred, 12, 271, 272
Daly, Herman, 75
Darkwater (Du Bois), 229, 230
Dasein, 20, 239–250, 290
Davis, Karen, 175
Davison, Victoria, 174, 175
D'Eaubonne, Françoise, 2
Decentralization, 2, 14, 15, 65–79, 147, 199, 287
de Certeau, Michel, 218
De Corpore (Hobbes), 83, 84
Deep ecology, 3, 12, 139, 144
Democracy, 2, 3, 29–33, 168, 169, 233, 276
Denaturalizing Ecological Politics (Biro), 6
Descartes, René, 85–87, 240–244
De-Shalit, Avner, 4
Devigne, Robert, 193–196
Dialogues (Rousseau), 137, 138
Dike (concept). 31, 35
Discourse on Origins of Inequality or *Second Discourse* (Rousseau), 133–139
Discourse on the Arts and Sciences or *First Discourse* (Rousseau), 133
Discourses on Livy (Machiavelli), 66, 67, 72, 73
Dissertation on the Duty of Mercy and Sin of Cruelty to Brute Animals (Primatt), 176
Dobson, Andrew, 3–5, 71, 117, 130, 136

Doctrine of the Mean (Confucius), 279
Donner, Wendy, 195, 200
Donovan, Josephine, 175
Douglass, Frederick, 226, 227
Dryzek, John, 3
Dualism, 30
  Aristotle and, 46–50
  Hobbes and, 15, 85–89, 94
  and human-nature relationship, 86, 173, 174, 185, 186, 287
  Marx and, 206
  Neo-Confucian alternatives to, 279, 280
  observer-object, 183, 184
  Plato and, 39, 40, 42
Du Bois, W. E. B., 5, 11, 18–20, 163, 180, 223–236, 288, 291

Eckersley, Robyn, 3–6, 15, 76, 77
Ecocentrism, 3, 6, 207, 282. *See also* Deep ecology
Ecofeminism, 2, 11, 174, 175
  Rousseau and, 139
  Wollstonecraft and, 18, 173–186
Economics
  Aristotelian, 47, 52, 57–59
  ecological, 58
Education, 31, 54, 56, 143, 146, 164, 173, 177–181, 197
Ehrlich, Paul, 6
Eighteenth Brumaire of Louis Bonaparte (Marx), 207, 216, 217, 274
Emerson, Ralph Waldo, 275
Emile (Rousseau), 136–145
Enclosure Acts, 167
Engels, Friedrich, 205, 206
Environmental ethics, 2, 3, 58, 59
Environmental history, 3
Environmentalism and Political Theory (Eckersley), 6
Environmental policy, 78, 79, 244–250
Equality. *See also* Inequality
  Burke and, 160–167
  gender, 173, 174

Equality (cont.)
  Hume and, 124
  Millian liberalism and, 195
  racial, 223
  as unnatural, 160, 161, 166
Equilibrium
  capitalism and, 210–213
  Machiavellian decentralization and, 68, 69, 73–76
  Platonic, 38–40
  Rousseauian, 136–139, 145
  stationary-state economies and, 18, 197–200
Essay Concerning Human Understanding (Locke), 100
Essay on Humanity to Animals (Young), 176
Euben, Peter, 8, 9, 273, 274
Eudaimonia, 55–57
Explorations in Environmental Political Theory (Kassiola), 6

Feminism, 2, 139
Feminism and Ecology (Mellor), 174
Filmer, Sir Robert, 16, 104, 106
Fortune
  in Aristotle, 50
  in Machiavelli, 14, 66–69, 73–77, 287
Foster, John Bellamy, 4, 5
Foucault, Michel, 5
Founding, of places, 257–266
Fourier, Charles, 6
Frankel, Charles, 192, 196
Freeden, Michael, 271
Freedom, 148. *See also* Liberty
  Arendt on, 255, 264
  Burkean, 153, 167
  Du Bois on, 225, 226
  Hobbesian, 2, 83
  Mill on, 191, 192
Freeman, Michael, 158
Free Market Environmentalism (Anderson and Leal), 169
Frost, Samantha, 87

Gadamer, Hans-Georg, 240
Galiani, Ferdinando, 210
Gandhi, Mohandas, 274
Garrett, Aaron, 126
Gender, 11, 18
  Burke on, 156
  Mill on, 189, 197
  Wollstoncraft on, 173–186, 287, 288
Globalization, 2, 4, 19, 21, 78, 207, 211, 217, 276
Godrej, Farah, 12
Godwin, William, 179, 180
Goethe, Johann Wolfgang von, 190
Good, 31, 34, 40, 138–144
Goodin, Robert, 3
Gore, Albert, Jr., 88
Gorz, André, 2
Great Chain of Being, 53, 176, 178
Greed, 33, 41, 42, 57, 58
Greenhouse gases, 122
Green politics, 1, 2, 8
  Arendtian, 266
  and civic republicanism, 66
  and convention or prejudice, 162
  and decentralization, 77, 78
  liberalism and, 189, 190
  and sustainability, 189, 190
  Wilson on, 154–169
Green State (Eckersley), 15, 76, 77
Growth
  Aristotelian *phusis* and, 48–51, 58, 59
  and Liebig's "Law of the Minimum," 211
  limits to, 78, 199, 200, 211
  Mill and, 192–200
  nature and cycles of, 254

Habitation
  Arendtian human artifice and, 21, 253–266
  Du Bois and, 235
  Locke and, 15, 16, 20, 21, 99–112, 261
  Rousseau and, 142
Hacking, Ian, 118
Haddad, Brent, 111
Hardin, Garrett, 1, 2, 58, 77, 168, 169
Hargrove, Eugene, 40
Harper, Lila Marz, 182, 183

Hayek, Friedrich, 166
Hegel, G. W. F., 243
Heidegger, Martin, 11, 20, 162, 211, 212, 239–250, 290
Herzog, Don, 162, 163
Hierarchy, 40, 53, 173–186, 287, 288
History of Animals (Aristotle), 53, 55
Hobbes, Thomas, 2, 6, 15, 47, 67, 83–95, 276, 287, 289
Holism
  Aristotelian, 45
  Confucian, 279, 280
  Hume and, 127–129
  Marx and, 19, 45, 208
Holland, Breena, 4, 5
Honig, Bonnie, 264
Hulliung, Mark, 134
Human Condition (Arendt), 253–265
Humanism, 16, 65–68, 85
Human-nature relationship
  ambivalence in, 289
  Christianity and, 104–107
  Dasein and, 20, 239–250
  dualism in, 86, 173, 174, 185, 186, 287
  gender oppression and, 173–186, 291
  Locke and, 99
  and science, 2, 3, 14, 47, 89
  as subject/object dichotomy, 183, 184
Humans
  as embodied animals, 16, 53, 117, 118, 130
  as fallen creatures, 137–142, 146
  as inseparable from nature, 206–211, 217, 218
Hume, David, 16, 22, 118–123, 174, 288
Hurston, Zora Neale, 230, 231
Husserl, Edmund, 240
Hust, Karen, 182

Identity, 7
  place and, 259
  racial, 19, 223, 224, 231–235
Individualism, 2, 169, 247
  Mill and, 18, 117

  possessive, 18, 189, 196
Inequality
  Burke and, 160, 161, 166, 167
  Locke on, 102, 103
  as root of abuse, 163, 164
  Rousseau on, 133, 139, 142
  Wollstonecraft on, 173–186
Interdependence, 1
  Aristotle and, 48
  Burke and, 157–160, 166
  Hume and, 129, 130
  Marx and, 19
  Rousseau and, 16, 17
Intergenerational obligation, 17, 21, 159, 206, 208, 280–282

Jaspers, Karl, 275
Jefferson, Thomas, 5
Jenkins, Joyce, 126
Johnson, James Weldon, 230, 231
Justice
  animals as entitled to, 117, 122–126, 175
  Burkean natural order and, 166
  dike, 31, 35
  environmental, 2, 4, 117–130, 169
  Humean, 117–130

Kant, Immanuel, 10, 275
Kassiola, Joel Jay, 3, 11, 12, 15, 21, 22, 31, 271–291
Kautz, Beth Dolan, 182
Kenyon-Jones, Christine, 176
Kirk, Russell, 167
Kosmos, 48, 51, 192

Labor
  agricultural, 225–234
  alienation of, 2, 209, 214, 215, 234, 235
  Arendt on, 254–256, 263–266
  commodification of, 19, 165, 166, 209, 214, 215
  Lockean theory of, 99–111, 214
  Marxian theory of, 205–219
  property rights and, 101–111
  and social status, 13, 31, 37–41, 234

Lane, Joseph H., Jr., 5, 16, 17, 133–149, 197, 276, 277, 289
Lane, Melissa, 5, 30
Latour, Bruno, 208
"Law of the Minimum," 211
Leal, Donald, 169
Leiss, William, 206
Leopold, Aldo, 1, 11, 16, 118, 127–129, 174, 224
Letter Concerning Toleration (Locke), 110
Letters Written during a Short Residence (Wollstonecraft), 174, 178–184
Letter to Beaumont (Rousseau), 137
Letter to D'Alembert (Rousseau), 146
Leviathan (Hobbes), 83–92
Leys, Simon, 275
Liberalism, political, 4, 11, 17, 22, 291
 Humean, 16, 117–130
 Lockean, 100, 101, 214
 Millian, 18, 19, 189–202
 modernity and, 134, 273, 287
 Rousseau and, 134, 287
 sustainability and, 189, 190
 thymos (spiritedness) and, 195
Libertarianism, 122, 163–169
Liberty. *See also* Freedom
 Burke and, 157, 158
 Earth's resources as constraint on, 2
 Locke and, 108
 Mill's principles of, 189–197
 and security, 66, 71, 75–77
Liebig, Justus von, 208–212
Light, Andrew, 4
Locke, John, 6, 9, 15, 16, 20, 261, 279, 287
 Arendt and, 255, 265
 Burke and, 158, 160, 163, 166, 167
 Hume and, 118–123
 Marx and, 207–214
 Mill and, 189, 193, 195
 Trachtenberg and, 99–112
Lorenz, Edward, 69
Luke, Timothy W., 3, 19, 159, 166, 205–221, 274

Macauley, David, 6
Machiavelli, Niccolò, 14, 15, 65–81, 287
MacPherson, C. B., 167, 189
Malthus, Thomas, 165, 166
Manifesto of the Communist Party (Marx and Engels), 205, 213, 214
Marcuse, Herbert, 5, 6
Marsh, George Perkins, 1
Marshall, Peter, 86
Marxism, 4, 19, 139, 206
Marx, Karl, 6, 19, 22, 159, 166, 205–219, 274, 288
Mary, A Fiction (Wollstonecraft), 173, 178, 180
Materialism, 4
 and commodification, 214–216
 Hobbesian, 85–90, 95
 Marxian history and, 205, 206, 208, 213–216
 Plato and, 30
 vital, 213
Mathews, Freya, 87
Mellor, Mary, 174, 176
Merchant, Carolyn, 2, 30, 87
Metaphysics (Aristotle), 48, 53, 57
Meyer, John M., 3–6, 10, 15, 83–95, 146, 148, 161, 289
Mill, James, 190
Mill, John Stuart, 9, 18, 19, 69, 117, 189–202, 288, 289
Miller, Charles, 5
Miller, Dale, 197, 198
Minding Nature (Macauley), 6
Modernity, 14, 17, 20, 264, 289
 Aristotelian thought and, 45–54, 59
 Confucian tradition and, 271–278, 282
 and mechanistic view of nature, 47, 59
 Rousseau and, 133–135, 141, 147
Moral economy, Aristotelian, 57, 58
More, Thomas, 38, 42
Moskal, Jeanne, 182
Muir, John, 1, 20, 229

Naess, Arne, 3, 143, 144
Natural Contract (Serres), 86

Nature. *See also* Human-nature relationship
    as Burkean authority, 160, 161, 168
    capitalism and, 217
    commodification of, 210, 288
    as Heideggerian resource, 20, 211, 212, 245
    and human artifice, 256
    as human construct, 148, 149, 160
    in Marx, 206–208, 211, 217, 218
    instrumentalization of, 14, 37, 47, 51, 59, 134, 184, 189, 215–217, 224, 254, 260–266, 279, 288
    kosmos as Presocratic concept of, 192
    "laws of," 89, 90, 101–102, 117–122, 137
    Machiavellian concept of, 68, 69
    mechanistic views of, 15, 30, 47, 59, 87, 88, 157, 196, 278, 287
    and politics, 15, 84, 87–95, 287, 289
    as principle of development, 192, 196
    as process, 48, 49
    as purposeful and orderly, 51
    racism and, 20
    Rousseauian, 135–137, 148
Nature (Mill), 69, 194, 289
Nazism, 239
Neo-Confucianism, 21, 22, 277–283
Nicholson, George, 176
Nicomachean Ethics (Aristotle), 54–56
Niemöller, Martin, 248
Nietzsche, Friedrich Wilhelm, 46, 243, 244
"Noble Savage" 139
Nominalism, 91–94
Norton, Bryan, 2, 3
Nussbaum, Martha, 5

Oakeshott, Michael, 84, 85, 89
Objectivity, 93, 95, 261, 265
Oelschlaeger, Max, 3, 30
Oikonomia, 52, 57, 58
O'Neill, John, 5
On Liberty (Mill), 189–197
Ophuls, William, 2, 77, 87, 88
Oppression

   gender, 173–186, 287, 288
   racial, 180, 223–236, 288, 291
Order. *See also* Equilibrium; Hierarchy
    complexity and, 157
    economic market and, 166
    nature as, 160, 161
Orhan, Özgüç, 14, 15, 45–59, 191 273, 278, 288
Original Stories (Wollstonecraft), 175, 178, 179
Ostrom, Elinor, 78, 79
Ott, Paul, 261

Paehlke, Robert, 3, 4
Paine, Thomas, 159
Parel, Anthony J., 271, 274
Parfit, Derek, 247
Parham, John, 198–200
Parts of Animals (Aristotle), 49, 51, 53
Passmore, John, 2, 3
Perkins, David, 176
Phaedrus (Plato), 38, 39
Phenomenology, 93, 240–243
Philadelphia Negro (Du Bois), 228
Philosophical Inquiry into the Origin of Our Ideas of the Sublime and Beautiful (Burke), 154
Phusis, 48–51, 58, 59
Physics (Aristotle), 49
Place
    Arendtian human artifice and, 21, 253–266, 288
    Burke and, 163
    Du Bois and, 19, 224, 230–236
    identity and, 259
Placelessness, 30, 35–43
Plato, 13, 14, 29–43, 46–50, 190, 234, 287
Plumwood, Val, 2–4, 86, 177
Pocock, J. G. A., 166, 167
Political economy, 165–167
Political Nature (Meyer), 6, 146
Political theory, 5–13, 271–274, 282, 287–292
    comparative, 271–274, 290, 291
    environmental, 3–6, 12, 21, 22, 290
    organic, 22

Political Theory and the Ecological Challenge (Dobson and Eckersley), 5, 6
Politics
 aestheticizing of, 156, 168
 Burke's theory of, 158, 159
 environmental, 271–283, 290, 291
 nature and, 84, 87–95, 287, 289
Politics (Aristotle), 51–55, 288
Pragmatism, 70–72, 161, 164, 165, 241–243, 248
Praxis, 46, 50–59
Precautionary principle, Burkean, 161–164
Preece, Rod, 176
Prejudices, 162
"Presentism," 8, 9, 273, 274
Preservation, 17, 18
 Arendtian place founding and, 260–267
 Burkean stewardship and, 163
 Du Bois and, 223, 232, 234, 291
 ecofeminism and, 175
 Mill's Romantic sympathies and, 201, 202
 Rousseauian foundations for, 135–137, 145
Primatt, Humphrey, 176
Prince (Machiavelli), 66, 67, 72
Principles of Political Economy (Mill), 189, 197, 198
Property rights
 Aristotelian theory of, 58
 Burke and, 166
 communitarian, 58
 and environmental protection, 112
 environmental regulation and, 102, 103, 122
 green capitalism and, 169
 Hume and, 118–122
 in Kallipolis, 13, 14, 29–43
 labor and, 101–111
 Lockean theory of, 99–112, 288
 Marxian intergenerational obligation and, 206, 207
 in More, 38
 and political corruption, 33, 34, 42
 as relationship between humans and natural world, 30
 and stewardship, 163, 225–228
 usufructory, 16, 107–111, 206, 207, 288
Pulido, Laura, 2

Quest for the Silver Fleece (Du Bois), 232–235

Race
 environmental justice and, 2
 Du Bois and, 180, 223–236, 288, 291
Racism, 11
Rawls, John, 5, 125
Reason
 Hobbes on, 85, 89
 Nietzschean "will to power" as, 244
 Platonic Good and, 40
 practical, 50, 53, 57
Reflections on the Revolution in France (Burke), 154, 155, 160, 166
Regulation
 Burke's opposition to, 166, 168
 Locke and, 102, 103, 110, 111
 property rights as obstacle to, 122
Regulatory takings, 102, 103
Republic (Plato), 13, 14, 29–43
Resources
 access to, 119–122
 commodification of, 184
 common-pool, 78, 79
 consumption of, 207, 210–212
 Heideggerian, 20, 211, 212, 245
 liberty to use, 2, 108
 scarcity and, 165, 166
Reveries of the Solitary Walker (Rousseau), 135, 144–146
Richardson, Alan, 179
Robin, Corey, 17
Robinson, Thomas, 30
Rolston, Holmes, III, 2, 3
Romanticism
 aesthetics and, 228
 Du Bois and, 228, 233
 and human-animal relationship, 176

Mill and, 18, 117, 190–202, 288
Rousseau's influence on, 144
and value of nature's beauty, 190, 228
Rousseau, Jean-Jacques, 5, 6, 16, 17, 133–149, 276, 277, 287, 289
Routley, Richard, 2, 3
Routley, Val. *See* Plumwood, Val
Ruston, Sharon, 177, 178

Sagoff, Mark, 3
Sale, Kirkpatrick, 2
Salleh, Ariel, 4
Sand County Almanac (Leopold), 127, 129, 144
Sandler, Ronald, 4
Scarcity, 111, 112, 119, 120, 125, 165, 200, 207, 211
Schlosberg, David, 4, 5
Science
 Aristotle and, 14, 46, 47, 50
 Burke and, 164, 169
 Heidegger on, 244, 245
 and human-nature relationship, 2, 3, 14, 47, 89
 and Humean justice, 122, 129, 130
 Locke's study of, 100, 111
 and mechanistic view of nature, 30, 47
 politics and, 85–88, 94, 95
 Rousseau on, 134, 141
Scientific Revolution, 47, 83, 87, 88, 141
Seeber, Barbara, 16, 18, 19, 126, 160, 161, 173–186, 288, 291
Seijo, Francisco, 14, 15, 65–79
Self-interest, 18, 55, 67, 129, 143, 193
Self-ownership, 101
Semmel, Bernard, 196, 197
Sen, Amartya, 122
Serres, Michel, 86
Shaver, Robert, 126
Shepard, Paul, 139
Shiva, Vandana, 2
Simplicity
 amour-propre and, 137–143
 Burke on, 157, 158, 197
 and emergence of complexity, 193, 194
Singer, Peter, 2, 3
Sinnott-Armstrong, Walter, 246–248
Slavery, 135, 154, 225–232
Slingerland, Edward, 275, 280, 281
Smith, Adam, 10, 207
Smith, Kimberly, 4, 5, 18–20, 223–236, 291
Snyder, Gary, 139, 144
Social being, and consciousness, 209, 210
Social class
 Burkean political economy and, 165–167
 in Kallipolis, 29–43
 Wollstonecraft and, 173–186
Social contract
 Burke's "complexity" and, 158–160
 Hobbesian, 83–86, 90, 91
 and Lockean property rights, 103
 Rousseauian, 135, 142–146
Social Contract (Rousseau), 135, 142–143, 146
Soper, Kate, 3
Souls of Black Folk (Du Bois), 223–226, 232
Speaking for Nature (Bowerbank), 179, 182, 185
Speenhamland Act, 165
Statesman (Plato), 29
Stationary-state economy, 18, 197–200
Stephens, Piers H. G., 9, 16–19, 117, 189–202, 289
Stewardship and trusteeship, 206
 Burkean, 17, 161–163, 168
 Du Bois on, 19, 223–231
St. John de Crèvecoeur, Hector, 227
Stone, Christopher, 2, 3
Strauss, Leo, 66, 84–89
Subjection of Women (Mill), 189, 197
Sublime, 154–157, 163
Sustainability
 Arendt and, 254, 262–265
 Aristotelian moral economy and, 57, 58

Sustainability (cont.)
  Burke and, 17, 159, 168, 169
  capitalism and, 217
  and common-pool resources, 78, 79
  environmental justice and, 169
  growth and, 77, 78, 199, 200
  and intergenerational obligation, 159
  liberalism and, 189, 190
  and "limits to growth," 78, 199, 200
  Lockean, 106–111
  Machiavellian decentralization and, 14, 67–79
  Marx and, 212, 217
  Mill's liberal ethics of, 189, 190, 197–202
  Rousseauian concept of nature and, 138–146
  usufructory rights and, 109–111, 288
Sweezy, Paul, 212
Sylvan, Richard, 2, 3
Sympathy, Humean, 118, 123, 126–129

Taylor, Dorceta, 2
Taylor, Paul, 2, 3
Technology, 45, 47, 141, 216, 244, 245, 249, 274
Thoreau, Henry David, 1, 8, 11, 144, 230
"Thoughts and Details on Scarcity" (Burke), 165
Thoughts on the Education of Daughters (Wollstonecraft), 178
Timaeus (Plato), 39
Todorov, Tzevetan, 134, 147
Toomer, Jean, 230, 231
Trachtenberg, Zev, 9, 15, 16, 20, 99–112, 117, 166
Tragedy of the commons, 1, 2, 58, 77, 78, 110
Treatise (Locke), 104
Trusteeship, Burkean, 162, 163
Tu, Wei-Ming, 278–282
Tully, James, 16, 107–109
Two Treatises of Civil Government (Locke), 100, 101

Utilitarianism, 141, 189–202
Utilitarianism (Mill), 189
Utopianism, 38, 42, 232

Valls, Andrew, 16, 87, 117–132, 174, 288
Value
  Aristotle and, 57, 58
  Lockean concepts of, 102, 214
  Marx and, 209, 210
Villa, Dana, 258, 259, 264, 266
Vincent, Andrew, 271
Vindication of the Rights of Brutes (Taylor), 185
Vindication of the Rights of Men (Wollstonecraft), 181
Vindication of the Rights of Woman (Wollstonecraft), 173–181

Wage Labor and Capital (Marx), 207
Wang Yang-ming, 280, 281
Warren, Karen J., 4, 174, 175
Westra, Laura, 30
Whitehead, Alfred North, 29
Whiteside, Kerry, 4, 5
Wilderness, 3, 4, 19, 20
  Du Bois and, 223, 229–235
  sublimity and, 154–156
Williamson, Thad, 4
Wilson, Harlan, 17, 153–171, 291
Winch, Donald, 199, 201
Wissenburg, Marcel, 4
Wollstonecraft, Mary, 11, 16, 18, 22, 126, 173–186, 282, 287–291
Women, as rational, 173, 177
Wood, Neal, 108
Wordsworth, William, 190, 198–201
Worster, Donald, 3
Wrongs of Woman (Wollstonecraft), 173, 180, 181

Young, Iris Marion, 5
Young, Thomas, 176

Zvesper, John, 195